I0135392

TO FACE DOWN DIXIE

TO FACE DOWN DIXIE

SOUTH CAROLINA'S WAR ON THE SUPREME COURT IN THE AGE OF CIVIL RIGHTS

JAMES O. HEATH

LOUISIANA STATE UNIVERSITY PRESS
Baton Rouge

Published by Louisiana State University Press

Manufactured in the United States of America
First printing

DESIGNER: *Mandy McDonald Scallan*
TYPEFACE: *Minion Pro*
PRINTER AND BINDER: *Sheridan Books, Inc.*

Chapter 5 was first published, in somewhat different form, as "The Boys Down There: Thurgood Marshall's Appointment to the Second Circuit Court of Appeals," *Journal of Political Science* 44 (July 2016). Chapter 6 was first published, in somewhat different form, as "A Colored Man with the Name of 'Marshall': South Carolina and the Confirmation of the Supreme Court's First African American Justice," *South Carolina Historical Magazine* 116:3 (July 2015): 180–97.

Library of Congress Cataloging-in-Publication Data

Names: Heath, James O., author.
Title: To face down Dixie : South Carolina's war on the Supreme Court in the age of civil rights / James O. Heath.
Description: Baton Rouge : Louisiana State University Press, [2017] | Includes bibliographical references and index.
Identifiers: LCCN 2017019260| ISBN 978-0-8071-6836-3 (cloth : alk. paper) | ISBN 978-0-8071-6837-0 (pdf) | ISBN 978-0-8071-6838-7 (epub)
Subjects: LCSH: United States. Supreme Court—Officials and employees—Selection and appointment—History—20th century. | Judges—Selection and appointment—United States—History—20th century. | South Carolina—Politics and government—1951– | Government, Resistance to—South Carolina. | Political questions and judicial power—South Carolina.
Classification: LCC KF8742 .H43 2017 | DDC 347.73/2634—dc23
LC record available at https://lccn.loc.gov/2017019260

The paper in this book meets the guidelines for permanence and durability of the Committee on Production Guidelines for Book Longevity of the Council on Library Resources. ♾

for thricea

CONTENTS

ILLUSTRATIONS

following page | 106

ACKNOWLEDGMENTS

It is perhaps logical that a man writing his first book while perched on a wooden chair held together by gaffer tape, typing on a borrowed laptop computer, and sitting next to an electric heater that hasn't worked in three years, probably needs all the help he can get. Nonetheless, it never occurred to me when I was completing this work that I would one day thank a significant number of people for assisting in what turned out to be a thrilling, yet also rather bleak, adventure.

The formidable Adunni Adams provided crucial support and assistance during the research trip. Through her loyalty, dedication, and efficiency, she played an integral part in my completion of interviews and primary research, and also helped to make everyday challenges, setbacks, and disappointments more bearable. She has also stuck with me in our Race in the Americas (RITA) collaboration, which began with the two of us organizing conferences in the UK (and, more recently, the USA) and now involves documentary filmmaking, all of which you can read about at www.raceintheamericas.com. Throughout several harrowing moments of self-doubt and psychological torment, I was able to function relatively smoothly just by reminding myself that Adunni always remembers to bring a second bucket of water when following me into the bowels of hell.

In addition to thanking my parents for their unwavering support, I wish to thank three men by the name of Robert. The unflappable Robert Greenhill gets the credit, or the blame, for starting me off on this journey, while Robert Mickey offered constructive comments and suggestions. Robert Mann (with assistance from Sheridan Wall) accessed vital research materials on my behalf and also provided words of advice and encouragement in guiding this work toward publication. No one else by the name of Robert has played any part in the completion of this book.

Several individuals assisted with the process of accessing the necessary research materials, specifically, Alan Burns at Clemson University, Herb Hartsook and Kate Moore at the University of South Carolina, Leigh McWhite at the University of Mississippi, and Sheryl Vogt and Jill Severn at the University of Georgia. Congressman James Clyburn and former congressman John Spratt generously gave up their time to speak to me, and Elizabeth Patterson was very gracious in discussing with me the life and career of her late father, Olin D. Johnston. Former senator Bill Brock of Tennessee provided useful remarks in writing.

This book has come to fruition largely because of the consistent support and encouragement of Rand Dotson, Jennifer Keegan, Catherine Kadair, and Lee Sioles at LSU Press, as well as freelance editor Gary Von Euer. Several other individuals helped to facilitate the completion of this work, for which I received no financial assistance from funding bodies, scholarships, governments, or educational institutions. In addition to the hospitality of Paula at Café Madeleine and Tony and Gardy at The Keg and Grill, I must acknowledge the remarkable faith and support of Mike Bennett, Amrit Bhogal, Sam Edwards, Philip Gill, Hiren Kanabar, Harvinder Makh, Katie Stevenson, and Carl Walton.

Finally, I wish to thank Adunni Adams once again (for obvious reasons), and also Andrea Clough (for reasons that will be obvious only to her).

TO FACE DOWN
DIXIE

INTRODUCTION

The Story of South Carolina and the Supreme Court

> There is a real spark of independence that ignites men once they become immune from all political pressures. As Justices, they sit as neither conservative nor liberal, but as intelligent human beings doing their utmost within their God-given capacities to search for and uphold the truth.
> —BARRY GOLDWATER, "Political Philosophy and Supreme Court Justices," 1972

> I think I ought to say that South Carolina realizes and appreciates your . . . influence in Washington. It is truly great.
> —EDGAR A. BROWN TO OLIN D. JOHNSTON, April 17, 1959

> As you know, I hate to identify with losing causes.
> —ERNEST F. HOLLINGS TO ROBERT S. SMALL, November 28, 1969

The United States Supreme Court is one of the world's most powerful political institutions. Comprised of nine justices, each appointed by the president and approved by a majority of the US Senate, the court has transformed the American polity on countless occasions by imposing its authority when five or more justices have believed the states or other institutions have violated the words of the United States Constitution.

Throughout the twentieth century and into the twenty-first, the justices of the Supreme Court have reached across the full spectrum of political issues, shaping the course of political development in gun politics, abortion, race and affirmative action, religion in schools, presidential authority during wartime, capital punishment, executive privilege, gay rights, and, in December 2000, the outcome of a presidential election. Inevitably, the polarized nature of American politics in the early twenty-first century has influenced debates over the Supreme Court's power. Conservatives tend to praise justices who remain faithful to the original meaning of the words in the US Constitution, while liberals condemn them for being out of touch, reactionary, and intolerant of minority rights. Liberals typically admire justices who adopt the theory of a "living Constitution," while conservatives criticize the same justices for exhibiting political, rather than judicial, behavior by creating a range of new rights and privileges that the nation's Founding Fathers would never have endorsed. Both liberals and conservatives adopt the term "judicial restraint" to indicate a particular perception of sensible behavior on the part of the justices, while both groups use the pejorative term "judicial activism" when they believe the court to have misused its authority and taken the policy-making process away from Congress, the legislative branch.[1]

During the twentieth century, the southern states' resentment of the landmark *Brown v. Board of Education of Topeka* decision became the ultimate example of a collective political resistance to the Supreme Court's power. The 1954 decision, in which the justices struck down racial segregation in public schools, proved to be a political bombshell for southern leaders, most of whom viewed the court's judgment as a direct threat to the "southern way of life." In the ensuing struggle to curb the court's power, the region's leaders made repeated efforts to impeach the justices; to link the court's decisions to the threat of Communism; to nullify the court's authority in matters relating to schooling; to change the conditions for appointing judges to the court; and to create a barrier between the South and the court's authority through the doctrine of "interposition," the notion of states retaining the right and duty to prevent unreasonable federal interference.

While Article I of the US Constitution provides for the legislature's power in ten lengthy sections, the paltry three sections of Article III leave the Supreme Court relatively unencumbered. Nonetheless, with seats on the Senate Judiciary Committee, southern senators James Eastland (Mississippi), John McClellan (Arkansas), Sam Ervin (North Carolina), Olin D. Johnston (South Carolina), and Strom Thurmond (South Carolina) used their powers under Article II, Section 2, of the Constitution to advise on and consent to the confirmation of presidential appointments to fill vacancies on the Supreme Court. Even if the Senate's "southern bloc" was unable to organize a majority of senators from other regions to oppose Supreme Court nominees when the time came for the full Senate to vote, the southern Judiciary Committee members were at least able to reassure their constituents at home that they were acting in their best interests. During the 1950s, southern senators intensified the committee's scrutiny of potential Supreme Court justices, offering the nominees a sharp, provocative, and angry line of questioning on issues relating to police powers, Communist subversion, and racial segregation. Several nominees would face down Dixie before taking their seat on the federal bench, including Thurgood Marshall, the charismatic black lawyer who had convinced all nine justices of the court to overturn racial segregation in schools.[2]

Senators from the state of South Carolina proved to be particularly indignant in responding to the *Brown* decision. They used a variety of methods, including advising the nominating president; triggering investigations into a nominee's background as a delaying tactic; or simply testing the nominee's composure, stamina, and constitutional knowledge in the form of grueling Q&A sessions before the Judiciary Committee. Senators Olin D. Johnston, Strom Thurmond, and Ernest "Fritz" Hollings each exerted a remarkable influence over the nomination of Supreme Court justices, occasionally going to extraordinary lengths to scrutinize or obstruct nominees, or influence the process of selection themselves.

The South Carolinian influence in the judicial nomination process was both consistent and controversial throughout the twentieth century. As far back as April 1930, an editorial in the *Buffalo Progressive Herald* identified Senator Coleman Blease as a ringleader in the fierce opposition to President Herbert Hoover's nomination of Charles Evans Hughes for the position of chief justice.[3] A more famous example is Strom Thurmond's melodramatic style of questioning when scrutinizing President Lyndon Johnson's nominations of Thurgood Marshall as an associate justice in 1967 and Abe Fortas as chief justice in 1968. More complex is the role of Fritz Hollings, whose suggestion to President Richard Nixon that he make the ill-fated nomination of South Carolinian Clement Haynsworth occurred at a time of press speculation that Nixon would "repay" the southern states for crucial support during the 1968 presidential election, with one newspaper noting Strom Thurmond's "passionate" interest in matters of the court.[4]

Perhaps more remarkably, South Carolina has the unusual distinction of being one of the few states in American history to elect a former Supreme Court justice as its governor. President Franklin D. Roosevelt had appointed Senator James F. Byrnes to the court in 1941, where he served for fifteen months before Roosevelt moved him to head the Office of Economic Stabilization. As governor of South Carolina in the early 1950s, Byrnes had the unenviable task of governing the state in the aftermath of the court's announcement of *Brown*. Byrnes became an outspoken critic of the court, condemning his former colleagues in a pamphlet entitled "The Supreme Court Must Be Curbed!," which supporters of segregation reprinted and circulated extensively throughout South Carolina during the mid-1950s.[5]

In waging a war on the court, South Carolina's senators employed a variety of measures aimed at restricting the court's power in order to reassure their constituents that they would succeed in maintaining racial segregation. Olin Johnston was an active participant in efforts to gather information to discredit the court's decisions, while Strom Thurmond advocated the impeachment of Supreme Court justices on an almost regular basis, making a special effort to target the elderly liberal, Justice William O. Douglas. In addition, Johnston and Thurmond unleashed a wave of legislation aimed at weakening the court's power, including a Johnston bill to eliminate the court's jurisdiction in matters relating to schools and a Thurmond bill requiring justices to hold a minimum of five years' judicial experience in order to be eligible for nomination. "Court-baiting," rather than race-baiting, was used by South Carolina's senators as a convenient means of asserting their state's independence by blaming presidents of both parties for making disastrous nominations. By using northern resistance as an excuse for the South's failure to prevent the court's interference in the practice of segregation, southern senators made a plausible case for their continuous reelection. Southern voters came to believe that reelecting their senators was the only means of containing the Supreme Court's dangerous influence. In winning continuous reelection, senators increased their seniority, and senior positions on the Judiciary Committee enabled those with an interest in judicial affairs to scrutinize and influence the very process used to select the individuals who sit on the court. As Keith Finley has explained, southerners were able to transform the Senate into "a citadel of their interests" through controlling a large number of the chamber's committees, giving them enormous influence in the passage—or obstruction—of legislation.[6]

American presidents have selected individuals to serve on the Supreme Court since 1789. The factors behind their selections have varied enormously. Presidents have favored some nominees due to personal friendship; others through general agreement on the nominee's suitability for the position; others through recommendations from individuals considered important enough for presidents to listen to. Presidents have often had specific ideological objectives in mind in selecting nominees, believing that the force of Supreme Court decision-making would meet those objectives. Some have made selections after taking time to gather together different perspectives before making an informed decision, while others have reached decisions while showcasing a stubborn refusal to listen to other views. It is quite common for a president's relationship with the other branches of government to determine a selection: indeed, presidents have chosen many nominees through a particular deference to, or antagonism toward, Congress, or to the Supreme Court itself.[7]

While all of these factors may influence the manner in which presidents select candidates, none is sufficient to explain fully the process of how individuals reach the Supreme Court, as there are an infinite number of external factors that have applied to the process since 1789. The one consistent feature of the selection process, regardless of all other factors, is the president's need for the United States Senate to confirm the nominee. Under the terms of Article II, Section 2, of the US Constitution, the president has the power to nominate, and "by and with the advice and consent of the Senate," to appoint justices of the Supreme Court.[8] With the Constitution requiring presidents to select and senators to approve each nominee, the Supreme Court nomination process has evolved into one of the most thrilling battlegrounds in US politics. The Senate has formally rejected a president's choice on twelve occasions and unofficially denied confirmation on many others. The controversial nature of the process was evident as recently as April 2017, when Republican Senate Majority Leader Mitch McConnell ensured confirmation for President Donald Trump's nomination of Judge Neil Gorsuch by sensationally pursuing the "nuclear option" of abolishing the Senate's requirement for a 60-vote majority. A Senate rejection of a nominee or the president's withdrawal of a nominee's name from consideration are both seen as political defeats, and when a vacancy remains unfilled for an extended period, leading to a backlog of deadlocked decisions, a president's political embarrassment is only exacerbated.[9]

Furthermore, a successful confirmation is not always a guarantee of presidential success: many nominees have failed to live up to the expectations of the presidents who nominated them, and there are some famous examples of presidents who later regretted their selections. These include Harry S. Truman's 1949 nomination of Tom C. Clark, Dwight D. Eisenhower's 1953 nomination of

Earl Warren and also his 1956 nomination of William Brennan, and George H. W. Bush's 1990 nomination of David Souter. On the other hand, scholars of the nomination process have noted that it takes an enormous amount of time and effort, not to mention some highly complicated considerations of a multitude of competing interests, for senators to unite in opposition to a president's nominee. Presidents tend to have a plethora of administrative tools and a large team of dependable staff to push a nomination, but an individual senator, carrying the burden of proof, will not succeed in winning support from other senators for a nominee's rejection without superior powers of persuasion and strong emotional issues to pursue.[10]

With these themes in mind, this study avoids the tendency in the current literature to focus on presidential selection, and will instead highlight the responses of senators from one particular state. A remarkable lack of Senate rejections during the lengthy period 1895–1967 does not indicate a nomination process free from controversy. Rather, it invites a closer inspection of the many intricacies of the process that have been neglected in the existing research, namely, the significance of southern senators on the Judiciary Committee; the question of how the "southern" agenda with regard to the selection of Supreme Court justices ultimately influenced judicial politics; and the question of how the Supreme Court's landmark decisions relating to the race issue may have held particular significance for the state of South Carolina.

From 1953 until his death in 1965, Olin D. Johnston proved well placed to influence the judicial appointments of presidents Dwight D. Eisenhower and John F. Kennedy. Senate Minority Leader Lyndon Johnson (who viewed his near-namesake as a natural ally as well as a loyal Democrat) used his influence to secure Johnston a place on the Judiciary Committee, and fellow southerner and committee chairman James Eastland frequently selected the South Carolinian to sit on subcommittees to assess the suitability of presidential nominations to the courts of appeal.[11] In using his position to delay the confirmation of any nominee he considered unsuitable, Johnston made a lasting imprint on the history of the US Senate, marking a period in which southern senators utilized Senate procedures to enforce a southern agenda on a national scale.[12] He was at his most obstructive when considering Eisenhower's nomination of Simon Sobeloff to the Fourth Circuit Court of Appeals and Kennedy's nomination of Thurgood Marshall to the Second Circuit. The Supreme Court proved to be the backdrop to both of these nominations: Kennedy made the latter selection amid speculation that he would eventually make Marshall the first African American Supreme Court justice, while Eisenhower supposedly saw the wisdom of "grooming" Sobeloff to replace the ailing Justice Felix Frankfurter. Johnston's tactics alienated his Senate colleagues and tested the patience of President Kennedy, who intervened personally to overcome Johnston's obstruction of the Marshall appointment.[13]

Strom Thurmond preferred a more confrontational approach toward nominees: his aggressive interrogation of Abe Fortas—inspired in part by his fury that the court had thrown out the conviction of Andrew Mallory, a black South Carolinian who choked and raped a white woman and went on to reoffend—is immortalized in his now-infamous outburst, "Mallory—I want that word to ring in your ears!" Fritz Hollings would carve out an equally distinctive record on Supreme Court nominations. Black leaders criticized his decision, only a few years after he established himself as one of South Carolina's more moderate governors, to oppose Lyndon Johnson's nomination of Thurgood Marshall to the Supreme Court. That vote remains, according to Hollings himself, one of his biggest personal regrets. Yet his record on Supreme Court appointments remained unusually conservative throughout his thirty-eight-year career in the Senate, most notably with regard to President Ronald Reagan's failed nomination of Robert Bork, which Hollings supported despite sixteen of his seventeen fellow southern Democrats voting against Bork's confirmation.[14]

One particularly notable aspect of this story is the manner in which Johnston, Thurmond, and Hollings always seemed to agree on the South Carolina position toward each nomination, although they rarely communicated formally on the relevant issues, and did not seem to discuss the formulation of a coherent strategy in the state's war on the Supreme Court. The relationship between Johnston and Thurmond remained strained following their bitter 1950 primary battle, and Johnston's reluctance to associate himself with Thurmond's racist posturing was summed up neatly in his (possibly apocryphal) remark to Harry Ashmore, editor of the *Arkansas Gazette:* "It's no use trying to talk to Strom. He *believes* that shit." Johnston's daughter, former congresswoman Elizabeth J. Patterson, recalls of her father that "I never heard him say anything bad about him, OK, but he did say 'poor Strom' a couple of times. He just sort of ignored him, I think." Johnston and Thurmond did not meet regularly, and maintained a cordial written agreement that each would not object to the other's judicial recommendations. Like Thurmond, Hollings would wage a bitter and ultimately unsuccessful attempt to unseat Johnston in the 1962 Democratic Party primary, and would clash openly with Thurmond during discussions over the extension of the Voting Rights Act in 1982.[15]

In addition to a lack of personal warmth among the three senators, each exhibited different political agendas. While Hollings crafted a reputation as a moderate, Thurmond filibustered against passage of the 1957 Civil Rights Act not only to assure his constituents that he could maintain segregation in South Carolina, but also to demonstrate to his southern colleagues that his commitment to preserving white supremacy was stronger and more authentic than theirs. South Carolina's politicians have defended their state with a testosterone-fueled energy that is quite evident in Thurmond's correspondence with his constituents during the debate over the Civil Rights Act during the summer of 1957, which includes his pledge to "speak at great length and to the full extent of my physical capacity." Thurmond's provocative promotion of the Southern Manifesto—signed by most of the southern congressional delegation in defiance of *Brown*—led to a physical altercation with Senator Ralph Yarborough of Texas. The leader of the southern delegation, Georgia's Richard Russell, condemned Thurmond's pursuit of "personal political aggrandizement" following his twenty-four-hour filibuster. Hollings later claimed that Thurmond's aggressive interrogation of Abe Fortas "had left even some of his own staffers shaking their heads," illustrating, as with Johnston's delay of Thurgood Marshall's Second Circuit appointment, that the actions of South Carolina's senators often proved deeply unpalatable to others in Washington, DC.[16]

South Carolina has arguably played the most important (yet overlooked) role in the development of Supreme Court nomination hearings into political, and confrontational, public events. Highlighting the enduring southern obsession with the Supreme Court in the twenty-first century, former South Carolina congressman John Spratt has referred to the influence of the nine justices as "one of the defining differences. If you want to know the difference between a Democrat and a Southern Democrat, my answer would be that it's about where you stand on the Supreme Court, particularly on recent rulings, such as those dealing with gay rights." Although ardent segregationists also represented the states of Arkansas, Mississippi, and North Carolina on the Senate Judiciary Committee during this era, none of those senators ever initiated a one-man crusade against a nominee, as in the case of Johnston's fight against the courts of appeals nominations of Marshall and Sobeloff, and Thurmond's obstruction of the Supreme Court nominations of Marshall and Fortas. The unyielding dissent of South Carolina's senators truly stands out from the actions of other southern segregationists in the nomination process. Thurmond virtually stood alone in refusing to back the Senate's confirmation of Abe Fortas as associate justice in 1965. He pursued a theatrical crusade to prevent Thurgood Marshall's confirmation in 1967, but Lyndon Johnson proved successful in convincing other southerners, including James Eastland and Richard Russell, to "take a walk" by abstaining from the final vote.[17]

The behavior of South Carolina's senators can be characterized as a "war on the Supreme Court" for three reasons. First, the expression refers, throughout this work, to the senators' attempts to achieve a variety of objectives. These include maintaining conservative segregationist credentials by regularly condemning the *Brown* decision; characterizing themselves as defenders of the South against an institution purported to be the region's number-one enemy; and attempting to obstruct liberal appointments to the judiciary while promoting the nomination of conservative judges who, supposedly, would defend southern interests through strict adherence to the words of the US Constitution. The expression does not refer to a consistent attack, as the state's senators did not remain on the offensive throughout the period under study.

Second, the term *war* seems appropriate given the Supreme Court's significance within South Carolina's broader response to the *Brown* decision. The term seems even more fitting when considering the influence of the man whose actions defined South Carolina's, if not the South's, politics throughout this era. Strom Thurmond's recent biographer, Joseph Crespino, has argued that the aforementioned Southern Manifesto "initiated for Thurmond a war on the Warren Court that became the most consistent theme of his politics for the next decade and a half."[18] Although the judicial selection process would eventually accommodate Thurmond's preferences during the 1970s and 1980s, the court's liberal majority would remain a threat to the southern way of life unless diluted by a long-term presidential commitment to appointing conservative judges.

Third, the nature of South Carolina's war varied throughout the period under study. For example, the senators' frequent criticism of the attitude, style, and judicial philosophies of the nine justices suggests that the state's war on the court was largely rhetorical. This was perhaps most evident in Thurmond's speech before the Citizens Committee for Constitutional Government in Augusta, Georgia, in November 1958, when, in one of many condemnations, he declared "total and unremitting war on the Supreme Court's unconstitutional usurpations and unlawful arrogations of power."[19] Alternatively, it might not be appropriate to refer to a South Carolinian "war" on the Supreme Court following Richard Nixon's inauguration as president in January 1969. As a Republican who won election on the back of a successful "southern strategy," Nixon set out to nominate the very brand of conservative judges sought by South Carolina's senators over so many years. On the other hand, the Senate's rejection in 1969 and 1970 of two southern Supreme Court nominees (including South Carolina's Clement Haynsworth) ensured that South Carolina's senators remained at war with northerners wishing to protect the liberal gains made during the 1960s. South Carolina's claims of an antisouthern bias suggested that the state would continue to fight for regional and state interests in the Senate.

Given the consistency of the state's senators in the nomination process, and the volatile nature of their actions and behavior, the case of South Carolina suggests that the frequent scholarly analysis of Supreme Court nominations as "one-off" events is restrictive and unhelpful. With a striking history of political dissent, and a unique relationship with the Supreme Court, South Carolina's influence on the judicial selection process offers a crucial example of a state's political agenda achieving national attention through the politics of the US Senate.

1. "TOTAL AND UNREMITTING WAR"

James Haw's view that South Carolina's antebellum leaders created an image of a superior southern civilization provides a useful starting point for an examination of the South Carolina sense of "exceptionalism" characterizing the state's history. As Jack Bass and Marilyn Thompson have argued, South Carolina's distrust of executive power originates from the colonial era, when the king of England was responsible for appointing the governor. This experience led political leaders to concentrate power within the state's legislature, making South Carolina's governor, until recently, one of the weakest governors in the United States. In addition to a sense of separatism, if not outright secession, a strong tradition of defiance permeates South Carolina's history. The soft, spongy palmetto log walls of Fort Sumter—which absorbed the shock of British cannonballs without shattering when nine British ships attempted to enter Charleston Harbor on June 28, 1776—inspired the choice of the palmetto tree as a prominent symbol on the state flag. The enormous success of South Carolina's slave economy, fueled by rice and indigo exports, gave the state an influential voice in national politics, which its leaders wished to maintain: with African slaves responsible for over half the annual value of South Carolina's exports, the state's leaders sought to ensure the continuation of a thriving slave economy while at the same time easing white fears of the state's black slave majority, which became a greater concern after the failed Stono Rebellion of 1739.[1]

The Nullification Crisis, during which Vice President John C. Calhoun led the state in rejecting the Tariff of 1828, damaged South Carolina's relationship with national party politics to the extent that, by 1860, Robert Barnwell Rhett, editor of the *Charleston Mercury,* expressed hope that Abraham Lincoln's election victory would create a southern backlash, leading eventually to the breakup of the Union and the establishment of a separate southern nation. Given its long tradition of independence, it is perhaps unsurprising that South Carolina became the first state to secede from the Union in December 1860, triggering the US Civil War.[2]

From the 1890s, South Carolina implemented one of the most savage and uncompromising systems of Jim Crow segregation in the South, and the principle of ensuring white supremacy continued to characterize the state's cultural and political identity long after the abolition of slavery and the failure of Reconstruction-era reforms. During the early twentieth century, South Carolina's politicians openly exploited the presence of a black majority in certain counties in order to secure reelection. Archsegregationist Senator Ellison D. "Cotton Ed" Smith won election to the US Senate continuously thanks to the conservative white voters of the state's "black belt" region, who backed him over a thirty-four-year period. Following the Supreme Court's announcement of *Brown v. Board of Education,* black belt cities such as Orangeburg, which had a 70 percent African American population in the mid-1950s, became centers of activity for white conservatives opposing racial integration through the White Citizens' Councils. The ongoing persistence of white supremacy had become so deeply ingrained in South Carolina's cultural identity by the 1950s that, in the words of C. Vann Woodward, African Americans felt "little need for Jim Crow laws to establish what the lingering stigma of slavery—in bearing, speech, and manner—made so apparent."[3]

South Carolina's demagogic politicians, in particular the notorious Coleman L. Blease, called frequently for the use of violence to maintain racial order, resulting in a total of 155 lynchings during the period 1880–1930. The state's notoriety for racial violence even stirred the presidency into action: after a white policeman struck black veteran Isaac Woodard in the face, blinding him in one eye, President Harry S. Truman created a Committee on Civil Rights. Yet racial violence persisted despite Truman's intervention, prompting one South Carolina minister to remark in 1957 that "fear covers South Carolina like the frost."[4]

The legendary V. O. Key, whose 1949 assessment of South Carolina remains the most insightful study of the state's politics after an incredible period of nearly seventy years, highlighted one particularly important reflection that assists in explaining the state's virulent defense of white supremacy. The state constitution of 1890 established that one senator would represent each county in the state Senate, giving the conservative politicians of the state's lowcountry counties an ironclad control over South Carolina's internal politics. Enjoying a higher rate of incumbency than congressmen from upcountry counties, the lowcountry politicians reaped the benefits of seniority through chairing various committees, leaving large numbers of white voters in upcountry counties disadvantaged in terms of their congressional representation. The white citizens of the lowcountry counties—with comparatively small numbers of whites but sizable, disenfranchised, black majorities—benefited from the state's most powerful politicians representing them in the legislature. As Bryant Simon has shown, the effects of South Carolina's malapportionment only worsened with large-scale migration from rural to metropolitan areas during the early twentieth century, constituting "a dilution of democracy, even racially skewed democracy" when compared to similar systems in place in other states.[5]

As a result, the preferences of whites residing in counties "with the highest proportions of Negroes" ultimately defined the state's political character, at least as it applied to their elected representatives. The result was a deeply conservative state legislature dominated by lowcountry politicians who, in the words of Key, "grasped firm control of the critical sectors of state administration" and effectively hamstrung a succession of relatively weak South Carolina governors. The politicians of Barnwell County, particularly Senator Edgar A. Brown, who served in the state Senate for forty-four years, and Speaker Solomon Blatt, who served in the state House of Representatives for a staggering fifty-four years (thirty-two of them as Speaker), became the embodiment of this phenomenon. The three senators studied in this work were forced to contend with the Barnwell effect during their terms as governor of South Carolina: Olin Johnston waged a bold but ultimately unsuccessful war with the legislature in a row over the state's Highway Division; Strom Thurmond railed against the "Barnwell Ring" during his successful election campaign of 1946; and Fritz Hollings was forced to charm state legislators with a bottle of bourbon in order to secure authorization for his ambitious program of technical training.[6]

It is perhaps unsurprising that Numan Bartley identified South Carolina, along with Mississippi and Georgia, as "the original hard core of resistance." Key and subsequent scholars have suggested that the South Carolina political elite not only succeeded in constructing an unbreakable conservative dominance of the state's politics but also managed to smother, or at least conceal, the potential for alternative, even moderate, political voices to emerge. This was a version of "massive resistance" to civil rights that created, in the words of Tony Badger, "a closed society, just as closed as Mississippi, in which dissent was not tolerated," but this is not to suggest that the state had been open to alternative political viewpoints prior to the 1954 ruling. As Robert Mickey has argued, South Carolina's response to *Brown* did not destroy "a burgeoning racially moderate public sphere," simply because "prior to *Brown,* none existed."[7]

The current South Carolina political scholarship suggests strongly that aspirants to political office would enjoy successful careers only if they conformed to an intolerant political system in which the racial prejudices of the lowcountry were deeply ingrained. If this is truly the case, it seems surprising that few scholars have considered the full reach of this effect by exploring the impact of South Carolina's racial politics in Washington, DC, particularly as Key has observed that the state's senators "used the floor of the United States Senate as a rostrum for white supremacy oratory, matched in virulence mainly by such Mississippi spokesmen as [James K.] Vardaman, [Theodore] Bilbo, and [John E.] Rankin."[8] In fact, the US Senate is a highly relevant aspect of South Carolina's history, in that many of the most violent, dramatic, and notorious events associated with the state's senators and the issue of race have taken place on the Senate floor itself, including the infamous Brooks-Sumner incident of 1856, when Congressman Preston Brooks subjected Senator Charles Sumner to a vicious beating with a cane; the aforementioned Coleman Blease's recitation in 1929 of the poem "N——s in the White House" in reaction to First Lady Lou Hoover taking tea with the wife of African American congressman Oscar DePriest; and Strom Thurmond's remarkable twenty-four-hour filibuster opposing the Civil Rights Act of 1957, which remains to date the longest recorded filibuster in US history.[9] With South Carolina's powerful conservative leaders unable to exert, at the federal level, a measure of influence on a par with their control over the state legislature, it was perhaps inevitable that the state's senators would clash repeatedly with senators from other states in their uncompromising defense of white supremacy.

The South Carolinian distrust of executive power, particularly in matters of race relations, makes it logical that the state's defiant politicians would target the US Supreme Court. The *Brown* decision drew together five cases relating to segregated schooling, among them *Briggs v. Elliott,* which originated from a challenge to segregated schools in Clarendon County, South Carolina. *Briggs* had been the first of the five cases, but, as Orville Vernon Burton has explained, the court's Texan justice, Tom C. Clark, suggested that the group of cases be named after the "Brown" case so that it would not be viewed as dealing solely with a "southern" issue, with the result that "Linda Brown and Topeka became famous, and Harry Briggs and Clarendon, South Carolina, did not."[10] Announced on May 17, 1954, *Brown* voided Article XI, Section 7, of South Carolina's constitution and suggested an overwhelming vote of no confidence in Governor James F. Byrnes's pledge to address racial inequalities in South Carolina's schools. While Eugene Cook, the attorney general of neighboring Georgia, tried to argue that his state had had nothing to do with the original group of cases and therefore would maintain segregation, South Carolina was in no position to make such a claim.[11] Further decisions followed: on February 25, 1963, the court ruled, in *Edwards v. South Carolina,* that South Carolina's authorities had violated the rights of African American protestors by forcing them to disperse. In January 1966 came *South Carolina v. Katzenbach,* which dismissed South Carolina's challenge to the preclearance provisions of the landmark Voting Rights Act of 1965. Chief Justice Earl Warren drafted the opinion himself, in an example of what Jim Newton has referred to as the chief justice's personal "campaign against Southern racism."[12] During oral arguments, Warren cited "an invidious and pervasive evil" in South Carolina's history of defying the Fifteenth Amendment of the Constitution through disenfranchising African Americans.[13] In December 1965, the court commanded South Carolina to completely reconstruct its system of representation in the state Senate in order to ensure the representation of African American voters, a challenge later upheld in the *Stevenson v. West* decision of 1973.[14]

However, the South Carolina senators' interest in judicial appointments went far beyond an agenda to preserve racial segregation. In the coming years, their participation in the nomination process would involve issues as diverse as religion, the Communist threat, crime and punishment, internal security and subversion, affirmative action, obscenity, and freedom of speech, all of which fueled their efforts, and those of other southern conservatives, to link the southern reaction to *Brown* to their perception of a growing national reaction to the Supreme Court's judicial activism. As will be shown, South Carolina's politicians targeted the court for a multitude of reasons: Johnston and Thurmond condemned the *Engel v. Vitale* decision, which ruled teacher-led prayer unconstitutional, while Thurmond would later blame the court for facilitating the proliferation of pornographic material throughout the United States. Having been heavily involved in the drive to regulate campaign spending in the early 1970s, Fritz Hollings blasted the court's *Buckley v. Valeo* decision in a chapter of his memoir, entitled "The Supreme Court Corrupts Congress." Savaging the justices for striking down the Federal Election Campaign Act, Hollings asked, "Does anyone think that James Madison intended free speech only for the rich? The Court had amended the First Amendment!"[15]

South Carolina's senators did not wage war on the Supreme Court through a defiant secessionist gesture worthy of John Calhoun's leadership during the drama of the Nullification Crisis, but instead chose to work within the existing system by invoking the senatorial right of "advice and consent" in the judicial confirmation process. Although the Nixon presidency marked the beginning of Thurmond's reinvention into a pillar of the Republican Party establishment, Hollings's record in maintaining a consistent streak of independence by supporting conservative nominees continued the tradition of South Carolina Democrats defying the national party. Hollings's record in the nomination process may not suggest that a war on the Supreme Court continued after 1970, but it does highlight the lengthy battle to protect the Democratic Party in South Carolina by using a conservative voting tendency to prevent Republican Party encroachment into the state's conservative white voting bloc. Despite the lack of agreement or coordination, and clear evidence of very different political agendas, the three senators, albeit unwittingly, maintained a clear solidarity over the course of each roll call vote.

Olin D. Johnston was destined to become a champion of South Carolina's textile community. Born on November 18, 1896, in Anderson County, in the heart of the Piedmont region, he worked as a youth in the Chiquola Manufacturing Company mill and earned his high school diploma at the Textile Industrial Institute. He entered politics while still enrolled at the University of South Carolina, serving in the state's House of Representatives prior to his election as governor in 1934. His support for President Franklin D. Roosevelt's New Deal produced many progressive policy outcomes, including South Carolina's comprehensive rural electrification program. A bold crusade to ensure the total exclusion of African Americans from the South Carolina Democratic Party primary system contributed in no small part to his election to the US Senate in 1944. In his opposition to the Supreme Court's *Smith v. Allwright* decision, Johnston declared that "white supremacy will be contained in our primaries—let the chips fall where they may."[16] In his final year as governor, he declined to intervene on behalf of the youngest person executed in the state's history, allowing George Stinney, a fourteen-year-old African American boy, to face the electric chair after an all-white jury found him guilty of murdering two white girls. In December 2014, Judge Carmen T. Mullen vacated Stinney's conviction, suggesting a miscarriage of justice seventy years after his execution.[17]

As governor, Johnston famously called out the state's National Guard to occupy the State Highway Division, but his senatorial career was largely free from dramatic behavior. He caused a minor stir in 1948 by refusing to attend a racially integrated Democratic fund-raising dinner.[18] While other southerners clashed with the Democratic Party or bolted it completely, Johnston remained a loyal Democrat throughout his life, putting his reluctant support behind Senator John F. Kennedy of Massachusetts, the party's liberal presidential candidate in 1960. Despite their differences on civil rights, Johnston retained a warm friendship with President Lyndon B. Johnson, as evidenced by a telephone call from December 26, 1963, when LBJ informed the senator, "I'm an Olin Johnston man. I'll work with you any way I can."[19] Until his death from cancer in 1965, Johnston's brand of economically progressive yet racially conservative Democratic politics proved sufficiently appealing to South Carolinians for him to win reelection over two decades. Despite his conservative position on race, Johnston was able to win a sufficient number of black votes to keep his Senate seat, even securing the endorsement of African American civil rights activist Modjeska Simkins during Strom Thurmond's challenge to his incumbency in the 1950 Democratic primary contest.[20] Few outside South Carolina have acknowledged Johnston's contributions to the state's agriculture and textile industries, but the lengthy, and successful, campaign to establish a miscarriage of justice in the George Stinney conviction has showcased his racial conservatism on a national scale.

Strom Thurmond was the last in a long line of controversial South Carolina senators. His birth on December 2, 1902, in Edgefield County links him to two other notorious figures born in the same county—the aforementioned Congressman Preston Brooks, and the enormously influential Governor Benjamin R. Tillman, who disenfranchised African Americans and called openly for the use of lynching to maintain white supremacy. Thurmond claimed he wished to run for governor after his father took him to a stump meeting in Edgefield, where the nine-year-old Strom witnessed Coleman Blease's demagogic, race-baiting oratory. Following a successful legal career, Thurmond won the governorship in 1946. Despite a relatively moderate position on segregation, he broke from the Democratic Party in disgust at President Harry S. Truman's civil rights plank in the 1948 presidential election and ran for president himself on a southern Democrat ("Dixiecrat") ticket, winning Electoral College majorities in four southern states. The campaign ensured the beginning of a confrontational relationship with the Democratic Party.[21]

A fitness fanatic who cultivated a macho persona, Thurmond seized on opportunities to showcase his physical fitness in order to impress his constituents, as in the case of his record-breaking filibuster against passage of the 1957 Civil Rights Act. Although still a Democrat at the start of 1964, Thurmond had not supported a Democratic presidential candidate for twenty years, and his decision to become a Republican and support Barry Goldwater's effort to reach out to disaffected white southerners proved to be a landmark event in the southern conversion to the Republican Party.[22] Thurmond retained his huge base of support despite his party defection, and Republican presidents Richard Nixon and Ronald Reagan found him to be a reliable and influential ally in securing southern votes.

The Voting Rights Act of 1965 effectively decapitated the southern crusade to maintain segregation, but Thurmond supported segregationist Albert Watson's unsuccessful 1970 gubernatorial campaign against the liberal John C. West. Nonetheless, his efforts to win over newly enfranchised black voters during the 1970s showcased his sense of political pragmatism. He continued to win reelection as a Republican until he left the Senate in 2003 at the age of 100. He died less than a year later. A fascinating postscript to Thurmond's life was the revelation after his death that, at the age of 22, he had fathered a mixed-race daughter with his family's 16-year-old black maid. Although he maintained contact with his unacknowledged fifth child and supported her financially, Thurmond concealed her existence to prevent accusations of hypocrisy, and spent years representing disaffected white voters while making a case that his commitment to racial segregation was more authentic than that of his southern colleagues. The discovery of a more "liberal" attitude toward black Americans in Thurmond's personal life was less surprising to those who recalled his womanizing, but for others, the emergence of Essie Mae Washington-Williams only added to the continuing fascination with the controversy surrounding Thurmond as an icon of the twentieth-century American South.[23]

Ernest "Fritz" Hollings is one of the more complex figures in South Carolina's political history. Born in Charleston on New Year's Day, 1922, he aimed for a career in law before pursuing politics. Following three terms in the state House of Representatives, he won election as lieutenant governor at the age of 32 before reaching the governor's mansion in January 1959. As governor, Hollings focused on education. Unlike Olin Johnston, who escalated a dispute with the State Highway Division by calling out the National Guard, Hollings used his charm to the full when making a case for the state's investment in technical training, a previously unheard-of innovation in the state's history. He secured his gubernatorial election victory by campaigning on a platform of maintaining segregation, but once elected, he proved more liberal on civil rights than any of his predecessors. Claiming that his views on race were influenced during World War II, when he saw black American soldiers standing outside being given food through a window while white German prisoners of war sat inside at tables, Hollings ensured the safety of demonstrators at lunch counter sit-ins and allowed the admission of African American student Harvey Gantt to Clemson University, offering his now-famous declaration that a process of desegregation "must be done with dignity. It must be done with law and order."[24] Through his energy and enthusiasm for business opportunities, he was able to attract a wealth of investment for subsequent South Carolina governors to build on.

As with his term as governor, Hollings carved out a moderate path during a thirty-eight-year career in the Senate, remaining a popular Democratic senator throughout a series of Republican challenges to his incumbency. His 1969 "hunger tour," his 1982 vote to renew the Voting Rights Act, and his 1988 endorsement of fellow South Carolinian Jesse Jackson during that year's presidential primary contests all served to solidify his moderate positions on race. With his dry, self-deprecating wit and heavy Charleston accent, Hollings stood out as a particularly colorful figure during his tenure on the Senate Commerce Committee, during which he questioned Frank Zappa on sexual and violent content in rock music lyrics and cited "Buffcoat and Beaver" (more commonly known as *Beavis and Butthead*) as an example of the unhealthy influence of television on American families. He discussed his passion for fiscal responsibility extensively in his 2008 memoir, *Making Government Work,* and he also aired his views on the Obama administration's handling of the global economic crisis.

Despite the similarities, there are many differences between the three senators that illustrate the unique facets of South Carolina politics. Johnston and Hollings represented different sides of the traditional divide between upcountry and lowcountry politics, while Thurmond's birthplace, Edgefield County, makes him the last in a long line of controversial South Carolina politicians. While all three claimed during their gubernatorial and senatorial campaigns to oppose integration, each reflected varying levels of enthusiasm for, and belief in, the principle of racial segregation. Johnston maintained a political stance against segregation as a matter of necessity, while Thurmond's aggressive opposition to integration reflected a more radical stance on the race issue which, although quite consistent with the careers of earlier "demagogic" South Carolinians, alienated some of his southern colleagues. While Thurmond defected to the Republicans in 1964 to campaign for Barry Goldwater (and later Richard Nixon), both Johnston and Hollings remained loyal to the Democratic Party throughout their careers in the Senate despite misgivings regarding the party's presidential nominees. Johnston was often unimpressed by the national party's more moderate positions on race, but Hollings risked deep unpopularity among South Carolina's voters with his enthusiastic support for John F. Kennedy's successful presidential campaign in 1960.[25]

The close and uniquely "southern" relationship each senator maintained with his constituents proved to be a significant influence in encouraging them to hold the conservative line on the race issue. John Spratt insists that Thurmond "had the best constituent service on the Hill, amongst Southerners at least. Back home, they remembered Strom calling on the telephone when somebody died, they remembered his wedding gifts, they remembered his telephone calls at critical moments, things like this."[26] As with their fellow southerner Herman Talmadge, who ensured that his constituents in Georgia received written responses within twenty-four hours, Thurmond, Johnston, and Hollings issued swift and affable communications with South Carolinians and other correspondents from elsewhere in the nation.[27]

Many of their constituents' letters represented the worst excesses of racism, particularly in the aftermath of the Little Rock integration crisis of 1957. One resident of Auburn, California, informed Thurmond that "unless white children can be educated in private schools . . . America will soon be a nation of mongrels." After J. H. Bickley, the grand dragon of the South Carolina Ku Klux Klan, wrote a letter to Johnston regarding the race issue, the senator scrawled a note in pencil, advising his staff to "tell him to rest assured of my efforts to defeat civil rights legislation," adding, "don't address him as Grand Dragon." After reading a detailed rant from a South Carolinian urging, "pray that God prevents the crime of 'negro' integration and 'colored' bastardism against the white race in America," Thurmond opened his response by stating, "Mrs. Thurmond and I sincerely appreciate your Christmas card."[28]

Yet some of the writers did engage the senators in discussions over complex and relevant political issues. When a resident of Florence, South Carolina, asked Thurmond if the southern states had accepted the Fourteenth Amendment—intended as a means of providing constitutional protection for black Americans—only "under force," the senator claimed that this was indeed the case, and provided a detailed and passionate response. Enclosing a speech he had made on the very same subject, Thurmond argued that "the radical Republican majority which was in power in the Congress following the War Between the States forced enough of the Southern states to agree to the ratification before they could be re-admitted into the Union so that the necessary majority was obtained for ratification purposes."[29] Aside from highlighting the manner in which the lingering bitterness over the South's treatment after defeat in the US Civil War would inform the region's resistance to civil rights, Thurmond's arguments in this letter would resurface in a range of obscure questions aimed at Thurgood Marshall during the latter's Supreme Court confirmation hearings in 1967.

In contrast to the letters of support were a great many letters from moderate South Carolinians who strongly disapproved of their senators' actions. In some instances, accusations of racism, sexism, anti-Semitism, and hypocrisy outweighed the many letters of praise for promoting the segregationist cause. South Carolina's war on the Supreme Court may have impressed the state's conservative political establishment during this period, but sufficient evidence exists to suggest that the attempts of Johnston, Thurmond, and Hollings to influence the judicial selection process did in fact antagonize, frustrate, and embarrass many South Carolinians. As will be shown, the sheer scale of voter disapproval expressed in letters to the three senators regarding their conduct in the fight over Supreme Court nominations suggests that each of them overestimated the extent to which their constituents expected them to invoke the spirit of John Calhoun. The marginalization of the state's more moderate voices forms a consistent theme in this complex story.

2. THE MAN FROM MARYLAND

Following Chief Justice Earl Warren's announcement on May 17, 1954, of the Supreme Court's *Brown v. Board of Education* decision, South Carolina's political leaders lined up to express their astonishment. Burnet R. Maybank, the state's senior US senator, commented that "the Supreme Court decision shocked me," while Ernest "Fritz" Hollings, the youthful speaker pro tempore of the South Carolina State House, claimed that the decision to end racial discrimination in public education came as "a real shock." In an article from the *Charleston News and Courier* entitled "Governor Byrnes 'shocked' by High Court Ruling," the state's governor expressed his own "shock" and urged "all of our people, white and colored, to exercise restraint and preserve order." US Congressman L. Mendel Rivers described the decision as "a tragic mistake," adding that it created "one of the gravest problems to confront the white people of the South since the days of Reconstruction." Olin D. Johnston, the state's junior US senator, offered a more optimistic reflection by claiming, "I have faith and confidence in the people of South Carolina and I know they are capable of solving this problem, although it is a perplexing one."[1]

As shocked and perplexed as South Carolina's politicians wished to appear, it is unlikely that the court's decision to rule racial segregation in public schools unconstitutional was entirely surprising. For South Carolina, the fight to maintain racial segregation in public places began long before *Brown*. Ten years earlier, as governor, Olin Johnston had reacted to the Supreme Court's *Smith v. Allwright* decision—which ruled the all-white Democratic primary system unconstitutional—by organizing the abolition of all state laws relating to the Democratic Party primaries. When the charismatic black lawyer Thurgood Marshall went to South Carolina to challenge Clarendon County's segregated school system in the *Briggs v. Elliott* case in 1951, Governor James F. Byrnes pledged to invest heavily to improve the quality of black schools as a means of encouraging the judges to uphold the doctrine of "separate but equal" established by the Supreme Court's *Plessy v. Ferguson* ruling of 1896. When Marshall and the National Association for the Advancement of Colored People (NAACP) brought *Briggs* and four other segregation cases before the Supreme Court in the form of *Brown,* Byrnes hoped that his massive long-term strategy to "equalize" South Carolina's schools would prove equally successful in encouraging the high court to affirm the 1896 decision. The governor utilized his political influence to the full by calling on John W. Davis, one of the most respected US lawyers, to defend South Carolina before the court, and persuading his friend President Dwight D. Eisenhower to prevent the Justice Department from filing an *amicus curiae* ("friend of the court") brief in support of Marshall and the NAACP.[2]

A colossal figure in South Carolina politics, Byrnes had represented the state in the US Senate before President Franklin Roosevelt appointed him to the Supreme Court in 1941 and the Office of Economic Stabilization in 1942. After heading Roosevelt's Office of War Mobilization, Byrnes served as secretary of state in President Harry S. Truman's administration during a pivotal era in the early Cold War. His reputation as a statesman is immortalized in the famous photographs of Truman, Clement Attlee, and Joseph Stalin sitting alongside each other in wicker chairs at the Potsdam Conference in August 1945. Byrnes is one of the four figures standing at the back, flanked by British foreign secretary Ernest Bevin and Russian foreign minister Vyacheslav Molotov, gently clutching Molotov's arm in the characteristic Byrnes gesture of friendship. In 1950, his election as governor of South Carolina, at the age of sixty-eight, constituted an overwhelming vote of confidence from both the traditional county communities and the new metropolitan elites.[3]

The implementation of the ambitious "equalization" project indicates Byrnes's long-held belief in the genuine possibility of court-ordered desegregation, not least because the justices had sided with Marshall and the NAACP in *Smith* and other landmark cases.[4] Given Byrnes's key role in attempting to prevent the justices from ruling segregation unconstitutional, it is unsurprising that he felt a sense of personal defeat following the court's announcement of *Brown.* Fritz Hollings, who had supported Byrnes's plan by authorizing legislation to "equalize" the state's schools through imposing a three-cent tax, and who accompanied John W. Davis at the oral arguments, recalled years later that "Byrnes was totally disillusioned when we lost that case. He'd been on the court itself, and said we had some dangerous fellows like [Justice] Felix Frankfurter, you couldn't tell which way they'd go, but he knew the court would find the right thing, and that there wasn't any chance of us losing and what have you, so when he lost in 1954, that was it."[5] The governor later published an article entitled "The Supreme Court Must Be Curbed!," in which he slammed his former colleagues for ignoring the legal precedent of *Plessy* and deciding instead to "legislate a policy for schools," offering a grave warning that "when the next court is called upon to 'read into' the Constitution something which was never there, another segment of the people may be the victim. It may be *you.*"[6]

As Tony Badger has argued, South Carolina's "preemptive" action of improving black schools as a means of offsetting court-ordered desegregation highlights the fact that southern conservatives pursued "the only coherent strategy on offer in the region in the years before the *Brown* decision," while southern liberals had yet to formulate a plan to implement gradual racial change. Although the "equalization" strategy ultimately failed, Jason Morgan Ward has argued convincingly that southerners believed they had accumulated a measure of moral capital for their attempt to showcase the "humane and orderly future of segregation," albeit in a manner that exposed a tension between moderation and militancy that would continue to characterize white southern resistance to civil rights. In the face of continuous black protest and northern pro–civil rights measures, southern white supremacy would remodel itself in response to new challenges.[7]

Plessy v. Ferguson had, for more than half a century, been the South's preeminent defense of its racial order, and following the Supreme Court's unanimous decision to nullify the 1896 decision through the *Brown* ruling, South Carolina's concerned white community began calling on a more radical figure in the state's politics. Although no longer in public office when the court announced *Brown,* ex-governor James Strom Thurmond had already established a national profile by breaking dramatically with the Democratic Party to run for president on an independent "states' rights" ticket in response to President Truman's adoption of a civil rights plank in the run-up to the 1948 presidential election.[8] To an audience of wild supporters who knew nothing of his twenty-three-year-old mixed-race daughter, whose identity remained secret until after his death, Thurmond had declared that "there's not enough troops in the army to force the Southern people to break down segregation and admit the n—— race into our theaters, into our swimming pools, into our homes, and into our churches."[9]

Having won Electoral College majorities in four Deep South states, Thurmond made a bold challenge to Olin Johnston's incumbency in the 1950 Democratic Senate primary contest, but the popular upcountryman proved immovable.[10]

Despite his failure to win election to the Senate, many white southerners sought Thurmond's advice on the best means of protecting segregation in schools, and the opportunistic Thurmond was happy to use South Carolina's outrage over *Brown* to make a second attempt at the Senate following Burnet Maybank's sudden death from a heart attack on September 1, 1954. He prevailed spectacularly, running as a write-in candidate to defy the efforts of the state's Democratic establishment to install state Senator Edgar A. Brown in Maybank's seat, defeating Brown by 145,444 votes to 83,525. Despite many of his adoring supporters misspelling his name on the ballot papers, "Strum Thormond" became the first candidate elected to the US Senate in a write-in victory.[11]

Thurmond, in his partnership with Olin Johnston, joined a bloc of southern senators that, for years, had resisted federal threats to the racial status quo. By grounding a consistent defense of segregation in the rhetoric of conservative Americanism, the southern senators had organized in response to the introduction of antilynching legislation during the 1930s, preventing passage of the Costigan-Wagner bill in 1935 and the Wagner-Van Nuys bill in 1938. They had condemned Franklin Roosevelt's introduction of the Fair Employment Practices Committee in 1941 and, despite misgivings about criticizing the American military establishment at the onset of the Cold War, protested Truman's desegregation of the US Army in 1948. To ensure a consistent southern presence on the Senate floor during the late 1940s, the highly influential Richard Russell of Georgia recommended to fellow southerners in 1949, "I think it is wise to have one Senator from the South responsible for watching the floor each day to see that no legislative trickery is employed," to which South Carolina's Johnston responded, "You may rest assured that I will co-operate with you in every possible way."[12]

With the practice of violent revolt and the creation of discriminatory legislation persisting back home in their respective states, southerners in Washington, DC, aimed to overcome their limited number, crafting a political rhetoric that would resonate with a national audience by claiming to represent disaffected white Americans throughout the entire nation.[13] As a member of the southern Democratic bloc, Thurmond's devotion to white supremacy was never questioned, but his fellow Democrats often ostracized him for his "lone wolf" tendencies, particularly his infamous 1957 filibuster. Thurmond struggled to bring himself to show deference to Richard Russell's leadership, or to the influence of Senate Majority Leader Lyndon Johnson. While some, such as Alabama's Lister Hill, commented on their dislike of Johnson behind the scenes, Thurmond was less inclined to conceal his resentment. He recalled years later that Johnson "was Chairman of the Steering Committee, he was Chairman of the Policy Committee, he was Chairman of just about every committee there was in the Democratic power structure. I was a little surprised to see that one man wanted that much power."[14]

Solidarity on the race question masked the fact that southerners often failed to see eye-to-eye on other issues of economic and social policy. On the workers' rights issue, Olin Johnston would distance himself from other southerners and align himself with northern liberal Democrats who sympathized with the civil rights movement, such as Jacob Javits of New York and Hubert Humphrey of Minnesota. Johnston argued that his political positions were logical rather than paradoxical. His continued defense of South Carolina's upcountry textile workers, despite the prevalence of hostility toward workers' rights elsewhere in the South, was often expressed in the form of resisting foreign imports and ensuring the strength of the US economy in the face of the very Communist threat that supposedly influenced the civil rights movement. When opposing a bill introduced by fellow southerner John McClellan to investigate union corruption, Johnston emphasized the problems of federal interference through legislation—a frequent argument used by segregationists when opposing civil rights—arguing that "to kill such legislation on civil rights matters and vote for such matters in the field of labor . . . this is inconsistency."[15]

Johnston was by no means the only Deep South Democrat to present racial conservatism as perfectly compatible with liberalism in other policy areas. When asked if his opposition to civil rights constituted a shift toward conservatism, Louisiana's Russell Long claimed, "I can be a liberal and still believe in the Constitution!" Given that their political future seemed to depend largely on the civil rights issue, southern senators were happy to put aside their ideological differences over matters such as government spending when the time came to stand together in resisting federal interference in race relations. With their frequent use of constitutional appeals and states' rights language, it seems logical that southerners feigned shock in the wake of the *Brown* decision, and equally unsurprising that the Supreme Court—at one time the defender of the very constitutional principles southerners claimed to uphold—became a focal point in the struggle to preserve segregation.[16]

Despite pressure to act following the 1954 decision, southern senators struggled to formulate a collective response, particularly as some felt inclined to wait for a ruling on how they would be expected to implement the desegregation of their schools. In the absence of a coherent strategy, Johnston and Thurmond set out to curb the Supreme Court's power during the mid-1950s. President Eisenhower's nominations to the court of John Marshall Harlan II, William J. Brennan, and Charles Evans Whittaker remained relatively untroubled by South Carolinian agitation, but Johnston's opposition to Eisenhower's nomination of Simon E. Sobeloff to the Fourth Circuit Court of Appeals offered an early, and much overlooked, indication of how the Supreme Court nomination process would intensify dramatically in the late 1960s. Although the justices had provoked South Carolina's war on the Supreme Court through the *Brown* decision, the Sobeloff case shows that the state's senators were as willing to obstruct presidential appointments to the lower courts. Johnston's tactics suggested a defensive strategy to prevent liberal judges from reaching South Carolina's territory, but his obstruction of President John F. Kennedy's appointment of Thurgood Marshall to the Second Circuit, covered here in chapters four and five, emphasized the insistence of both Thurmond and Johnston that the Supreme Court threatened Americans on a national, not just regional, scale.

South Carolina's involvement in many failed attempts to introduce court-curbing legislation reflected a concerted effort to weaken the court as an institution, yet the battle that emerged in the nomination process suggests that Johnston, Thurmond, and, later, Senator Ernest "Fritz" Hollings considered the liberal ideologies of the individual justices to be the root cause of the threat posed to the South. As history would prove, this belief was particularly relevant in the case of Chief Justice Earl Warren, the man who led the Supreme Court throughout this most turbulent period of political transformation.

Southern suspicion of Warren began brewing long before his announcement of *Brown*. After President Eisenhower nominated him to replace the late Fred Vinson as chief justice of the United States on October 5, 1953, Warren served for three months on a recess appointment prior to his official nomination on January 11, 1954. The Senate Judiciary Committee began scrutinizing the appointment, with Olin Johnston of South Carolina, James Eastland of Mississippi, and

Chairman William Langer of North Dakota all voting against confirmation. Johnston joined Eastland in criticizing Warren's lack of judicial experience, and claimed that the committee had requested a Federal Bureau of Investigation report on Warren, which had failed to materialize. Drew Pearson speculated in the *San Francisco Chronicle* that Eastland's concern over Warren's position on segregation was in fact at the heart of the request for the investigation, but the opposition of Johnston and Eastland became overshadowed when the press condemned Chairman Langer's repeated delays of Warren's confirmation, motivated solely by his continued irritation that no president had ever chosen a judge from his home state of North Dakota to sit on the Supreme Court. "Wild Bill's" antics ultimately achieved little—he reportedly "chewed on his ever-present unlighted cigar but said nothing" while the Senate confirmed Warren by a unanimous voice vote—but the chairman's eccentric behavior masked the emerging southern obstructionist tendency that would later define the Judiciary Committee's scrutiny of Supreme Court nominees.[17]

A former Republican vice presidential candidate and governor of California who had used his influence to assist Dwight Eisenhower in securing the Republican nomination for the 1952 presidential election, Earl Warren remained an unpopular figure in the South following the Senate's confirmation of his appointment as chief justice. For two reasons in particular, southerners remained adamant that Warren was primarily responsible for the court's landmark ruling in *Brown*. The first was that Warren himself had read the ruling from the bench, making it inevitable that he would become the "face" of the decision. Back in 1952, Governor Byrnes might have had good reason to expect the Supreme Court to uphold the constitutionality of South Carolina's segregated schools in that Warren's predecessor, Chief Justice Vinson, and several others on the court, including justices Stanley Reed, Felix Frankfurter, Robert Jackson, and Tom C. Clark, had all expressed serious concerns over whether the court could or should overturn *Plessy v. Ferguson*. Vinson's death from a heart attack and his replacement by Warren proved critical six months later when the justices reargued the case, with the new chief justice utilizing his skills as diplomat, umpire, and negotiator to steer the other justices toward a unanimous opinion, partly through convincing his brethren that if one of them produced a dissenting opinion, segregationists would almost certainly use it as a rallying cry for their cause. Fritz Hollings claimed, when marking the fiftieth anniversary of the *Briggs v. Elliott* case in 2002, that when Warren arrived on the Supreme Court in late 1953, "he didn't want to hear about 'separate but equal.' He wanted the case reargued on the constitutionality of segregation itself." This proactive approach in changing the course of history ensured Warren's notoriety in the minds of southerners during the mid-1950s.[18]

The second reason for laying the blame for *Brown* at Warren's door was his inclusion in the opinion, in the form of footnote 11, of a reference to Gunnar Myrdal's *An American Dilemma*, a critical sociological study of US race relations that had infuriated many in the South when published in 1944, largely for its attack on white prejudice toward African Americans. As Jim Newton has argued, the Myrdal footnote appeared to suggest "what many Southerners suspected: the court was striking down school segregation not because the law commanded it but because modern experts no longer approved of it," particularly as Warren had added the words "see generally" to the footnote. Two of the court's southerners, Hugo Black of Alabama and Tom Clark of Texas, had anticipated this highly negative reaction months earlier, and both had advised Warren against citing Myrdal.[19]

Their fears proved well-founded. In June 1955, Olin Johnston initiated a southern effort to gather information on the sources of recent court decisions, teaming up with James Eastland to introduce Senate Resolution 104 as a means of investigating what Johnston described as the "pink, red or actually communistic sources" of information that he believed to be the inspiration for the justices' legal reasoning. So keen was Johnston to investigate the court's sources that he wrote to his Mississippi colleague one year later, advising Eastland, by now chairman of the Senate Judiciary Committee, to set up a subcommittee to implement the resolution. Johnston felt compelled to point out, even in a friendly letter to a colleague of the same ideology, that the *Brown* decision was "illegal from the Constitutional point of view, unlawful in a jurisprudential sense, and was purely a political pronouncement based upon psychological, sociological and other non-judicial, un-factual theories and fallacies."[20]

For many in the South, Warren's authorship of the *Brown* ruling, and his insistence on quoting "generally" a controversial work such as Myrdal's, suggested that the chief justice had brought his private motivations into the decision to order the desegregation of schools. Strom Thurmond, who had proved his willingness to lead disenchanted southerners out of the Democratic Party when he headed the "Dixiecrat" presidential ticket in 1948, put his criticism of Warren at the center of his warning of a second southern "bolt" from the party, arguing that "Democratic Presidents appointed eight of the nine judges on the court at the time of the [*Brown*] decision, and President Eisenhower appointed the man who wrote the opinion. . . . The South blames both parties."[21] The truth of Eisenhower's position on segregation was more complex. Mindful of southern fears of a desegregation order well before *Brown*, the president had considered at least two southern judges as a replacement for the Kentuckian Vinson. With John W. Davis's advanced age ruling him out, and Judge John J. Parker of the United States Court of Appeals for the Fourth Circuit tainted by the Senate's rejection of his nomination to the Supreme Court in 1930, Eisenhower chose instead to honor a private promise, made long before, that Earl Warren would be put forward for the first court vacancy to come up during his presidency.[22]

The Senate Judiciary Committee hesitated when, on November 9, 1954, Eisenhower nominated Judge John Marshall Harlan II of the US Court of Appeals for the Second Circuit to replace the late Robert Jackson on the Supreme Court. Having failed to prevent the Senate from confirming Earl Warren over their objections, southerners Johnston and Eastland were determined to ensure a full background check on Eisenhower's second nominee. The committee initially declined to act on the nomination, made only one week after the 1954 congressional elections, forcing Eisenhower to renominate Harlan in January 1955. By then, the Democratic Party had taken control of the Senate, with Democrat Harley Kilgore of West Virginia replacing Republican William Langer as Judiciary Committee chairman. The way the Harlan nomination was handled indicates that southern senators, still reeling from the court's announcement of *Brown* and still considering methods of counterattack, were not yet prepared to oppose Supreme Court nominations by declaring openly their concern over a nominee's position on segregation. While happy to speak at length on their reservations regarding Harlan, southerners obscured, or at the very least blunted, the true motivation for their obstruction during the committee hearings.[23]

Supreme Court nominees had appeared before the Senate Judiciary Committee only rarely up until the mid-1950s, but the southern influence on the committee was sufficient to bring Harlan before them to testify.[24] The one mention of segregation throughout two days of hearings occurred during a round of questions from James Eastland, who, when putting to Harlan a query "requested by a member of the Senate to propound," appeared adamant that the segregation issue had no relevance to his interrogation:

Senator Eastland: I do not think you understood the question. This is not a case—this is not a question that would come before the court. It says—

Do you believe that the Supreme Court should change established interpretations of the Constitution to accord with the economic, political and sociological views—that is, the personal views—of the judges who from time to time constitute the membership of the court?

Judge Harlan: I misinterpreted the question.

Senator Eastland: I knew you did.

Judge Harlan: The purport of your inquiry. To lay the inquiry bare, as I understand it, you are asking me how I would have voted on the segregation issue?

Senator Eastland: No, sir. That has not anything to do with it. What he is asking you is this—it is not my question—do you think that a judge should interpret the Constitution in accordance with the personal views of that judge on economic, political, or sociological questions?

Judge Harlan: That gives a different thrust to the question. No, sir.[25]

The Senate's ongoing debate regarding the Bricker Amendment—a proposed adjustment of the US Constitution that would have reduced the president's authority in signing future treaties with foreign powers—led senators to focus on the nominee's views regarding "world government" throughout most of the hearings. But the brief mention of "the segregation issue," which Harlan, rather than Eastland, brought into the hearings, is significant for providing the first example of a southern Judiciary Committee member probing a nominee's attitude toward *Brown* by offering questions that supposedly referred only to the issue of constitutional interpretation.[26]

On the Senate floor, Eastland maintained that he was opposed to Harlan for his views on US sovereignty, his lack of judicial experience, and the fact that he came from the state of New York, a state whose people, according to Eastland, "possess views and philosophies which are different from the viewpoints of the rest of the country." Given that Harlan had spent only one year on the Second

Circuit, his relative lack of judicial experience was an obvious weakness for southerners to exploit. Both Eastland and Johnston were happy to press this point, as they had done the previous year with the Warren nomination, and the fact that the nominee's grandfather was the earlier Justice John Marshall Harlan of Kentucky, who had rejected the "separate but equal" doctrine in the sole dissenting opinion in *Plessy*, was unlikely to inspire reverence among other Deep South Democrats. Johnston also concurred with Eastland regarding the "world government" issue, claiming he feared that Harlan "would put the United Nations above the United States Constitution." Richard Russell of Georgia, the leader of the southern bloc in the Senate, echoed the concerns regarding Harlan's judicial experience and added, "I do not propose, Mr. President, to vote to advise and consent to the nomination of any judge to the Supreme Court bench who has not had considerable judicial experience under the restraint of precedent." Senator Sam Ervin of North Carolina asked Russell, his southern colleague, to yield so he could point out that "of the eight present members of the Supreme Court of the United States, only one had as much as a single second's judicial experience on an appellate court or a court of general jurisdiction prior to his elevation," to which Russell responded, "I am quite confident that the statement made by the distinguished senator from North Carolina is correct."[27]

Away from the Senate deliberations, Johnston's South Carolina colleague, Strom Thurmond, suggested that the Supreme Court nomination process would soon emerge as an arena of battle between the Eisenhower administration and the South. With his belief that "there is little apparent concern over whether the new members of the courts will follow the Constitution instead of the psychology books," the junior senator made a speech before the Southern Society at the Plaza Hotel in Harlan's home state of New York only days after the nomination was announced. Thurmond pledged, in a bold statement of intent that only hinted at his controversial future in the Supreme Court nomination process, "to consider carefully every nomination made by the Chief Executive to the courts and to other positions of power. If I find the appointee, by his actions and statements, to be disqualified for the trust he would assume, I shall vote against his confirmation." In the final words of the speech, Thurmond announced that "the Supreme Court by its decree has impeded the progress made in seventy-five years of work to provide equal and adequate public education for the white and Negro children of the South. No accuser can point his finger in any other direction with as much accuracy."[28] With these words, South Carolina finally declared war on the Supreme Court.

Despite their reluctance during the Harlan hearings to push the segregation issue, or even mention it by name, southern senators had registered their first significant protest against a Supreme Court nominee in the aftermath of *Brown*. In contrast to the unanimous voice vote for Warren, nine southern Democrats voted against John Marshall Harlan's confirmation. Senators Lister Hill of Alabama, John McClellan of Arkansas, George Smathers of Florida, John C. Stennis of Mississippi, and the newly elected freshman senator from South Carolina, Strom Thurmond, all joined with Johnston, Eastland, Russell, and Ervin in opposition. Republican William Langer maintained his cigar-chewing bitterness over the fact that the president had once again failed to choose anyone from North Dakota. With only one other member of Langer's party, Senator Herman Welker of Idaho, joining him in opposition, the final vote, on March 16, 1955, stood at 71–11 in favor of confirmation. The two Republicans aside, the vote seemed to reflect Olin Johnston's view, expressed in a letter to a South Carolina constituent, that "the Southern states are alone in this battle against the Supreme Court decision." As with Eastland's criticism of the state of New York, the ambiguous Russell/Ervin comments did not prevent the *New York Times* from making the rather obvious observation that "all of the Senators who voted against confirmation come from states where opposition to integrated schools is strong." Just as southern senators sought to offset charges of racism by arguing that Earl Warren's opinion in *Brown* contained no references to precedent or legal text but did refer "generally" to a sociological study written by a non-American author, the southern bloc would adopt an obstructive position to Supreme Court nominees by emphasizing concerns with judicial interpretation, the wording of the US Constitution, and, of course, the justices' "economic, social or political" views.[29]

Following arguments from school boards requesting relief from the desegregation order issued in the *Brown* ruling, the Supreme Court ruled, in a decision commonly referred to as "Brown II," on May 31, 1955, that school authorities must ensure desegregation "with all deliberate speed." Justice Hugo Black later regretted the use of that term, recognizing that the court's ambiguous language would effectively "authorize" southern leaders to drag their heels in implementing desegregation. Blaming Justice Felix Frankfurter for the inclusion of "all deliberate speed" in the ruling, Black frequently claimed to his law clerks, "I should never have let Felix get that into the opinion."[30] Thanks to the court's leniency, Judge John J. Parker of the Fourth Circuit Court of Appeals declared that the justices were merely forbidding segregation, rather than demanding integration. Thurmond praised the efforts of his former speechwriter, Robert M. Figg Jr., who had defended the Clarendon County school district that had been the original setting for the *Briggs* case, and who had argued before the justices in "Brown II" that "the handling of this problem should be left to those familiar with local conditions." In the event, the court sided with Solicitor General Simon E. Sobeloff, who, in arguing on behalf of the federal government, laid out an assertive plan for *Brown*'s enforcement, albeit in wording that President Eisenhower felt compelled to tone down, reportedly in his own handwriting, to avoid "rhetoric that might shame the South."[31]

Thanks to the outcome of "Brown II," South Carolina's senators were now acquainted with a brand-new nemesis in the struggle over segregation—Solicitor General Simon E. Sobeloff.

President Eisenhower's nomination, on July 14, 1955, of Simon Sobeloff to the US Court of Appeals for the Fourth Circuit signposted South Carolina's first truly significant battle in the lengthy war provoked by the high court's ruling in *Brown*. The state's outrage over the Sobeloff nomination was logical, despite the fact that it concerned a lower court vacancy rather than a vacancy on the Supreme Court. No South Carolina judge had served on the Fourth Circuit Court of Appeals (which comprised the states of Maryland, Virginia, West Virginia, North Carolina, and South Carolina) since Charles A. Woods's death in 1925, and now President Eisenhower was proposing to appoint Sobeloff, from Baltimore, Maryland, to replace the recently promoted Judge Morris A. Soper, also from Maryland. Whereas South Carolina's senators considered *Brown* an insult to the South, they were able to portray the Sobeloff nomination as an insult to the state of South Carolina specifically. In so doing, Johnston and Thurmond could play down claims that their opposition was due to Sobeloff's role in presenting the federal government's brief before the Supreme Court in the "Brown II" arguments.[32]

The uncertain positions of Warren and Harlan on the race issue offered little opportunity for attack during the debates over their appointments to the high court, but Sobeloff's role in "Brown II" appeared to confirm what South Carolina's senators had suspected: the president of the United States was prepared to back the appointment of judges who openly supported the *Brown* ruling. If Eisenhower genuinely believed that his selection of such a nominee would prove less controversial because the vacancy existed on a lower court rather than the Supreme Court, his prediction proved ill-judged. As if the imposition of such a judge on their own turf was not enough, Johnston and Thurmond were no doubt mindful of the fact that Sobeloff's appointment to the Fourth Circuit made his elevation to the Supreme Court an increasingly likely possibility. As David A. Nichols has claimed, Eisenhower and his attorney general, Herbert Brownell, were "grooming" Sobeloff for the Supreme Court's "Jewish seat" in the event that the elderly Justice Felix Frankfurter decided to retire.[33]

Johnston and Eastland blocked the Sobeloff nomination immediately in order to initiate a thorough investigation into the nominee's background. Of particular concern was Sobeloff's claim before the Judicial Conference of the Fourth Circuit that "the Supreme Court is not merely the adjudicator of controversies, but in the process of adjudication, it is in many instances the final formulator of national policy." The *Washington Post–Times Herald* claimed that Sobeloff's argument on behalf of the federal government in "Brown II" formed the "real" objection of both Johnston and Eastland, who remained "wholly unappeased by the fact that [Sobeloff] advocated a course of statesmanly moderation in applying the segregation decision." The nomination would ultimately meet the same fate as Harlan's, with the delay causing Sobeloff's nomination to expire under Section 6 of Rule 38 (Standing Rules of the Senate), forcing Eisenhower to renominate him at the start of the next Congress.[34]

Never one to miss an opportunity to influence events in a manner that might raise his public profile, Thurmond proposed, as an alternative nominee, his former speechwriter, Charleston resident Robert M. Figg Jr., and continued to push for Figg's appointment throughout the controversy. In so doing, Thurmond was setting up Sobeloff and Figg—the two men who had argued against one other during the South Carolina segment of "Brown II"—as opponents once again, this time as potential nominees for a vacancy on the Fourth Circuit. One frequently overlooked yet notable aspect of the Sobeloff episode is the fact that Thurmond, in offering his personal recommendation of Figg, was effectively pushing Eisenhower to choose between the man who had argued for the desegregation of southern schools in "Brown II" and the man who had made South Carolina's counterargument in the same case.[35]

When Eisenhower renominated Sobeloff in January 1956, Olin Johnston—

who, like Thurmond, was facing reelection—remained determined to use his position on the Senate Judiciary Committee to defend South Carolina's honor. With Thurmond dismissing Sobeloff by claiming "I do not know the appointee or his qualifications," Johnston composed a detailed letter to Judiciary Committee chairman Harley Kilgore, declaring, "since I am vitally interested in any nomination to the Fourth Circuit Court of Appeals, I would sincerely appreciate your instructing the staff member handling receipts of such nominations to immediately and personally notify me of receipt of any new nomination, because I may not be present on the floor of the Senate to hear them read when they come over."[36] Only two days later, Johnston wrote a longer and more detailed letter to the chairman, requesting that Kilgore set up a subcommittee to look into the fact that Sobeloff had been paid $30,000 to investigate the Baltimore Trust Company, and later represented clients with claims against the same company. Sobeloff, in response to Johnston's request for careful scrutiny of the nomination, was quoted in the press as declaring, "it is undoubtedly the privilege of the Senator to inquire, and it will be my pleasure to answer his questions, and the sooner the better."[37]

Two crucial developments complicated the nomination during the month of February. First, at the start of the month, Judge Armistead M. Dobie's elevation to senior status created a second vacancy on the Fourth Circuit Court of Appeals. The Eisenhower administration could now use the opening up of the second vacancy as an olive branch to satisfy South Carolina's demands, and potentially undermine Johnston's principal argument against Sobeloff. Secondly, at the end of the month, Harley Kilgore's sudden death from a cerebral hemorrhage made way for archsegregationist Eastland of Mississippi to become chairman of the Judiciary Committee. This development marked a significant victory for southern senators, who for years had understood the tactical advantages of establishing a reliable southern presence on that body, particularly given the committee's jurisdiction over antilynching legislation during the 1930s. Olin Johnston now had his closest ally on the committee in the most influential role of all.[38]

In a newsletter dated April 12, 1956, Johnston made clear to his supporters that he was entirely committed to opposing the Sobeloff nomination, taking the trouble to point out, in terms worthy of Thurmond, that "I believe it is vital for every South Carolinian to know that President Eisenhower is directly to blame for the farm woes, the civil rights turmoil, our textile industrial problems, our failures in international diplomacy, the steady destruction of our states' rights and the many other serious problems that face our people today." The senator submitted a full account of the conflict-of-interest charges, as offered by a Mr. Charles Shankroff of Baltimore, Maryland, to a Senate judiciary subcommittee chaired by Senator Joseph C. O'Mahoney of Wyoming, which began public hearings into the nomination on May 5, 1956. Sobeloff refuted Shankroff's charges before the Senate subcommittee while sitting alongside Senator J. Glenn Beall of Maryland, and composed a five-page letter to Chairman O'Mahoney, in which he provided detailed responses to each of the charges. Without commenting on Johnston or the other southerners opposing his nomination, the solicitor general concluded that "it is sheer presumption of [Mr. Shankroff] to suggest after two decades that he has found irregularities that have been overlooked by a community and its press that were watching these proceedings with keenest interest." An impressive range of judges, lawyers, and businessmen from Washington, DC, and his home state joined with Maryland's two senators in backing Sobeloff.[39]

Several newspapers, including the *Washington Post–Times Herald,* recognized Johnston as Sobeloff's "arch challenger" and criticized the senator for his obstructionism, yet he showed no sign of relenting in his crusade. Johnston hit back against his critics in a newsletter and took the opportunity to reassure his constituents that he would continue to block the nomination. The Columbia-based law firm of Tompkins, Tompkins and McMaster aided Johnston's investigation of Sobeloff's background, with John Gregg McMaster forwarding to the senator a "revelation" that Sobeloff had spoken favorably of recording jury deliberations, a practice that Attorney General Herbert Brownell had allegedly condemned. According to McMaster's account, Sobeloff had attended a judicial conference in Denver, Colorado, at which a delegate played an audio recording of jury deliberations and Sobeloff reportedly "made no protest." Before long, President Eisenhower became frustrated with the delay, criticizing the Senate Judiciary Committee during a news conference on May 23 and defending his selection of the controversial nominee. The aforementioned Senator Beall of Maryland observed that "it is doubtful if any judicial nomination has received more minute examination."[40]

The Sobeloff nomination divided the members of the Senate Judiciary Committee. Minutes from a committee meeting that took place on June 25, 1956, suggest that some members' discomfort with Johnston's agenda must have been palpable. Chairman Eastland began by recognizing Senator O'Mahoney, who requested a special meeting to take a roll call vote on Sobeloff's nomination. Perhaps unsurprisingly, the cantankerous, cigar-chewing William Langer of North Dakota recalled a similar experience regarding the Eighth Circuit Court of Appeals, and queried the details of the last occasion on which a president had appointed a South Carolinian to the Fourth Circuit, receiving Johnston's confirmation that the last appointment of a South Carolina judge occurred in 1913. Senator Langer then raised the complicated issue of the second vacancy. The fact that the Eisenhower administration was refusing to nominate a judge for this vacancy until the committee acted on the Sobeloff nomination must have put pressure on O'Mahoney, who was chairing the subcommittee.[41]

In order to confirm the administration's position, Chairman Eastland read to the committee a letter from Herbert Brownell, in which the attorney general assured Eastland that the matter of the second vacancy was "under active consideration." Adding a "respectful" reminder that the first vacancy had been outstanding for over a year, Brownell urged that "anything that the committee does to expedite action on [the Sobeloff] nomination, which is still pending before it, would considerably alleviate the pressure on the court." Senator O'Mahoney moved that the committee make a vote on the Sobeloff nomination the first order of business at a special meeting later in the week. The committee took a roll call vote on O'Mahoney's motion, with southern Democrats Johnston, Eastland, and Price Daniel of Texas—joined by one Republican, Langer—registering "no" votes. Estes Kefauver, the moderate southern Democrat from Tennessee, joined fellow Democrat O'Mahoney and Republicans Everett Dirksen of Illinois, Arthur V. Watkins of Utah, and John Marshall Butler of Maryland in voting "yea."[42]

The minutes suggest that committee members were prepared to respect senatorial courtesy by recognizing Johnston's right as a South Carolina senator to withhold consent on a nomination to the Fourth Circuit, but the roll call vote suggests that most members were keen to draw the ongoing obstructionism to a close. Furthermore, the minutes indicate that Johnston's position was supposedly fireproof, not only because Chairman Eastland was bound to sympathize, but also because Johnston could simply insist that South Carolina had missed its turn rather than be deprived of a judicial appointment altogether. He was able to press the point further the very same day, in a detailed written response to Senator Langer's query, in which he informed the North Dakotan that "there have been two judges [on the Fourth Circuit] from every state except Maryland, which has three. If Mr. Sobeloff is confirmed, Maryland will have had four in comparison to two from every other state . . . according to the rotation of appointments, South Carolina should be recognized."[43]

Despite the lukewarm feelings within the committee, several letters from Johnston's constituents suggested widespread support for his actions in South Carolina. One anonymous writer urged the senator to "call upon all available help" to prevent Sobeloff's confirmation, observing that "some politicians seem determined to set the South up for a raping." Others focused on Sobeloff's religion, with one resident of Lexington writing, "Tell me who the honorable man is, please: Name sounds like a Greek, or other foreigner. Is he a churchman? Or what?" The senator responded that Sobeloff "is active in the Jewish faith," adding that "the press reported that he received the 'Man of the Year' Award last year from the B'Nai B'rith fraternity." One resident of Columbia presumably hoped that Johnston would agree with his view that "when one reads of the success of certain 'Jewish groups' in running the government in this country . . . it just seems that they are so well-mobilized, and organized, that it's almost impossible to 'sidetrack' any important matter which concerns them." Perhaps inevitably, Johnston's continued opposition to the nominee led to suggestions of anti-Semitism, to which the senator responded, "I have never persecuted the Jewish race at any time," claiming that, in South Carolina, "the Jewish people have supported me as near as 100 percent as any race of people."[44]

Senate Majority Leader Lyndon Johnson persuaded Chairman Eastland to allow a vote on the Sobeloff nomination in committee, on June 29, despite Olin Johnston twice objecting. On July 6, eight Judiciary Committee members voted to send the nomination to the Senate for a vote, with only Chairman Eastland joining Johnston in opposition. Lyndon Johnson allowed a lengthy debate to take place on July 16 as a means of drawing the Sobeloff controversy to a close while also accommodating the disgruntled southerners. Making his final stand, Johnston began by asking other senators not to interrupt him during his speech, before addressing the press criticism aimed at Eastland and himself for their handling of the nomination. Claiming to have a threefold objection to the nominee, Johnston led with "tradition and every consideration of the rights of the state of South Carolina," followed by Sobeloff's involvement in the alleged conflict of interest, and concluding with the nominee's philosophy concerning states' rights, which "are repugnant to me and the overwhelming majority of the good people whom I have the honor to represent." Turning to the disrespect shown to South Carolina with regard to the rotation of appointments, the senator pointed out that Eisenhower had won more than one hundred thousand votes in South Carolina in the 1952 presidential election, and argued that "the nomination now pending is an insult" to most of the president's supporters in the state. In discussing the Shankroff charges, Johnston conceded that "the majority report states that the charges against the nominee are baseless," but switched the focus of the argument to suggest that senators had discredited Charles Shankroff as a witness when he had had a right to be heard, before launching into a lengthy and interminable discussion of the facts surrounding the alleged conflict of interest.[45]

James Eastland asked Johnston to yield in order to engage his southern colleague in a familiar routine of using pointless queries to ensure an emphasis on certain points. The Mississippian asked, "We are in an era of judicial tyranny, are we not?" to which Johnston replied, "There is no question about that in my mind." Perhaps inevitably, the discussion turned to the Supreme Court, with Eastland wondering if Sobeloff "has the same philosophy as Chief Justice Warren and Associate Justice Black and Associate Justice [William O.] Douglas," to which Johnston responded, "His philosophy of life is very closely aligned with their philosophy of life." The South Carolinian concluded by urging the Senate "to be practical" by denying Sobeloff confirmation. Throughout the debate, Johnston was able to point to the solid support of southern Democratic senators from the other Fourth Circuit states, who had signed a petition protesting Sobeloff's confirmation. He later wrote to Senators Sam Ervin and W. Kerr Scott of North Carolina, and Harry F. Byrd and A. Willis Robertson of Virginia, to thank them for their "meritorious assistance" in signing the petition. Throughout their opposition to the nominee, both Johnston and Eastland had minimized their references to segregation, but this did not prevent Thurmond, South Carolina's unpredictable junior senator, from pointing out that Sobeloff was "a strong advocate of integration of races in the public schools."[46]

Following Johnston's complaint that the Judiciary Committee had failed to make satisfactory investigations into Sobeloff's background, the Senate defeated his motion to send the nomination back to committee by a vote of 63–20. Senators confirmed the nomination shortly afterwards, by a vote of 64–19—with four Republicans joining fifteen southern Democrats in opposition—but this did not discourage praise from back home for Johnston's stand. State Senator L.

Marion Gressette believed that Johnston's fight against Sobeloff "was an excellent job and will in the long run prove most helpful to our cause," while former state Senator Huger Sinkler felt that "the fight demonstrated both to the country and to Sobeloff himself that we are seriously concerned over the progressive encroachment of the Federal Judiciary."[47]

Reflecting on his year-long crusade to prevent Sobeloff from reaching the Fourth Circuit, Johnston wrote in a letter to attorney James H. Hammond that "without additional support in the final stages it proved impossible," but added that "possibly the fight against him, though, and the publicity given it, will make the people realize what his views are, and I sincerely hope that it may lead him toward the path of conservatism, although that seems unlikely." To Huger Sinkler, he declared, "it is good to know that my people realize the efforts extended in the Senate. As you know, people do not often take the time to write letters of commendation, and I therefore doubly appreciate your courtesy." In writing to acknowledge Johnston's communication regarding the introduction of a new federal judgeship for South Carolina, Governor George Bell Timmerman Jr. quipped, in his own handwriting at the bottom of the letter, "I hope Brownell doesn't attempt to force a Marylander on us." To fill the second vacancy on the Fourth Circuit, Strom Thurmond renewed his effort to engineer Robert Figg's appointment, but Olin Johnston—who recalled Figg's role as Thurmond's speechwriter during the latter's challenge to his incumbency in 1950—did nothing to support his colleague's effort. Attorney General Brownell finally approved the appointment of a South Carolina judge in the form of Clement F. Haynsworth of Greenville. Few, if any, during this era would have recognized Haynsworth's significance in the story of South Carolina and the Supreme Court. A little over a decade later, he would find himself at the center of one of the most controversial judicial nomination battles in US history.[48]

Senator Johnston had established his credentials as a no-nonsense investigator of judicial nominees, leading the nation's press to focus on him once again following President Eisenhower's selection of William J. Brennan to replace the outgoing Justice Sherman Minton on the Supreme Court. Despite calling for careful scrutiny of the nominee's background, Johnston claimed that he was not planning to initiate a concerted opposition to Brennan on a scale similar to his crusade against Sobeloff, maintaining simply that "I just don't know anything about him one way or another . . . but the Supreme Court is so important we should be very careful on all these nominations."[49] Eisenhower employed a programmatic method of sourcing judicial nominees, with the search for a conservative Democratic judge from the east coast, preferably younger than sixty-two years of age, culminating in Brennan's selection. With the upcoming presidential election in mind, Eisenhower was keen to target the Catholic vote by reinstating the "Catholic seat" that had disappeared from the court following Justice Frank Murphy's death in 1949. For Johnston's supporters, Brennan's faith would become the most controversial aspect of his nomination, with one writer declaring "never before in the history of our country have we been faced with such grave danger as there exists today . . . I refer to ROMAN CATHOLICISM," and another, who wished to remain anonymous, citing Massachusetts Senator John F. Kennedy's unsuccessful campaign for the Democratic vice presidential nomination as an example of how "the Roman Catholic church wants to control this country of ours, and make us slaves to the Pope." As with the anti-Semitic comments he had received during the summer, Johnston declined to dignify the anti-Catholic views of his supporters.[50]

Johnston's reluctance to unleash hell on the comparatively inoffensive Supreme Court nominations of William Brennan and Charles Evans Whittaker proved that the South Carolinian knew how to pick his battles. Senator Joseph McCarthy of Wisconsin, already a notorious figure for his anti-Communist "witch-hunts," asked to appear before the Senate Judiciary Committee so that he could question Brennan at length on the manner in which the nominee had supposedly "used the Supreme Court of New Jersey as a privileged sanctuary from which to . . . conduct guerrilla warfare against anyone who would dare attempt to expose individual communists." McCarthy's interrogation provoked tense exchanges with Chairman Eastland and also Senator O'Mahoney, but failed to convince senators of Brennan's lack of suitability for the court. The Senate confirmed both Brennan and Whittaker by unanimous voice vote on March 19, 1957.[51]

It may seem ironic that Olin Johnston pursued a lengthy battle to prevent Simon Sobeloff from reaching the Fourth Circuit Court of Appeals while showing little or no interest in Eisenhower's nomination to the Supreme Court of William Brennan, a man who would later prove to be a formidable progressive influence. On the other hand, while Sobeloff's role in "Brown II" appeared to confirm the federal government's sympathy with the Supreme Court's desegregation order, there was little in Brennan's judicial record to indicate that he would become one of the court's most consistent and influential liberal forces throughout the 1960s, 1970s, and 1980s. Furthermore, the fact that Eisenhower's choice of Brennan resulted partly from the president's preference for filling Supreme Court vacancies with judges not known to him personally—in contrast to the choice of Sobeloff, whose role as solicitor general had him marked as an administration insider—might well have minimized suspicion of one nominee and increased suspicion of the other. Few have contested Mark Silverstein's claim that, during the Eisenhower years, "the appointment of federal judges remained a low-key affair, with Senators typically unwilling or unable to invest substantial political capital in any attempt to challenge judicial nominations." But Johnston's behavior throughout the Sobeloff controversy suggests that the state of South Carolina does not conform to this narrative. The senior senator's obstruction of President Kennedy's appointment of Thurgood Marshall to the Second Circuit Court of Appeals in 1962 would further emphasize South Carolina's role in the intense politicization of lower court, as well as Supreme Court, nominations.[52]

With two new justices joining Earl Warren and John Marshall Harlan on the bench, President Eisenhower appeared to be reshaping the Supreme Court with remarkable speed. Yet the occurrence of two landmark events in 1957 would only increase the likelihood of Olin Johnston living up to his reputation as a formidable southern presence on the Senate Judiciary Committee.

3. "A RENDEZVOUS WITH REALITY"

The bitterness of the 1950 Democratic Party primary battle lingered on in South Carolina's senatorial partnership. Despite the cordial relationship established in the late 1940s, when Olin Johnston was the junior Senator and Strom Thurmond served as governor, the two men never developed a genuine friendship after 1950 and preferred to conduct their business separately whenever possible. Yet a sense of mild antagonism characterized the relationship, rather than outright hostility. Each reportedly ran a "nuisance" candidate against the other during the Senate elections of 1956, when both men were seeking reelection but running unopposed in the Democratic primaries, in what the *Charleston News and Courier* described as "a skirmish to determine which of the men will emerge as the state's number one political boss." Former congresswoman Liz Patterson recalls that her father, Olin Johnston, "would take people to the Senate dining room and Strom would come over and sit down and join them, and then Strom would leave and Daddy would pay the check for Strom and everyone. I do remember Daddy would really get sort of upset."[1]

Regardless of any ill feeling over one hoodwinking the other into paying for dinner, Johnston and Thurmond remained united in their condemnation of the US Supreme Court. It was during this era that South Carolina's conservative political community responded to the *Brown* decision with discussions of "interposition," which derived from James Madison's notion of each state retaining the right and duty to "interpose" themselves between their citizens and the federal government in order to prevent unreasonable political interference. With James J. Kilpatrick, editor of the *Richmond News Leader,* effectively resurrecting the doctrine, the nation's press began discussing the significance of "interposition" following Senator James Eastland's visit to South Carolina in January 1956. During his address before the state's Association of Citizens'

Councils, Eastland was joined onstage by, among others, Johnston and Thurmond, Governor George Bell Timmerman Jr., State Senator Edgar A. Brown, and also Ernest "Fritz" Hollings, who was elected lieutenant governor in 1954.[2]

Endorsements of interposition may have reassured the state's concerned white conservative voters that racial segregation would not be compromised, but the involvement of Thurmond, and, to a lesser extent, Johnston, in the creation of the Southern Manifesto of 1956 suggested that both men saw sense in Alabama senator John Sparkman's insistence that Democratic solidarity in the Senate remained the only realistic means of preventing the Senate's introduction of legislation that might undermine southern state autonomy. Introduced on the Senate floor by Walter F. George of Georgia on March 12, 1956, the manifesto condemned the Supreme Court while providing a clear southern statement of opposition to the *Brown v. Board of Education* ruling, and included signatures from ninety-nine Democrats and two Republicans, including the entire congressional delegations of all five Deep South states (Louisiana, Mississippi, Alabama, Georgia, and South Carolina) in addition to Arkansas and Virginia. Thurmond's boisterous promotion of the manifesto among senators, particularly his provocative, yet unsuccessful, attempt to goad racial moderate Senator Albert Gore of Tennessee into signing the document in front of reporters, only reinforced Richard Russell's claim that the South Carolinian played a particularly significant role in drafting the document. Scholars of southern politics have recognized the significance of the Southern Manifesto in Thurmond's segregationist crusade against the Supreme Court, with Joseph Crespino claiming that the document "initiated for Thurmond a war on the Warren Court that became the most consistent theme of his politics for the next decade and a half," and Tony Badger noting that Thurmond's aim "was to stir up popular segregationist feeling by convincing wavering politicians and their constituents that the Supreme Court could, and should, be defied."[3] Yet Olin Johnston's brand of simmering cynicism is generally overlooked, despite the fact that his position on the Senate Judiciary Committee would became a powerful weapon in South Carolina's lengthy anti–Supreme Court campaign, in which Thurmond was only one participant.

The impression of unity and strategy that southern congressmen aimed to convey with the Southern Manifesto may have masked the challenge of uniting conservative southerners behind a coordinated plan of action, as Jason Morgan Ward has claimed, yet Americans from outside the South sent a great many supportive letters to South Carolina's senators, awarding some degree of legitimacy to southern claims of representing "a national majority of ignored and discontented white Americans." In addition, a conference of state chief justices—of which Judge Taylor H. Stukes of South Carolina was the only Deep South representative—boosted their cause further by introducing a resolution urging the Supreme Court to exercise judicial restraint in matters relating to federalism. In their report, the chief justices echoed Olin Johnston's view that "there seems to be a tendency for the Supreme Court to get into the legislative field" by declaring that "we are not alone in our view that the Court, in many cases arising under the Fourteenth Amendment, has assumed what seem to us primarily legislative powers."[4]

Yet these developments did not prevent South Carolina's senators from pointing to the pro–civil rights liberalism of their northern counterparts as an excuse for their limited gains. This was particularly the case during 1958, when both men were advising their supporters to manage their expectations, with Johnston telling one resident from Hammond, Indiana, that passage of a bill to introduce a constitutional amendment requires "a two-thirds vote, which is the problem we Southern Senators have faced recently" and Thurmond complaining to a married couple from Chappells, South Carolina, that "I am afraid the odds will be more strongly against us in the new Congress." In other letters, Thurmond was keen to emphasize his own contribution over those made by other southerners, telling a Greenville, South Carolina, resident that "I am sure that you are aware that one of the main difficulties we face in this fight is the fact that many of our Southern leaders are not willing to stand up and fight for the principles of constitutional government."[5]

Thurmond had channeled his enthusiasm over the Southern Manifesto on behalf of the entire southern delegation, but his behavior during the debate over the Civil Rights Act of 1957 was for many, not least Richard Russell, the leader of the Senate's southern bloc, an example of the South Carolinian's willingness to use the race issue to further raise his public profile. Despite initially agreeing with fellow southerners that a filibuster would be unwise, Thurmond informed his constituents that he was "prepared to speak at great length and to the full extent of my physical capacity when the bill is brought before the Senate for consideration." In complete contrast, Johnston offered a more reserved declaration that he would not "burn down the barn to destroy the rat." In the event, Thurmond set a record, which remains unbroken, by speaking against passage of the act for twenty-four hours and eighteen minutes on August 28 and 29, 1957. Some fellow southerners were enraged, particularly those who had been insisting on the need to maintain solidarity after Thurmond's divisive "Dixiecrat" presidential run in 1948. Russell, who feared that Thurmond's antics would compromise his negotiations over the bill with President Eisenhower, slammed the South Carolinian for pursuing "personal political aggrandizement," to which Thurmond remained indignant, arguing that "each Senator individually was free to fight the bill as he chose."[6]

With the battle over the Civil Rights Act raging on in the Senate, two landmark events from 1957 escalated South Carolina's war on the Supreme Court. On June 24, the court handed down its decision in *Mallory v. United States,* which involved black South Carolinian Andrew R. Mallory's conviction and death sentence for the rape and assault of a white woman. Finding that police had arrested Mallory without probable cause and then interrogated him for hours prior to arraignment, the court overturned the conviction, despite the existence of an apparently voluntary confession, and Mallory walked free. Thurmond employed a predictable choice of words to illustrate his disgust, arguing that "the Supreme Court shows more concern for the rights of communists and criminals, including rapists and murderers, than it does for the protection of the innocent American citizens." As a frequent reoffender, Andrew Mallory would unwittingly provide Strom Thurmond with years of future opportunities to condemn the court's liberal judicial activism.

The following year, Thurmond read to the Senate an editorial in the *Washington Evening Star,* which reported that police were again hunting Mallory on suspicion of housebreaking and assault. The same year, the House of Representatives passed a so-called "anti-Mallory" bill, essentially a means of allowing the submission of evidence obtained during a delay of arraignment, but the Senate stalled the measure. By the end of April 1960, when Mallory was facing a new trial for rape and burglary charges, Senators Sam Ervin of North Carolina, Harry F. Byrd of Virginia, and Olin Johnston of South Carolina had added their voices to the southern outrage over the court's original decision to set Mallory free, and collaborated in introducing legislation to permit trial judges to determine whether a confession was truly voluntary, in a decision that would be binding in any future process of judicial review.[7] The ongoing controversy over the Supreme Court's consideration of criminal justice cases only fueled Strom Thurmond's rage, and his attempt to use *Mallory v. United States* as one of the more potent weapons in his interrogation of Supreme Court nominee Abe Fortas in 1968 would once again emphasize Andrew Mallory's significance in the story of South Carolina and the Supreme Court.

President Eisenhower's decision to use federal troops to remove Little Rock Central High School from the hands of Arkansas governor Orval Faubus, who was using the National Guard to prevent the enrollment of nine African American students, proved to be the second key event in 1957 that intensified the war on the Supreme Court. The outcome of the Little Rock crisis held particular significance for the course of twentieth-century racial politics: although segregationists were able to exploit the event as a means of discrediting southern moderates and promoting further resistance, the extraordinary nature of Eisenhower's intervention seemed to rule out the possibility of the federal government reversing its interference in southern politics and society. Deep South senators offered a chorus of condemnation to welcome Eisenhower's dramatic gesture, which seemed only to confirm once again his willingness to ensure the integration of southern schools through implementation of *Brown*. An appalled Olin Johnston urged Governor Faubus to "proclaim a state of insurrection," and declared in a letter to Leroy Collins, governor of Florida, that "it is impossible for me to fully express my concern over the action taken by President Eisenhower to use brute force and troops armed with bayonets and guns at Little Rock." Johnston's insistence that the Supreme Court was failing to protect the United States from communism was evident in his remarks in the Senate, not least when he declared, "Mr. President, one wonders when the gentlemen of the high court will have a rendezvous with reality and recognize the communistic conspiracy in America for what it is: a clear and present danger. I recommend to the membership of the Supreme Court that no matter how heavy their workload, no matter how pressing the demands of their judicial duties, that they take time out and read and ponder and reflect on the contents of Mr. J. Edgar Hoover's bestseller, *Masters of Deceit: The Story of Communism in America and How to Fight It*."[8]

The outrage over Little Rock served to prolong the delay over W. Wilson White's appointment as head of the Justice Department's new Civil Rights Division, a post created by the 1957 Civil Rights Act, which would empower White to ensure the enforcement of voting rights. In outlining his opposition, Thurmond complained that, as assistant attorney general, the nominee had advised President Eisenhower to send federal troops to Arkansas, claiming that "Mr.

White is known in the South as one of those who badly bungled the affair in Little Rock. I do not understand how the Administration can believe that a man of this reputation will be able to inspire confidence and respect with the Southern people in his work." Observing that White had remained unconfirmed for eight months, Richard Lyons commented in the *Washington Post–Times Herald* that "the Southerners . . . have put their views on the record again for the folks back home."[9] The intervention in Little Rock, combined with the grossly unpopular *Mallory* decision, served to remind southern Democratic senators of their disgust following the announcement of *Brown* in May 1954. The justices' decision in September 1958 to reject the ongoing delay in the desegregation of Little Rock's schools underlined the sharp ideological divide between North and South in the US Senate. Thurmond claimed that "no one will rejoice more from this decision than Nikita S. Khrushchev and his cohorts," while Senators Jacob K. Javits of New York and Clifford P. Case of New Jersey praised the ruling, with Case arguing that the court had "admirably restated the settled doctrine that interpretations of the Constitution by the Supreme Court are the supreme law of the land."[10]

With conservative white voters handing out "Impeach Earl Warren" leaflets all over the South, the region's senators stepped up their efforts to investigate the Supreme Court in the hope of finding any scraps of information they could use to discredit the individual justices and also the NAACP. Richard Russell requested a complete breakdown of Thurgood Marshall's record of cases before the court, while his fellow Georgian, Herman Talmadge, compiled biographical details of all justices serving as of May 1958, noting that five of them had never served on a state Supreme Court or a US Court of Appeals. Talmadge's curiosity even extended to enquiries into the origins of Earl Warren's family name: the senator learned that the chief justice's father, whose surname was originally Varran, came to the USA as an infant from Stavanger, Norway. The details of Warren's Scandinavian heritage would no doubt have reminded Talmadge of the chief justice's reference to Gunnar Myrdal in *Brown*'s footnote 11, which provoked years of resentment among Deep South senators. As late as 1987, Talmadge was unrelenting in his loathing of the Myrdal influence, describing Sweden in his memoirs as "the biggest cesspool of social pathologies this side of the Iron Curtain."[11]

Having called for the impeachment of Supreme Court justices who had "curtailed the anti-communist campaigns of Congress," Thurmond called for "total and unremitting war on the Supreme Court's unconstitutional usurpations and unlawful arrogations of power" in a speech before the Citizens' Committee for Constitutional Government in Augusta, Georgia, adding that "the Federal Government does not have enough troops to police the entire South, and even if it did, race mixing still could not be forced upon a determined, organized and united people." The outrage of his South Carolina colleague was just as evident, with Johnston pressing for passage of a new bill requiring the Senate to reconfirm all Supreme Court justices every four years, and warning, in a manner recalling his reservations over the John Marshall Harlan nomination, that "unless the Supreme Court is halted on its infamous road, some day it will rule that United States law and our beloved Constitution and Bill of Rights will be subservient to some United Nations agreement or rule."[12]

With a growing number of senators believing that the justices had begun to ignore the Constitution by pursuing judicial activism, the late 1950s saw an increase in the number of bills introduced to curb the Supreme Court's power. For South Carolina's senators, this was nothing new, as they had been attempting to restrict the court's jurisdiction since 1955. One of their early attempts, essentially a means of preventing *Brown*'s enforcement, involved a bill giving final authority in school segregation cases to the district courts. Senator Paul Douglas of Illinois criticized these and other efforts, claiming that Johnston and Thurmond "want to make the Senate a Super Supreme Court to override the language of the Fourteenth Amendment that equal protection shall be granted under the law to all citizens." Republican senator William Jenner's introduction of the Jenner-Butler bill provided South Carolina with the first realistic opportunity to get behind a serious effort to reform the court's power. Many throughout the Senate, including southern segregationists and conservative northerners concerned about Communist subversion, favored the bill. At the same time, southerners supported a House Resolution known as "HR3," introduced as a "pure states' rights" measure, which civil rights advocates feared would allow southern bar associations to disbar attorneys accepting race-related cases. As Stephen Engel has shown, the House's passage of the "anti-Mallory" bill only encouraged southerners to pursue further court-curbing initiatives.[13]

Under pressure from Thurmond, who threatened to attach the more aggressive HR3 to every remaining bill on the calendar unless a vote was allowed on the Jenner-Butler bill, Majority Leader Lyndon Johnson agreed to bring the bill before the Senate following the Judiciary Committee's favorable vote of 10–5.

The cunning Texan allowed Jenner to attach his legislation to another bill dealing with federal appellate procedure, safe in the knowledge that he had enough votes to defeat the latter bill. In the event, the Senate rejected Jenner-Butler by a vote of 49–41. Shortly afterwards, Johnson abruptly adjourned the Senate in order to prevent passage of HR3 and managed to block its passage the following day by convincing a sufficient number of senators to vote to return the bill to the Judiciary Committee, by a vote of 41–40.[14]

Despite Lyndon Johnson's success in using his mastery of the Senate to defeat the anti-Court legislation, the wide support for the Jenner-Butler bill and the near-passage of the notorious HR3 provided the first strong indication that the liberalism of the Supreme Court's justices now constituted a national concern—a claim that Johnston and Thurmond had been making for years. The war that began in a Charleston courtroom in 1951, when Thurgood Marshall had argued against Clarendon County's segregated school system, had now been played out in the US Senate for half a decade, during which South Carolina's senators, through dogged determination, had contributed to a serious anti-Court agenda to the point where the South had very nearly succeeded in denting the awesome power of the nine unelected justices. By the beginning of John F. Kennedy's presidency in January 1961, southern conservatives were chairing nine of the Senate's fifteen standing committees. With neither death nor retirement a likely prospect for any of the aging chairmen, Lyndon Johnson, who would become Kennedy's vice president, was reported to have told Senate liberals that a desperate ploy of "killing off" a number of elderly southerners remained their only hope of introducing a new civil rights bill.[15]

By the beginning of 1959, both President Eisenhower and Chief Justice Warren were beginning to feel the strain of the continued southern onslaught that *Brown v. Board of Education* had kick-started almost five years earlier. In February, Warren tendered his resignation from the American Bar Association in protest at the association's criticism of the Supreme Court and a perceived failure to back the court in the war over *Brown*. The same month, the president gave a clear indication of his antipathy toward South Carolina's senators in a letter to Ralph McGill, editor of the *Atlanta Constitution*, describing Olin Johnston and Strom Thurmond as "so entrenched in the prejudices and racial antagonism that they never show so much as a glimmer of readiness to see the other side of the problem."[16]

Johnston and Thurmond seemed only too willing to live up to Eisenhower's characterization of them following the crisis in Little Rock. Early in 1959, Johnston was using his position on the Senate Judiciary Committee's Subcommittee on Constitutional Rights to resist the advancement of civil rights measures. In March, he seized upon an announcement that several members of the Commission on Civil Rights, including Chairman John A. Hannah, were to resign, advising Senator Thomas C. Hennings of Missouri, chairman of the subcommittee, to postpone hearings on all civil rights bills pending before it until members of the commission could testify regarding their resignations. Johnston was happy to put on record his skepticism over the commission—established by the 1957 Civil Rights Act—in a letter to Hennings, in which he claimed that testimony from those members planning to resign "may save our committee tremendous time, money and effort, and will probably indicate, as I have personally believed, that there is no useful purpose to be served by the existence of the Commission on Civil Rights." In his response, Hennings reminded Johnston that the commission "is a distinct entity separate and apart from our subcommittee" and argued, "to the contrary, I believe that such announcements by the commissioners indicate the need that the subcommittee proceed as planned with the hearings so that we may study the proposed bills and recommend needed legislation without unnecessary delay."[17]

Johnston may have proved ineffective in curtailing the Civil Rights Commission's activities, but he was at least able to use his position to guarantee the prominence of South Carolina voices during subcommittee hearings. The senator worked closely with South Carolina's political establishment to create a sizable delegation of state dignitaries, with the aim of making an impact in Washington, DC, during hearings on civil rights measures. In addition to Thurmond, the delegation included South Carolina's Lieutenant Governor Burnet R. Maybank (son of the late senator); Thomas R. Waring, editor of Charleston's *News and Courier;* attorney Thomas H. Pope; Representative William Jennings Bryan Dorn; Representative Robert E. McNair, chairman of the state House Judiciary Committee; Representative L. Mendel Rivers; Senator L. Marion Gressette, chairman of the state Senate Judiciary Committee; Senator Edgar A. Brown, president of the state Senate; Solomon Blatt, Speaker of the state House of Representatives; and Attorney General Daniel R. McLeod. But Johnston clearly believed that South Carolina's newly elected governor, the youthful and dynamic Charlestonian Ernest "Fritz" Hollings, would be the star of the show.

In addition to Hollings's lengthy, impassioned speech in support of South Carolina's position in the civil rights debate, the visit to Washington, DC, would also include a luncheon to "honor" the governor, for which Congressman Rivers would contribute a turkey and Congressman Dorn a ham.[18]

Significantly, former governors James F. Byrnes and George Bell Timmerman Jr. did not attend the hearings. Byrnes claimed to have a business engagement, and Timmerman cited a family member's illness as the reason for his nonappearance, but also expressed concern that the hearings might aid sponsors of civil rights proposals "in their efforts to advertise their political activities among groups who oppose the South."[19] Others in the delegation, such as Speaker Solomon Blatt, shared the concern that unfriendly witnesses would use the hearings to dilute the impact of South Carolina's segregationist message and further the cause of civil rights. To offset this possibility, Johnston, Hollings, and McNair agreed with Thomas Pope's suggestion of splitting the delegation into two, keeping some friendly witnesses back "for possible rebuttal testimony."[20]

In making his speech before the subcommittee on April 14, 1959, Governor Hollings began by citing racial conflict in other nations, such as "Great Britain having difficulty in trying to integrate the Turk with the Greek on the island of Cyprus," before characterizing South Carolina as "a state of tolerance and understanding." Claiming that "we don't just speak of opportunity, we give it," Hollings argued that only "understanding, tolerance, and respect" can create "good race relations," but warned that "good race relations can be disturbed by law, and today we have only to look to Little Rock to see its destruction by the so-called 'law of the land.'" Building on his "law of the land" theme in an obvious condemnation of *Brown,* the governor cited Supreme Court historian Charles Warren's claim that "however the Court may interpret the provisions of the Constitution, it is still the Constitution which is the law and not the decision of the Court." Naming Chief Justice Warren in addition to Justices Hugo Black and William O. Douglas, Hollings railed against the court's willingness to overturn legal precedent. He would later return to his "law of the land" arguments, in a very different form, in his famous farewell address as governor in 1963.[21]

Hollings sounded sincere when he stated, "I beg of you not to destroy the friendship, education, culture, and opportunity of both races by enacting the proposed civil rights bills in this subcommittee," but some "unfriendly" witnesses, such as Rev. I. DeQuincey Newman, South Carolina's foremost black civil rights leader, challenged the governor's claim to represent "all the people of

South Carolina, the Negroes as well as the white people."[22] Acknowledging his hometown of Spartanburg—also that of Senator Olin D. Johnston—Newman made a mockery of Hollings's characterization of South Carolina as "a state of opportunity," informing the subcommittee that while Hollings had claimed that the state boasted "outstanding members of the legal and medical professions," the governor had neglected to mention that neither the University of South Carolina Law School nor the South Carolina Medical College permitted the enrollment of African American students. Where Hollings had put forward bold claims of positive race relations, Newman provided detailed statistical evidence to support his claims of racial discrimination, claiming, in one example, that "in Calhoun County, home of Senator Marion Gressette, Chairman of the School Segregation Committee, 95.8% of whites over 21 have registered [to vote] while 4.2% of the Negroes were registered." In his concluding remark, Newman rubbished Hollings's references to racial tensions in other nations, particularly his mention of India's caste system, claiming, "I do not think it takes too much imagination to ascertain which caste, which race, the South Carolina law relegates to the jobs of scrubbing and cleaning lavatories." Following the close of hearings, Hollings advised Johnston against bringing further witnesses to respond to Newman's testimony. Johnston agreed, believing that he had "refuted most of their major points when they appeared before the committee," but sent to Hollings the statements made by Newman; Billie S. Fleming, president of the Clarendon County Improvement Association; and John H. McCray, publisher of the militant black publication *Lighthouse and Informer,* who had established himself as an enemy of South Carolina's political establishment with his active support for Thurgood Marshall's *Briggs* suit.[23]

Hollings's remarks indicated the growing resentment of the Supreme Court among South Carolina's political establishment, but the appearance of the state's delegation before the Constitutional Rights Subcommittee did little to convince supporters of civil rights that their efforts were in vain. Nonetheless, despite Eisenhower's antipathy toward Johnston and Thurmond, there is evidence that the influence of southern senators was beginning to make an impact on the president's selection process for Supreme Court justices. In a letter to William P. Rogers, his new attorney general, Eisenhower sounded skeptical of Rogers's recommendation of his predecessor, Herbert Brownell, as a replacement for the outgoing Justice Harold Hitz Burton, on the grounds that southerners "would point out that [Brownell] was Attorney General when the Supreme Court's integration orders conforming to the decision of 1954 were promulgated." If David A. Nichols is correct that Eisenhower and Brownell were "grooming" Simon Sobeloff for a seat on the high court in 1956, the president's comment to Rogers regarding Brownell suggests that Eisenhower had almost certainly reconsidered this move in the wake of Johnston's anti-Sobeloff crusade, and also the crisis in Little Rock. Conscious of the fact that Hugo Black was the only remaining southern justice on the court by the summer of 1958, the president added the name of Judge Elbert Tuttle, of the Fifth Circuit Court of Appeals, to the shortlist of candidates, in addition to that of Kenneth Royall, also "of Southern origin," who had served as Harry Truman's secretary of the army. Ultimately, Eisenhower decided against both southern candidates: Tuttle's support for *Brown* would have proved fatal when Eastland's Judiciary Committee began scrutinizing him, while the president ruled out Royall because "he is a Democrat and I do not want to further overbalance the Court as between the two major parties."[24]

Eisenhower eventually decided to nominate Judge Potter Stewart, of the Sixth Circuit Court of Appeals, who, like the outgoing Justice Burton, was from the state of Ohio. By the time of his official nomination, Stewart had served on the Supreme Court on a recess appointment for three months, a situation that, according to the *Philadelphia Inquirer*, caused concern among northern and southern senators that "Mr. Eisenhower had robbed the Senate of some of its control over the nomination." One particularly unhappy northerner was freshman senator Philip A. Hart of Michigan, who complained that recess appointments "hamper the Senate in performing its constitutional duty of confirmation" in the sense that a Supreme Court nominee who has already served for several months can always argue that his service prevents him from answering questions relating to his judicial positions on issues currently before the court. Hart, who would later introduce a Senate resolution to discourage the use of recess appointments to the Supreme Court, also observed that the presidential practice of placing individuals in office months before the Senate is able to scrutinize and confirm them "had not been used for more than a century until Mr. Eisenhower named Earl Warren as Chief Justice in 1953."[25]

Southern Democrats, led by Richard Russell, were only too happy to emphasize the recess appointment controversy, if only as a means of demonstrating that their concerns over Stewart's views on segregation did not constitute the sole reason for their opposition. Nonetheless, southern senators began discussing the segregation issue far more openly than before. While Chairman Eastland expressed doubt that Stewart would offer fair rulings on "the greatest domestic question before the country today: racial integration," Russell complained that the nomination was part of a Justice Department scheme to "perpetuate some recent decisions of the Court in segregation rulings, which were partly based on *amicus curiae* briefs submitted by the Justice Department." The Georgian offered little in the way of evidence, but, as both Michael Kahn and David A. Nichols have argued, Eisenhower remained committed to the appointment of judges who would support desegregation, and, in the process, constructed "a judicial edifice that would withstand Southern and conservative efforts to undermine *Brown v. Board of Education.*" Stewart's own remarks during his confirmation hearings would appear to support this view: when prompted to comment on the *Brown* ruling, he declared, "I would not like you to vote for me on the assumption . . . that I am dedicated to overturning that decision. Because I am not."[26]

The Stewart confirmation hearings proved to be a landmark event, first, because of the willingness of southern senators, five years on from the court's announcement of *Brown,* to discuss the segregation issue openly during deliberations over nominations to the Supreme Court. Olin Johnston provided an example early on during the hearings:

Senator Johnston (South Carolina): Let us get down to the question in my state, the public school question there. In what way was it changed in 1954—the law—in what way was it changed? How was the Constitution changed? The interpretation of what the Constitution meant?

Mr. Stewart: Well, as I understand that decision—as I understand that decision, it held that it was a denial of equal protection of the laws for a state in the public school system to discriminate against school children exclusively on the basis of race. To my knowledge—I may be mistaken—there never has been a decision of the Supreme Court of the United States contrary to that. I don't know that I agree that the Constitution was changed by that decision.[27]

Second, with Stewart continuing to respond carefully to questions on the same subject, the hearings took a bizarre and confrontational turn. The aforementioned Thomas Hennings of Missouri raised a point of order, claiming, "I do not think it proper to inquire of a nominee for this court or any other his opinion as to any of the decisions or the reasoning upon decisions which have heretofore been handed down by that court."[28] When Chairman Eastland implied that Hennings was attempting to "gag" members of the committee, the hearings descended into chaos, with a standoff emerging quickly and dramatically:

Senator Hennings: Mr. Chairman, I did not use the word "gag."

The Chairman: All right. It means that the committee is censoring Senator McClellan in denying him the right to ask a question that he thinks is necessary in order for him to ascertain how to officially act in this matter.

Senator Hennings: I did not interrupt him.

The Chairman: You did not interrupt. If the committee says he can't ask such a question, if it so rules, of course, he is—

Senator Hennings: May I complete my statement?

Senator O'Mahoney: Will the Senator from Missouri yield to me?

Senator Hennings: Please, I do not believe, Mr. Chairman, that the word "gag" is an appropriate one.

The Chairman: All right.

Senator Hennings: Many, many questions have been asked by members of the Committee of the gentleman who presented himself here—many proper questions. I do not believe it is gagging, as the Chair is pleased to use the word, when a court overrules a question in a trial. That is not gagging counsel.

The Chairman: I know, but I don't think that you can—

Senator Hennings: I believe this Committee is proceeding in a lawyer-like fashion.

The Chairman: If this Justice decides that the question is improper he can decide that.[29]

The controversial Supreme Court nominations of the 1960s and beyond, covered in future chapters, often showcased a confrontation between a senator and a nominee, but the Stewart hearings are unique for the manner in which committee members argued among themselves throughout a dispute that reportedly lasted for an hour—and very nearly had to be settled by Senator William Langer's proposed roll call vote—while the nominee sat patiently and waited. The Hennings point of order, although one of the less distinguished moments in the history of Supreme Court confirmation hearings, was, for L. A. Scot Powe, a watershed moment, as the court's dramatically increasing significance in American life now began to demand that senators apply a more rigorous form of scrutiny with regard to nominees.[30] With southerners now prepared to discuss *Brown* openly during confirmation hearings, future confrontations over Supreme Court nominations simply became inevitable.

James Eastland delayed the committee's consideration of the Stewart nomination long enough for Olin Johnston to compile a twelve-page report condemning the practice of recess appointments. As the *Washington Post–Times Herald* noted, it was not until the final sentence of the report that senators opposed Stewart personally on the grounds that the nominee "thinks the Supreme Court has the power to legislate and to amend the Constitution of the United States."[31] Following Committee approval by a vote of 12–3, the Senate confirmed Stewart by a vote of 70–17, with the opposition consisting of all senators from the states of Alabama, Arkansas, Georgia, Louisiana, Mississippi, North Carolina, South Carolina, and Virginia, joined by Senator Spessard Holland of Florida. Strom Thurmond spoke for many in the southern bloc by speculating that Stewart would be "an improvement over the other occupants of seats on the Supreme bench; but when I make that statement, I must add that, in my opinion, he would not have to be too good a lawyer to be an improvement."[32] Michigan senator Philip Hart ultimately voted to confirm, despite his agreement with southerners on the recess appointment issue, as did the moderate Estes Kefauver of Tennessee.[33] As the roll call tally demonstrated, the nomination—perhaps in part because of Stewart's candor—united southern senators in a particularly impressive segregationist opposition bloc in the wake of the Little Rock crisis. While the court-curbing bills and the issue of recess appointments had temporarily brought together senators from all regions, the Stewart hearings provided a stark reminder that *Brown v. Board of Education* remained a powerful source of intense disagreement between North and South. Thanks in no small part to the southern influence on the Senate Judiciary Committee, the confrontational era of the Senate's consideration of Supreme Court nominations had arrived.

For most of the 1950s, with southern states showing a strong interest in reducing the Supreme Court's power as a means of preserving their regional autonomy, Olin Johnston and Strom Thurmond formed only part of a collective anti–Supreme Court crusade to assure the folks back home of an unwavering drive to protect racial segregation. Although it would not be until the 1960s that the South Carolina senators truly stood out in the conflicts over judicial nominations, it is clear from Johnston's crusade against Simon Sobeloff and Thurmond's determination to talk himself hoarse when opposing the Civil Rights Act that the South Carolina trait of resistance was alive and well during the 1950s.

In watering down segregationist rhetoric to offset northern dismissal of their region's priorities, southern senators aimed to expand their attack on judicial nominees by pinpointing a lack of judicial experience, which became relevant in the case of John Marshall Harlan, or a lack of "etiquette" on the part of Eisenhower in making his appointments, which became a critical issue with both Simon Sobeloff and Potter Stewart. In the event, southerners appeared to achieve little success in using their powers of advice and consent in the judicial nomination processes of the 1950s. They failed to engineer any rejections, and their obstructionism failed to convince Eisenhower to select Supreme Court nominees favored by the South. The president's commitment to naming justices who would uphold the *Brown* ruling was painfully clear during Arkansas senator John McClellan's questioning of Potter Stewart: as the *Washington Post–Times Herald* reported, "Stewart said that coming from Ohio, he had not been 'shocked' by the decision."[34]

On the other hand, it would be inaccurate to conclude that South Carolina's crusade proved entirely unsuccessful during this decade, for two important reasons. Firstly, the insistence of Johnston and Thurmond that the Supreme Court posed a national, rather than regional, threat to American interests appeared to gain legitimacy before the end of the decade, with northern senators joining the southern bloc in criticizing Eisenhower's recess appointments. The southern insistence that the Warren-led Supreme Court was facilitating Communist subversion became a powerful weapon in the fight over the court-curbing bills introduced throughout this era, which came close to compromising the court's power in the summer of 1958. Secondly, although southern senators failed to convince the administration, the press, and northern senators that their obstruction was not due solely to the segregation issue, Johnston and Thurmond were nonetheless able to create a comprehensive anti–Supreme Court agenda during the 1950s, which contributed to the emergence of the highly politicized nomination process of the 1960s. The strategy of linking the court's power to concerns over states' rights, US sovereignty, and Communism would broaden over the next decade to include crime and punishment, prayer in schools, legislative apportionment, obscenity, voting rights, and freedom of speech. The greatly expanded range of political issues would give further potency to continued southern complaints over the justices' lack of judicial experience, and their continued criticism of the court for not following the "strict constructionist" doctrine of applying only the words of the Constitution in line with their original meaning as intended when the nation's Founding Fathers drafted them. Although Eisenhower refused to nominate judges who would endanger the survival of *Brown*, his consideration of John J. Parker, John W. Davis, Elbert Tuttle, and Kenneth Royall, and his agreement to appoint Clement Haynsworth to the Fourth Circuit Court of Appeals, suggests that the president was forced to acknowledge and tolerate pressure from southern Democrats to name judges with judicial philosophies that would accommodate the segregationist agenda. John F. Kennedy, his Democratic successor in the White House, would also make his judicial nominations in the shadow of the southern segregationist influence.

Potter Stewart's success in facing down Dixie suggested that increasing demands were being placed on Supreme Court nominees during the era of civil rights, but the Stewart hearings ultimately gave little indication of the lengths to which Olin Johnston, Strom Thurmond, and later, Ernest "Fritz" Hollings were prepared to go in defending the southern—and South Carolinian—way of life.

4. HOME OF THE WHITE MAN'S SOUL

On August 20, 1962, an incredulous Senator Philip Hart of Michigan predicted that "when historians of the future write about weird proceedings in the Senate, this hearing will occupy a most peculiar chapter."[1] He did not aim his comments solely at future historians of US politics with an unusual passion for judicial nominations. The statement was one of the milder criticisms aimed at Senator Olin D. Johnston for using his seniority on the Senate Judiciary Committee to delay and obstruct President John F. Kennedy's appointment of Thurgood Marshall—black lawyer, civil rights hero, and future justice of the Supreme Court—to the US Court of Appeals for the Second Circuit. In attempting to keep Marshall from the federal bench, South Carolina's senior senator provoked a wave of criticism that united President Kennedy with various members of the US Senate from the Democratic and Republican parties, several national newspapers, and a great many black and white Americans throughout the United States.

With Strom Thurmond yet to take a seat on the Judiciary Committee, it was left to Olin Johnston to stand between Thurgood Marshall and a position on the Second Circuit, even if this obstruction counted for little more than assuring white South Carolinians that he had not forgotten Marshall's argument before the Supreme Court during the *Brown v. Board of Education* hearings. As chairman of the subcommittee scrutinizing Marshall's appointment, Johnston had the power to determine the scheduling of hearings; to call witnesses; to decide on the relevance of submitted materials or particular lines of questioning; and, most importantly for South Carolina's political establishment, to ensure the inclusion of southern voices in the debate over Marshall's suitability for the federal judiciary. While his opposition to Eisenhower's nomination of Simon Sobeloff to the Fourth Circuit represented the first hotly contested judicial nomination following the announcement of *Brown,* the mild-mannered Johnston adopted an altogether more blatant form of obstruction with regard to Marshall.

Although Kennedy had nominated Marshall for a circuit court rather than a Supreme Court position, the nation's highest court remained the backdrop to this drama, for three reasons. First, South Carolina's ongoing war on the Earl Warren–led Supreme Court would influence Johnston's tactics to a great extent. During the ten-month period in which Marshall served on a recess appointment while waiting for the Judiciary Committee to confirm him, the court handed down two of the most important rulings of the Warren Court era. Southern politicians condemned both *Baker v. Carr,* which gave federal courts the power to intervene in matters relating to malapportioned legislatures, and *Engel v. Vitale,* which ruled teacher-led prayer in public schools to be unconstitutional, viewing these rulings as dangerous developments in the Supreme Court's repeated encroachment into southern state autonomy. The sheer magnitude of such rulings meant that southern senators would handle a presidential nomination of any prominent liberal to a position on the federal judiciary with extreme caution.

Second, it is clear that a further influence on Johnston's obstructionism was a concern that if he gave Marshall an easy ride for a circuit court appointment, there may be a risk of Kennedy or a future president promoting him to the Supreme Court.[2] If this was the case, his fears proved well-founded: Marshall would succeed in facing down the quiet but determined Johnston to secure his Second Circuit appointment in 1962, but would later face an onslaught of sustained provocation at the hands of the abrasive Strom Thurmond after President Lyndon Johnson selected him as the first African American Supreme Court nominee in the nation's history, in 1967. Johnston's lonely campaign during the 1962 Second Circuit hearings provided only the first stage in South Carolina's resistance to Marshall's career advancement. By 1967, the stakes were even higher, and, as future chapters will illustrate, both Thurmond and Ernest "Fritz" Hollings would make their own unique contributions to Marshall's long journey to the Supreme Court.

Third, given that Johnston and Thurmond had placed such a great emphasis on standards of qualification for Supreme Court nominees during the late 1950s, it was imperative that Johnston pursued these standards ruthlessly when scrutinizing Marshall, who in 1961 was only the second African American appointed to a federal judicial position, and the first since the court announced the much-hated *Brown* decision in 1954. As with the Sobeloff episode, the demands of South Carolina's internal politics temporarily shifted Johnston's attention from the Supreme Court nomination process to lower court appointments, yet with the Supreme Court's influence continuing to provide the impetus for his obstructionism. The Marshall Second Circuit controversy highlights not only the importance of lower court appointments in South Carolina's war on the Supreme Court, but also the contribution of the state's senators to the intensification of the judicial nomination process as it applied to the courts of appeal.

Of all the men and women who have sat before the Senate Judiciary Committee, none has known better the experience of facing down Dixie than Thurgood Marshall. Few were better prepared for the cynicism, attempted smears, and grueling questions that Southern Judiciary Committee members were hurling at nominees by the early 1960s. Marshall had argued thirty-two cases before the US Supreme Court during his time as chief counsel for the NAACP Legal Defense Fund, winning on twenty-nine occasions. Each of these cases proved to be a landmark decision in the court's history, establishing Marshall's reputation as a hero of the civil rights movement in the process. With *Shelly v. Kraemer* (1948), Marshall persuaded the court to strike down the enforcement of racially restrictive covenants, while in the cases of *Sweatt v. Painter* and *McLaurin v. Oklahoma State Regents* (both 1950), he convinced all nine of the court's justices to strike down racial discrimination in graduate education institutions.[3]

Although the groundbreaking *Sweatt* and *McLaurin* triumphs had given him the confidence to seek out a new case involving segregated education in schools, Marshall understood that each victory he scored for African American rights also constituted a hammer blow to the "southern way of life." Psychologist Kenneth Clark, whose research into child psychology proved vitally important in Marshall's successful *Brown* argument a few years later, recalled traveling with Marshall by train to South Carolina in 1951. It was not Marshall's first visit to the state, as he had already argued successfully for equal pay for black teachers there in 1944, and also for an end to the state's all-white primary system in 1947. But Clark noticed Marshall's demeanor change as the train went deeper into the South: he began to look more and more serious, and offered little other than the solemn declaration that he was "tired of trying to save the white man's soul."[4]

Marshall's visit to South Carolina to argue against Clarendon County's system of segregated schooling proved to be one of the defining moments of the civil rights era. Having found twenty black parents in the state who were willing to attach their names to an NAACP legal brief despite the risk of losing their employment, Marshall had planned only to criticize the disparities between black and white schools in Clarendon County. Of the three-judge panel hearing the case, one judge would prove to be sympathetic toward, even enthusiastic for, Marshall's argument. Judge J. Waties Waring had established himself as a notorious figure in the South only a few years earlier when he had nullified Olin Johnston's attempt to abolish the South Carolina Democratic primary system following the Supreme Court's *Smith v. Allwright* decision. As if that act of defiance had not been enough, Waring had made no secret of his sympathy with Thurgood Marshall's antisegregation arguments when the latter came to South Carolina to challenge the state's treatment of black teachers.[5]

One particularly notable irony in the story of Thurgood Marshall and South Carolina is the manner in which Judge Waring inspired Marshall to question the constitutionality of segregation per se. Having once again defied the white southern establishment by inviting Marshall to dinner at his home, Waring shared with Marshall his personal view that the original NAACP brief—dealing solely with the racial inequalities in Clarendon County's school system—did not go far enough. Despite being startled by the judge's suggestion that he make a case for the unconstitutionality of segregation itself, Marshall followed Waring's advice, and, after redrafting his brief, argued in court that the entire system of segregated schooling had a corrosive effect on black children, causing lasting emotional damage.[6]

South Carolina's counsel, Robert M. Figg Jr., was able to neutralize Marshall's argument by making the surprising concession that the quality of the state's black schools was not on a par with schools for white children, adding that the state could and would address the differences through a comprehensive investment scheme. The other two members of the three-judge panel—South Carolina's George Bell Timmerman, and North Carolina's John J. Parker—sided with Figg, indicating an expectation that the state would "equalize" its schools within six months. Waring remained supportive of Marshall on the bench: not only did he reiterate Marshall's arguments during the hearing, he also requested that Chief Judge Parker order repairmen to cease work on the street outside, as the sound of pounding jackhammers mysteriously started up every time Marshall began speaking. Following the final presentations of the hearing, Waring returned home and complained bitterly to his wife about the manner in which the other two judges had dismissed Marshall's argument, claiming he had told them that Governor James Byrnes—who had instructed Figg to offset Marshall's case by admitting to the disgraceful state of South Carolina's black schools—was "no better and even worse than Thurmond."[7]

It is highly significant that a member of South Carolina's white legal establishment inspired, encouraged, and even pushed Thurgood Marshall to make his groundbreaking argument in *Briggs*. The fact that Marshall used the same argument three years later to change the course of American history with *Brown v. Board of Education* only emphasizes Judge Waring's courage in the face of enormous social and political pressure. Yet the judge paid a heavy price for siding with Marshall in *Briggs*. His refusal to go along with Judge Timmerman and Chief Judge Parker provoked an onslaught of personal abuse that eventually drove him out of Charleston and into retirement. With the segregationist Judge Ashton H. Williams replacing Waring on the bench, the panel reconvened to hear the appeal in March 1952 and rejected Marshall's case unanimously, concluding that the state of South Carolina had improved the quality of its black schools sufficiently. Spectators had traveled miles to watch the NAACP hero face down the white legal establishment, and over five hundred of them had attempted, in ninety-degree heat, to squeeze into a courtroom that would seat only seventy-five. Marshall, who was asked at one point by Chief Judge Parker to instruct the excitable crowd to settle down, later pointed out that this chaotic scene made a mockery of white southern claims that black Americans were content to live under segregation. Despite the enormous black crowd viewing him as a messiah figure, Marshall was reminded of the white southern attitude toward his crusade at the close of proceedings, when one South Carolina lawyer shouted out, "If you ever show your black ass in Clarendon County again, you'll be dead."[8]

Although defeated in South Carolina, Marshall's experience there provided the momentum for a bigger challenge to segregated schools that would have far greater implications. When, in 1953, he was given another opportunity to make the argument that Judge Waring had suggested to him, it would be before the justices of the US Supreme Court. These hearings grouped together *Briggs* and four other cases relating to schools, and resulted in the landmark *Brown* decision, which invalidated completely all systems of segregation in public schools. Although delighted by his triumph, Marshall almost certainly knew that years of trouble lay ahead—with most of it in all probability originating in the southern states—particularly as his opponent, the legendary lawyer John W. Davis, had shaken his hand and conceded defeat with the words, "I hope you realize that the only way you can win a case is somebody has to lose."[9]

While the politicians of the South Carolina lowcountry, with its dense African American population, were unable to escape what V. O. Key has characterized as the state's preoccupation with race issues, the enigmatic upcountryman Olin D. Johnston was able to win election as governor of South Carolina in 1934 by focusing on New Deal and class-related matters, and capitalizing on his popularity within the state's textile communities. With segregated unions muzzling black activism, white upcountry millworkers had little reason to prioritize the race issue during the 1930s, yet the apparent freedom of campaigning on a New Deal platform without acknowledging racial tensions within the mill communities proved to be a temporary luxury for Governor Johnston. In the run-up to the 1938 Senate election, President Franklin Roosevelt endorsed Johnston as his candidate in an attempted purge of Senator and New Deal critic Ellison D. "Cotton Ed" Smith. Despite Roosevelt's popularity in South Carolina, his endorsement proved fatal for Johnston, with voters resenting the president's interference in the campaign. Although Johnston won the mill precincts overwhelmingly, voters in other regions, many of whom remained hostile to workers' rights, were unimpressed by his support for the Congress of Industrial Organizations (CIO). His attempt to dismiss the race issue, by claiming that the Costigan-Wagner antilynching bill was "not an issue in this campaign," counted against him in the "black belt" counties, where Smith maintained his support base with an uncompromising stand for white supremacy.[10]

The rapidly increasing membership of the NAACP fueled the growing intensity of the race issue during the 1940s. In addressing the need for candidates to appeal to voters in all regions of the state, not least the deeply conservative lowcountry counties, Johnston reconsidered the extent to which he would use race in a future run for the Senate. In a rematch with the ailing Smith in 1944, Johnston made the Supreme Court's *Smith v. Allwright* decision a central theme in his campaign by leading the fight against the ruling of the nine justices that the all-white primary system was unconstitutional. His reluctance to promote his white supremacist credentials is evident in various versions of a speech from the 1944 campaign, with a draft dated June 14 containing the claim that "I am not now, and have never been, in favor of social or political equality of the white and black races," while still making clear that "I do not intend to base my campaign to the high office of the United States Senate on this issue." However, by July 24—the day before polling day—Johnston had expanded the paragraph in question to include the claim that "as soon as the Supreme Court handed down its decision . . . I immediately called a special session and recommended legislation that was passed by a unanimous vote of both the House and Senate which assured the people of South Carolina white Democratic government. Had it not been for my action, tomorrow you would be walking along with Negroes to the ballot box."[11]

The governor's stand against the Supreme Court proved popular with conservative voters, who elected him as the Democratic Party candidate (and, therefore, the state's next senator) the following day, but Johnston failed to reform the state's primary system. In his ruling in *Elmore v. Rice* (1947), Judge Waring declared that "it is time for South Carolina to re-join the Union. It is time to fall in step with the other states and to adopt the American way of conducting elections." The decision, which torpedoed Johnston's dramatic attempt to defy the *Smith* ruling, established Waring's controversial reputation long before his open support for Thurgood Marshall in the *Briggs* case. With South Carolina's newspapers condemning the ruling and the Ku Klux Klan leaving burning crosses outside Waring's home, Congressman L. Mendel Rivers led an unsuccessful impeachment attempt, while Governor Strom Thurmond offered a brief preview of the southern reaction to *Brown* seven years later with the claim that he was "shocked" by the *Elmore* decision. Johnston would later refer to the controversial Charlestonian as "the obnoxious Judge J. Waties Waring of Charleston, who . . . left his party and our way of life."[12]

Alongside fellow New Deal liberal southerners such as Lister Hill of Alabama, Johnston signed the Southern Manifesto without question. He kept up, albeit carefully, a relationship with conservative organizations such as the White Citizens' Councils, formed as a means of community resistance in response to *Brown*. He also appeared regularly at anti-integration rallies across South Carolina, and responded courteously to letters from Council officials. The senator's handling of President Dwight D. Eisenhower's judicial nominations—particularly the appointment of Simon Sobeloff to the Fourth Circuit—provided an early indication of Johnston's willingness to use his influence on the Senate Judiciary Committee to maintain his segregationist credentials.[13]

Eisenhower's successor in the White House had declared an intention to promote black judges to the federal bench during his presidential campaign in 1960, but John F. Kennedy hesitated before nominating Thurgood Marshall to fill a vacancy on the Second Circuit Court of Appeals. Louis Martin, the administration's chief black advisor, supported Marshall—as did a majority of Kennedy's black supporters—but the president's brother, Attorney General Robert Kennedy, advised him that he would succeed in appointing Marshall only if he was prepared to risk alienating southern senators, which might prove politically costly if and when the administration required southern support for its legislative proposals. After Marshall refused a District Court appointment, Kennedy nominated him to the Second Circuit over the objection of his brother, only for the Senate Judiciary Committee, under Chairman James Eastland's leadership, to put an immediate delay on confirmation hearings. Knowing that the committee would hold up the nomination indefinitely, Kennedy gave Marshall a recess appointment on October 5, 1961, allowing him to serve on the Second Circuit on the condition that the committee would scrutinize and confirm him when Eastland finally agreed to hold hearings.[14]

The President resubmitted Marshall's name on January 15, 1962, but the nomination was still in limbo on April 1, when Justice Charles Evans Whittaker announced his retirement from the Supreme Court. Whittaker's departure gave the president and his brother the brand new dilemma of whether or not to nominate another black judge, this time for a vacancy on the nation's most powerful court. The obvious candidate was Judge William H. Hastie, who in 1949 had become the first black judge ever appointed to a US Court of Appeals after President Harry S. Truman nominated him for the Third Circuit. Despite Robert Kennedy's enthusiastic support, Hastie eventually lost out to Deputy US Attorney General Byron White, as President Kennedy did not wish to risk another confrontation with southern senators following their blockage of his attempt to create a Department of Housing and Urban Development under the leadership of black economist Robert C. Weaver. Southerners might have recalled that Hastie had stood shoulder-to-shoulder with Marshall when making the NAACP's case for the unconstitutionality of the all-white primary during the Supreme Court's hearings in the *Smith* case. Furthermore, both Hastie and Weaver had been members of Franklin Roosevelt's "black cabinet" in the 1930s, a group which—as aging southern senators would have recalled—gathered together prominent African Americans in a loosely coordinated collective that would theoretically influence federal policies relating to race relations. In addition, Kennedy remained concerned that a Hastie nomination would jeopardize the support of senior southerners such as Senate Finance Committee Chairman Harry F. Byrd of Virginia, whose influence was necessary to ensure that the administration's economic reforms passed through Congress smoothly. Kennedy was also mindful of the fact that the Senate had still not approved Marshall's Second Circuit appointment after six months, and that Chairman Eastland might perceive a Hastie Supreme Court nomination as a provocative gesture.[15]

In late February, Eastland handpicked three senators to sit as a subcommittee to scrutinize Thurgood Marshall's Second Circuit nomination: Democrat John McClellan of Arkansas, Republican Roman Hruska of Nebraska, and, as chairman, Democrat Olin Johnston of South Carolina. Johnston's appointment as chair proved critical in determining the course of events. With southern voters urging him to support the John Birch Society's campaign to impeach Chief Justice Earl Warren, the pressure mounting on Johnston to pursue a war on the court only grew throughout 1961. Despite adopting a cautious tone in some of his responses by reminding his constituents that the House of Representatives, rather than the Senate, must initiate all impeachment proceedings, Johnston was more sympathetic in other letters, telling one impeachment enthusiast from Orangeburg, South Carolina, "I shall certainly bring your suggestion to the attention of the other members of the Senate from the Southern states, and I know that they will be glad to have your suggestion. I certainly agree that many of the recent decisions of the Supreme Court are contrary to our way of thinking."[16]

To complicate matters further, Johnston's fixation with the power of the Supreme Court only intensified during Marshall's six months on a recess appointment. On March 26, 1962, the court handed down its landmark *Baker v. Carr* decision, which made the unprecedented judgment that federal courts were entitled to intervene in matters relating to malapportioned legislatures. In a newsletter released four days later, Johnston denounced the court's opinion, arguing that "by allowing federal district courts to step into strictly legislative affairs, the nation's entire election system may well be destroyed."[17] The huge importance of *Baker* in the evolution of the relationship between the states and the federal government makes Johnston's outrage at the court's action unsurprising. Gordon Silverstein has compared *Baker*'s significance with that of *Brown* in that the justices, in both decisions, "commanded" other institutions to act, offering a dramatic illustration of the Supreme Court's profound political power.[18] Considered by Earl Warren to be the most important case of his tenure as chief justice, *Baker* dispensed with the notion of a "political question doctrine" as a limit to judicial power, a development which Justice Felix Frankfurter feared would increase accusations of judicial activism and trigger an enormous political backlash.[19]

Baker presented a particularly grave problem for South Carolina's conservative political establishment. The legislators representing counties in the low-country region, with black majority populations, maintained an ironclad control over the state's legislature thanks to the very principle of malapportionment that the court had invalidated in *Baker.* The announcement of the decision was inevitably met with condemnation by the state's leaders, notably Senator Edgar A. Brown—long associated with the so-called "Barnwell Ring" and described by V. O. Key as the state's "Prime Minister"—who referred to *Baker* as "the political crisis of my time."[20] As Brown and others well understood, the establishment of a "one person, one vote" system of apportionment would only aid the emergence of a two-party system by revealing the true extent of Republican Party support in the south during the early 1960s. This predicament proved equally intimidating to Democratic leaders in other southern states: as Bill Frist and Lee Annis have explained, *Baker* "portended the rise of the Republican Party in Tennessee" by allowing "the equitable representation of city-dwellers and suburbanites" in that state. Even in the case of Georgia, where the Democratic Party proved particularly resilient, Charles Bullock and Ronald Keith Gaddie have shown that mass redistricting was producing "unprecedented rewards for the Republicans" by the 1990s. South Carolina embarked on a lengthy battle against the order to reconstruct its system of representation, refusing to accept the inevitability of a more democratic form of apportionment until the Supreme Court's announcement of *Stevenson v. West* in 1973.[21]

With Olin Johnston and other outraged South Carolinians describing *Baker* in typically apocalyptic language, the Kennedy brothers openly embraced the ruling, with the president claiming at a press conference that "to have each vote count equally is, it seems to me, basic to the successful operation of a democracy," a comment which would have given Johnston little incentive to schedule Thurgood Marshall's confirmation hearings with any urgency. Johnston's frequent delays of Marshall's hearings provide a useful example of how South Carolina's internal politics were influencing political controversy at the national level with regard to the Supreme Court. By the end of April, Fritz Hollings, the state's youthful and highly popular governor, had launched a strong primary challenge to Johnston's incumbency, and the senior senator did not wish to jeopardize his reelection by appearing to show mercy to the notorious black lawyer who had spoken so eloquently against the southern way of life during the *Brown* arguments. Furthermore, it was crucial for Johnston to address increasing white anxiety over frequent incidents of racial unrest on South Carolina's streets: during 1960 and 1961, the sit-in movement came to South Carolina, with demonstrators triggering protests at various establishments throughout the state, including branches of S. H. Kress in Orangeburg, Columbia, and Charleston. Particularly significant was the groundbreaking "Friendship Nine" protest at McCrory's in Rock Hill, which made history when nine protesters chose to serve time in jail, rather than make bail, in order to cause administrative inconvenience while saving the civil rights movement money.[22]

While Governor Hollings was ensuring public safety through crowd control and the use of black police officers to maintain calm, Senator Johnston condemned civil rights protests such as the "Freedom Rides," claiming that "the real courage does not exist . . . in the actions of the Freedom Riders, but lies with the Southern people, both white and Negro, who have lived together quietly and peacefully and who have solved in harmony their differences and achieved progress through the years. This sentiment built on themes covered in "The Good Side of the South," an article attributed to Johnston (but ghostwritten by his press secretary, Tom Chadwick) and published in September 1961 in the *New York Times,* which made the dubious claim that "in South Carolina . . . there has not been one case where a Negro has been denied the right to register or vote since records have been maintained showing the race of voters."[23] Under pressure to win reelection in a tense climate of increased racial unrest—and with the *Baker* decision striking the biggest blow to the survival of South Carolina's political establishment since *Brown*—Johnston refused to grant Thurgood Marshall an opportunity to legitimize his selection before the subcommittee, forcing him to continue serving on a recess appointment.

Elsewhere in the Senate, the two Republican senators from New York, Jacob Javits and Kenneth Keating, strongly supported Marshall's nomination. Aside from the fact that the state of New York fell within the boundary of the Second Circuit, both senators had personal reasons for supporting the nominee. Javits, who had attended Marshall's swearing-in ceremony on October 23, 1961, had already established a track record of standing up to South Carolina's senators in the ongoing war over the Supreme Court: in May 1958, he had condemned proposals in the Jenner bill to reduce the court's power, provoking an angry response from Olin Johnston, while more recently, he had debated Strom Thurmond in the December 1961 issue of the *American Legion Magazine* on the issue of whether judges should acquire five years' experience on the federal bench before being eligible for service on the Supreme Court. Keating, who served alongside Johnston on the Senate Judiciary Committee, contacted his South Carolina colleague to urge him to schedule confirmation hearings as quickly as possible due to Marshall's ongoing service on an unconfirmed appointment. When this suggestion proved ineffective, Keating was sufficiently enraged that he released a statement criticizing Johnston heavily and claiming that Marshall was being "victimized." Noting that a "majority" of the subcommittee was opposed to civil rights (singling out the chairman, the "Senator from South Carolina," for special mention), Keating made the serious allegation that Judiciary Committee staff had been briefed to prepare material that would discredit Marshall during his confirmation hearings. He claimed that he had "protested the delay and procedures to Senator Eastland . . . but my protests have fallen on deaf ears." Thanks to New York's WNEW-TV station, Charleston's *News and Courier,* and other media outlets, Keating's comments, criticisms, and accusations were well known and well documented by the end of April.[24]

While Johnston did not respond to these charges, his frequent delays did suggest a deliberate effort to keep Marshall's appointment on ice until after South Carolina's Democratic Party Senate primary. Having set a date of April 16, he delayed the hearings until April 24, and then delayed them again until May 1, when neither Johnston nor John McClellan showed up, despite the fact that Johnston had set the date himself. McClellan was attending a session of the Senate Appropriations Committee and Johnston claimed that a train journey had delayed him, but these explanations convinced few that their nonattendance constituted anything other than a typical southern attitude toward civil rights. In their absence, Marshall made a brief statement while Senator Hruska sat and listened. The two senators from New York, Javits and Keating, spoke in Marshall's defense, with Keating asserting that "the controversy about Judge Marshall centers not about the man, but the results he has achieved."[25]

The question of whether or not President Kennedy made a political gesture in order to persuade James Eastland to ensure Marshall's safe passage through the confirmation hearings remains somewhat shrouded in mystery. One well-documented anecdote involves Kennedy's agreement to nominate

Eastland's college roommate, the segregationist Judge W. Harold Cox, as a federal district judge in Mississippi. Eastland's alleged remark to Robert Kennedy—"tell your brother that if he will give me Harold Cox, I will give him the n——"—has never been substantiated, despite frequent scholarly references to it. Arthur Schlesinger believes that Kennedy's nomination of Cox "softened" Eastland, but Mark Tushnet has argued that Kennedy had selected Cox prior to his decision to nominate Marshall. Juan Williams has claimed that Eastland simply assured Robert Kennedy that the committee would confirm Marshall after southern senators had made as much political capital as possible out of the nomination. Regardless of the accuracy or detail of the story, Victor Navasky has argued persuasively that a notional Cox/Marshall trade-off symbolizes the profound systemic problem endured by the Kennedy brothers with regard to judicial nominations. The southern bloc had become sufficiently immovable under President Eisenhower—who was willing to accommodate the southern influence and who did not name a single black judge to any federal position during his presidency—that the Kennedys were ultimately doomed to nominate a string of undesirable segregationist judges as "sweeteners" for southern senators.[26]

Kennedy's prediction that the process of Marshall's confirmation would be a marathon rather than a sprint proved accurate when Johnston proceeded to spend the rest of May campaigning against Fritz Hollings in South Carolina, refusing to deal with Marshall until he had secured renomination. Perhaps recalling Hollings's willingness to use race-baiting tactics during his successful 1958 run for governor, Johnston refused to allow his youthful opponent the opportunity to accuse him of giving the notorious Marshall an easy ride—a claim that might have played well with the conservative South Carolina voters calling for Earl Warren's impeachment. Aided by his seniority in the Senate, and his claim to have prevented the closure of Donaldson Air Force Base, Johnston's hard work on the campaign trail during the months of May and June 1962 paid off handsomely when he defeated Hollings in a landslide victory, winning 216,918 votes to 110,023, securing a majority in all but one of the state's counties, with Hollings winning Calhoun County by 34 votes.[27]

With the Democratic nomination now secure, Johnston showed no greater sense of urgency in scheduling Marshall's confirmation hearings, but did continue to demonstrate his antagonism toward the US Supreme Court by joining with Senators James Eastland, John McClellan, and Herman Talmadge to introduce a constitutional amendment to nullify the court's *Engel v. Vitale* decision, which ruled teacher-led prayer in public schools to be a violation of the First Amendment. He would later find the time to preside as acting chairman over Judiciary Committee hearings on the *Engel* decision, which included testimony from Senators John Stennis of Mississippi, A. Willis Robertson of Virginia, Vance Hartke of Indiana, J. Glenn Beall of Maryland, and his South Carolina colleague, Strom Thurmond. Just in case a reminder was needed of South Carolina's attitudes toward the Supreme Court, Thurmond issued a newsletter in which he argued against permitting the court "to interpret God out of our national life." In observing that Karl Marx aimed "to dethrone God and destroy capitalism," Thurmond concluded solemnly that the court, through the school prayer decision, was "helping Marx attain those objectives."[28] As with *Baker v. Carr,* the *Engel* decision only encouraged southern senators to be more vigilant in their duty to their constituents on the question of judicial nominations.

The three members of the Johnston subcommittee finally met on July 12, 1962, to assess Thurgood Marshall's Second Circuit nomination. Chairman Johnston employed a hostile strategy from the start by unleashing the committee's special counsel, L. P. B. Lipscomb of Mississippi, who proceeded to interrogate Marshall at length regarding an obscure Texas District Court decision finding the NAACP guilty of practicing law illegally. Senator Keating of New York pointed out that Marshall had not been associated with the case, and Republican senator Everett Dirksen of Illinois joined his protests. Johnston defended Lipscomb throughout the hearing, even insisting that he proceed to interrogate Marshall regarding another NAACP case relating to Virginia, provoking Republican senators into making further objections. Dirksen and Keating protested that it would be inappropriate to discuss cases still pending before the Supreme Court on appeal:

Senator Keating: Well, Mr. Chairman, may I make a comment, that we are not here concerned with investigating the NAACP. We are here concerned with the investigation of the qualifications of this nominee, as to his character, ability, and integrity to be a US circuit judge.

Senator Johnston: That is true, but at the same time, the question is before this committee as to whether or not, in his activities and as a witness and attorney for the NAACP, just what he has done in that line.

Senator Keating: Well, we could spend the rest of this session doing nothing but examining and investigating the NAACP, and I would hope that counsel would make more progress than he has up to the time or up to date.

Senator Johnston: I think when he brings in the Virginia case and ties in the two, you will see the connection in the two cases.[29]

Following further fruitless questioning from Lipscomb, Johnston decided to adjourn the hearings at noon without setting a date for the next hearing. The frustration of Marshall and others in the room was palpable:

Senator Keating: Has the time been fixed, Mr. Chairman for—

Senator Johnston: No, it has not. The subcommittee is adjourned.

Judge Marshall: Well, Mr. Chairman, would it possibly be tomorrow? I wonder whether I should stay over or not.

Senator Johnston: Well, not tomorrow. I can tell you that right now.

Judge Marshall: Well, I would like to get back to my work. That is the only reason—

Senator Johnston: It will not. We will notify you in advance. We will arrange it as early as possible. The committee is adjourned.[30]

Having defended the subcommittee lawyer's interrogation, Johnston maintained a correspondence with Lipscomb and even encouraged him to undertake further investigations. After a Mrs. E. Sinclair Eaton of Gainesville, Florida, wrote to the senator to inform him of a television film focusing on Marshall and the US Constitution, Johnston forwarded the letter to Lipscomb (without informing Mrs. Eaton), telling him, "I thought you might be interested in looking into this matter."[31]

Perhaps sensing support for Marshall among other senators, Dirksen and Keating attempted to obtain the Senate's permission to force a hearing on the afternoon of August 8. Despite Dirksen's seniority among Republican senators,

Johnston used his seniority as subcommittee chairman to object, claiming that one morning session would be sufficient, and also that the Judiciary Committee would be meeting that afternoon to discuss President Kennedy's plans for tighter drug control legislation. Although Johnston's veto over scheduling remained his trump card, the shambolic July 12 hearing suggested he had very little in the way of credible ammunition to use against the nominee. He informed the *News and Courier* two days later that the full Judiciary Committee might soon withdraw his authority to question Marshall, leaving him powerless to scrutinize the nominee or prevent confirmation. Referring to this possibility as "the sharpest piece of political strategy in 1962," the paper's editorial concluded that "Sen. Johnston has to ask himself whether South Carolina voters would accept full committee action as straightforward, or see it as a political trick for the benefit of a fellow politician."[32]

As the state's press commented on the remarkably low voter turnout in the June primary, Johnston looked ahead to his reelection battle. With columnist W. D. Workman launching a strong Republican challenge to his Senate seat, Johnston kept in mind his responsibility, as South Carolina's senior senator, to ensure that the tens of thousands of white voters who had failed to vote in June's Democratic primary would not now defect to the Republican Party in November.[33] His fruitless obstruction of Thurgood Marshall's Second Circuit appointment could only continue.

5. "THE BOYS DOWN THERE"

By July 1962, the Thurgood Marshall affair had stirred emotions among the South's white conservatives. Many of them wrote to Olin Johnston to express their disgust at President Kennedy's appointment of a black judge to the Second Circuit, with one Spartanburg, South Carolina, resident claiming that "the whole South will always love and respect you if you will help keep the Negroes and the Jews out of office," and a Biloxi, Mississippi, resident hoping for further delays while expressing the view that, in the event of Marshall's confirmation, "let's hope they'll keep him in the East and North—JFK will probably put him on the US Supreme Court."[1]

More surprising is the huge number of letters advising Johnston to cease delaying the hearings and simply allow the Judiciary Committee to confirm Marshall's appointment. Many of these writers claimed to have voted for Johnston, rather than Governor Ernest "Fritz" Hollings, in June's Democratic Party Senate primary, while other correspondents had campaigned actively for the senator's renomination. Former state senator Calhoun Thomas, whose influence had helped to secure Johnston's victory in Beaufort County, warned that the senator would lose crucial black support in the November election if he continued delaying Marshall's confirmation, declaring that "I have talked to a number of the Negro leaders in this vicinity. They understand what you are doing and your reason for your actions. They feel, though, that you are hurting yourself by this because it is not being understood by the mass of the Negro voters. They and I feel that you have very little to gain and will run a possible loss of a great many votes if you continue to delay an action."[2] Johnston conceded that the letter contained "a mighty strong well-taken point," but Thomas was not alone in making this argument. One Augusta, Georgia, correspondent reminded Johnston that "the Negroes in South Carolina have been largely responsible for your going to the Senate in Washington and since Mr. Marshall is qualified and had been cleared by the Justice Department before his nomination, we cannot understand your move in this matter."[3]

Black voters sent a great many letters to Johnston's office during the summer of 1962, often combining supportive statements for the senator's reelection with an enthusiastic backing for Marshall's confirmation. The Rock Hill chapter of the much-hated NAACP endorsed Marshall, as did John H. McCray, publisher of *Lighthouse and Informer,* who explained that "we South Carolina Negro voters won our status in the Democratic Party largely through the efforts and ability of Mr. Marshall." C. B. Bailey, who—as "the only Negro postal employee from South Carolina"—had met with Johnston during a pay raise rally, advised Johnston that embarrassing Marshall "will be of no advantage to you in the fall election, or in any other situation." Further endorsements for Marshall (from both black and white sources) continued flooding in to Johnston's office from outside South Carolina. By the end of the first week of July, the managing editor of the *Birmingham (AL) World,* the treasurer of the *Philadelphia Inquirer,* and the chairman of the "Thurgood Marshall Confirmation Committee" of the Washington Bar Association of the District of Columbia had all urged Johnston to instruct the committee to approve Marshall's appointment.[4]

Given the outpouring of enthusiasm for Marshall's confirmation in Johnston's correspondence, it seems surprising that the senator opted to defy so many of his supporters by continuing to delay and inconvenience the nominee with his hostile tactics as subcommittee chairman. On the other hand, his actions seem logical in the context of his correspondence with South Carolina's conservative political establishment. Despite Johnston's sensational primary victory over Fritz Hollings in June, South Carolina's Democrats were mindful of the disappointing white turnout, and viewed with concern the potential for W. D. Workman's segregationist campaign to secure Republican votes in November's Senate election. As in most southern states, victory in the Democratic Party primary usually guaranteed election in November—given the lack of credible Republican opposition—resulting in the additional risk of white voters staying at home, viewing the November election result as a foregone conclusion. Since Johnston's last election victory six years previously, the Republican Party had begun making electoral inroads in the South by capitalizing on white disillusionment with civil rights measures. In March 1962, South Carolina Republicans had welcomed Barry Goldwater at the largest Republican convention in the state's history, where the influential conservative senator from Arizona implored the adoring crowd to elect W. D. Workman in order to "help Strom Thurmond represent conservatives" in Washington, DC. As a Republican opponent, Workman seemed unusually formidable. Through defending the racial status quo in *The Case for the South* (published in 1960), the veteran journalist embodied, in the words of Jason Morgan Ward, "the ethos of responsible segregation that had guided South Carolina's resistance campaign for over a decade." In a further suggestion of a growing Republican threat, State Representative Floyd Spence announced in April that he was switching to the Republican Party to challenge Democrat Albert Watson's incumbency as US representative for the state's Second Congressional District.[5]

Senior Democrats pressured Johnston to use his influence to ensure continued Democratic dominance in the state, and do everything within his power to slow the rapid emergence of a two-party system.[6] Senator Edgar A. Brown, president pro tempore of the South Carolina Senate, wrote to Johnston frequently during the second half of 1962, informing him optimistically that "we are making an all-out drive to get out a full vote which is the answer to the Republicans. If the same vote is polled in this election as was polled in the primary, you will beat Workman in the same proportion you beat Fritz." Charles A. Lafitte, president of the Carolina Commercial Bank, reminded Johnston of his importance in resisting the Republican insurgency, claiming that "some of my good friends who have always voted Democratic with me have changed and will vote otherwise in November. The situation to me appears serious and I strongly urge you to immediately get busy in South Carolina and try to counteract some of this trend." Congressman Charles E. Simons expressed particular concern over Republican support in his home county, warning Solomon Blatt, Speaker of the South Carolina House of Representatives, that "we are having a terrible fight here in Aiken County as I am sure you are aware. Everywhere I turn I find strong Workman-Spence supporters, which has me very much concerned about our carrying Aiken County." Johnston attempted to whip up Democratic Party support at a major rally at the Aiken High School Stadium, but Senator Brown advised Charles Lafitte that "Olin is not going to have time to cover every county and they are going to try to make Aiken a rousing one to break the ice in this Goldwater political atmosphere in our area."[7]

In addition to the growing anxiety over the Republican threat, there is evidence to suggest a lingering resentment over President Eisenhower's dismissal of Strom Thurmond's recommendation of South Carolinian Robert Figg for a vacancy on the Fourth Circuit Court of Appeals in 1956, favoring instead the appointment of Marylander Simon Sobeloff. By the spring of 1962, Thurmond and Walter Brown, one of his most trusted political advisors, were aiming to secure Olin Johnston's endorsement of Figg for a vacancy on the United States District Court for the Eastern District of South Carolina, left by the death of Judge Ashton H. Williams. As Brown outlined in a letter to Thurmond, "as I see it, there cannot be a greater travesty of justice than for Thurgood Marshall, who represented the NAACP before the court, to be put on the Circuit Court of Appeals and for Bob to be denied even a district judgeship in South Carolina."[8] While understanding that Johnston's lukewarm attitude toward Figg resulted from Figg's role as Thurmond's speechwriter during the latter's challenge to Johnston in the bitter Democratic Party primary battle of 1950, Brown's view neatly summed up the outrage that would have ensued in the Thurmond camp if Johnston had appeared willing to accept Marshall but unwilling to accommodate Figg, who had argued against Marshall in the *Briggs v. Elliott* case.

One particularly striking aspect of the correspondence between the key members of South Carolina's political establishment during this period is the manner in which influential Democrats were goading Johnston and Thurmond into attacking the Supreme Court. Despite Thurmond's years of aggressive "court-baiting" since the mid-1950s, Walter Brown declared, "I would like to see you go after the Supreme Court with the same zeal and determination you have demonstrated in exposing the 'no-win' policies in the State Department," while one month later, Edgar Brown advised Johnston to "take a blast at Hugo Black and the Supreme Court on the anti-prayer decision," perhaps as a means of capitalizing on accusations that Alabamian justice Black had "betrayed" the South with his role in *Brown v. Board of Education*.[9] The attitude of the state's Democratic politicians toward South Carolina's black population was evident in Edgar Brown's letter to Johnston on June 14, in which he stated, "The 'n——' has more civil rights now than he can use, and if some of our friends would only realize that a citizen must be capable of exercising the rights which are inherently his before he can start a riot to obtain those rights we would be much better off."[10]

The overwhelming support for Marshall from black and white South Carolinians suggests that a sizable community of racial moderates may have finally begun to emerge in South Carolina by the early 1960s. On the other hand, the members of South Carolina's political establishment expressed virulent anti–Supreme Court sentiments that drowned out the huge wave of enthusiasm for Marshall's confirmation, with the kingpins of the state legislature remaining determined to keep an iron grip on the state's political affairs, even after the court's announcement of *Baker v. Carr.* As Johnston's correspondence suggests, many of the more liberal-minded voters continued to reelect the senior senator, but the pressure exerted by the state's most powerful political figures ensured that Johnston's seniority would continue to function as an extension of their racially conservative agenda on a national scale.

By the middle of August 1962, Olin Johnston felt that he had delayed Thurgood Marshall's Second Circuit confirmation hearings sufficiently. During that month, he would allow himself and his allies further opportunities to scrutinize Marshall, forcing the nominee to face down Dixie in three further hearings.

During the first August hearing, Senator Kenneth Keating maintained the onslaught of criticism he had been directing at Johnston for months, arguing that other recent nominees—specifically Robert J. Elliott of Georgia and W. Harold Cox of Mississippi—had not been investigated with the same rigor, nor were the activities of their law firms scrutinized in a manner similar to Johnston's focus on the NAACP. Before long, the press picked up on the double standard argument. As James Marlow noted in the *Nashua Telegraph,* there had been no subcommittee investigation into Byron White's nomination to the Supreme Court: "Although the full committee probably knew far less about White than it did about Marshall, a brief hearing was held April 11 and White got unanimous committee approval. That same day, the full Senate approved." By the end of August, other public figures began targeting Johnston, including baseball legend Jackie Robinson, who threw accusations of racism at the subcommittee in his news column, and former First Lady Eleanor Roosevelt, who considered the hearings a worldwide embarrassment.[11]

At the second August hearing, Marshall's critics persisted with the familiar tactic of linking the NAACP to communism. Losing patience, Republican senator Kenneth Keating of New York and Democratic senator John A. Carroll of Colorado announced that they would consider moves to discharge the subcommittee if Johnston allowed further pointless hearings to continue. The quiet man from South Carolina responded, "I do hope the two senators that have spoken are not making that in the form of a threat to the subcommittee." At a further hearing held on August 17, the subcommittee challenged Marshall on his alleged remark that the NAACP had "the law, religion and God" on its side. Marshall denied making the remark but made his views on the South quite clear when he declared to the subcommittee that "anybody who takes a man out and lynches him, I believe is working with the devil."[12] A more newsworthy result emerged during the next hearing, held on August 20, when the subcommittee focused on a speech delivered by Dr. Alfred H. Kelly, professor of history at Wayne State University in Detroit, Michigan, at the annual meeting of the American Historical Society, which the *US News and World Report* published as an essay.

In the speech and essay, Kelly, who had assisted with NAACP research into the school segregation cases, claimed that Marshall was prone to making racially charged jokes, offering one choice quote as an example: "When us colored folk take over, every time a white man draws a breath, he'll have to pay a fine." It is unclear how or when the three members of the subcommittee learned of this potentially explosive remark. If Senator Keating's allegations regarding research into Marshall's background were correct, it remains possible that a member of the Judiciary Committee staff may have unearthed the speech. What can be confirmed is that a constituent alerted Johnston to the speech as early as July 9, and Ralph B. Kolb, chairman of the South Carolina Citizens' Council, reminded him of it when he wrote to the senator on August 7.[13] Among the remarks in the speech were the following reflections on the *Brown* case: "The problem we faced was not the historian's discovery of the truth, the whole truth, and nothing but the truth. It is not that we were engaged in formulating lies; there was nothing as crude and naïve as that. But we were using facts, emphasizing facts, sliding off facts, quietly ignoring facts, and above all, interpreting facts in a way to do what Marshall said we had to do—'get by the boys down there.'"[14]

Johnston may or may not have agreed with Kolb's view that the text of the speech "furnishes sufficient ammunition to forcibly bring before the nation the fraud involved in the court's decision in the schools cases."[15] He had, however, along with other southerners, always questioned the legitimacy of the *Brown* decision's reliance on "sociological" sources such as Gunnar Myrdal's *An American Dilemma.* The remark concerning the white man paying a fine for drawing a breath proved sufficiently offensive to justify Johnston's call for a further hearing, during which the subcommittee would question Dr. Kelly in person. The request triggered one of the more tense exchanges of the hearings:

Senator Johnston: I will call the subcommittee together, the three of us, and I will lay this before them to see what they want to do. I think that is the logical thing for me to do as one member here of the committee, and that is what I am going to do.

Senator Hart: Mr. Chairman, if I could, neither Senator Keating nor I are members of this subcommittee.

Senator Johnston: You are visitors. I am glad to let you make a statement, but just remember you are not on the subcommittee.

Senator Keating: But we are on the full committee.

Senator Johnston: But you are not on the subcommittee.

Senator Keating: It will be in the hands of the full committee unless this meeting is quickly closed. This is a ridiculous procedure and an unlawyer-like procedure, and it will be my intention to raise the problem before the full committee.

Senator Johnston: You have a perfect right to do that, but as far as the subcommittee, we want to get the facts before the full committee. I don't know what the man who wrote the articles in the newspaper will come and say.[16]

Having decided he had had enough, Keating claimed he would request that Chairman Eastland terminate the subcommittee hearings and allow the full Senate to vote on Marshall's appointment, taking the matter to the Senate floor if necessary. Senator Philip Hart of Michigan, who by now had added his voice to Keating's objections, defended the nominee by claiming that Marshall's "reputation in American jurisprudence is established. We will indict ourselves if we fail to acknowledge it."[17]

Despite his reluctance to antagonize southern senators, President Kennedy finally opted to use his influence to draw the hearings to a close. Given that the one-year anniversary of the recess appointment was approaching—meaning that Marshall would stop getting paid if the Senate did not confirm him—the president had already taken action to ensure that Marshall would not have to work without a paycheck. At a press conference, Kennedy said that confirmation had been "too much delayed" and expressed confidence that the Senate would not adjourn without taking action on Marshall's appointment. However, even the President's intervention did not deter Chairman Johnston from pursuing one final hearing on August 24, during which the subcommittee questioned Dr. Kelly on Marshall's "pay a fine" quote. To those who knew Marshall personally, Kelly's claim that the remark was "mordant humor, given exclamation by a man possessed of a powerful sense of humor" would have seemed quite plausible. Bob Woodward and Scott Armstrong have claimed that Marshall would typically use humor to unsettle well-to-do white people in his company, such as Warren Burger. When Burger and Marshall were both on the Supreme Court some years later, Marshall would address Chief Justice Burger with the idiosyncratic greeting, "What's shakin', Chiefy-baby?" Another anecdote has an amused Justice Marshall responding "yowsa, yowsa" to a man mistaking him for an elevator operator in the Supreme Court building. While Johnston may have been skeptical of Kelly's explanation, the newspapers did not express horror at the idea of Thurgood Marshall's "mordant" sense of humor, with Mary McGrory commenting in the *Atlanta Constitution* that "nobody has ever said this quality would be unbecoming in a federal judge." The *Washington Post* argued that Marshall's remark "could have been only a jest" while ridiculing the "flimsiness of Senator Johnston's opposition," asking the reader, "is a notoriously prejudiced Senator to be allowed to defeat the appointment of a well-qualified Negro to the federal bench simply by endlessly stringing out his hearings?"[18]

After Kelly's testimony failed to yield any negative material to use against the nominee, L. P. B. Lipscomb, the subcommittee's counsel, read from a section of *Newsweek,* which recorded Marshall as declaring, "We've negotiated too quietly and too reasonably for too long. We've made up our minds to harass the legal hell out of the school boards. From here on out, we're going to be unreasonable, un-decent, and un-everything else." The inclusion of this quote on the record brought further protests from Marshall's exasperated supporters:

Senator Keating: Is this—might I enquire whether this is offered as proof of the facts stated?

Senator Johnston: This is offered as being printed in *Newsweek* of September 18, 1961, for whatever it is worth.

Senator Hart: What's it worth? What's it worth, then, in light of the problem facing the committee?

Senator Johnston: This is a very prominent magazine, and I think a lot of us read it, and I know I read it, and try to keep up with what's going on in the world, like a lot of other people do.

Senator Keating: I might comment it is in line with some of the other legal antics which have taken place in these hearings.

Senator Hart: Mr. Chairman, if this concludes the hearing—

Senator Johnston: Yes, this concludes the hearing, is that right?

Senator Hart: Amen and thank heaven, and let's not berate or review the chronology.[19]

With the nation's press continuing to criticize him and the president and several outspoken senators pressuring him to desist, Johnston finally announced that he did not intend to question Thurgood Marshall further, but caused another tense exchange with Keating and Hart with his insistence on printing the hearings before the subcommittee reached a decision. As if to signal the end of Johnston's crusade, the *New York Times* noted that Keating's move to end the subcommittee hearings and bring the nomination to the Senate floor for a vote "would enable Senator Johnston to tell South Carolinians that he had done all in his power to resist the nomination."[20]

Despite Strom Thurmond's gloomy prediction that "if the nomination reaches the floor, there will be a fight," the Senate confirmed Marshall by a vote of 54–16. The subcommittee had voted privately to reject Marshall following the conclusion of hearings, with only Senator Roman Hruska supporting the nominee. When the full committee took a vote, Chairman Eastland and Senator Sam Ervin of North Carolina joined Johnston and McClellan in opposing Marshall, and fourteen other southern Democrats joined them in dissent when the full Senate voted.[21] Senators had finally legitimized Thurgood Marshall's appointment to the Second Circuit, but, as he would discover before the end of the decade, his days of facing down Dixie in the US Senate were far from over.

As with Johnston's prioritization of the Sobeloff appointment to the Fourth Circuit over the selection of William Brennan for the Supreme Court, the senator evidently considered the Marshall Second Circuit nomination far more important than President Kennedy's decision to nominate Arthur J. Goldberg to fill the Supreme Court vacancy left by the retirement of Justice Felix Frankfurter. Former justice Charles Evans Whittaker briefed Goldberg in advance, as did Jim Adler, a former law clerk to Chief Justice Warren, enabling Goldberg to charm the Judiciary Committee in hearings lasting only one day, in stark contrast to the drawn-out confrontation involving Thurgood Marshall.[22]

As explained in the previous chapter, President Eisenhower's letter to his attorney general in September 1958 highlighted an acknowledgment of the strong southern influence within the Senate Judiciary Committee. The existence of a Justice Department briefing paper, prepared for Goldberg prior to his Committee hearings in 1962, offers further compelling evidence that the Kennedy administration also acknowledged the southern influence as a highly significant potential roadblock to confirming Supreme Court nominations. Extracts from this paper provide great insight into the administration's expectation of the content and style of Judiciary Committee questioning during this period. Given the tense nature of Potter Stewart's confirmation hearings in 1959, Justice Byron White—Kennedy's first Supreme Court appointee—recommended that the Justice Department provide Goldberg with a transcript of the Stewart hearings as a guide to what he might expect at his own hearings.

The briefing paper offered a series of hypothetical yet "ritualistic" questions for which "pavlovian answers" were expected. As part of its highly detailed advice, the paper explained that a question asking "do you think that the courts should cite as authority for decisions, books or documents written by individuals which have never been part of the record in the case?" would be aimed essentially at the infamous footnote 11 of the *Brown* decision, referring to Myrdal's *An American Dilemma.* Noting that "this question was asked of both Justice Brennan and Justice Stewart and both had trouble with it," the paper recommended an answer emphasizing the value of "relevant constitutional and statutory provisions" whilst noting that "the Court did not, in our view, cite Myrdal as precedent, but your questioner's opinion will be otherwise." The paper pointed out that the committee's line of questioning could easily place a nominee in a difficult position: denying that the court had cited Myrdal as precedent "will simply initiate a detrimental sideshow," but on the other hand, accepting that the justices had treated Myrdal as precedent would be interpreted as criticism of the *Brown* decision. The paper advised Goldberg against offering evasive answers when committee members raised the *Brown* decision, and also pointed out that senators might seize upon the brief he had filed on behalf of the CIO for the *Brown* case. The paper reminded Goldberg of a speech he had given before the annual meeting of the American Jewish Committee in 1961, condemning racial segregation in private clubs, which the committee might also wish to scrutinize, particularly as the Supreme Court had dealt with a number of "sit-in" cases during the past term.

Significantly, the paper referred to both *Baker v. Carr* and *Engel v. Vitale* as areas of concern for committee members, and suggested that Goldberg offer diplomatic responses in order to demonstrate a sound knowledge of the cases in question.[23] With such meticulous preparation, Goldberg faced the committee with confidence, and the Senate confirmed him by a voice vote with only one objection—South Carolina's Senator Strom Thurmond, who demonstrated his state's consistent skepticism of the Kennedy administration's judicial nominees by opposing Goldberg's confirmation.[24] The existence of a detailed and well-researched Justice Department briefing paper, intended to advise nominees on how to face the Senate Judiciary Committee, illustrates the extent to which marathon judicial hearings had become an institution by the end of 1962. As with the Sobeloff controversy, Olin Johnston's obstruction of Thurgood Marshall's Second Circuit appointment serves as a reminder of South Carolina's prominent role in the swift development of judicial nomination hearings into confrontational events of increasing public interest.

Following the Senate's confirmation, Marshall's supporters continued to send letters of criticism to Johnston, many of them from the state of New York. Perhaps taking the protests of their senators as their cue, New Yorkers expressed varying degrees of outrage over Johnston's handling of Marshall's nomination, one declaring, "I am white and I'm deeply ashamed of some of my kind, you included"; another stating, "your constituents in South Carolina may be proud of your efforts . . . as for me, I think they are disgusting," and one New York–based southerner asking Johnston "not to add to the stigma under which the South labors as the alleged hospitable home of bigotry."[25] It is unlikely that any of these sentiments would have moved the senior senator from South Carolina, particularly given that he had already blamed the state of New York for inciting racial unrest through forced integration. He reminded southerners of his views when making a speech in Alabama, arguing that "as soon as you develop a strong two-party system in the South you are going to get the same minority vote baiting that you have in cities like New York." Making full use of an opportunity to take aim at his New York critics, he added, "How would you like living on the civil rights issue with Jacob Javits, Kenneth Keating, Barry Goldwater or another Eisenhower?"[26]

It was with pep talks such as these that Johnston succeeded in defeating Republican W. D. Workman in November's Senate election. With his victory over Workman, of 178,712 votes to 133,930, Johnston secured himself another six-year term and eased, temporarily, Democratic fears of a Republican insurgency. Through his rough treatment of Thurgood Marshall, he was able to maintain segregationist credentials and maximize white conservative turnout while at the same time minimizing the civil rights issue to give the impression of being the more moderate of the two candidates. He was able to emphasize his loyalty to the Democratic Party as a means of discouraging a voter exodus to the Republicans, while at the same time distancing himself from President Kennedy, who had angered many white southerners by sending federal troops to the University of Mississippi in October 1962 to ensure the safe enrollment of black student James Meredith, albeit amid scenes of violent resistance and chaos. Johnston still managed to win Kennedy's endorsement, thanks to his seniority on Senate committees, and also managed to convince a sufficient number of South Carolina's registered black voters to stick with him despite his treatment of Marshall. In Charleston, approximately nine out of ten registered black voters supported his reelection.[27]

Recalling Johnston's success in attracting black support over the more conservative Strom Thurmond during the 1950 Democratic primary, John H. McCray was quick to attribute the senator's 1962 victory to the black vote: "Take 25,000 Negro votes away from Sen. Johnston in the last general election and Mr. Workman would now be on his way to the US Senate in Washington."[28] The logic of supporting Johnston simply for being the more moderate candidate was evident even in the letters of criticism sent to the senator in the run-up to the election, with one pro-Marshall student telling him "you have my support against Workman . . . I consider you the lesser of two evils."[29] Nonetheless, Johnston's victory did not make him complacent. Frank E. Jordan, in his famous study of South Carolina's elections from 1896 to 1962, argued that "although Johnston was successful against W. D. Workman, that race concluded the story of the one-party system."[30] The state of South Carolina was now a hotbed of dramatic Republican Party growth, thanks in no small part to the unpredictable Strom Thurmond's growing influence during the 1960s.[31]

With his opposition to Marshall's Second Circuit appointment, Olin Johnston ensured national recognition of South Carolina's response to *Brown* through the federal nomination process. With a far more challenging reelection effort to face in 1962 than his most recent contest in 1956 (the year of his sustained objection to Sobeloff), it is difficult to deny that the political situation in South Carolina was the primary influence on Johnston's behavior throughout the Marshall controversy. Yet the nationwide scale of his actions was evident in a national chorus of condemnation that included a president, several senators, a sporting hero, a former first lady, and several influential African American political activists. Johnston's obstructionism offered a fascinating suggestion of future events in the story of South Carolina's war on the Supreme Court. His masterful understanding of the state's electorate—and his success in appealing to conservative white voters with a gesture guaranteed to antagonize African Americans without compromising his share of the black vote—would be evident twenty-five years later, when his successor, Fritz Hollings, found himself in a similar situation when supporting Ronald Reagan's controversial Supreme Court nomination of Robert Bork. Furthermore, the 1962 Second Circuit affair provides a useful prologue to President Lyndon Johnson's landmark selection of Marshall to become the first African American justice on the nation's highest court—an episode in which South Carolina's role in the judicial nomination process would become only more controversial.

Following the events in Dallas on November 22, 1963, the new president set up a commission to investigate John F. Kennedy's assassination. Even under such traumatic conditions, Lyndon Johnson was reminded of the ongoing southern hatred of Chief Justice Earl Warren only one week after Kennedy's death, when both James Eastland and Richard Russell advised him to appoint Justice John Marshall Harlan, rather than Warren, as head of the new commission, with Russell even refusing to serve on the commission if it meant working alongside Warren.[32] The new president would also have to address South Carolina's fixation with judicial nominations by filling a District Court vacancy that Kennedy had neglected, in addition to a second vacancy that had appeared after Judge George Bell Timmerman announced his retirement in September 1962. The increasing restlessness of South Carolina's politicians for the appointment of their two new judges is evident in a note sent by Edgar Brown to Olin Johnston twelve days after Kennedy's assassination, which read: "Am I right in the grapevine information which I have received that no further appointments are going to be announced until after the mourning period? Also, if you will be a little confidential, are our two agreed upon?"[33]

6. "A COLORED MAN WITH THE NAME OF MARSHALL"

"As we meet, South Carolina is running out of courts. . . . We of today must realize the lesson of one hundred years ago, and move on for the good of South Carolina and our United States. This should be done with dignity. It must be done with law and order . . ."

In declaring these words to the South Carolina General Assembly on January 9, 1963, outgoing Governor Ernest "Fritz" Hollings signaled the beginning of the end for the state's resistance to civil rights. In a bid to avoid the violent protests over the University of Mississippi's desegregation in October 1962, Hollings had overseen the safe enrollment of Clemson University's first black student, Harvey Gantt, and, in contrast to scenes of fire hoses and German shepherds subduing black protestors in Birmingham, Alabama, he had maintained law and order during South Carolina's sit-in protests. Only four years earlier, he had used arguments relating to "law and order" when testifying on behalf of the South Carolina delegation attending hearings of the Senate Judiciary Committee's Subcommittee on Constitutional Rights. Having slammed the court's desegregation rulings such as the landmark *Brown v. Board of Education* by citing Charles Warren's claim that "it is still the Constitution which is the law and not the decision of the court," Hollings now claimed, in his farewell address in 1963, that "we have all agreed that the Supreme Court decision of 1954 is not the law of the land. But everyone must agree that is the fact of the land."[1]

Hollings's skill in preparing South Carolina for a transition to integration "with dignity" appeared to count for little in the governor's own career trajectory: with state law preventing him from running for a second consecutive term as governor, he had made a bold challenge to Olin D. Johnston's incumbency, only for the veteran senator to thrash him in the 1962 Democratic primary.

Hollings paid a heavy price for his friendship with the liberal-minded President John F. Kennedy, and scraped a victory in only one of the state's forty-six counties.[2] Following a second, this time successful, run for the Senate in 1966, Hollings would face a dilemma over whether or not to support the confirmation of the first African American nominee for the US Supreme Court. Thurgood Marshall was already a nationally known figure, particularly after President Lyndon Johnson appointed him as US solicitor general in 1965. His controversial relationship with the state of South Carolina had been played out in the courts in the form of *Briggs v. Elliott* and *Brown v. Board of Education,* and also before the Senate Judiciary Committee, where Olin Johnston had provoked mass condemnation for using his seniority to delay President Kennedy's nomination of Marshall to the Second Circuit Court of Appeals.

Fritz Hollings had been far more closely involved in the *Brown* case than either Johnston or Strom Thurmond. In December 1952, as Speaker of the South Carolina House of Representatives, Hollings had authorized the necessary legislation to substantiate Governor James Byrnes's pledge to "equalize" the quality of the state's school system in order to comply with instructions from the three-judge panel presiding over the *Briggs* arguments.[3] Byrnes had asked Hollings, prior to his election as lieutenant governor, to accompany South Carolina's counsel, John W. Davis, at the *Brown* hearings, during which Davis argued before the Supreme Court that South Carolina had sufficiently improved the standard of its black schools. Through his involvement in *Brown,* Hollings claimed to have developed a friendship with Thurgood Marshall that would last until Marshall's death at age 84, on January 24, 1993. His vote against the confirmation of Marshall's Supreme Court nomination, which threatened to alienate his black supporters in South Carolina, serves to illustrate the influence of persistent regional issues on the politics of the US Senate, and, at the same time, the potential consequences for state politics when senators face difficult choices in their role in the judicial nomination process.

The Marshall nomination signposted a new phase in South Carolina's anti–Supreme Court crusade, with Strom Thurmond taking his place on the Senate Judiciary Committee and escalating the southern attack on any liberal nominee seeking confirmation. From 1967, each nominee faced an even greater physical and emotional strain in facing down Dixie, as the committee hearings showcased not only the ongoing southern tension over the race question, but also the growing significance of the Supreme Court nomination process in US politics. Although Hollings aimed to bring South Carolina through a peaceful process of desegregation, his judgment in the nomination of Supreme Court justices threatened to jeopardize his liberal record as the state's governor. Thurmond, meanwhile, in his role as chief antagonist, would take the confirmation process out of the judicial realm and into the murky world of personal animosity, once again with the state of South Carolina at the center of events.

Fritz Hollings's dramatic farewell speech to the General Assembly led to a great deal of media discussion on the theme of an emerging "New South." Earl Mazo noted in the *Charleston News and Courier* that "Negro enrollment—and turnout on election day—is increasing at a considerably faster rate than the white," due in no small part to Thurgood Marshall's historic triumph in arguing against the state's white primary system back in 1947. The *New York Times* acknowledged the peaceful desegregation of South Carolina's universities, colleges, schools, lunch counters, and hotels, with a professor of education at South Carolina State College suggesting that many white politicians would welcome the rapidly increasing black registration and turnout, as a significant rise in black participation would ultimately relieve them of the "burden" of running on a racist platform. Yet, despite the relative calm of South Carolina's civil rights protests during the early 1960s, the state's Democratic political establishment remained aware that the segregationist Republican Senate campaigns of W. D. Workman in South Carolina and James D. Martin in Alabama had resulted in sharp increases in Republican voting during the 1962 Senate elections.[4] These unusually strong Republican challenges to long-serving southern Democrats Olin Johnston and Lister Hill provided much encouragement for the Republican Party in its ongoing effort to win over the southern states, but the South Carolina Democratic Party continued to fight for political control of its territory regardless of increasing Republican popularity and growing momentum in the civil rights movement.

For Strom Thurmond, the Republican Party encroachment of the early 1960s presented a more positive set of possibilities. Aware that his base of support comprised a particularly conservative variety of white voter, Thurmond felt a greater kinship with conservative Republicans such as W. D. Workman and Senator Barry Goldwater of Arizona than the "liberals, intellectuals, would-be socialists, and bloc-vote appeasers" in the national Democratic Party, whom he had been forced to tolerate since his first election to the Senate. By the early 1960s, Thurmond's ongoing determination to fight desegregation at all costs sat uneasily with the political agendas of more liberal-minded southern Democrats such as Lister Hill, John Sparkman, Russell Long, and George Smathers, who, as Keith Finley has argued, "would not risk jeopardizing the influx of federal money into the impoverished South based on the unproven assumption that a caucus counter-offensive as Thurmond proposed would prolong the existence of segregation." Whereas Johnston and Hollings aimed to convince southerners to stick with the Democratic Party in the face of the other party's gradual and ultimately successful takeover, Thurmond believed that until Americans sent a Republican, such as former vice president Richard Nixon, to the White House, there was simply no hope of ensuring the appointment of reliable conservative judges to the federal judiciary. His sensational defection to the Republican Party in September 1964 ushered in a new era for the state of South Carolina, providing the minority party with an enormously influential figure to spearhead its rapid development into a formidable electoral force in southern politics. In maintaining his political following despite the change of party affiliation, Thurmond became a valuable asset to the Republican presidential campaigns of Barry Goldwater, Richard Nixon, and Ronald Reagan, making a sizable contribution to the successful long-term Republican effort to convince the South that the Democratic Party no longer represented conservative white interests. As a Republican senator and a new addition to the Senate Judiciary Committee, Thurmond would now have the opportunity to oppose liberal judicial nominees on his own terms, without the inconvenience of senior Democrats, such as Georgia's Richard Russell, keeping him in check.[5]

Thurmond's failure to see eye-to-eye with national Democratic figures had been evident for many years, not least in his refusal to support any Democratic presidential candidate since 1944.[6] By complete contrast, Olin Johnston's loyalty to the Democratic Party had paid off handsomely by the early 1960s, with the mild-mannered senior senator achieving even greater seniority on his Senate committees. A telephone call between Johnston and President Lyndon Johnson in December 1963 indicates clearly the new president's attitude toward Thurmond's true political allegiance, despite the fact that the call took place nine months before his party defection. The fact that the president was happy to accept Johnston's choice of Charles E. Simons for a new District Court vacancy (rather than Thurmond's preference for Robert Figg, his former speechwriter, now dean of the University of South Carolina Law School) serves as a reminder of Thurmond's failure to build a productive working relationship with Lyndon Johnson during the latter's tenure as Senate majority leader:

LBJ: They say that you want that Hemphill boy, don't you?

Johnston: Oh yeah, he's alright.

LBJ: Uh, and they, somebody told me you want a fella named Simons.

Johnston: Simons would be alright, uh—

LBJ: They tell me that, that, the head of the law school, though, is not too hot.

Johnston: Well, he's not. You can't appoint him.

LBJ: Well, that's who Strom wants. That's who Strom wants appointed.

Johnston: He's too old.

LBJ: Strom wants him appointed.

Johnston: I know.

LBJ: He says he's his number one choice.

Johnston: Yeah, but uh, you'll find with him that, see, they don't appoint usually when they're over sixty.

LBJ: Sixty-two.

Johnston: Is that right?

LBJ: Yeah, that's what the [*indecipherable*] . . . but they make exceptions, they made one, they made one in Texas, sixty-four.

Johnston: Oh yeah?

LBJ: But uh, I want, I don't want, I don't want to appoint anybody that you don't want 'cause you're a Democrat.[7]

As a loyal party man, Olin Johnston stood by the president. Despite his opposition to the Civil Rights Act of 1964, he set out on the campaign trail in the face of growing Republican popularity in the run-up to that year's presidential election. Despite his success in holding back a Republican encroachment into the South during his 1962 Senate campaign, the famous Johnston "pep talks" failed to prevent Barry Goldwater from winning South Carolina and the other four Deep South states in his unsuccessful presidential bid. Lyndon Johnson's landslide victory over Goldwater provided little consolation for the South Carolina Democratic Party. Johnston's daughter, Liz Patterson, recalls her father's disappointment on election night: "That broke his heart, when South Carolina went for Goldwater. They have a picture of Daddy from when the results came in, and you can just tell he's really broken-hearted. Daddy campaigned a lot, but not enough probably." One likely reason for his failure to campaign as vigorously in 1964 was a battle with cancer, which required an operation to remove a carcinoid tumor from his right colon in January 1965. Following a second operation in early April, Senator Edgar A. Brown, leader of the state Senate, wrote to Johnston to tell him, "We have all been greatly concerned about your condition and have been thinking and praying for you throughout this tragic period in your life. Do what the doctors say, get well, and I am sure there are a lot of good years ahead for you." One week later, Johnston lapsed into a coma and died, aged 68, at Providence Hospital in Columbia, South Carolina.[8]

Governor Donald S. Russell was responsible for appointing a replacement for Johnston before the scheduling of a special election to elect a new US senator. Deciding that he wished to go to the Senate himself, Russell resigned the governorship and allowed his successor, Robert E. McNair, to appoint him as Johnston's replacement, a move that received a mixed reaction in the state. The *Spartanburg Herald-Journal* reported that while South Carolinians had much respect for Governor Russell, and little doubt about his ability to represent the state in Washington, DC, the swift and opportunistic manner in which he had seized a Senate seat occupied until recently by one of the state's most popular political figures did raise some eyebrows, particularly as he had done so without consulting Gladys Johnston, widow of the late senator, and without asking any of Johnston's employees to join his staff. Fritz Hollings had returned to practicing law after Johnston defeated him in 1962, but was only too happy to make a political comeback by challenging Russell in the Democratic primary, held on June 14, 1966. Having already defeated Russell during the gubernatorial race of 1958, Hollings entered into a rematch with relish, believing his opponent to be "brilliant and accomplished, but he was not a very good politician. . . . He didn't seem to enjoy mixing it up with the voters. By contrast, I really enjoyed barnstorming the state. I was on a 'Fritzkrieg,' as the *New York Times* put it."[9]

One key difference between the 1958 Hollings/Russell gubernatorial contest and the 1966 Senate primary rematch was an increase in African American voter registration following the passage in Congress of the landmark Voting Rights Act of 1965. By 1971, the percentage of voting-age African Americans in South Carolina had more than doubled since 1960. The significance of a growing black South Carolina electorate was evident in a remarkable event that took place on April 30, 1966, in Orangeburg, during which the chairmen of the Democratic and Republican parties debated one another at the predominantly black South Carolina State College. In reporting the event, the *New York Times* predicted that the Goldwater campaign, and Thurmond's defection to the Republican Party, would ensure black support for the Democrats in that year's elections, but ultimately, "the Democrats' assurance and the Republicans' concession that most Negroes will vote Democratic this year focuses both parties' attention on white voters, who still make up 80 per cent of the electorate."[10]

To ensure white conservative support in his challenge to Donald Russell, Hollings arranged for his supporters to distribute a photograph of Russell shaking hands with black civil rights leader I. DeQuincey Newman as a means of damaging Russell's segregationist credibility. The fact that Newman and Hollings were friends was not well known among white South Carolinians, and Newman's decision to supply Hollings with the photograph for use in his campaign highlights his usual tactic of backing the more moderate candidate during primary elections. In taking full advantage of the discontent over Russell's "self-appointment," Hollings's "Fritzkrieg" proved enormously popular, and he scored a convincing victory over Russell to become the Democratic Party's nominee for the special Senate election, winning by 196,405 votes to Russell's 126,595. In the special election, held on November 8, 1966, Hollings managed to defeat a strong challenge from Republican Marshall Parker to become South Carolina's choice to replace Olin Johnston, in a victory of 223,790 to 212,032 votes.[11]

Republicans may have failed to solidify the white vote in South Carolina, but the party did succeed, unwittingly, in unifying black voters behind the Democratic ticket. With black residents now accounting for an estimated 20 percent of the voting turnout in 1966, the need for Fritz Hollings to continue winning over black voters while at the same time maintaining sufficient segregationist credentials to secure white conservative support would only persist, offering a useful illustration of James C. Cobb's view that, during the mid- to late 1960s, southern politicians "walked a tightrope in trying to convince white voters that their interests remained paramount" in order to overcome fears that the region's politicians were becoming too attentive to the growing black vote.[12]

During the 1960s, a string of landmark Supreme Court decisions would reduce the likelihood of Strom Thurmond mellowing as he reached sixty years of age. While southerners had condemned many of the more controversial opinions handed down since the 1940s—notably, *Smith, Brown,* and *Baker*—for threatening the "southern way of life," the court was now tackling a series of cases dealing with the state of South Carolina specifically. These included *Edwards v. South Carolina* (1963) and *Bouie v. City of Columbia* (1964), both of which upheld the rights of protestors in the state capital, and *South Carolina v. Katzenbach* (1966), which nullified the state's challenge to the "preclearance" provisions of the Voting Rights Act. It is unlikely that Justice Hugo Black, historically one of the court's more liberal members, offered Thurmond any consolation with his growing preference for judicial restraint. Having already dissented in *Bouie v. City of Columbia,* Black—a native of Alabama whose "betrayal" of the South provoked death threats following the *Brown* ruling—dissented once again in the *Katzenbach* case, viewing as patronizing the Voting Rights Act's inclusion of a provision that empowered the federal government to approve southern voting registration procedures. The South's attempt to resist the Voting Rights Act failed, and, as one study has argued, "the increased African American voter registration and turnout almost immediately eliminated the white supremacist rhetoric that had been a hallmark of the state's political leaders." These new political conditions would, in time, force even the likes of Strom Thurmond to make concessions to the state's growing African American voting bloc.[13]

The ongoing southern effort to curb the power of the Supreme Court continued to appear in the correspondence between South Carolina residents and their senators. Voters reminded Fritz Hollings, only one month after he took office, of their passionate desire to curb the court's power, in various letters to which he responded, "there are currently many bills under consideration by the 90th Congress to restrict the power of the Supreme Court, and I intend to look these bills over carefully with an eye towards revising the Supreme Court to a greater degree of efficiency and curtailing the number of poor decisions which have recently been handed down." Thurmond, in a letter sent a few days after the court's announcement of *Katzenbach,* complained to a constituent that his frequent attempts to introduce a judicial qualification bill in Congress had failed. He claimed he would now sponsor a constitutional amendment to create a "Court of the Union," to be composed of the chief justices of the highest courts of all fifty states, which "would be empowered to hear and determine cases of appeal from the Supreme Court which affect the rights reserved to the states or to the people."[14] Despite the strong likelihood of other senators blocking this ambitious idea, as with all of his previous attempts to restrict the justices' power, Thurmond had lost none of his rage. Having become South Carolina's senior senator following Olin Johnston's death, he would now adopt a more militant approach in the war on the court by using his position on the Senate Judiciary Committee to scrutinize and obstruct judicial nominations.

Unlike most presidents, who have made nominations to the Supreme Court upon the death or retirement of a serving justice, Lyndon Johnson—a southern president with a legislative agenda aimed at furthering civil rights for African Americans—was happy to simply create his own vacancies. During the summer of 1965, he persuaded Justice Arthur J. Goldberg to become US ambassador to the United Nations as a means of creating a space on the court for Abe Fortas, his close friend and confidant. Thanks to the Justice Department's businesslike preparation of nominees for facing the tough questions offered regularly by southerners on the Judiciary Committee, Fortas sailed through his confirmation hearings. In praising the nominee for winning unanimous approval from the committee, Johnson told Fortas by telephone, "I want to congratulate you. Damned if you don't show them all up."[15]

The close friendship between Johnson and Fortas appeared to raise no alarm bells among southern Democrats, who offered no resistance to the nomination. With only Carl Curtis of Nebraska and John J. Williams of Delaware joining him in opposition, Thurmond's public comments suggested an intense personal dislike of the nominee.[16] As with his unexplained opposition to President Kennedy's nomination of Arthur Goldberg to the court three years earlier, it seemed that Thurmond was prepared to oppose any nominee who did not express a clear willingness to uphold the autonomy of the states, offering in support a track record of legal hostility toward civil rights. Cynics might have concluded that Thurmond was bound to oppose any nominee failing to express this willingness in a Deep South accent. With Abe Fortas now on the Supreme Court, Thurmond had lost the battle but not the war. As future chapters will illustrate, he would get another chance to face down his nemesis.

While Johnson was able to put Abe Fortas on the court as a long-term means of protecting his Great Society programs, his plan to appoint the first African American Supreme Court justice was, in itself, a long-term project. David A. Yalof has argued that Johnson appointed Thurgood Marshall as solicitor general in 1965 as a first step in getting him onto the Supreme Court, yet Johnson always denied any connection with a future appointment. Bob Woodward and Scott Armstrong have claimed that the president persuaded Marshall to take the position of solicitor general by telling him, "I want folks to walk down the hall at the Justice Department and look in the door and see a n—— sitting there." Two years on from the Fortas appointment, Johnson's promotion of Ramsey Clark to the post of US attorney general created a serious conflict of interest, in that Clark's father was a serving Supreme Court justice. As the president hoped, his appointment of the younger Clark as head of the Justice Department forced Justice Tom C. Clark's retirement, allowing another convenient space for Johnson to fill on the Supreme Court.[17]

After Justice Clark's retirement became public knowledge, Thurmond wrote a letter to the president, requesting that he give "earnest consideration to filling the impending vacancy on the Supreme Court with an appointee who has had prior judicial experience, preferably at the trial level." Regardless of whether or not Johnson interpreted the letter as a thinly veiled southern warning against appointing Thurgood Marshall, he would most likely have been amused by the next paragraph, in which Thurmond stated, "I realize that appointments to the Supreme Court are entirely within the prerogative of the President of the United States, and I hope you will not construe this letter as interference in that domain. It is meant only as a friendly suggestion." At a press conference on June 13, 1967, Johnson made no attempt to disguise his pride in nominating Thurgood Marshall to replace Tom Clark, declaring, "I believe it is the right thing to do, the right time to do it, the right man, and the right place."[18]

Marshall had gone to South Carolina to argue against segregated schools in 1951, and ended up changing the course of history with the *Brown* case in 1954. He had successfully faced down South Carolina's Olin Johnston on his way to the Second Circuit Court of Appeals, and ended up becoming the nation's first African American solicitor general. Strom Thurmond, now the voice of South Carolina on the Senate Judiciary Committee, was determined to make Marshall's journey to the US Supreme Court as difficult and uncomfortable as possible. Responding immediately to the president's announcement, the senator complained that "this appointment to the Supreme Court will unquestionably tip the scales overwhelmingly in favor of the so-called liberal viewpoint on the court." He elaborated on this argument in letters to his constituents, telling a married couple from Florence, South Carolina, that "in many instances on basic constitutional questions, the vote is now 5 to 4 for the liberal viewpoint." Referring to the outgoing Justice Clark, he claimed that, "The Justice that Marshall is being named to replace is usually found voting with the 4 on issues of this nature, and I fear that the appointment of Marshall will make the future line-up to be 6 to 3. This means that it will require two conservative appointments before Court decisions will reflect true adherence to both the letter and the spirit of the Constitution."[19]

In his correspondence during the summer of 1967, Thurmond maintained the argument that Marshall would provide one extra liberal vote on the court with his "completely erroneous" interpretation of the Constitution. His responses to constituents during the month of June often included a statement acknowledging a similarity between the correspondent's views and his own, such as "I am glad that you agree with my observations," "I am pleased to know of your agreement with me," or "I am very glad that we are in agreement on this issue."[20] However, his statements of agreement began to disappear from his responses later in the month, when some of the letter writers adopted an overtly racist message. These included a New Yorker who expressed hope that the Senator would "VOTE NO ON THE SEATING OF A NEGRO TO THE SUPREME COURT"; a Washington, DC, resident who considered the Marshall nomination "an INSULT to every white citizen in the US!"; a South Carolinian who asked, "Is there such a dearth of white lawyers in the US (qualified ones) that we come to this?," and also a Texan correspondent, wondering what the court will become "with a n—— there," adding her view that "the white man does not owe the n—— one cotton pickin' thing."[21] To each of these messages, Thurmond expressed only his acknowledgment of the writer's views, and an assurance of his opposition to the nomination.

The only occasion on which Thurmond declared agreement with an openly racist letter was in his response to New York–based "research historian" Edward R. Cusick, who wrote to the senator on June 13 and 26 to argue that the Masonic lodge to which Thurgood Marshall belonged was "an illegitimate and clandestine Grand Lodge." Addressing the senator as "Brother Thurmond," Cusick pointed out that southern senators John Stennis of Mississippi and Sam Ervin of North Carolina, and former South Carolina Governor and Senator Donald Russell, were all "regular" Masons. In mentioning "Brother Thomas Clark" and his retirement, Cusick referred to the long history of a Masonic presence on the Supreme Court: "To think a colored man with the name of Marshall who is a clandestine may sit on the bench which was so glorified and honored as it was by Brother John Marshall!" Noting Thurmond's listing in the *Royal Arch Mason* magazine as a member of a "regular" Masonic fraternity, Cusick urged Thurmond to inform other Masons in the Senate of Marshall's membership of one of the "colored or Negro" lodges that the Grand Lodge of South Carolina had condemned in 1898. To emphasize his concern, Cusick enclosed a bulletin entitled "Important for Regular Masons!" which pointed out that "none of the 40 regular Masonic Grand Lodges in the United States, all being recognized by the Mother Grand Lodge of England, has ever extended any recognition to any of the colored or Negro Grand Lodges in the United States," adding "(PLEASE let other regular Masons read this)."[22] Whether or not Thurmond raised the issue of Marshall's "illegitimate" Masonic affiliation with his "brothers" in the Senate is not known, but it is significant that he would openly express agreement with Cusick's argument when failing to acknowledge agreement with other racist sentiments expressed to him in letters during this period.

Meanwhile, some very different letters were arriving at the office of South Carolina's junior senator. One particularly remarkable aspect of South Carolina's war on the Supreme Court is the fact that Hollings maintained a written correspondence with Thurgood Marshall throughout the latter's confirmation hearings. Knowing that he would have to vote for or against the nominee's confirmation following the close of the Judiciary Committee hearings, Hollings wrote to Marshall on June 19, 1967, telling him that "early this morning the Reverend Martin Luther King stated on television that he believed it was the citizen's moral right and duty to violate laws that he believed were unjust. I would appreciate you letting me know your agreement or disagreement with this statement or belief."[23] Marshall provided a detailed response:

> Dear Senator Hollings:
>
> You ask whether I agree with the statement that "it was the citizen's moral right and duty to violate laws that he believed were unjust." That proposition misconceives, I believe, the nature of our "government of laws and not of men." I believe that in our democratic society the ways to challenge an unjust law are (1) by intelligent use of the vote in order to spur elected officials to change the law, and (2) by action in the courts if its

validity is doubtful. In sum, the citizen has a fundamental duty not to disobey the law while seeking to accomplish desired change through normal political and legal processes.

This does not mean that I discount the value of dissent. It was the design of the Framers that there should be no impairment of the rights of speech and assembly, and the responsible exercise of those First Amendment rights provides an avenue to peaceful change. But I cannot accept the view—implicit in the statement you asked me to comment upon—that any man stands above or beyond the law.

I appreciate this opportunity to express my views.

Sincerely
Thurgood Marshall[24]

Perhaps because this first letter did not satisfy him, or perhaps because Marshall's candor led him to ask more specific questions, Hollings turned to the subject of recent Supreme Court decisions in his next letter. Despite not being a member of the Judiciary Committee, Hollings had more compelling reasons than other freshman senators to investigate Marshall's nomination, particularly given the very careful balancing act he had performed as governor by appearing conservative on civil rights while at the same time guiding South Carolina through a peaceful process of desegregation. His next letter highlighted South Carolina's interest in the Supreme Court's power, particularly with regard to the impact of recent decisions relating to crime and punishment:

Dear General Marshall:

I do not mean to besiege you with letters or pre-empt your hearings before the Judiciary Committee but in that I am not a member of the Committee, I would appreciate your letting me know whether or not you agree with the philosophy of the majority opinion in the following cases:

1. Miranda vs. State of Arizona—June, 1966
2. Walker vs. City of Birmingham—June, 1967
3. Reitman vs. Mulkey—May, 1967
4. Berger vs. State of New York—June, 1967

It is quite apparent with the recent trend of the court, a man's competence as an attorney should not only be weighed but also his basic concept of the Constitution. I respect your ability as an attorney and in addition to my first inquiry of June 19, I would also appreciate your response to this.

Sincerely
Ernest F. Hollings[25]

Earlier the same month, conservative southern columnist James J. Kilpatrick had pointed to the significance of Justice Clark's vote in the *Walker v. City of Birmingham* case, and questioned whether Thurgood Marshall, like Clark, would have voted to sustain Martin Luther King's 1963 conviction in Birmingham, Alabama.[26] In his response, Marshall refused to comment on specific cases due to a likelihood of the issues involved in those cases returning to the Supreme Court, highlighting a pattern that would reemerge frequently during his confirmation hearings:

Dear Senator Hollings:

I apologize for not responding sooner to your letter of June 21; I was out of town over the weekend.

I am sure you will understand when I say that you place me in a difficult position by asking me if I agree with the majority opinions in some recent cases. Should I become a member of the Court, I would of course be called upon to pass on similar issues to those decided in the cases you cite, and indeed, to determine the application of those cases. Therefore, I think it would be improper for me to express specific agreement or disagreement with specific cases.

I have, however, enclosed the briefs for the United States in *Westover* v. *United States* (a companion case to *Miranda*), *Walker* v. *City of Birmingham*, and *Reitman* v. *Mulkey*.

Sincerely
Thurgood Marshall
Solicitor General[27]

Ultimately, Marshall's second response provided Hollings with the ammunition he required to justify voting against confirmation. While he may have struggled to reach a decision during the week following Johnson's announcement of the nomination, the existence of a draft of a speech, dated June 20, 1967, suggests that Hollings was preparing himself to justify his reasons for opposing the nomination at least three weeks prior to the commencement of confirmation hearings, and at least two months before the nomination would reach the Senate floor. The draft contains his confession that "when the President recommended Marshall for the United States Supreme Court this week, I thought it was a good opportunity to vote for a competent Negro. . . . But I hesitated." After mentioning his correspondence with the nominee, Hollings declared that "it is obvious from his answers that Mr. Marshall has no idea of restricting himself to interpreting the Constitution and statutory law. Rather, he, like some of the other brethren on the Court, [is] prepared to re-write the Constitution. I think this is one of the greatest dangers facing the Republic and while I was prepared to vote for him on other scores, he flunked the main exam. I voted no."[28]

For all his forward-looking moderation, Hollings's reservations over confirming Marshall's appointment seemed to echo the familiar constitutional appeals and states' rights rhetoric employed by southern senators in their struggle against civil rights prior to, and during, the 1950s. Nonetheless, he was able to use his correspondence with Marshall as a means of assuring his supporters that he was considering his vote on the nomination very seriously. Despite having declared "I voted no" in a draft of a speech dated June 20, he claimed in a response to a constituent from Bishopville, South Carolina, dated June 29, that "before I make a final decision, I want to make certain that [Marshall's] philosophy does not conform with some of the recent opinions of the Court, and particularly the recommendation of anarchy by Martin Luther King. Rather than awaiting the Committee hearings, I have written directly to the Solicitor General, and my vote will depend on his response and the Committee hearings." At the same time, the senator seemed reluctant to tell his constituents that he had known Marshall for many years. An earlier draft of the letter to the Bishopville resident, dated June 23, includes the statement, "I stated to the press that I knew Mr. Marshall to be a competent attorney because I had tried cases against him," but this line had been removed by the time the letter was sent to the constituent six days later.[29]

In a letter dated June 20, 1967—the same day on which Hollings drafted his comments regarding his "hesitation"—fellow Charlestonian and former state senator Huger Sinkler put forward a strong argument in favor of Hollings casting a dissenting vote. Sinkler claimed to be "seriously concerned about the effect that a favorable vote would have on your race in 1968 . . . the sure way to beat you is to tie you with Johnson, and an issue of this sort would be just what your opposition is looking for. I have talked to several of your friends on this subject and I think definitely the consensus share my views." Sinkler advised that "you don't have to be extreme about it and your decision can rest on the solid ground of qualifications and philosophy. Perhaps this is what your inquiry into Marshall is intended to develop but in any event, it is my judgment that a vote for Marshall would have a serious effect upon your race in 1968."[30]

Sinkler's argument seemed logical given the nature of the expanding southern electorate. Despite the surge in African American voter registration from 1965, Earl Black and Merle Black have pointed out that, throughout the 1960s, "three new whites were enrolled in the Deep South for every two new blacks," offering a range of compelling reasons for southern whites to vote in greater numbers, including rising levels of education, greater party competition, the politicization of working-class white women, and, possibly, a measure of racist counter-mobilization.[31] Although the Voting Rights Act had triggered the creation of a greatly increased black southern electorate, an equally impressive increase in white voter registration would blunt the impact of the "black vote," preserving the existence of a sizable white voting majority in South Carolina.

Whether Hollings genuinely hoped that his correspondence with Marshall would convince him to support the latter's confirmation, or whether he hoped to use the correspondence simply as a means of sticking to his original position of dissent, the Sinkler letter summarized Hollings's ultimate course of action. South Carolina's black voters could only decide for themselves if they would be as sympathetic to Hollings's position as his friends in the conservative political establishment were.

The US Supreme Court in 1941, including Justice James F. Byrnes of South Carolina. *Standing, left to right:* Byrnes, William O. Douglas, Frank Murphy, and Robert Jackson. *Seated, left to right:* Stanley Reed, Owen J. Roberts, Chief Justice Harlan Fiske Stone, Hugo Black, and Felix Frankfurter. (Louis Bachrach/Clemson University Libraries' Special Collections and Archives)

An informal gathering of Deep South Democrats. *Left to right:* Richard Russell of Georgia, who led the southern bloc in the Senate; Olin Johnston of South Carolina; and James Eastland of Mississippi, who chaired the Senate Judiciary Committee from 1956 through 1978. (F. Clyde Wilkinson/James O. Eastland Collection, Archives and Special Collections, University of Mississippi Libraries)

Senate Majority Leader Lyndon Johnson welcomes South Carolina's political leaders as they gather in Washington, DC, in April 1959. *Left to right:* State Senator Edgar A. Brown, Senator Olin Johnston, Governor Ernest "Fritz" Hollings, Johnson, and Senator Strom Thurmond. (Clemson University Libraries' Special Collections and Archives)

John F. Kennedy facing Olin Johnston. (Olin D. Johnston Papers, South Carolina Political Collections, University of South Carolina)

Vice President Hubert Humphrey administers the oath of office to the two senators from South Carolina in January 1967. *Left to right:* Everett Dirksen of Illinois, Mike Mansfield of Montana, Humphrey, Fritz Hollings, and Strom Thurmond. (Clemson University Libraries' Special Collections and Archives)

Thurgood Marshall, the first African American Supreme Court nominee, departs following a round of questions from the Senate Judiciary Committee, July 14, 1967. (John Rous/Press Association)

A cheerful Abe Fortas, accompanied by Senator Albert Gore of Tennessee, awaits the commencement of his turbulent chief justice confirmation hearings, July 16, 1968. (Press Association)

Flanked by Strom Thurmond and Fritz Hollings, South Carolina's Clement Haynsworth ponders his future before the Senate Judiciary Committee, September 16, 1969. (Press Association)

Strom Thurmond meets Harry A. Blackmun, the man who replaced his arch nemesis, Abe Fortas, on the Supreme Court in 1970. (Clemson University Libraries' Special Collections and Archives)

The first female justice, Sandra Day O'Connor, shortly after the Senate's confirmation of her nomination to the Supreme Court, September 10, 1981. Standing behind O'Connor, *left to right,* are Senator Barry Goldwater of Arizona, Attorney General William French Smith, Strom Thurmond, and Senator Dennis DeConcini of Arizona. (Scott Applewhite/Press Association)

7. BETWEEN THURMOND AND THURGOOD

As Fritz Hollings continued to assure his constituents that he would cast a responsible vote on Thurgood Marshall's Supreme Court nomination, Senate Judiciary Committee member Sam Ervin of North Carolina was ordering his staff to begin researching Marshall's background, while Strom Thurmond began preparing a multitude of obscure questions in a bid to test and, wherever possible, ridicule the nominee's legal knowledge.[1] When the confirmation hearings commenced, on July 13, 1967, John McClellan of Arkansas took the lead in interrogating the nominee, with most of his questions relating to the landmark *Miranda v. Arizona*, one of the four cases Fritz Hollings had cited in his second letter to Marshall. In the *Miranda* decision, the Supreme Court, by a five-to-four margin, had ruled that evidence used in a criminal prosecution would be inadmissible if arresting officers did not make defendants aware of a constitutional right to an attorney and a right against self-incrimination, obtaining a firm acknowledgment of the defendant's understanding of those rights.

McClellan made clear at the outset that his questions "do not go to the legal ability or training of the nominee, but they do deal with a critical condition in this country," namely the problem of crime and disorder in the streets. In responding to McClellan's questions regarding his position on *Miranda*, Marshall maintained, as in his correspondence with Hollings, that he was not able to give his views on matters that would soon be under consideration by the courts.[2] His refusal to provide a straight answer eventually agitated McClellan:

Senator McClellan: Do you subscribe to the philosophy that the Fifth Amendment right to assistance of counsel requires that counsel be present before the police can interrogate the accused?

Judge Marshall: That is part of the Miranda rule.

Senator McClellan: Yes.

Judge Marshall: And as I say, I can't comment, because it is coming back up.

Senator McClellan: I have to wonder, from your refusal to answer, if you mean the negative.

Judge Marshall: Well, that is up to you, sir. But I have never been dishonest in my life.

Senator McClellan: I did not say that. But you lead me to wonder why I cannot get the answer.[3]

Senator Philip Hart of Michigan, who had defended Marshall throughout his troubled Second Circuit confirmation hearings in 1962, made the first of many interjections, and took the opportunity to put on record his support for the nominee.[4] Hart and other Marshall supporters would have cause to interject over several days of hearings. On July 14, Marshall went head-to-head with Sam Ervin, who was distinctly unimpressed by the nominee's description of the US Constitution as a "living document." In taking up McClellan's *Miranda*-based attack, Ervin pressed Marshall on the original meaning of the words in the Fifth Amendment. Marshall, recognizing this line of questioning as simply another means of probing his views on *Miranda,* stuck to his original line of defense by asserting that he was unable to comment on issues due back for review in the Supreme Court. Marshall's evasiveness eventually led Ervin to refer to the potential consequences of the hearings:

Senator Ervin: I will tell you, Judge, if you are not going to answer a question about anything which might possibly come before the Supreme Court some time in the future, I cannot ask you a single question about anything that is relevant to this inquiry.

Judge Marshall: All I am trying to say, Senator, is I do not think you want me to be in the position of giving you a statement on the Fifth Amendment, and then, if I am confirmed and sit on the Court, when a Fifth Amendment case comes up, I will have to disqualify myself.

Senator Ervin: If you have no opinions on what the Constitution means at this time, you ought not to be confirmed. Anybody that has been at the bar as long as you have, and had as distinguished a legal career as you have, certainly ought to have some very firm opinions about the meaning of the Constitution.

Judge Marshall: But as to particular language of a particular section that I know is going to come before the Court, I do have an opinion as of this time. But I think it would be wrong for me to give that opinion as of this time. When the case comes before the Court, that will be the time. I say with all due respect, Senator, that is the only way it has been done before.[5]

The Ervin/McClellan style of questioning showcases the southern tactic of trying to expose a nominee's sympathy with the court's "liberal" decisions by pushing them into debates over the wording of the US Constitution. Given Marshall's refusal to answer a specific question on *Miranda,* Ervin continued to press him on the wording of the Fifth Amendment, which includes a specific provision, relevant to the *Miranda* ruling, that no person "shall be compelled in any criminal case to be a witness against himself."[6] While Ervin insisted that he was not asking Marshall to comment on any particular case that had come before the court, and claimed that he was merely questioning the nominee's views on the wording of a particular section of the Constitution, Marshall eventually made light of Ervin's tactics and reasserted that he was not in a position to comment on any issues likely to come before the court in the future:

Senator Ervin: Judge, how can the words "no person shall be compelled in any criminal case to be a witness against himself," apply to anything except testimony given in a court?

Judge Marshall: I would say, Senator, that we know, you and I, that you are talking about a matter which was in the Miranda cases, and there will be many more cases dealing with the Miranda ruling and the use of confessions. Those cases are now in the Supreme Court or on their way to the Supreme Court.

Senator Ervin: Well, Judge, I would respectfully suggest that I am talking about fifteen words which have been in the Constitution since June 15, 1790. Am I to take it that you are unwilling to tell me what you think those words, which have been in the Constitution since 1790, mean?

Senator Hart: Would the Senator yield just briefly?

Senator Ervin: Yes.

Senator Hart: It would be interesting to know from the record how many cases have been litigated since 1790 over those very fifteen words. It would be an enormously long hearing.

Senator Ervin: Yes, sir.

Judge Marshall: It certainly would.[7]

Despite the fact that the southern tactic clearly held no credibility with Senator Hart and others, it did at least allow southern senators the opportunity to portray the nominee's refusal to answer questions on specific cases as a refusal to answer questions on the US Constitution. In offering the claim that the nominee before them appeared to have no views on what the Constitution means, southerners were also making the unspoken accusation that, if confirmed, the nominee would not adhere to the basic principles of that document. In the event, Ervin hinted at his reluctance to confirm Marshall, and also pointed out that Potter Stewart had provided more straightforward answers during his tense confirmation hearings in 1959. By the end of the second day, both McClellan and Ervin had indicated that neither would approve Marshall's appointment, with the former complaining of a lack of sufficient information to confirm, and the latter criticizing Marshall for apparently having no views on the wording of the Constitution. Meanwhile, Strom Thurmond remained silent, and continued to remain silent throughout a third day of hearings, during which Ervin questioned Marshall on issues relating to the Voting Rights Act, including the Supreme Court's *Katzenbach* case.[8]

The Committee reconvened for a further session on July 19, which opened with a remarkable exchange between Thurgood Marshall and Chairman James Eastland of Mississippi, adding an even stronger southern flavor to the hearings:

The Chairman: Now, you have been in a lot of institutions in the Southern states.

Judge Marshall: Yes, sir.

The Chairman: Are you prejudiced against white people in the South?

Judge Marshall: Not at all. I was brought up, what I would say, way up South in Baltimore, Maryland. And I worked there for white people all my life until I got into college. And from there most of my practice, of course, was in the South, and I don't know, with the possible exception of one person that I was against in the South, that I have any feeling about them.

The Chairman: Now, if you are approved, you will give people in that area of the country, and the states in that area of the country, the same fair and square treatment that you give people in other areas of the country?

Judge Marshall: No question whatsoever.

The Chairman: Senator Thurmond.

Senator Thurmond: Thank you, Mr. Chairman.[9]

With Eastland handing over to Strom Thurmond, the hearings took an extraordinary turn, resulting in one of the most unique confrontations in the history of the Supreme Court confirmation process. Having prepared thoroughly for the hearings, Thurmond unleashed an arsenal of carefully worded and mind-bogglingly complex questions, which would build in intensity in a sustained effort to frustrate and confuse the nominee. Beginning with a fairly straightforward line of inquiry, Thurmond asked Marshall if he knew who had drafted the Thirteenth Amendment, despite the fact that the Thirteenth Amendment did not constitute a significant part of any case that Marshall had been involved in.[10] While it was clearly the case that an advanced level of legal expertise was required in order to satisfy Thurmond, it was apparent from the very first question that the relevance of each topic he opted to raise was at best questionable with regard to the nominee's suitability for a seat on the Supreme Court.

The senator turned to the question of the constitutionality of the Civil Rights Act of 1866 prior to the ratification of the Fourteenth Amendment. With Marshall maintaining that he had not researched, nor been called upon to research, any of these issues since the early 1950s, Thurmond proved relentless, moving swiftly from a discussion of theories prevalent in the Republican Party during the 1860s regarding the constitutionality of the 1866 Act, to a question regarding the significance of Congress copying the act's enforcement provision from the Fugitive Slave Law of 1850.[11] Whatever his concern may have been over Marshall's suitability, it is significant that none of the questions related to the nominee's experience or judicial background. When a law professor from the University of Alabama wrote to Thurmond following the conclusion of the hearings to request material on Marshall's work on civil rights cases, the senator admitted that no such material was included in the preparation he had done prior to the hearings.[12]

The questions reached new levels of obscurity and complexity when Thurmond asked, "What constitutional difficulties did John Bingham of Ohio see, or what difficulties do you see, in congressional enforcement of the privileges and immunities clause of Article IV, Section 2, through the necessary and proper clause of Article I, Section 8?"[13] Following Marshall's confession that he did not understand the question, Thurmond simply repeated the question word-for-word. At this point, Senator Edward M. Kennedy of Massachusetts interjected in order to bring clarity to Thurmond's line of inquiry:

Senator Kennedy: Could we just have some further clarification so all of us can benefit? I really don't understand the question myself. I was just wondering if the Senator, so we could all benefit from both the question and response, if we could have some further clarification of the question, because I really am confused as to what actually you are driving at, and I would like to hear the answer of the person that is called upon to answer.

Senator Thurmond: Well, I repeated the question twice. Would you like me to repeat it again?

Senator Kennedy: I thought rather than repeating the question maybe there was some other way that you could arrive at it.

Senator Thurmond: I don't think I can make it any plainer, if you know the answer.

Senator Kennedy: I see.

Senator Thurmond: It is just a question of whether you know the answer.

Senator Kennedy: I see. Could you tell us how the Solicitor is—

Senator Thurmond: Well, I could tell you that Article IV, Section 2, did not set forth the powers vested in the United States. That's the answer.

Senator Kennedy: That's the answer. I see.[14]

Following an outbreak of laughter, Chairman Eastland called the room to order, and Thurmond continued in his humorless crusade.[15] When Marshall managed to provide an answer to Thurmond's question on the 1866 abolition of the Slave Codes, Thurmond asked, "Is there anything else you wish to add?"[16] From this point, the question-and-answer routine fell into a pattern of Thurmond asking a question that Marshall was unable to answer, whereby he would simply move on, occasionally pausing to ask Marshall if he understood a particular question. Each time Marshall was able to answer, Thurmond asked him if he wished to add anything further, as if to imply that the answer had been unsatisfactory:

Senator Thurmond: What provision of the Slave Codes in existence in the South before 1860 was Congress desirous of abolishing by the civil rights bill of 1866?

Judge Marshall: Well, as I remember, the so-called Black Codes ranged from a newly-freed Negro not being able to own property or vote to a statute in my home state of Maryland which prevented these Negroes from flying kites.

Senator Thurmond: Is there anything else you wish to add?

Judge Marshall: No, sir.

Senator Thurmond: Now, on the 14th Amendment, what committee reported out the 14th Amendment and who were its members?

Judge Marshall: I don't know, sir.

Senator Thurmond: Why do you think the framers of the original version of the first section of the 14th Amendment added the necessary and proper clause from Article I, Section 8, to the privileges and immunities clause of Article IV, Section 2?

Judge Marshall: I don't know, sir.

Senator Thurmond: What purpose did the framers have, in your estimation, in referring to the incident involving former Representative Samuel Hoar in Charleston, South Carolina, in December 1844, as showing the need for the enactment of the original version of the 14th Amendment's first section?

Judge Marshall: I don't know, sir.

Senator Thurmond: Why do you think the framer said that if the privileges and immunities clause of the 14th Amendment had been in the original Constitution, the war of 1860–65 could not have occurred?

Judge Marshall: I don't have the slightest idea.

Senator Thurmond: Why do you think the equal protection clause of the original draft of the first section of the 14th Amendment required equal protection in the rights of life, liberty and property only?

Judge Marshall: I don't know.

Senator Thurmond: Did you understand that question?

Judge Marshall: Yes, sir.[17]

Scholars such as Keith Finley and Jason Morgan Ward have discussed in depth the southern tactic of framing political arguments in the language of constitutional authenticity. True to his reputation for insisting that his commitment to defending segregation went further than that of any of his colleagues, Strom Thurmond took the southern preference for constitutional rhetoric in a more confrontational direction throughout the Marshall Supreme Court hearings. While other southerners used constitutional appeals as a means of winning support from outside the South, Thurmond promoted himself as an authority on the US Constitution in an attempt to portray others as ignorant. One famous anecdote has him presenting Attorney General Robert Kennedy with an annotated, pocket-size version of the Constitution with the words, "It's written in such an interesting way that anyone can understand it."[18]

Marshall's ploy of remaining calm and admitting that he did not understand most of Thurmond's well-prepared but occasionally inexplicable questions simply exposed the emptiness of the senator's plan to prove the nominee unqualified. Even if Marshall had, for example, been able to name the committee that reported out the Fourteenth Amendment, in addition to the names of all of the committee members, his detailed answer might have embarrassed Thurmond and amused others in the room, but it would have demonstrated only an impressive academic knowledge, rather than legal ability or judgment. When Marshall did provide a detailed answer to Thurmond's question on the equal protection and due process clauses of the Fourteenth Amendment—issues relevant to several cases he had been involved in throughout his career—the senator still insisted on making his inquiry into whether or not Marshall had anything else to "add."[19]

Eventually, Thurmond's style of attack backfired when he turned to the subject of constitutional interpretation, asking Marshall, "Do you think that the Supreme Court must adhere to the original understanding of the Constitution as set forth by its framers, or may it ignore the intent of the framers and hold that a provision of the Constitution means whatever the Court chooses to have it mean at the moment?"[20] The question failed to back Marshall into a corner:

instead, he challenged the premise of the question while at the same time asserting his true belief that the Constitution is a "living" document for judges to interpret differently over time:

Judge Marshall: I don't agree with the end of your statement that the Supreme Court has a right to interpret the Constitution any way they see fit at that moment.

Senator Thurmond: So you do agree that they are bound to adhere to the original understanding of the Constitution as set forth by its framers?

Judge Marshall: As set forth by its framers, and I am not trying to get around the question. My point is that I take the position, which I think is contrary to what you intend in your question, that this is a living Constitution, and its—you can't expect the Court to apply the Constitution to facts in 1967 that weren't in existence when the Constitution was drafted. That I think is how it differs.[21]

At the conclusion of Thurmond's interrogation, Senator Hart made a brief statement, announcing, "I think all of us were impressed by the research that Senator Thurmond has done. The questions he raised were interesting. I will have to get his answers before I know what the answers are to most of them. I did learn that there was a Michigan Senator I never heard of before who said something a hundred years ago which time has proved probably would have been wrong."[22]

Hart's dry humor may have lightened the mood in the room temporarily before Chairman Eastland called Michael D. Jaffe, general counsel for the conservative Liberty Lobby organization, to make a statement in opposition to Marshall's confirmation. In making the case that Marshall was unqualified to sit on the Supreme Court, Jaffe reminded others in the room of Dr. Alfred Kelly's remarks, which had become controversial during Marshall's 1962 Second Circuit hearings. He also pointed out that, following those hearings, the late Senator Olin D. Johnston had declared in the Senate that "in studying the background of Thurgood Marshall, we discovered that, although he had practiced law in the state of New York, he had never been licensed to conduct this practice in that state. . . . The practice of law without a license by Thurgood Marshall certainly denotes a careless attitude towards the law of the land."[23]

With Strom Thurmond committed to proving Marshall's ignorance and Olin Johnston appearing to condemn Marshall from the grave, Fritz Hollings continued debating the arguments concerning his vote against Marshall's confirmation in the Senate. He frequently mentioned his correspondence with the nominee in his letters to supporters, telling one concerned Anderson, South Carolina, resident of "letters I have written the Solicitor General asking for his position on recent Supreme Court decisions," adding that he had stated publicly that "if the Solicitor General could not find it within himself to disagree with these recent [Supreme Court] decisions [then] I did not feel I could vote for his confirmation."[24]

Senator McClellan presided over the final day of confirmation hearings, in James Eastland's absence, on July 24, 1967. The development of Supreme Court nomination hearings into major political events of huge public interest was evident when McClellan asked Marshall at the start of the hearings if the presence of photographers bothered him. Black and white photographs from these hearings—showing a nonchalant Marshall gazing across the room through a cloud of cigarette smoke, his eyes giving away no indication of his thoughts on those facing him—are reminiscent of images of jazz musicians from the 1950s and 1960s, particularly Julian "Cannonball" Adderley.[25] Having spent more than two decades facing down Dixie before the nation's press, Marshall declared that he had no objections to the photographers, whereby the acting chairman proceeded to question him at length on the use of wiretapping.[26] Thurmond, having used up his arsenal of complex questions on obscure footnotes in the history of the Thirteenth and Fourteenth Amendments, grilled Marshall on possible circumstances in which congressmen might impeach Supreme Court justices. The solicitor general was not shy in expressing his view on this subject:

Judge Marshall: I don't believe Congress has the right to impeach any judge if in the opinion of some Congressmen they wrongly interpret the Constitution.

Senator Thurmond: I am not speaking of some Congressmen. You know that impeachment would have to originate with the House, they would have to bring the impeachment proceedings. The Senate would sit as a jury and act upon the proceedings. So you would have the House originating the proceedings and the Senate acting by a two-thirds majority to convict on the impeachment. But I just wondered what your thinking was, if a Supreme

Court member does not follow the Constitution, if you felt he ought to be impeached.

Judge Marshall: I have no position on that because I can't conceive of a situation you are talking about. If you mean that a Supreme Court justice, or indeed the Supreme Court itself, interprets the Constitution differently from the way Congress wants it interpreted, that Congress has a right to impeach, I don't believe that.

Senator Thurmond: I was afraid you would take that position. I have no more questions.[27]

With his unique onslaught of questions finally at an end, Strom Thurmond had succeeded spectacularly in leaving his mark on the history of the Supreme Court nomination process. But the reactions of Hart and Kennedy suggested little likelihood that senators from outside the South would be convinced to oppose Marshall's confirmation. Even among the southern delegation, some senators were looking to the future, among them Fritz Hollings, who remained painfully aware that the southern brand of obstructionism that Johnston and Thurmond had inflicted on Thurgood Marshall during two separate sets of Senate Judiciary Committee hearings was looking increasingly out-of-date. By the summer of 1967, black Americans were voting in greater numbers, many were taking to the streets and speaking of "black power," and the US Supreme Court would soon be welcoming its first African American justice.

On the very same day that his Senate Judiciary Committee hearings concluded, Thurgood Marshall sent to Fritz Hollings three news clippings to illustrate the manner in which he had distanced himself from the philosophies of several key figures in the civil rights movement. The clippings consisted of articles from the Newark, New Jersey *Star-Ledger,* the *Chattanooga Times,* and the *Youngstown (OH) Vindicator,* all reporting an interview in which Marshall had repudiated Martin Luther King's advice to black Americans that they refuse to fight in Vietnam. He had also dismissed "black power" by declaring, "I could do without Stokely Carmichael," and disputed the meaning of the term by claiming that "from the time the NAACP was organized, it was urging Negroes to vote, and if that's not black power, I don't know what is. But throwing Molotov cocktails is not black power. That's black anarchism."[28] Hollings acknowledged receipt of the clippings with a polite response, but the information proved too little, too late, for South Carolina's junior senator. In responding to concerned constituents who expected him to confirm the appointment, Hollings once again commented on his correspondence with Marshall, declaring, "I wanted to know Mr. Marshall's position on four fundamental points and wrote him, but he refused to answer. . . . Of course, this refusal puts a Senator at a loss to judge the qualifications. I therefore decided to vote not to confirm."[29]

The correspondence relating to the Marshall Supreme Court appointment arriving at Hollings's office during his first summer as a US senator exposes the political divide in South Carolina during this particular period. In writing to express their support for the Marshall appointment, several Hollings supporters made clear their preference for Hollings's brand of racial progressivism over Strom Thurmond's persistent racist posturing. One Marshall enthusiast claimed that "with you in Washington, South Carolina has the best opportunity it has ever had to be the most outstanding state in America . . . but if you follow the same selfish ideas of our other Senators, you will find that South Carolina will remain on the bottom." Hollings received a particularly poignant letter from a Mr. Samuel B. Hudson, a Georgetown resident writing "in quest of an answer to a twelve-year-old Negro boy's question, 'Do we ever win?'" In making the case that "this boy knows the accomplishments of Judge Marshall" and "how hard he has struggled to prepare himself and . . . become the best constitutional lawyer of his time," the writer implored Hollings to "send an open letter to all Negro boys of South Carolina," even if only to prevent them from joining black nationalist groups in reaction to the racism of white politicians. He claimed that "this boy understands Senator Thurmond's position for there is a long list of racist-type statements from him," and added that the boy "is worried because your vote of 'NO' would make the Senatorial delegation of South Carolina 100% against the progress of the Negro, and the Negro of South Carolina in particular."[30]

After a member of Hollings's staff pointed out that Mr. Hudson was in fact the assistant director of the Office of Economic Opportunity (OEO)—set up as part of President Johnson's War on Poverty—and also "a responsible Negro with some political influence," Hollings composed a lengthy response, arguing that "the main point I would make to you and your twelve-year-old friend is that you do not lessen your faith or enthusiasm for the belief that regardless of color in America, you can reach the top," adding that "our twelve-year-old friend should realize that it is Mr. Marshall's cause rather than his race that I disapprove." Hollings would have been fully aware of the significance of Hudson's seniority in the OEO: in 1967, the senator was involved in negotiations with OEO director R. Sargent Shriver to obtain a $17,000 contribution for a food stamps office that black leaders were setting up in Williamsburg County, South Carolina. Meanwhile, Hollings responded to James W. McPherson—described in an office memo as "the biggest vote-getter" in the predominantly black city of Orangeburg—by claiming that "it boils down to a question: Will the appointee judge the law or attempt to make new law? But I wanted to give him every opportunity to dispel this concern. He refused."[31]

These and Hollings's other responses highlight his careful political judgment on the Marshall question. In using Marshall's refusal to give a satisfactory answer to his questions as a reason to vote against confirmation, Hollings claimed that he admired Marshall for "the fact that he took his grievances to the courts rather than to the streets" while also making clear that Marshall's race played no part in his decision. Significantly, he argued that Marshall's "legal ability, of course, is eminently more distinguished than that of Chief Justice Warren prior to his appointment, and I do not hesitate to state that I would vote for Mr. Marshall before I would vote for Chief Justice Warren," which reads as a reminder to South Carolinians that their real enemy was in fact the man who had presided over the court's unanimous decision in *Brown,* rather than the man who made the winning argument. In making such statements, Hollings aimed to convince his constituents that he was committed to the state's war on the Supreme Court but also that he remained unopposed to the cause of black advancement in the era of civil rights—a balancing act quite evident in the early draft of his comments from June 20. Perhaps more significantly, some of Hollings's letters included the claim, "I did not ask silly questions," even when the writer did not mention the Judiciary Committee hearings.[32] As if Hollings's recognition of Marshall's qualifications and achievements were not enough, the inclusion of his "silly questions" comment was clearly an attempt to distance himself from another distinguished senator from South Carolina.

Thurmond, meanwhile, was receiving a mixed reaction to his extraordinary interrogation of Marshall during the committee hearings. Having read Thurmond's questions in a newspaper, a "Mrs. Arthur B. Ward," from Darien, Connecticut, wrote to the senator to ask, "Can you honestly say you could answer those questions, and that you would have asked those questions of a white, conservative Southerner? I don't believe it—like the South's 'fair' voter registration forms!" Thurmond's response suggested a certain degree of tetchiness:

> Dear Mrs. Ward:
>
> Your card of recent date has been received.
>
> Yes, I can answer the questions I posed to Mr. Marshall since I did extensive research for these hearings. Although I would not expect the average person, the average lawyer, or the average judge to be capable of answering these questions, I would expect intelligent answers from a lawyer who has devoted his entire practice to the area of constitutional law concerning the 13th and 14th Amendments.
>
> I feel that Mr. Marshall has displayed a great lack of comprehension of his own area of expertise. I intend to vote against confirmation of his nomination.
>
> With best wishes,
>
> Sincerely,
> Strom Thurmond[33]

In reporting on the hearings, Fred P. Graham noted in the *New York Times* that "the hearings cast some doubt over Mr. Marshall's mastery of constitutional history, but none at all on his dignity as a man. . . . They also proved to many observers the need for new ground rules to avoid questioning that does no more than punish a future Supreme Court justice." When a constituent sent this article to Thurmond, the senator responded that he did not consider Graham's views "to be a fair evaluation of the hearings. The questions I asked were ones which were on some rather obscure constitutional principles. However, Mr. Marshall is noted as one of the foremost attorneys in the area of the Fourteenth Amendment, and I expected him to be knowledgeable enough to provide answers to my questions." Mrs. Ward and others may have been skeptical of Thurmond's laughable claim that Marshall "lacked comprehension in his own area of expertise," but others wrote to congratulate the senator on his line of questioning. One Spartanburg, South Carolina, resident expressed the view that, "I am quite sure the press expected you to question Marshall on the race issue, and planned to conjure up their usual biased reporting of the confrontation. Your line of questioning reflected not only a knowledge of constitutional law, but was a credit to yourself and to the stature of the entire South."[34] As Thurmond had known all along, he clearly represented a very different brand of voter from the more moderate South Carolinians who had supported Olin Johnston, and more recently, Fritz Hollings.

Press endorsements of Marshall's appointment seemed to suggest that South Carolina's senators were on the wrong side of history. Editorials from the nation's newspapers—including the *Atlanta Journal,* the *Chattanooga Times,* the *Denver Post,* the *Miami Herald,* and the *Washington Star*—described the appointment as a major step forward in race relations. The *Deseret News,* of Salt Lake City, Utah, even argued that "Marshall brings with him more impressive courtroom experience than most other appointees of recent years." James J. Kilpatrick attempted to downplay the significance of Marshall's race and instead pointed to the danger that, in replacing Tom Clark, Marshall would "upset the rough balance of liberalism and conservatism that recently has prevailed upon the high tribunal." Nonetheless, an editorial in Alabama's *Times Daily* argued that "fair-minded Southerners . . . are probably not going to denounce or applaud the action. They will want to wait and see how he conducts himself on the bench."[35]

The Judiciary Committee approved the Marshall nomination by a vote of 11–5, with Senators Eastland, McClellan, Ervin, and Thurmond voting against confirmation, along with Senator George Smathers of Florida.[36] On August 30, 1967, Thurmond delivered a lengthy speech on the Senate floor in opposition to the nominee. Conceding early on that "it may seem to some, as it has subsequently been alleged, that the questions I posed to the nominee were either immaterial or irrelevant or exceeded that which any reasonable person would be expected to know about the Thirteenth or Fourteenth Amendments," the senator reiterated his belief that "any person who has spent the bulk of his adult life studying the Fourteenth Amendment" would be well equipped to provide detailed answers to his questions.[37] Thurmond proceeded to justify the complexity of his questions—and also reveal the correct answers—in a speech lasting for a total of thirty-six pages. Highlights included his reference to a question he had asked Marshall regarding the Thirteenth Amendment, and how the Framers copied the language from "a prior provision" of the law:

> The answer, of course, is that the Thirteenth Amendment was a virtual carbon copy of a provision contained in the Northwest Ordinance of 1787, and the legal significance of the fact that it was copied from a prior provision of the law is the fundamental doctrine that when a new provision is copied from an older one, the understanding and interpretations of the older are considered to be carried over into the new.[38]

Referring to the infamous "John Bingham of Ohio" moment, Thurmond acknowledged that "Judge Marshall did not understand the question, but he was not alone in failing to grasp the import of the question." For the benefit of fellow senators, Thurmond clarified his meaning:

> The privileges and immunities clause of Article IV, Section 2 is self-executing; its enforcement is dependent on the judicial process and it does not authorize legislation by Congress. This provision of the Constitution is similar in that respect to the very next section of Article IV of the Constitution, dealing with the extradition procedures for fugitives from one state to another. Both have been held to be responsibilities of the states but neither is subject to Congressional enforcement. Therefore, this provision does not delineate a power of Congress which can be legislated upon through the authority of the necessary and proper clause of Article I, Section 8 of the Constitution.[39]

Drawing his speech to a close, Thurmond lamented that Marshall seemed to believe he was free to interpret the Constitution as he wished, concluding, "this is probably the popular attitude, but it is an attitude that has wreaked havoc within our Constitutional structure of government, and one which we here in the Senate should not be parties to perpetuating."[40]

Senators confirmed Marshall by a vote of 69–11. Eight southern Democrats—Allen Ellender and Russell Long of Louisiana, Lister Hill and John Sparkman of Alabama, Herman Talmadge of Georgia, Robert C. Byrd of West Virginia, Spessard Holland of Florida, and, of course, Ernest "Fritz" Hollings of South Carolina—all joined Thurmond, Ervin, and Eastland in opposition. However, their southern Democratic colleagues, William Fulbright of Arkansas, Albert Gore of Tennessee, Ralph Yarborough of Texas, and William B. Spong of Virginia, joined with Republicans John Tower of Texas and Howard Baker of Tennessee in approving Marshall's appointment. Juan Williams's claim that Lyndon Johnson persuaded twenty more senators not to vote may explain why southern dissent was diluted further, with Richard Russell of Georgia, John Stennis of Mississippi, and John McClellan of Arkansas all abstaining.[41]

The roll call tally on Marshall's nomination highlights the changing nature of southern voting in Congress following the passage of the Civil Rights Act of 1964 and the Voting Rights Act of 1965. In their research on congressional voting behavior, Keith Poole and Howard Rosenthal have argued that the need for southern politicians to seek the votes of black constituents effectively ended the influence of the civil rights issue in separating northern and southern Democratic voting on economic issues. However, Robert Mann has pointed out that a generational divide was emerging among southerners prior to the landmark legislation of the mid-1960s, with younger senators, including Talmadge, Long, Fulbright, and Smathers, feeling "tired of being outcasts in the Democratic Party and weary of swimming against the tide of history," as well as less inclined to follow Richard Russell's leadership wholeheartedly in the drive to maintain segregation.[42] Yet, with only Fulbright choosing to support Marshall, the enormous symbolic quality of voting to approve the appointment of the Supreme Court's first African American justice proved to be a step too far even for a "younger" generation of southerners, particularly those from Deep South states.

In his 2008 memoir, Fritz Hollings described his vote against Marshall's confirmation as "the most difficult decision in my political career." Although his explanation that "the South looked upon Johnson's appointment of Marshall as nothing more than a political down payment for the black vote" sounded similar to the arguments southern politicians were making forty years earlier, he did concede that "I knew if I voted to confirm him, my political career would be over." In mentioning that Marshall's son, Thurgood Jr., later worked on the staff of the Commerce Committee on which he served, Hollings concluded, "I am sure that he and his father understood my vote. As I look back at my years in the Senate, that is the one vote I regret."[43] He did not mention their correspondence, nor did he reflect on the fact that his dissenting vote aligned him unwittingly with Strom Thurmond's aggressive and opportunistic style of questioning. Despite being convinced that the Marshall controversy could have resulted in fatal consequences for his career, Hollings has never discussed the issue of where the pressure was coming from to oppose Marshall's confirmation. As with the letters sent to Olin Johnston during his sustained opposition to Marshall's Second

Circuit appointment, the content of Hollings's correspondence during the summer of 1967 suggests once again that the state's political establishment ultimately shouted down South Carolina's racially moderate voices, with the anti–Supreme Court sentiments of lowcountry politicians only increasing following the court's order to reconstruct malapportioned legislatures in *Baker v. Carr.*

Furthermore, Hollings has said very little regarding the reaction of the state's black community to his vote against Marshall. As the *New York Times* reported in September 1967, Vernon Jordan, of the Voter Education Project, told a meeting of black leadership figures in Columbia that "Fritz Hollings must understand one thing: The Negro vote giveth, and it taketh away." Wiley A. Branton, special assistant to Attorney General Ramsey Clark and director of the Voter Education Project, "drew shouts of 'No' from the audience when he asked, 'Did Senator Hollings vote for you when he voted against Thurgood Marshall?'"[44] Far from suggesting that black South Carolinians had short memories, Hollings's reelection victory in November 1968 served as yet another indication that black southern voters faced little choice but to side with the more moderate of the two candidates on offer in each round of elections.

As governor of South Carolina, Hollings had led the way in guiding the South through a complex and delicate process of desegregation, but his vote to deny Thurgood Marshall's confirmation implied that nothing had changed in the outlook of South Carolina's senators since Olin Johnston cast his dissenting vote against Earl Warren's nomination as chief justice in March 1954. By the end of the summer of 1967, there was ample evidence to suggest that Senators Thurmond and Hollings represented very different constituencies, yet, throughout the course of deliberations over the Marshall Supreme Court nomination, neither senator was able to make a positive gesture to reassure the state's sizable black community. While each demonstrated very different attitudes toward the nominee as a human being, both men ultimately voted for the same outcome. Despite Hollings's success in guiding South Carolina toward accepting the *Brown* decision and allowing black students to enroll peacefully in traditionally white universities, the South Carolina trait of resisting federal interference in the southern way of life was still perfectly intact in the troubled development of Supreme Court confirmation hearings into controversial public events. Thurmond's passion for his new opportunity to interrogate Supreme Court nominees face-to-face as a member of the Judiciary Committee recalls W. J. Cash's description of the southern man's "love of self-assertion and battle—a chance to posture and charge and be the dashing fellow," and his style of attack would reach truly obnoxious proportions the following year, when his role on the committee proved critical in Lyndon Johnson's failure to elevate Justice Abe Fortas to the position of chief justice following Earl Warren's retirement.[45]

Other than allowing further national exposure for South Carolina's war on the Supreme Court, the struggle over Thurgood Marshall's Supreme Court appointment appeared to signal another defeat for the state's senators. On the other hand, Thurmond had offered a graphic demonstration of a unique brand of dogged determination that would ultimately prevail in the case of Abe Fortas. The Fortas episode would confirm that South Carolina's war on the court could be effective in scoring significant victories, but only when working in tandem with other potent political forces. With Thurmond escalating his attack and Hollings continuing to carve out a unique conservative record on judicial nominations that would last for nearly four decades, South Carolina's influence in the federal judicial nomination process had reached unprecedented heights.

On September 1, 1967, in a private ceremony, Justice Hugo Black, a former member of the Ku Klux Klan from Alabama, was responsible for swearing in Thurgood Marshall as an associate justice of the Supreme Court.[46] A resident of Massachusetts wrote to Strom Thurmond a few days later over his concern that Marshall had told a reporter, "I sorta got sworn in." The writer asked "What did he mean? Did he or did he not take the oath to support the Constitution? Was he sworn in or was he not?" Thurmond responded that "reliable sources" had informed him that all aspects of the procedure involved in Marshall's swearing-in ceremony had been perfectly legal, adding, "as to what he meant by his statement, I am afraid you would have to ask him that."[47]

8. "AND YOU REFUSE TO ANSWER THAT QUESTION?"

With his concern for future historians once again evident, Senator Philip Hart of Michigan employed an idiosyncratic choice of words to clarify Senator Strom Thurmond's comments regarding unwelcome "demonstrations" during hearings to determine Justice Abe Fortas's suitability for the position of chief justice of the United States: "Now, Mr. Chairman, for the reader of the record, he will be completely fogged up by that exchange. All that happened was that some people were pleased that the Justice did not agree that, whatever the crime rate is, it is a consequence of Supreme Court decisions. As I look over the room, everybody looks nice and clean and fine and fresh."[1]

Having sat through Olin D. Johnston's interminable stalling tactics during Thurgood Marshall's Second Circuit hearings in 1962, and also Thurmond's barrage of carefully worded and occasionally inexplicable questions during Marshall's Supreme Court hearings in 1967, Senator Hart observed Thurmond's attack on Fortas during his chief justice hearings, with the South Carolinian's preambles, questions, and diatribes merging occasionally into one barely coherent tirade. Unable to conceal his amusement at the reaction of some in the room to Fortas's blunt response to Thurmond's staggeringly lengthy and complex framing of one particularly straightforward question, Hart clarified for the record that the "demonstration consisted of mild scattered applause for a statement that I would have applauded myself," preventing future historians from misreading the "demonstration" as the work of antiestablishment youths, whose protests against the Vietnam War had already begun to characterize the USA of the late 1960s.[2]

Lyndon Johnson's failure to engineer Fortas's rise to the highest judicial position in the land proved pivotal in the development of Supreme Court confirmation hearings into controversial, heavily politicized events of great public interest. Previous studies have examined in depth the significance of the Fortas affair, focusing in particular on Johnson's failed judgment in the final, troubled year of his presidency. Scholars such as Thurmond's recent biographer, Joseph Crespino, have discussed the importance of judicial politics in fashioning the conservative movement of the late twentieth century, but no one has analyzed Thurmond's behavior in the context of South Carolina's long-standing war on the Supreme Court. From Olin Johnston's campaign to defy the court's *Smith v. Allwright* decision to Fritz Hollings's hesitation in rejecting the court's first African American justice, the full extent of South Carolina's war on the court has remained an overlooked characteristic of postwar conservatism. For Mark Silverstein, the Fortas rejection marked the beginning of the "modern" era of conflict in the Supreme Court nomination process, showcasing "a new generation of Senate Republicans [who] understood that highly visible public battles to bring the court back to the 'silent majority' could produce real electoral dividends that would outweigh the consequences of any breach of timeworn patterns of Senate decorum and behavior."[3] One might argue that several southern Democrats—preeminently those from South Carolina—had been pioneering this practice for years prior to the events of 1968.

As with previous nominations, Thurmond set out to attack the Supreme Court's liberal jurisprudence under Chief Justice Earl Warren's leadership, but in the case of Johnson's 1968 selection of Fortas, the senator's actions represented a tactical shift from an obstructive role to an interventionist role in the nomination process. As Thurmond himself was fond of telling constituents, he had opposed the confirmation of every individual nominated to the Supreme Court since the beginning of his service in the Senate in 1955. His opposition to Fortas involved not only resistance to the nominee's confirmation, but also a concerted political effort to infiltrate the selection process by using his growing influence as a member of the Senate Judiciary Committee. For Thurmond, the complex political situation within the Senate during the summer of 1968 offered an opportunity to prevent the outgoing Lyndon Johnson from replacing Warren, with a view to the incoming president filling the role instead. Rather than following his earlier approach of opposing the nominee alone or in collaboration with the southern Democratic bloc led by Georgia's Richard Russell, this time Thurmond allied himself with Richard Nixon, the Republican presidential hopeful, and Robert P. Griffin, Michigan's recently elected Republican senator. Ultimately, Thurmond's role in Abe Fortas's rejection was a key element of his growing influence in the Republican Party, which proved critical in the gradual Republican takeover of the South, culminating in a political dominance over the region that remains in place to this day.

With the Fortas episode, Thurmond made a significant political impact in the Supreme Court nomination process despite, or perhaps in part as a result of, his obnoxious and provocative behavior in confronting the individuals chosen to serve on that most powerful political institution. Yet, as previous chapters have shown, the persistent influence of South Carolina's senators in the appointment of Supreme Court justices transcends the issue of whether or not the full Senate ultimately voted to reject the nominee. As will become clear, the Fortas controversy represents one of several landmark events in the state's war on the court, suggesting that analyses of nomination hearings as "one-off" events fail to take account of the consistency in state and regional agendas. These studies also tend to obscure the long-term escalation of the tensions that defined and shaped the development of the nomination process throughout this era.

Following Chief Justice Warren's announcement that he had informed President Johnson of his intention to retire from the Supreme Court, Strom Thurmond spoke for many in the South when he claimed that Warren had done "more harm to the American way of life than any other one man holding public office in the history of our country." In contrast to the deferential tone of his letter to Lyndon Johnson following Justice Tom C. Clark's retirement the previous year, Thurmond told the press in plain terms that as Johnson had announced on television that he would not be running for reelection in the 1968 presidential election, he should now refrain from making any further nominations to the Supreme Court. His letter from the previous year had offered "friendly advice," but Thurmond now declared that he was "unalterably opposed to a lame duck president attempting to fill the vacancy on the Court to designate a new Chief Justice," making clear his intention to "strongly oppose any attempt by President Johnson to do so."[4]

Republican senator Robert Griffin of Michigan soon added his voice to Thurmond's public comments by declaring that "never before has there been such obvious political maneuvering to create a vacancy so that a 'lame duck' president can fill it."[5] There was some degree of credibility in Griffin's comments: Johnson and Warren were indeed discussing the question of whom Johnson would name as Warren's replacement. Keen to ensure that Johnson, rather than a potential Republican successor, named the new chief, Warren proposed that the president bring back Arthur J. Goldberg, who had resigned from the court two years earlier to become ambassador to the United Nations. Johnson opted instead to elevate Justice Abe Fortas, his long-time counsel, to the chief justiceship, and, to complicate matters further, he decided to name Congressman Homer Thornberry, another loyal Johnson man, as a replacement associate justice, to step in when Fortas became chief. Given the ambiguity over whether or not Warren had in fact submitted a formal resignation, an incredulous Thurmond resented the possibility that Johnson had engineered a situation whereby senators would be stuck with Warren if they refused to confirm Fortas.[6] By Thurmond's logic, if Warren was still serving, then there was no vacancy for a new chief justice, and if Fortas was still serving, then no vacancy existed for an associate justice. He responded by refusing to recognize the Thornberry nomination altogether.

The announcement in May 1968 of the *Green v. County School Board of New Kent County* decision—ruling that an eastern Virginia school board's admissions policy did not comply with the legal requirements of a desegregated school system—exacerbated Thurmond's hostility toward the Supreme Court. In declaring to his supporters that he was "very much opposed to [Fortas's] appointment and will do whatever is necessary, including taking part in a filibuster, to block this nomination," Thurmond outlined clearly a determination, after tolerating Earl Warren for fourteen bitter years, to prevent the Supreme Court from falling into the hands of another dangerous liberal chief justice.[7]

By contrast, Fritz Hollings's position on the Fortas nomination appeared ambiguous. In response to constituents urging him to join Thurmond's opposition, Hollings claimed that "the proposed filibuster is for political shenanigans and does not involve the Fortas qualifications. Long before I came to Washington, the Senate confirmed Justice Fortas for the Supreme Court. His qualifications were considered then, but no one suggested a filibuster. A filibuster is proposed now on the basis that the President, having only six months left in his term, is a 'lame duck' and therefore has no right to appoint. He not only has the right but the duty." Having hailed Johnson's recent appointment of General William Westmoreland as US Army chief of staff, Hollings protested that he could not claim the very next week that the "lame duck" Johnson had no right to make any further appointments. He maintained that "if the Republicans thought Fortas should be filibustered against because of his qualifications, they could have well done so on August 11, 1965, when he was confirmed for the Supreme Court. They didn't then, and I won't join in their shenanigans now."[8]

Although he may have been successful in preventing his constituents from confusing him with Strom Thurmond, the state's junior senator faced challenges in negotiating his position, just as he had experienced one year earlier when arriving at the difficult decision to vote against Thurgood Marshall's confirmation as an associate justice. After Hollings told the *News and Courier* that he would vote against Fortas and Thornberry, former State Senator Calhoun Thomas, of the Beaufort County Democratic Committee, reminded him that "in Beaufort County, we are going to have to depend on a large Negro vote in your behalf, if you are going to make a real showing in this county. Right now, I am of the opinion that the Negroes are extremely lukewarm as to your race for re-election. . . . You may not be aware of it, but there is a lot of resentment toward you, because of such positions taken by you in respect to these nominations." In his brief response, Hollings outlined his belief that the Democratic Party could maintain its control of South Carolina through adopting a conservative position on the Supreme Court. As he explained to Thomas, "I can't in conscience confirm the Warren philosophy. I made this crystal clear in the primary, and I believe my position on the Supreme Court would help build me as a stronger Democrat, and, in turn, build a stronger party in our state." In referring to the continued southern defection to, or at least sympathy with, the Republican Party, Hollings added that "our strongest Democratic candidate, Mendel Rivers, curses these things outright and supports the candidate of the other party. I am squeezed in the middle and do my best, and I do appreciate your concern."[9]

While Hollings's dismissal of the "lame duck" argument constituted a deliberate move to distance himself from Thurmond, the similarity of their political outlook on other issues was quite evident in their letters and news releases during the summer of 1968. In response to letters from concerned South Carolinians, urging them to reject gun control legislation, both senators released communications that combined the Supreme Court's threat with a personal endorsement of the right to bear arms. In his correspondence, Thurmond would frequently follow up a statement of his willingness to filibuster the Fortas nomination with a declaration that "I believe that the states have the prime responsibility to legislate controls on firearms." In response to a letter from Jack C. Hawe, chief of police in Santa Barbara, California, who offered information on gun control matters while condemning "the permissiveness and extreme liberal attitudes that prevail in our democracy," Thurmond claimed that the information would assist him in blocking Fortas's nomination on the Senate floor, adding, "I want you to know that I am truly appreciative of the tremendous task facing law enforcement personnel at this particular time."[10] Hollings, true to his reputation for a folksier style of communication, opened his June 20 newsletter by declaring:

> Last Christmas was the best ever. I gave my 17-year-old son a 12-gauge Browning automatic, and we went hunting together. It's difficult to get on the same frequency with these teenagers. We did on these hunts, and I wouldn't want to pass any law that would mar this pleasure. Moreover, I can understand the home owner, the store owner, and the bus driver wanting a weapon. With militants and the church leadership recommending civil disobedience . . . and with the Supreme Court decisions, the average man has lost confidence in the law.[11]

One reason for the increasing concern of South Carolinians over law and order was the violence witnessed during the Orangeburg Massacre, which, on February 8, 1968, ended the relatively peaceful nature of South Carolina's civil rights movement when a tragic outburst of police gunfire killed three students and injured twenty-eight others during a protest at the segregated All-Star Bowling Lane. Governor Robert E. McNair responded by describing the incident as "one of the saddest days in the history of South Carolina." The massacre proved to be, for civil rights activist Rev. I. DeQuincey Newman, "an indication that despite all that might be considered progress in terms of interracial co-operation, beneath the surface South Carolina is just about in the same boat as Alabama and Mississippi."[12] With the continued southern resentment over the court's *Miranda v. Arizona* decision, and the growing public hysteria over outbreaks of racial violence in the streets, the law and order issue became a significant aspect of the Fortas hearings, particularly as both Thurmond and Nixon were discussing the issue frequently on the campaign trail. Following Thurmond's statement in an interview during the 1968 Republican Convention in Miami that "the number one issue in this campaign is law and order," NBC's

David Brinkley remarked that the American voter was "free to interpret the true meaning of that phrase however he likes."[13]

Lyndon Johnson built his reputation as a master of congressional politics largely through his understanding of individual senators' wants and needs, and his skillful use of such wants and needs as political carrots. Only six weeks after Johnson took over the presidency following John F. Kennedy's assassination, South Carolina's then-lieutenant governor, Robert McNair, wrote to the new president to point out that the continued delay in filling two judicial vacancies for the state's Eastern District was causing concern among members of the General Assembly and the South Carolina Bar Association.[14] It was not until April 1964, when Johnson became impatient over the passage of a Civil Service payment bill—which South Carolina's Olin Johnston would oversee as chairman of the Post Office and Civil Service Committee—that he began talking seriously about nominating the two South Carolina judges.

But the president had inadvertently waded into a muddle of competing interests that highlighted the complex political situation in South Carolina during the early 1960s. The growing distance between Johnston and Thurmond was evident in Thurmond's ongoing effort to promote Robert Figg, now serving as dean of the University of South Carolina Law School, for one of the two outstanding Eastern District vacancies. There was a consensus over the selection of Johnston's friend, Congressman Robert W. Hemphill, for one vacancy, but, with regard to the second, the Thurmond camp assumed that Johnston's sour memories of the 1950 Senate contest would lead him to withdraw his tepid support for Figg and endorse Congressman Charles E. Simons as a means of denying Figg the second vacancy.

In a letter to Walter Brown, Thurmond outlined the formal nature of his agreement with Olin Johnston over South Carolina's federal judicial appointments. In 1961, the two senators had met, along with Thurmond advisor Harry Dent and also Baxter Funderburk, Johnston's administrative assistant, to agree that if either senator objected to the other's recommendation, it would not be interpreted as "personal obnoxiousness." Under the terms of the agreement, which Dent recorded in writing shortly after the meeting, neither senator would push a nomination if the other man objected, and both would submit nominations to the Justice Department only if both men approved. Thurmond claimed that "if Olin should object to Bob, I shall suggest another name . . . If

Olin objects to Simons, I shall name another person and shall keep on naming persons until I get one to whom he does not object."[15] Thurmond was happy to accept Simons, his former law partner, as his second preference, but Simons later embarrassed Thurmond by supporting Olin Johnston in the 1962 Senate primary. Furthermore, given that Simons supposedly switched his allegiance from Fritz Hollings to Johnston after finding out that the latter might object to Figg's nomination and therefore back him for one of the two vacancies, Brown advised Thurmond that "if Olin turns down Bob and accepts Simons, then a lot of people in South Carolina will conclude there was a political deal on this judgeship."[16]

By October 1963, Thurmond was growing impatient with the delay, telling State Senator John C. West that "I will not give consideration to any nomination to fill the Timmerman seat until the Senate also has before it a nomination to fill the Williams seat, which has been vacant since early in 1962," adding his view that "it is in the interest of all South Carolinians that the 'advice' as well as the 'consent' of the Senators be sought and heeded . . . particularly in view of the sensitive and important issues now being decided by the federal courts."[17] But it was Olin Johnston who would reach an agreement with Lyndon Johnson over the two judgeships. Knowing how badly the South Carolina Democrats wanted Hemphill and Simons confirmed by April 1964, the president telephoned Johnston to urge swift passage of the pay bill, telling the senator, "Alright now, Olin, I'll tell you, we've gotta do this in a hurry because I'm losing the best men I've got in the government." After assuring him that "I'll get your judges up there simultaneously and I'll call you and then I'll call Strom, and they'll be who you want," an irate Johnson pressed the senator to use his influence on the Judiciary Committee to confirm the two judges as quickly as possible:

LBJ: Alright, you get 'em to have permission to let you waive the hearing on these judges so you can get 'em confirmed quick.

Johnston: Good. I'll do everything—

LBJ: Now, if you don't, they tell me that the NAACP is liable to come in and protest.

Johnston: Well, we'll get 'em right through.

LBJ: They, they, they, they, they say your boy Simons is not qualified.

Johnston: Well, I think he is.

LBJ: Well, I know he is if you want him, and, and you don't want that professor and that's why I'm naming [*Simons*].

Johnston: Yeah.

LBJ: So you just get, you get that, hell, I put you on that committee, uh, uh, as leader, to help old man McCarran and help us with some of our plans. So you just get John McClellan and Sam Ervin and some of your buddies and tell them that dammit, you want a subcommittee and you want it to meet and report 'em right quick.

Johnston: Well, we'll do everything we can.

LBJ: Alright.

Johnston: Good.

LBJ: I can count on you now to get that pay bill out in a week or so?

Johnston: I'll do it.

LBJ: Alright, goodbye.[18]

Later that day, the president was irritated to find that someone had announced the two nominations to the press before he could make them official. He again telephoned Johnston, whose "surprised" response—"Oh, my"—may or may not have convinced Johnson of the senator's view that newspapermen were getting ahead of themselves:

LBJ: They quote you and Thurmond both saying they're quite imminent and all about what's gonna happen and now they're jumping on me and I'll get all, uh—

Johnston: Well, I think the news has gone a little far on it.

LBJ: Well let me read you what the, the press boys are asking us about, and we're telling them we don't know a damn thing about it: "President Johnson today was reported on the verge of nominating Hemphill and Simons." All that does is just notify anybody who wants to protest and raise hell—

Johnston: Well—

LBJ: —which they're doing.

Johnston: —you won't get anything coming from me, names, any particular people.

LBJ: "Senator Olin Johnston issued a statement quoting the president as saying he would release his nominations if possible tomorrow"—

Johnston: Well—

LBJ: —"for two long-vacant judgeships. Johnston said the president promised one nomination would go to Hemphill, a congressman since '57, and Senator Thurmond agreed the nominations were imminent, and said the other nominee would be Simons, 47, a lawyer in Aiken."

Johnston: I haven't talked to Thurmond anything about it either.

LBJ: "Simons is a former law partner of Thurmond."

Johnston: Uh-huh.[19]

With his concern over the best men in his government "quitting like flies," Johnson again reminded Johnston to ensure passage of the civil service pay bill, before making a much calmer and more businesslike call to Strom Thurmond, with whom he had never enjoyed a particularly cordial relationship:

LBJ: Strom.

Thurmond: Mr. President, how are you?

LBJ: Fine. Bill Moyers already talked to you, I find out, I ju . . . while I was calling you, he called you from the other office.

Thurmond: Uh, he just called me and said that you're gonna send the judgeships up tomorrow.

LBJ: We're gonna try to get both of them out tomorrow. I'd, I'd wait 'til, uh, uh, well, I guess y'all can go ahead and say so, we'll . . . uh, we'll, uh, notify 'em and uh, uh . . . I think . . . uh, they're . . . I think we'll try to get 'em out by the twelve o'clock meeting.

Thurmond: Fine.

LBJ: OK, Str—

Thurmond: Thank you very much, Mr. President.

LBJ: Right, Strom. 'Bye.

Thurmond: 'Bye. Goodbye.[20]

Shortly after the call, Thurmond sent a telegram to Lieutenant Governor McNair to confirm the president's agreement to name the two nominees.[21]

Following Olin Johnston's death, Thurmond's defection to the Republicans, and Barry Goldwater's victory in South Carolina in the 1964 presidential election, Lyndon Johnson's relationship with South Carolina's senators would never again be quite so straightforward. Only four years after he had played second fiddle in the Hemphill and Simons appointments, Strom Thurmond's influence over the nomination process had transformed. As South Carolina's senior senator, he now held a place on the Senate Judiciary Committee as a Republican during the party's rapid expansion in the southern states. The combined effect of Johnson's televised announcement that he would neither seek nor accept the Democratic Party nomination for that year's presidential election, along with the escalating Vietnam War, growing concerns over crime and disorder in the streets, and a developing white conservative resentment over civil rights legislation, only encouraged Republican hopes for taking back the White House. Tennessee Republican Bill Brock, who won election to the Senate in 1970, remembers the 1960s as a critical period for the South, with the region's transition to the Republican Party becoming evident in the growing number of successful Republican candidates: "The elections of John Tower in Texas, Howard Baker in Tennessee, and myself, along with a number of other Southern Senators and members in the 1960s, created an excitement with Republicans in general, and President Nixon, in particular. All felt that the South posed an enormous new opportunity for party growth."[22]

In leading South Carolina through this transition, Thurmond used his considerable influence to build on the hard work of white upcountry activists in revitalizing the state's Republican Party during the 1950s and 1960s. Congressman Albert Watson and former congressman Arthur Ravenel Jr. both followed Thurmond into the Republican Party during the 1960s, and many other South Carolinians, including former governor James F. Byrnes, had supported Republican Dwight D. Eisenhower's presidential campaigns in the 1950s. Although Byrnes opted to remain a Democrat, he gave Thurmond a private blessing to defect to the Republican Party, and also criticized the "punishment and humiliation" that senior Democrats inflicted on Albert Watson by stripping away his congressional seniority following his endorsement of Barry Goldwater's presidential campaign in 1964.[23] South Carolina's Democratic establishment may have fought tooth and nail to maintain Democratic control over the state, but many in the party fought equally hard to maintain a South Carolina tradition of independence—a trait that, ironically, led many to endorse Republican Party candidates before eventually defecting to that party themselves.

As a result of this transition, South Carolina became a crucial state in the expanding US conservative movement, with the Abe Fortas chief justice nomination providing an early example of the "culture wars" that fueled conservative mobilization during the late twentieth century.[24] For Thurmond, who had gnashed his teeth in frustration when the Senate approved Fortas as an associate justice three years earlier, the 1968 hearings provided, for the first time ever, an opportunity for him to confront a serving Supreme Court justice. Although Hollings would play no part in the hearings, the nomination once again placed him in a difficult position. With his acknowledgement of being "squeezed in the middle" as a conservative Democrat during the state's dramatic shift toward the Republican Party, Hollings continued to distance himself from his South Carolina colleague by taking advantage of the fact that, unlike Thurmond, he had not been in the Senate when that body had first confirmed Fortas for a seat on the court. His portrayal of filibuster plans as Republican "shenanigans" recalled the late Olin Johnston's spirited resistance to the development of the state's emerging two-party system. Meanwhile, the role of Thurmond and South Carolina in the process of conservative mobilization cannot be overstated. The importance of this episode in the history of the state's troubled relationship with the Supreme Court was never more evident than in Thurmond's explosive behavior during the infamous Fortas confirmation hearings.

While an unimpressed Thurgood Marshall had faced down his southern adversaries through a haze of cigarette smoke, and the combative Robert Bork would respond to his critics twenty years later with a fierce, devil-may-care attitude, Abe Fortas was a quiet man whose temperament was ill suited to the ordeal of Supreme Court nomination hearings. His voice, barely audible in Lyndon Johnson's crackly telephone recordings, was often so quiet during the hearings that the aging Senator John McClellan of Arkansas complained that he could not hear Fortas's responses. With his reserved, soft-spoken persona, the Tennessean was a perfect foil to the boisterous Lyndon Johnson, but his cerebral, academic approach was never likely to sit well with a Senate Judiciary Committee characterized by the cigar-chewing cynicism of Chairman James Eastland, the simmering bulldog demeanor of Sam Ervin, and especially the unfiltered theatrics of Strom Thurmond.

The Department of Justice had prepared Fortas thoroughly, and he knew to expect questions regarding his long friendship with Johnson, whom he had first met while serving as general counsel of Franklin Roosevelt's Public Works Administration in the 1940s. After heading Johnson's successful legal strategy during the fight over the contested Senate election in Texas in 1948, Fortas had become one of Johnson's most trusted political advisors. The relationship between the two men became a vital ingredient in Johnson's rise to power, with Bruce Allen Murphy noting that "together, they had learned how to operate the wheels of government."[25]

Despite the obvious concerns over the relationship between the president and the man he had nominated to become chief justice of the United States, the

Judiciary Committee chose to focus initially on the question of whether or not a vacancy did in fact exist on the Supreme Court. On the first day of hearings, July 11, 1968, Attorney General Ramsey Clark—whom Johnson had appointed as a means of forcing Justice Tom Clark into retirement so that Johnson could send Thurgood Marshall to the Supreme Court—had the unenviable task of clarifying for the committee the issue of whether or not Chief Justice Warren had in fact resigned, or whether his resignation would become effective only when the Senate confirmed Fortas as his replacement. Some of the southern committee members, who had loathed Warren openly since his announcement of *Brown v. Board of Education* in 1954, were particularly keen to confirm that the current chief justice genuinely intended to leave the Supreme Court. Chairman Eastland inquired as to whether Warren's resignation was "irrevocable," while North Carolina's Sam Ervin read from a newspaper report suggesting that Warren would remain chief justice if senators did not confirm Fortas.[26] Thurmond also expressed an interest in the issue, albeit in the form of his typically confrontational style of questioning:

Senator Thurmond: In a news conference held by Chief Justice Warren, he stated that he could serve on and would be willing, I believe, to do so. Did you see that statement by him?

Attorney General Clark: I have read his statement, yes. I have seen newspaper clippings on it.

Senator Thurmond: Therefore, does it not come down to this. Chief Justice Warren is virtually saying to the Senate, "You confirm Justice Fortas or I will continue to serve." And if that is the case, how can there be a resignation of Chief Justice Warren? How is there a resignation if he can continue to serve? Either there is a resignation, or there is not a resignation. I ask you which is it?

Attorney General Clark: Well, there is no resignation. The question is whether his retirement is effective. If so, when it will be.[27]

The southern suspicion over whether or not Johnson and Warren had made a deal as a means of encouraging the Senate to confirm Fortas guaranteed that

Fortas would endure lengthy, tense confirmation hearings. Earl Warren only added to the complexity over his proposed departure from the court at a press conference, after which Senator Robert C. Byrd of West Virginia announced that he was "reconsidering his position in light of Warren being able to choose his successor."[28]

Before long, senators were debating the potential problems of the unusually close relationship between Fortas and Johnson.[29] During the second day of hearings, Michigan's junior senator, Republican Robert Griffin, put forward his opposition to Fortas in bold terms when he claimed that "the argument has been advanced that if a 'crony'—nominated because he is a 'crony'—is 'qualified,' he should be approved. I reject such a view because it demeans the Senate and the Supreme Court."[30] Republican senator Everett Dirksen of Illinois, who, as the most influential Republican leader in the Senate, enjoyed an amicable and productive relationship with Lyndon Johnson, responded to Republican criticism by claiming that he found the "lame duck" term "offensive," pointing out that most if not all of President Harry S. Truman's Supreme Court nominees were also "cronies," including Justice Harold Hitz Burton, whom Truman had sat next to in the Senate, and Chief Justice Fred Vinson, with whom Truman had regularly played poker.[31] Nonetheless, Griffin proved fearless in opposing the nominee, making clear that "I do not condemn Mr. Fortas because he has been Mr. Johnson's personal lawyer and his advisor throughout much of his personal career. . . . But, Mr. Chairman, I do raise the question [of] whether Mr. Fortas should be rewarded with the position of Chief Justice of the US Supreme Court because he performed such services as a friend of Lyndon Johnson."[32] Michigan's senior senator, the inimitable Democrat Philip Hart, expressed regret that his Senate colleague felt so strongly in his opposition to Fortas, declaring, "I just happen to think that America can be a little proud of itself that there is a man like Abe Fortas in our land, and that this nation affords to such an individual full opportunity to advance. But, having said that, I know that Bob will not say Amen, so I have no more to say."[33] Three days later, President Johnson discussed his concerns over the Republican opposition with Everett Dirksen in a telephone call, urging his ally, "don't let them filibuster this." Dirksen assured him that he would not, but also admitted, "I couldn't straighten out Strom, and neither could Jim Eastland."[34]

As with the events of Thurgood Marshall's confirmation hearings, Thurmond initially had little to say, almost as though he considered John McClellan and Sam Ervin to be warm-up acts. When Fortas finally appeared before the committee on July 16, 1968, Democratic senator Albert Gore, from Fortas's home state of Tennessee, formally introduced the nominee.[35] James Eastland kicked off, in a line of questioning that seemed to have changed little since he became the committee's chairman in 1956, by enquiring into the nominee's relationship with the president, and then asked Fortas for his view on whether the Supreme Court should "bring about social, economic, or political changes."[36] John McClellan picked up this line of interrogation, before Sam Ervin began a lengthy dialogue with the nominee on various aspects of constitutional law. By the following day's hearings, Ervin was pursuing a familiar line of inquiry by grilling the nominee on the *Miranda* decision—in which the court had underlined the necessity of law enforcement officers making suspects aware of their constitutional rights—with Fortas's uncomfortable responses sounding eerily similar to those of Marshall:

Senator Ervin: The thing that puzzles me, and it is beyond my power of comprehension, is that if the Constitution means what it was meant to mean in the Miranda case, why one of the smart judges who had sat on the court during the preceding one hundred and seventy-six years did not discover that.

Justice Fortas: Senator, again, much as I would like to discuss this, I am inhibited from doing it.[37]

When Thurmond's chance to question the nominee finally came, on July 18, he preceded his interrogation with the declaration that, "in the last decade and a half, the Court has made so many decisions affecting the lives of the American people in very fundamental ways that it would seem to me that the Senate, as representatives of the people, is entitled to consider these views."[38] While he may have intended his brief statement as a preemptive strike against the same voices that had condemned Olin Johnston's and his own behavior as Judiciary Committee members during previous hearings, Thurmond's words gave little warning of what was to follow. Without wasting time on the technicalities of the US Constitution, Thurmond cut straight to one of the most controversial issues in the South following the passage of the Voting Rights Act in 1965, namely, the issue of state control over voting procedures. In targeting the court's *Katzenbach v. Morgan* decision (1966), which recognized, and ruled as constitutional, Congress's power to enforce the Voting Rights Act's equal protection guarantees, Thurmond was not shy in referring to the use of literacy tests in southern state voting regulations:

Senator Thurmond: Under the reasoning of the majority in the Morgan case, are not the states prevented from exercising an otherwise constitutional legislative prerogative, such as the requirement of literacy in the English language, merely because the Congress declares otherwise?

Justice Fortas: Senator, with all deference, I must ask you to understand and to excuse me from addressing myself to that question. I do so only because of my conception of the constitutional limitations upon me . . . as a justice of the Supreme Court, I am under the constitutional limitation that has been referred to during these past two days, and must respectfully ask to be excused from answering.[39]

Fortas, having been briefed by the Justice Department on how to conduct himself during the hearings, continued to provide diplomatic answers that acknowledged, albeit apologetically, his limited ability to offer his views on the issues under discussion.[40] In attempting to portray Fortas's noncommittal responses as an outright refusal to clarify his views, Thurmond segued happily into the issue of Fortas's close relationship with Lyndon Johnson:

Senator Thurmond: You have expressed your views to the president when he has called you down there, and over the telephone, haven't you?

Justice Fortas: No, sir. Never.

Senator Thurmond: And he got the benefit of your views on these matters, did he not?

Justice Fortas: Never.

Senator Thurmond: Why shouldn't a senator have the benefit of your views?

Justice Fortas: I have never, never been asked by the president. Nor have I expressed my views on any pending or decided case. Never, Senator, never.[41]

This line of questioning succeeded in provoking Fortas into more definite responses, but Thurmond soon returned to the subject of literacy tests. In yet another parallel with the Marshall hearings—during which the senator asked the nominee repeatedly if he understood the question, and also inquired into whether or not he had "anything to add" to his more detailed answers—Thurmond began a routine of hurling questions at Fortas and following up the nominee's noncommittal answers by asking repeatedly, "and you refuse to answer the question?"

Senator Thurmond: Mr. Justice Fortas, if Congress were to pass a law prohibiting literacy tests for voting in all states—and I gather you believe such tests to be unwise—would it be your opinion that, if this matter came before the court, the proper questions would be whether this was appropriate legislation under Section 5 of the Fourteenth Amendment, even if such legislation were constitutional in the absence of congressional action?

Justice Fortas: I am afraid I have to make the same answer, if I have followed that correctly, Senator.

Senator Thurmond: You refuse to answer the question?

Justice Fortas: Yes, sir.

Senator Thurmond: What is your answer?

Justice Fortas: I said, yes, sir, for the same reason.

Senator Thurmond: Mr. Justice Fortas, in all but a very few states, a person must be 21 years of age in order to vote. Suppose Congress passed legislation, not an amendment to the Constitution, lowering this to 18, based on findings that certain racial groups have a greater percentage of persons in the 18-to-20 age bracket. Is there anything in the reasoning of the majority in the Morgan case which would prevent congressional action overriding the state's judgements on this matter?

Justice Fortas: For the same reason—because of constitutional limitations upon me—I must decline to address myself to that.

Senator Thurmond: So you refuse to answer that question?

Justice Fortas: I have so stated. Yes, sir.[42]

With Fortas following successfully the same calm and collected approach demonstrated by Marshall the previous year, Thurmond eventually became agitated, with his comments bordering on sarcasm:

Senator Thurmond: Would you consider your dissent in *Fortson v. Morris* to be an example of translating a personal preference into a constitutional requirement?

Justice Fortas: I most certainly would not, but I should not say that. I must stand on the constitutional position. I cannot respond to that, Senator.

Senator Thurmond: I thought you did respond.

Justice Fortas: I am sorry. It was inadvertence.

Senator Thurmond: Well, maybe we need more inadvertent answers here this morning.

Justice Fortas: It is pretty hard not to make them, Senator, as I am sure you will understand. I just repeat—this is not a pleasant role for me.[43]

With the senator offering no sympathy for the nominee's situation, Thurmond moved swiftly on to a range of other cases from the Warren Court era, from the controversial *Miranda* to the much-hated *Baker v. Carr* (1962) and to the lesser-known case of *Berger v. State of New York* (1967), which Fritz Hollings had flagged up in one of his letters to Thurgood Marshall the previous summer. Despite having told a supporter that "I have decided that my questions should be limited to the record which Justice Fortas has made since coming to the Court," Thurmond could not resist raising the case of *Mallory v. United States* (1957), which, for him, constituted perhaps the most blatant example of the justices' "concern for the rights of Communists and criminals, including rapists and murderers."[44] The inclusion in the hearings of questions relating to the *Mallory* decision is significant if only because, as Jim Newton has explained, "the facts [of the case] were so clear that even the court's conservatives joined the opinion, and Fortas had absolutely nothing to do with it."[45] The justices had thrown out Andrew Mallory's rape conviction eight years prior to Fortas taking his seat on the Supreme Court, but Thurmond had continued citing the case in speeches and newsletters in the years since. His questions on *Mallory* soon cascaded violently into the infamous rant that has, over time, become the defining moment of the Fortas hearings:

Senator Thurmond: Does not that decision—Mallory—I want that word to ring in your ears—Mallory—the man happened to have been from my state, incidentally—shackle law enforcement? Mallory, a man who raped a woman, admitted his guilt, and the Supreme Court turned him loose on a technicality. And who I was told later went to Philadelphia and committed another crime, and somewhere else, another crime, because the courts turned him loose on technicalities. Is not that type of decision calculated to encourage more people to commit rapes and serious crimes? Can you, as a justice of the Supreme Court, condone such a decision as that? I ask you to answer that question.[46]

Thurmond's obsession with the theme of the Supreme Court standing in the way of punishment for a black male who raped a white woman recalled the rage of Coleman Blease, his boyhood hero, who had endorsed the lynching of African Americans as a means of defending the honor of southern white women. Blease had infamously declared, "Whenever the Constitution comes between me and the virtue of the white women of the South, I say to hell with the Constitution!"[47] Like Blease, Thurmond defended the honor of southern white women, but never endorsed lynching and never dismissed the Constitution. Rather, he employed the very opposite tactic of speaking of the Constitution as a sacred document in order to hold judicial nominees to account. While Blease preached from the stump, Thurmond channeled his aggression into an institutional process of interrogating the individuals responsible for determining the outcome of judicial questions relating to race relations, crime, and other issues that remained as relevant in the South Carolina of the 1960s as they had been when Blease occupied Thurmond's Senate seat during the 1920s.

Reporters noticed Fortas glance over at Chairman Eastland, who was apparently reading and did not look up. As with the previous year's Marshall hearings, the Mississippian seemed happy to allow Thurmond off the leash.[48]

Justice Fortas: Senator, because of my respect for you and my respect for this body, and because of my respect for the Constitution of the United States, and my position as an associate justice of the Supreme Court of the United States, I will adhere to the limitation that I believe the Constitution of the United States places upon me and will not reply to your question as you phrased it.

Senator Thurmond: Can you suggest any other way in which I can phrase that question?

The Chairman: Let us have order.

Justice Fortas: That would be presumptuous. I would not attempt to do so.

Senator Thurmond: Would you care to make any comment at all on this question?

Justice Fortas: Not as phrased, no, sir.

Senator Thurmond: Well, as phrased differently, would you care to make any comment?

Justice Fortas: No. No, Senator.[49]

As with his record-breaking filibuster against the 1957 Civil Rights Act, Thurmond's outburst over *Mallory* confused, rather than satisfied, many who would ordinarily have sided with him. As Fritz Hollings later commented, his colleague's theatrical interrogation of Fortas "had left even some of his own staffers shaking their heads."[50]

On the very same day that Thurmond made political history with his *Mallory* outburst, South Carolina's junior senator was offering a more dignified explanation for opposing the Fortas nomination. In a lengthy speech in the Senate, Hollings linked Fortas to Chief Justice Warren and the "Warren philosophy," but at the same time condemned Republican filibuster plans. Significantly, he opted not to mention his fellow senator from South Carolina even once during the speech, and instead claimed that those behind the filibuster plans chose Senator Bob Griffin of Michigan and the Republican presidential candidate, Richard Nixon, as the leaders of their "manifesto."[51] As with his cautious statements on Thurgood Marshall, Hollings's Senate speech on Fortas indicated his well-developed skill in occupying tricky political positions. Having received several letters urging him to support Thurmond's filibuster efforts, Hollings was careful not to mention, let alone criticize openly, his fellow South Carolinian, while at the same time emphasizing the relevance of party politics in order to distance himself from the filibuster plans.

Similarly, Hollings was careful to keep up a united South Carolina front by linking Fortas repeatedly to the much-hated Earl Warren while at the same time refusing to recognize the "lame duck" description of the incumbent Democratic president.[52] By Hollings's logic, defeating Fortas's nomination may have been in South Carolina's best interests, but it was also true that certain Republican senators, aiming for the same outcome, were using shabby political tactics that he could never endorse. Perhaps inevitably, his complex position left him open to criticism, particularly as Republican Marshall Parker, whom Hollings had narrowly defeated in the 1966 special election following Olin Johnston's death, was keen to use the Fortas affair to criticize Hollings during a second run against him in 1968. Claiming that "this is another case where Hollings is talking out of both sides of his mouth," Parker remarked that "Hollings has attacked Supreme Court decisions on many issues and now he won't do enough to change them by helping block the nomination."[53]

Thurmond's outburst over the *Mallory* case played a critical role in the development of Supreme Court nomination hearings into major public events, but it was not the only notable exchange to take place during the lengthy Fortas chief justice hearings. On the following day, Thurmond continued to question Fortas on matters relating to law and order. One of the questions proved to be remarkably straightforward, yet Thurmond preceded it by quoting an incredibly lengthy extract from a speech entitled "Law, Order, and the High Court," which

Chief Justice John C. Bell of the Supreme Court of Pennsylvania had delivered ten days earlier. In what must have been an excruciating experience, Fortas waited patiently for over ten minutes for Thurmond to complete the extract, after which the senator asked if the nominee agreed "that the recent decisions of a majority of the Supreme Court of the United States, which shackle the police and courts and make it terribly difficult to protect society from crime and criminals, are among the principal reasons for the turmoil and near-revolutionary conditions which prevail in our country and especially in Washington." Finally, Fortas was able to respond, and his polite one-word answer—"No"—provoked an outburst of applause from some in the room, leading Chairman Eastland to call for order.[54] An unimpressed Thurmond commented, "I understood there had been recruiting actions to bring people here today which would try to cause such a demonstration, Mr. Chairman, but I did not believe it until I now see what is happening in the back of the room," prompting Senator Philip Hart to offer his clarification:

The Chairman: We are not going to have demonstrations at these committee hearings.

Senator Hart: The demonstration consisted of mild scattered applause for a statement that I would have applauded myself.

The Chairman: But you did not, Senator.

Senator Hart: Happily, I can speak for the record. My impression of the Bill of Rights is that it was intended to handcuff government. That is the whole purpose of the Bill of Rights. It might mean one thing—if you cannot hit somebody over the head or hold him for as long as you want—for a policeman but we are all better because you cannot.

Senator Thurmond: Mr. Chairman, I have not yielded, but I will be glad to yield to the senator from Michigan if he wishes to say any more.

The Chairman: Proceed.

Senator Thurmond: Would you care to say anything further?

Senator Hart: Yes. But I will resist the temptation, just the way Justice Fortas has.[55]

On August 3, a bruised Abe Fortas made a speech before the American College of Trial Lawyers, during which he claimed that the role of politicians in holding justices of the Supreme Court to account for their views ultimately threatens the judiciary's independence. As James A. Thorpe has noted, Fortas did not mention Thurmond by name but "the text of his speech left little doubt that the Justice was referring to the line of questioning followed by the Senator and the Committee."[56] The outbreak of applause for Fortas's "No," along with Hart's comments, suggested strongly that some were rooting for Fortas in his showdown with Thurmond, but the senator's personal goal of preventing Fortas's confirmation was still within reach. Despite concluding his interrogation by assuring Fortas that his questions "have not been the result of personal ill will toward you," Thurmond would soon find a new and surprisingly effective angle in his war on the Supreme Court, ensuring that his plan to make Abe Fortas the prize casualty would ultimately be fulfilled.[57]

9. NO ORDINARY TIME

The correspondence sent to Strom Thurmond's office during the summer of 1968 showcased a very mixed reaction to his *Mallory* outburst. While one writer declared that "I am ashamed for myself and my country that you are a United States Senator" and another claimed that "I think your actions concerning Justice Fortas are reprehensible," Arthur J. Ravenel Jr., a former South Carolina congressman and fellow defector to the Republican Party, offered "just a quick line to tell you what a great job you're doing on Abe Fortas—give him hell—he deserves it." Another writer requested a copy of "Senator Thurmond's recent speech," to which Thurmond responded with the unintentionally amusing clarification that "the discussion of the *Mallory* decision was not in a speech but rather in the form of my questioning of Justice Fortas in the Judiciary Committee."[1]

Thurmond maintained his view that no vacancy existed for an associate justice while Abe Fortas continued to serve on the Supreme Court. He skipped the July 20 Judiciary Committee hearing, during which senators questioned Homer Thornberry, the man President Johnson had chosen to replace Fortas following Senate approval of the latter's elevation to chief justice. Thurmond reappeared on July 22 but declined to question Thornberry on the grounds that "Chief Justice Warren has never submitted a firm resignation. The President of the United States has never made a firm acceptance. So in my opinion, there is no vacancy."[2] Following objections to Fortas's confirmation from Michael D. Jaffe of Liberty Lobby, who had also opposed Thurgood Marshall's confirmation the previous year, James J. Clancy, attorney for the executive board of the National Organization for the Citizens' Council for Decent Literature, Inc., began his testimony before the Committee, condemning the justices' inconsistent rulings on the obscenity issue and placing Abe Fortas at the center of the Supreme Court's supposedly liberal attitude toward "obscene" materials. Clancy highlighted a range of "sex paperback books" that the justices had scrutinized in 1966, with titles such as *Lust School, Orgy House, Flesh Pots, Passion Priestess, Sin Warden,* and *Flesh Avenger,* and also a fourteen-minute striptease film by the name of *0-7*—which Fortas had not considered obscene in *Schackman v. California* (1967)—and requested that "the individual Senators view and consider these materials before they cast their votes in this matter."[3]

Thurmond questioned Clancy with enthusiasm, exploring the manner in which the court's obscenity rulings might determine the nature and proliferation of the materials under discussion:

Senator Thurmond: Now, as long as the publishing houses who produce this smut material can get decisions like were handed down by the Supreme Court, will not this encourage them to go even further and further, and produce even more obscene material if it is possible to do so?

Mr. Clancy: Yes, sir. They have already done that. Not only that. They have gone further in the area of exhibition, as I have mentioned. Previously, these films would be sold in certain locations. Now they are going into the liquor, into the bars. You will see signs in Los Angeles which say "Girlie Films." In a bar, they have a little projector, and will throw these films on the wall. This has replaced the topless situation. This is one use of the film.[4]

On the issue of judicial interpretation, Clancy commented that the justices appeared to reach very different conclusions when studying the materials despite all of them applying the same judicial tests. He explained to Thurmond that Justices Warren, Brennan, Harlan, and Clark had all branded the *0-7* film as obscene, "but when it came to still photographs of the same type of activity, for example, a woman thrusting her vagina forward, or showing an invitation to sexual intercourse in still, Justice Brennan said that it was not obscene."[5] Clancy's testimony proved sufficiently compelling for Thurmond to undertake further investigations, the result of which became evident the following day, when members of the Judiciary Committee questioned Deputy Attorney General Warren Christopher. Thurmond accused the Justice Department of sending Christopher to the hearings as a deliberate ploy to defend Fortas from criticism, and raised the provocative question of whether Fortas had effectively exercised his right to silence under the Fifth Amendment by "refusing" to answer the Committee's questions, which Christopher refuted. But Thurmond's real agenda became clear when he declared to Christopher that he had sent a member of his staff to find out if obscene material was available to purchase on the streets of Washington, DC. As he made full use of the exhibits before him, Thurmond's line of questioning once again reached theatrical proportions:

> Isn't that disgraceful? Hand that down, let him see that. And here is another one entitled *Friendly Females.* Now, the last three that we just handed you were picked up by a member of my staff today, Tuesday, the 23rd of July, 1968. . . . Mr. Christopher, how much longer are the parents, the Christian people, the wholesome people, the right-thinking people, going to put up with this kind of thing? How much longer should they do it?[6]

In arguing that the justices were facilitating the distribution of obscene materials in various five-to-four decisions, Thurmond turned his questioning into a lengthy and impassioned plea for decency:

Senator Thurmond: Does it shock you that this material is so readily available in the city in which you live and in most of the cities of the nation?

Mr. Christopher: No, I am not surprised by it, Senator.

Senator Thurmond: You are not surprised by it, in view of the decisions by the Supreme Court permitting it to be sold?

Mr. Christopher: Were you asking a question, Senator?

Senator Thurmond: You say you are not surprised because the decisions of the Supreme Court permit it to be sold, or do you think the material is alright for the public to buy?

Mr. Christopher: I just answered, Senator, that I was not surprised to see that magazines like this were on sale at newsstands.

Senator Thurmond: I ask you why, upon what your answer is based. Why are you not surprised at this filthy, obscene material which you are now looking at, or were just a moment ago?

Mr. Christopher: Because it has become commonplace in our society, not only in the United States, but elsewhere for there to be magazines of a girlie character.

Senator Thurmond: And why is it commonplace? Because the Supreme Court has made it commonplace, hasn't it?

Mr. Christopher: No, I think the Supreme Court is only following the Constitution as best they know how to do so, sir.[7]

It is perhaps ironic that Thurmond's forceful condemnation of materials "of a girlie character" overshadowed James Clancy's valid, if not altogether powerful, arguments regarding the justices' inconsistent interpretation of "obscene" materials. The recurring problem of how to define obscenity was never more evident than in the *Jacobellis v. Ohio* decision of 1964, in which Justice Potter Stewart had declared, "I know it when I see it"—a phrase that became so infamous that Stewart later predicted it would be engraved on his tombstone. Justice Hugo Black later commented that "I understand that 'pornography' sounds bad. It really sounds bad. But I never have seen anybody who can say what it is."[8] While it was easy for Thurmond to prove that "this filthy, obscene material" was easily accessible, it was difficult for the Justice Department or anyone else to defend the court's obscenity decisions because, as Senator George Smathers of Florida explained to President Johnson by telephone, so few of these cases included written opinions. He might have added that the individual justices' vague and amusing statements on the obscenity issue could hardly be held up as examples of judicial restraint or sound constitutional theory, nor could Fortas's supporters use them to offset Thurmond's laughable claim that "the effect of the Fortas decisions has been to unleash a floodtide of pornography across the country."[9]

With the Fortas hearings generating huge publicity, the nation's press soon began focusing on the political relationship between Richard Nixon, the Republican presidential nominee, and South Carolina's senior senator. Harry Dent, chairman of the state's Republican Party and Thurmond's former advisor, had invited Nixon to South Carolina as far back as February 1966 to build on Barry Goldwater's victory in the five Deep South states in the 1964 presidential election. During the Republican National Convention in Miami, where Thurmond made his controversial "law and order" comments, Drew Pearson authored an article claiming that Nixon had given Thurmond an assurance that, as president, he would nominate Supreme Court justices "agreeable to the South," and also that Thurmond would "corral southern delegates" in return for an assurance that Nixon would not appoint a liberal northerner as his running mate. In the article, published in various newspapers, Pearson made light of South Carolina's ongoing war on the court by pointing out that "Thurmond is passionately interested in the Supreme Court [and] feels that the worst blot on American history in this century was the Supreme Court's desegregation ruling of 1954."[10]

Although Thurmond denied that a deal had taken place, he would later become candid about his discussions with Nixon in letters to constituents, telling one resident of Great Falls, South Carolina, that "I have discussed the matter of appointing men who are dedicated to the Constitution to the Supreme Court with Richard Nixon. I am confident that his election would mean much sounder appointments to the Supreme Court than we have had recently."[11] Whether or not an official agreement was reached, it was obvious to Thurmond and other Republicans that if they could debate the Fortas nomination throughout marathon hearings, they might succeed in denying the "lame duck" Johnson a sufficient period of time in which to make another nomination, allowing the incoming President Nixon to appoint a "sound" conservative chief justice.

Yet Thurmond was unimpressed by Nixon's inconsistent stand on the Fortas nomination during the summer of 1968. Despite criticizing the Supreme Court regularly, the Republican candidate refused to support unequivocally the Republican effort to prevent Fortas's confirmation. At a meeting of southern delegations, Nixon told the audience that he had urged President Johnson not to make the appointment, and offered his view that a chief justice "should represent the mandate of the future and not the Johnson mandate of the past." However, he then declared an interest in nominees "who are for civil rights" but who also understand the importance of law and order, adding, "I think we need that kind of balance on the courts."[12] Despite being knee-deep in pornographic material in his ongoing campaign against Abe Fortas, Thurmond was keen to ensure that the Fortas affair did not compromise Nixon's electability. In a letter to John Mitchell, Nixon's future attorney general, the senator made the case that "in my judgment, it hurts Nixon, particularly in the South, when he takes a stand and then the next day appears to back off from it. With regard to the Fortas matter, he should stick to his original statement that it is a matter for the Senate to decide." He also passed on the message to his supporters that Nixon considered the Fortas nomination "a matter for the Senate. . . . With a majority of the Republicans and some Democrats, this nomination will be stopped."[13]

The Republican candidate's "southern strategy" on the campaign trail and the senator's intensifying anti-obscenity drive proved to be a winning combination. With Nixon's groundbreaking presidential campaign kick-starting the Republican political takeover of the southern states, and Thurmond's "anti-smut" campaign highlighting an issue that would galvanize conservatives and influence the rise of the modern Religious Right, the Nixon-Thurmond partnership formed an unstoppable political force in US politics, with Abe Fortas becoming a symbol of liberal America gone out of control.[14]

During a press conference, a frustrated Lyndon Johnson compared the Fortas affair to the struggle over Woodrow Wilson's controversial nomination of Louis Brandeis to the Supreme Court in 1916, thus making the unspoken suggestion that anti-Semitism was behind southern senators' obstructionism. Significantly, some Fortas supporters accused both Thurmond and Hollings of anti-Semitism.[15] Alan Banov, special assistant to Senator Hollings, responded to one constituent to explain that Hollings was "very concerned" over accusations of anti-Semitism. He argued that "Senator Hollings is *not* and has *never* been anti-Semitic. He has long had many close Jewish friends and supporters, including myself. . . . There are many reasons for opposing the appointment of Fortas, and the Senator's own rationale is clearly delineated in his speech. That speech . . . cannot by any measure of imagination be construed as anti-Semitic. I, as a Jew, wanted to make that clear to you in this letter."[16]

The injection of anti-Semitism accusations into the Fortas affair recalled Olin Johnston's defense against the same charge during his opposition to President Eisenhower's nomination of Simon Sobeloff to the Fourth Circuit Court of Appeals in 1956.[17] However, on this occasion, there were unexpected and further-reaching implications. According to Bruce Allen Murphy, one Jewish leader telephoned Hollings to make a halfhearted attempt to request support for Fortas's confirmation, only for Hollings to turn him down. Undeterred, he asked the senator if he would arrange to send fifty F-4 Phantom jets to Israel. When the news reached Lyndon Johnson that Jewish leaders were now bargaining for arms to Israel rather than corralling support for Fortas—whose devoutness as a Jew was questioned, particularly as he had "married outside his faith"—one presidential aide made the desperate, but apparently serious, suggestion that a picture of Fortas in a yarmulke might win over some prominent Jews.[18] Meanwhile, Johnson's suggestions of anti-Semitism failed to discourage Thurmond, who responded simply by announcing that "if President Johnson would take the necessary time to review four films—*Flaming Creatures; 0–7; 0–12*, and *0–14*—or any of them, it would be interesting to know if he still favors Mr. Fortas's appointment." Thurmond had certainly been proactive in sharing the material with other senators: following James Clancy's testimony before the committee, he had been arranging regular screenings of the material, dubbed the "Fortas Film Festival"—a move that Johnson claimed to James Eastland was making senators look ridiculous.[19]

With an imminent Senate filibuster, the Fortas nomination was now a major political event. On the other side of the Atlantic, in London, the *Times* reported that "Senator Ernest Hollings (Democrat, South Carolina) says that 16 southern Democrats are ready to oppose the nomination [and] with the 18 Republicans claimed by Senator Robert Griffin, of Michigan, this would be enough to thwart any attempt to block a filibuster." The Republican determination to obstruct Fortas's nomination would only develop further momentum after Senator Gordon Allott of Colorado alleged that Fortas had played a part in amending an appropriations bill to provide for Secret Service protection of presidential candidates. While the charges appeared to lack concrete evidence, the allegation did remind senators of the unusually close relationship between the nominee and the president.[20]

Far more serious was the revelation, leaked by Bob Griffin to the press, that Fortas had been paid $15,000 to teach a law school course at American University's Washington College of Law. Inevitably, the Judiciary Committee asked Fortas to reappear before them. Facing the dilemma of whether to appear for further hearings and look as though he was there to answer for wrongdoing, or simply not appear at all and risk looking as though he had something to hide, Fortas opted for the latter move, which dented his credibility and offended members of the committee. It seemed that those willing to defend Fortas publicly were thin on the ground. As Thurmond commented in a letter to a constituent, "In my judgment, had any member of the Executive Department been able to testify in such a way [as] to help Justice Fortas, they would surely have done so. Instead, they allowed damaging evidence to go unrefuted. While their failure to appear does not 'prove' the allegations, I believe it is reasonable to infer that it indicates they were in no position to contradict the charges."[21] In the absence of anyone offering to respond to the accusation of financial impropriety with regard to American University, Thurmond was free to demand further hearings as part of his anti-obscenity crusade.

President Johnson tried to pressure James Eastland to conclude the hearings, but Eastland claimed that Thurmond's determination to block a vote on the nomination in order to call further witnesses made it impossible for him to get the nomination out of committee. Philip Hart's own attempt to end the hearings proved equally unsuccessful. Having prepared a letter to Eastland with the intention of generating a sufficient number of signatures to persuade the Mississippian to allow the nomination to go to the full Senate, Hart came up one signature short. Committee members Thomas Dodd of Connecticut, Hiram Fong of Hawaii, and, significantly, Republican leader Everett Dirksen of Illinois, all turned down his request that they sign the letter.[22]

With Fortas refusing to make another appearance before the committee, Thurmond wasted no time in calling Dean B. J. Tennery of Washington College of Law. His interrogation of Tennery revealed that donations from high-profile business leaders who "could easily become involved in any number of suits which might reach the Supreme Court" had ultimately provided Fortas's honorarium. In the words of Bruce Allen Murphy, "the new set of hearings was now Strom Thurmond's show . . . it was Thurmond who would become Abe Fortas's prosecutor. And destroying the nomination to him meant destroying the man himself." A cartoon in *The State,* showing the senator kneeling on a casket, wielding a hammer, with the caption "A Coupla More Nails Should Do It," summed up the public perception of Strom Thurmond by September 1968. Everett Dirksen, Johnson's crucial Republican ally in the Senate, provided one additional nail by withdrawing his support, conceding that the "dirty movies" had damaged Fortas's credibility. Nonetheless, Jim Newton has argued persuasively that the Fortas episode threatened to reveal Dirksen's waning influence over his party in the Senate, while Murphy has cited, in particular, "the upstart Griffin's challenge to [Dirksen's] authority as a major factor in sealing Fortas's fate."[23]

As Lyndon Johnson was discovering, the Senate was now a strikingly different institution from the one he had taken over as majority leader in 1955. Concerned that his chances of building a filibuster-proof majority were ebbing away with alarming speed, he resorted to vintage bargaining methods as a last-minute effort to whip up support for Fortas's confirmation. As illustrated by the example of his nominations of Robert Hemphill and Charles Simons to South Carolina's Eastern District, the president was masterful in his understanding of individual congressmen and their wants and needs, particularly when it came to southern requests for nominations of favored individuals to influential positions. In addition to agreeing to appoint a postmaster as a favor to Senator Russell Long of Louisiana, the president agreed to make a federal Court of Appeals appointment in Alabama in order to curry favor with Senator Lister Hill. Although Johnson's tactics had proved effective on countless occasions, his gestures proved woefully insufficient to save Abe Fortas in the complicated political climate of 1968. Despite the sudden renewal of the president's support for Arkansas's milk industry, Senator John McClellan voted against Fortas in committee, while Justice Hugo Black, whose rivalry with Abe Fortas has been well-documented, succeeded in discouraging Lister Hill, his old friend from Alabama, from voting to confirm Fortas in the Senate.[24]

The death rattle sounded when Senator Richard Russell of Georgia, Johnson's long-time friend and mentor, and leader of the Senate's southern Democratic bloc, fell out with the president after growing tired of Johnson's repeated failure to nominate an old Russell family friend to Georgia's Southern District. Interpreting Johnson's reluctance to nominate Alexander Lawrence as an arm-twisting tactic to guarantee his support for Fortas, the Georgian became so enraged that he told the president by letter that "in view of the long delay in handling and the juggling of this nomination, I consider myself released from any statement I may have made to you with respect to your nominations," after which he telephoned Bob Griffin to declare his support for the anti-Fortas campaign. In announcing that he would oppose Fortas, Russell referred to the $15,000 payment for the American University lectures as "an exorbitant and unreasonable honorarium, even had it come from the resources of the school, but the evidence developed the fact that this money was raised by Fortas's former law partner from a handful of the wealthiest clients of this firm, who have some interest, direct or indirect, in almost every decision touching the economy of the country." Johnson never succeeded in repairing their friendship.[25]

When a motion to bring the Senate filibuster to a close and move the Fortas nomination to a vote failed to get the necessary two-thirds majority, Abe Fortas wrote to the president and formally requested that he withdraw his name from consideration. Johnson reluctantly complied, making Abe Fortas the first unsuccessful nominee for a seat on the US Supreme Court since President Herbert Hoover's ill-fated nomination of John J. Parker in 1930.[26] With Homer Thornberry's nomination now a moot point, Fortas would continue to serve on the court, as an associate justice, while the president resumed the process of selecting a new chief justice from scratch. In addition to the question of who the next nominee would be, there was now a much more serious question concerning which president would make the nomination.

Mark Silverstein has attributed the Fortas nomination failure in part to the decline of the "whales and minnows" system of seniority in Congress. The congressional elections of the 1960s had introduced a new breed of "minnow" senators—with modern political perspectives of US society, and a closer relationship with special interests—which reduced considerably the impact of Richard Russell, Everett Dirksen, and others who had achieved "whale" status through the Senate's seniority system. This argument suggests that the Fortas affair signposted the decline of a rigid hierarchical Senate, resulting in the emergence of a volatile and unpredictable process for confirming judicial nominations. The fact that Lyndon Johnson, with his traditional understanding of the structure of Congress, "simply could not imagine that a band of renegade young Republican Senators would consider defying Everett Dirksen or that Richard Russell was no longer the behind-the-scenes master of the Senate" offers yet another in the long list of reasons for his failure to promote Fortas to the chief justiceship.[27]

On the other hand, the Senate's rigid hierarchical structure had never compromised the South Carolina senators' dogged determination. As previous chapters have shown, the southern "whale" Richard Russell proved no more effective in keeping Olin Johnston and Strom Thurmond in check during the years leading up to the Fortas debacle. The South Carolinians exercised little restraint—and little regard for what Silverstein describes as the "timeworn patterns of Senate decorum and behavior"—when obstructing Eisenhower's nomination of Simon Sobeloff (to the Fourth Circuit), Kennedy's nomination of Thurgood Marshall (to the Second Circuit), and Johnson's nominations of Marshall and Abe Fortas as associate justices of the Supreme Court.[28] Joseph Crespino has noted that when Thurmond arrived in the Senate in 1955, he "chafed at the Senate custom of newcomers lying low" and soon developed a frosty relationship with Lyndon Johnson, then Democratic majority leader. His filibuster against the 1957 Civil Rights Act serves as a particularly potent reminder of his failure to show deference to Richard Russell as leader of the southern bloc, and it is unlikely that Lyndon Johnson would have been surprised by Everett Dirksen's admission that neither he nor James Eastland could "straighten out Strom" during the escalation of tensions during the Fortas hearings.[29]

It could be argued, however, that Senate "whales" were able to minimize dissent rather than stamp it out completely. In this regard, the fact that South Carolina elected particularly cantankerous senators who were largely unmoved by, if not immune to, the Senate's hierarchical tradition does not suggest a failure on the part of Russell, Dirksen, or Lyndon Johnson. Some southern Senators proved more open to the influence of presidents than others, as evidenced by Johnson's cordial relationship with James Eastland, and his success in convincing Eastland, John Stennis, and John McClellan to miss the final vote on Thurgood Marshall's confirmation in 1967. The events of each controversial nomination suggest that Presidents and Senate "whales" may have accepted the behavior of South Carolina's senators as inevitable, constituting a level of damage worth accepting if it meant avoiding the proliferation of dissent elsewhere in the Senate. It is notable that no senator from any other southern state pursued a public one-man crusade against a judicial nominee throughout this era.

The emergence of a new wave of Republican senators who did not identify as "minnows" clearly did contribute to the outcome of the Fortas affair, but South Carolina's role in the breakdown of senatorial seniority, at least with regard to judicial nominations, had begun long before the mid-1960s. In fact, the traditions of seniority and hierarchy might actually have facilitated their uncompromising behavior. As part of the "whales and minnows" system, presidents would deal first and foremost with the Chairman of the Judiciary Committee when attempting to speed action on their nominations and ensure safe passage to confirmation for their nominees. James Eastland, a Deep South Democrat who shared the South Carolina senators' segregationist ideology, allowed Johnston and Thurmond free reign in waging war on the court while at the same time maintaining cordial relationships with presidents through his own dignified and diplomatic conduct as Judiciary Committee chairman. Had either Johnston or Thurmond assumed the position of chairman, it is highly unlikely that their actions would have resulted in explosive consequences for the judicial nominations process.

Strom Thurmond had long possessed the necessary drive, determination, and ability to take advantage of complicated circumstances in a changing political environment. With his victory in the Fortas debacle, he proved that senators could still sabotage a Supreme Court nomination after nearly forty years of relatively smooth confirmations. It also ensured, in spectacularly provocative southern anti-Supreme Court rhetoric, that South Carolina's role in the judicial nominations process was far more evident in 1968 than at any time since the state's delegation had condemned *Brown v. Board of Education* in 1954. Despite declaring "I feel that this is a great victory for our country" in letters to constituents, Thurmond did not appear satisfied by his hard-won effort, telling the Senate, "I suggest Mr. Fortas now go a step further and resign from the Court for the sake of good government."[30] As the following chapter will illustrate, this proved to be a prescient remark.

Given Thurmond's influential role in the Fortas affair throughout the summer of 1968, it seems fitting that Richard Nixon was campaigning in South Carolina in the days leading up to President Johnson's official withdrawal of Fortas's nomination for chief justice. During stops in Greenville and Spartanburg, Nixon remained focused on his strategy of winning over the South, without adding his voice to the Republicans' gloating over Fortas. As the *New York Times* reported, "under the watchful eye of Senator Strom Thurmond . . . the Republican presidential nominee stuck to the themes that stir the Southland—law and order, the Vietnam War, the alleged collapse of American prestige abroad, and the need for a change in Washington."[31]

Nixon won the presidency of the United States on November 5, 1968. Although his margin of victory over the Democratic candidate, Vice President Hubert H. Humphrey, constituted only 511,944 votes, the Republican "southern strategy" paid off handsomely, with Nixon winning the states of Virginia, North Carolina, South Carolina, Tennessee, Kentucky, Oklahoma, and Florida, with Alabama Governor George Wallace's independent segregationist campaign winning over the remaining Deep South states, and Humphrey securing victory in only Texas and West Virginia.[32]

On the same day that Nixon triumphed in the nation, Fritz Hollings won reelection in South Carolina against a second challenge from Marshall Parker. Having beaten Parker by 11,753 votes in 1966, he increased his majority to a more convincing 155,280 votes two years on. Although Parker had attempted to characterize Hollings's caution over Fortas as "talking out of both sides of his mouth," the senator had succeeded in cultivating a masterful demonstration of South Carolina independence during his first two years in the Senate, revealing a liberal tendency in his support for the state's textile industry but also a conservative streak in his opposition to Lyndon Johnson's nominations of Thurgood Marshall as an associate justice and Abe Fortas as chief justice. With his well-crafted defiance of the Democratic establishment, and a well-developed understanding of South Carolina's conservative white voters, Hollings neutralized Parker's attempt to link him with the liberal figure of Hubert Humphrey. Yet, at the same time, Hollings did benefit from Humphrey's popularity among black South Carolinians: the *New York Times* noted that while Hollings's vote against Marshall had angered African Americans, there remained "considerable enthusiasm for Mr. Humphrey in the Negro community in South Carolina, and some leaders have dropped opposition to Mr. Hollings to ensure that no votes are lost for the Vice President."[33]

Hollings's first two years in the Senate, and his role in facilitating South Carolina's peaceful desegregation, provided ample evidence of a strong political contrast with Strom Thurmond. But the Fortas affair demonstrated yet again the difficulty in finding a meaningful ideological difference between the two Senators when it came to South Carolina's war on the Supreme Court. While Hollings claimed on July 18, 1968, that "the Warren Court has not followed the principle of judicial restraint . . . It has substituted the principle of judicial activism," Thurmond, two months later, outlined the view that "judicial activism is one of the most dangerous legal concepts to appear on the scene in this century. The Supreme Court is supposed to interpret the law rather than create new law by amending the Constitution as it did in the *Miranda* case."[34]

Within a very short space of time, Hollings had established a conservative record on the nomination of Supreme Court justices that he would develop throughout his lengthy career in the Senate. As he explained in a 1968 newsletter when discussing the court's judicial philosophy, "since the Justices do not run for office, how do the people 'get at' the judges? How can this wrong be righted? The only way is for the United States to withhold confirmation."[35] These words suggested strongly that Hollings understood only too well that the Supreme Court nomination process was, and remains today—years after the speeches, legislative efforts, and provocative interrogations pursued by Thurmond and

Olin Johnston—the ultimate political arena for questioning, challenging, and scrutinizing the power of the US Supreme Court.

Thurmond's victory in the Fortas affair signposted a turning point in South Carolina's war on the court, for two reasons. Firstly, his tactics shifted from a defensive/obstructive role to an outright attempt to determine the selection of a new chief justice: not content simply to stop Abe Fortas from succeeding Earl Warren, Thurmond continued hammering the Johnson administration in a bid to ensure that Nixon, his political ally, made the next appointment. Secondly, the court's record of exercising raw judicial power in a wide range of policy areas over the preceding decade allowed Thurmond to broaden and deepen his attack. By shifting the focus away from race and the "southern way of life" and emphasizing constitutional interpretation, crime and punishment, and decency and obscenity, the South Carolinian was able, for the first time since 1955, to make a convincing case for the use of senatorial "advice and consent" to restrict the Supreme Court's power and political influence through the judicial nominations process. His tactics proved considerably more successful than those employed by southerners in the 1950s, when they were unable to convince their fellow senators that the comparatively noncontroversial Eisenhower nominees offered an equally dangerous threat. The fact that the southern objections had rested so heavily on regional interests in a period prior to the court's rulings in *Baker, Engel, Miranda,* and *Schackman* proved to be a further obstacle in overcoming their limited numbers in the Senate. The defeat of Fortas and the subsequent Republican success in preventing Johnson from naming the new chief constituted a groundbreaking victory for conservative America. South Carolina could now build on this achievement following the inauguration of the new Republican president, who remained keen to build on his support in the South. Thurmond's role in the Fortas rejection, and his influence in securing the Republican presidential victory, suggested strongly that South Carolina voices would now be heard in the selection process for Richard Nixon's nominations to the Supreme Court.[36]

The failure of Abe Fortas's chief justice nomination constituted another disaster for Lyndon Johnson in the final year of his presidency, but the outgoing president had not yet given up. Returning to Earl Warren's suggestion from nine months previously, the president began giving serious consideration to naming Arthur Goldberg as an interim chief justice in a recess appointment as part of a last-ditch attempt to take Warren out of the equation and prevent Richard Nixon from naming Warren's successor. Ironically, Johnson had lured Goldberg away from the court in 1965 with the United Nations offer in order to create a vacancy for Abe Fortas. Goldberg was now happy to accept the post of chief justice, but Johnson soon reconsidered the plan when an aide discovered a statement in which the president had criticized recess appointments.[37] Nonetheless, Johnson continued weighing up his chances of making another nomination. Briefly, he flirted with the idea of bringing back former justice Tom Clark, who had vacated the Supreme Court the previous year in order to avoid a conflict of interest with his son, the newly appointed attorney general, Ramsey Clark. Following the suggestion of Johnson's friend Willard Deason that the nation would have "a glow in its heart at the thought of the son now stepping down in deference to the father," Johnson telephoned Everett Dirksen, whom he still considered his only realistic point of contact among Senate Republicans, and floated the idea of Clark's return, stressing that the appointment of the elder Clark as chief justice would be an attractive prospect for southern Democrats and would also remove accusations of Republican opportunism:

LBJ: It would unify the country and wouldn't look like you all are playing politics trying to get a justice. You're going to get Black, he's eighty-four, and he can't go on, and nobody on the court really wants him to act because they don't know the stability there, they've got a problem.

Dirksen: Yeah.

LBJ: You've got Douglas, who's got a bad heart. You've got, uh, Harlan, who's got eye trouble. So you got three right there.

Dirksen: That's right.

LBJ: But a lot of folks feel that the Griffin effort was a pure political effort, particularly in the light of what you said. And he said nobody should serve, that the lame duck shouldn't appoint anybody.

Dirksen: Yeah, right.

LBJ: Now, if we took Clark, who just retired on account of his son and sent him up there as chief, instead of letting Warren go on acting . . . uh, the southerners all urge me to name Clark as chief because of his crime record and so on and so forth. McClellan and Eastland and them thought that he would be good.

Dirksen: Yeah.

LBJ: I would have to get me a new attorney general.[38]

Despite suggesting that he would support a Clark nomination, Dirksen soon became skeptical of his party's accepting any Johnson nominee, regardless of qualifications or suitability, while James Eastland confirmed to White House assistant Mike Manatos that a "flat Republican policy of opposition" had indeed taken hold. Thurmond, having spent little time celebrating his victory in the Fortas affair, was now opposing a new batch of five nominees for the lower courts, including Texas judge and longtime Johnson associate, Barefoot Sanders. On December 10, 1968, the *New York Times* published Thurmond's claim that Johnson's request for Congress to return for a "special session" was motivated not so much by the president's interest in ratifying the Nuclear Non-Proliferation Treaty, signed in July, but his determination to get Arthur Goldberg back onto the Supreme Court.[39] On the very same day, Johnson revealed to Chief Justice Warren—who was likewise inclined to prevent Nixon from naming his successor—the true extent of the Republican pressure on him to avoid making a further appointment, claiming that Thurmond was now attempting to use the lower court nominations as a bargaining chip to secure Nixon the opportunity to name the new chief:

LBJ: Strom Thurmond tried to get me, he agreed to confirm some of our recommendations, like Barefoot Sanders to the District Court, Circuit Court—

Warren: Yes.

LBJ: —if I agreed not to name an interim chief justice, recess appointment, or if I would agree not to send one up from January the third to the twentieth.

Warren: Mm-hm.

LBJ: I told him I couldn't do that, that, uh, I couldn't trade off the powers of the presidency for the confirmation of anybody.

Warren: Of course you couldn't.[40]

Claiming, "I don't wanna have a tragedy as we did in the case of Abe," Johnson explained to Warren that he remained unconvinced that a Goldberg nomination would win over a majority of senators: "People like Griffin and people like Fulbright and others who opposed Abe have said they would accept Arthur, but I have never felt that Russell and the southern bloc and the Republican bloc would ever let him be confirmed, and Dirksen in effect told me that."[41] In the event, Johnson nominated neither Goldberg nor Clark as an interim chief justice. President-Elect Nixon asked Warren to continue serving as chief justice until June 1969, allowing the new president plenty of time to make a careful selection of a "strict constructionist" nominee, as he had promised throughout his campaign. The intensity of the Republican determination to deny Lyndon Johnson the chief justice appointment was underlined three days after Nixon's inauguration, when, in yet another victory for Thurmond, the new president withdrew the nominations of Barefoot Sanders and the other four lower court judges.[42]

In announcing that he would "ordinarily" have made another chief justice nomination but finally decided not to—as Warren's continued service would be in the best interests of government for the time being—a tired and dejected Lyndon Johnson noted that "these are not ordinary times."[43]

10. "THE LITTLE FELLA THAT STUTTERED"

Republican Senator Marlow Cook of Kentucky spoke for many southerners when, in one of the more overlooked speeches in the history of the US Senate, he claimed that senators had effectively created a "new standard" of qualification when considering President Richard Nixon's nomination of Judge Clement F. Haynsworth for a vacancy on the US Supreme Court. With African American groups and organized labor criticizing the nominee's conservative legal record, Haynsworth was certainly one of the more controversial figures nominated to the nation's highest court. Yet skeptical senators chose to focus on accusations of his ethical impropriety, provoking some such as Cook to respond angrily with the claim that the southern nominee was guilty of nothing other than being southern.

After reminding his colleagues that none of them ever proved any charges of ethical impropriety, Cook claimed in his speech that their rejection of Haynsworth constituted "a low point in the history of the United States Senate." Perhaps as a gesture of how firmly he believed his colleagues to have created "new standards" in the judicial nomination process, Cook offered what he referred to as his "Haynsworth test," claiming, "I have tried to exercise my individual judgment in advising and consenting to presidential nominees to the Supreme Court in a responsible manner. These guidelines, I now leave behind. A fitting epilogue, I hope, to an unforgettable era in the history of the Supreme Court."[1]

The outcome of the Haynsworth nomination proved disappointing for two southern senators in particular—South Carolina's Strom Thurmond and Ernest "Fritz" Hollings, both of whom had been satisfied with the nominee's capability and impeccable conservative track record. Perhaps more importantly, President Nixon had chosen a judge from their home state. The existing literature suggests agreement among scholars that Nixon selected Haynsworth as a calculated move to "repay" the South for his 1968 election victory and also encourage support for his 1972 reelection, but the fact that Nixon's first southern nominee happened to be from South Carolina only reinforces Thurmond's significance in bringing Nixon to the White House.[2] What makes this story somewhat unique is the fact that Democrat Fritz Hollings was ultimately the primary sponsor of the Republican nominee, rather than Thurmond, the state's Republican senator.

Thurmond had been the chief antagonist in the 1967 Marshall hearings and the 1968 Fortas chief justice hearings, and, with his leading role in denying Lyndon Johnson the opportunity to replace the outgoing Earl Warren, the South Carolinian could claim a small, indirect influence in Nixon's eventual appointment, in the spring of 1969, of "strict constructionist" Judge Warren Burger as the new chief justice of the United States. By contrast, Hollings had maintained a low profile in the process, choosing the wording of his public statements carefully and ensuring that each position taken would not harm his political future as a Deep South Democrat. With the Haynsworth nomination, Hollings adopted a more interventionist role in the process, with the intention of establishing a sound conservative ideology on the court while also guaranteeing South Carolina's representation on that body for the first time since 1943, when Justice (later Governor) James Byrnes departed the court to head Franklin Roosevelt's Office of Economic Stabilization.[3]

As noted previously, many studies have focused on presidential failure in the judicial nomination process. Richard Watson's views on Herbert Hoover, Mark Silverstein's comments on Lyndon Johnson, and John Maltese's reflections on Richard Nixon would appear to suggest that if a scholarly consensus does exist regarding the question of responsibility when a Supreme Court nomination fails, it is that the president is usually the one to blame, either because he made his selection poorly or because he failed to marshal a sufficient army of supporters to ensure confirmation.[4] Rarely, if ever, has a scholarly work examined the failure of a Supreme Court nomination by focusing on the intentions, actions, and ideologies of the two senators from the nominee's home state, and never has a previous study examined such a failure within the context of that state's history in the nomination process.

With Nixon's nomination of Haynsworth unleashing a more outspoken Fritz Hollings—happy to dive head-first into a heated debate over a controversial nominee—Strom Thurmond began something of a mellowing process during the first term of the Nixon presidency. With President Ronald Reagan eventually building on Nixon's Court strategy by nominating a string of conservative judges, with whom the aging Republican senator had no quarrel, Thurmond would never again, after 1968, find a reason to unleash his inner rage as a participant in the nomination process. Thanks to his dedicated participation in the conservative movement of the late twentieth century, he had finally succeeded in establishing a nomination process that produced the very brand of Supreme Court justice he had always longed for. There would be a far less happy outcome for his colleague's involvement in the Haynsworth nomination: the Senate's rejection of the nominee, by only five votes, left a sour taste in Hollings's mouth, and he would remind his fellow senators of their treatment of Haynsworth eighteen years later during the tense debate over Ronald Reagan's controversial nomination of Robert Bork. Hollings appeared to have mellowed very little when recalling the Haynsworth episode in his memoirs in 2008, concluding that "the country was denied the services of a first-rate jurist on the Supreme Court. Bare-knuckled politics had triumphed over substance."[5]

As both Mark Silverstein and Joseph Crespino have noted, the intense debate over the Supreme Court's role in US society proved vital to Thurmond and other Republican politicians in their electoral success from the mid-1960s, and this chapter serves as another reminder of South Carolina's prominent role in that complicated story.

A Republican Senate filibuster succeeded in destroying President Lyndon Johnson's attempt to elevate Justice Abe Fortas to the chief justiceship, with Senators Strom Thurmond and Bob Griffin bringing the Johnson presidency to a tragic and bitter end by denying Johnson the opportunity to name a new chief justice. The Republican success was only emphasized by the fact that the Fortas affair provoked an outbreak of debate amongst scholars and politicians over the Senate's role in confirming Supreme Court justices.[6] Among the early examples of the debate is a pair of articles published in *Prospectus* in the aftermath of the Fortas debacle, in which the two senators from Michigan—the aforementioned Griffin, a Republican, and Philip Hart, a Democrat and member of the Senate Judiciary Committee—put forward two opposing arguments. Griffin, in his article, "The Broad Role," outlined his opposition to the Fortas nomination by opening with Alexis de Tocqueville's comment that "if the Supreme Court is ever composed of imprudent men or bad citizens, the union may be plunged into anarchy or civil war," before arguing that only a "broader and more purposive interpretation" of the Senate's power to "advise and consent" on Supreme Court nominations will ensure the "quality" of the nine justices.

The inimitable Hart, who had continued to support Abe Fortas's nomination as Lyndon Johnson's Democratic coalition in the Senate was falling apart, argued in his article, "The Discriminating Role," that the "broader" role of the Senate had never prevented the confirmation of "mediocrities whose names are better left unremembered." While Griffin believed that the Senate's power of advice and consent, as covered by Article II, Section 2, of the US Constitution, "is not only real but is at least as important as the power of the President to nominate," Hart declared, with characteristic understatement, "I appear to be advocating that the Senate continue to muddle along as it has done in the past: approving most appointments, but occasionally being cantankerous." The friendly debate between the two Michiganders illustrates clearly the polarizing effect of the Fortas rejection on the Senate's role in the nomination process, with senators adopting markedly different perspectives on their personal and professional responsibilities in consenting to, or denying, a presidential selection of a Supreme Court justice.[7]

South Carolina's significance during this pivotal era was perhaps more evident than usual during the remarkable month of May 1969, during which four highly important developments occurred. The first was the dramatic decision of a sitting Justice to resign from the Supreme Court. Thurmond had declared to the Senate the previous October his recommendation that Justice Abe Fortas resign from the court "for the sake of good government" after the Senate rejected his chief justice nomination. Following an investigation aided by the Justice Department under the leadership of John Mitchell, Nixon's attorney general, the revelation that Wall Street financier Louis Wolfson had been paying Fortas a $20,000 retainer caused a storm in Washington, DC, when published in *Life* magazine. Chief Justice Warren proved successful in persuading Fortas to resign from the court as a means of avoiding impeachment proceedings. Seven months after facing down Dixie in his now legendary confirmation hearings, Abe Fortas submitted his resignation from the court on May 4, 1969, marking yet another victory for Thurmond and the Nixon administration.[8]

The second event provided another example of Thurmond's growing confidence. Having successfully prevented an undesirable liberal nominee from reaching the chief justiceship, Thurmond attempted, in May 1969, to use his influence to remove a serving justice by calling for the impeachment of William

O. Douglas—long associated with the court's liberal bloc—by criticizing Douglas's role as chairman of the "overtly political" Center for the Study of Democratic Institutions, and his role as director of the Parvin Foundation, which multimillionaire Albert Parvin had supposedly created as "a front for gambling enterprises and persons of anti-democratic character." In a clear indication that he was using Fortas's resignation as an opportunity to push for the removal of another liberal justice to create space for Nixon to make another nomination, Thurmond, according to the *New York Times,* believed that "the case of Abe Fortas, who recently resigned as an Associate Justice, and the controversy over Justice Douglas's connection with the Parvin Foundation 'are intertwined.'" On the very same day that he made this claim, Thurmond explained in a letter to Claude Ragsdale Jr. that "Fortas should never have been appointed by Lyndon Johnson to be Associate Justice and I am glad that we stopped him becoming Chief Justice in that he is now off the Court altogether. Douglas should also get off." Never one to drift unexpectedly into modesty or self-doubt, Thurmond claimed in another letter that "I am more convinced than ever that my position was correct in strongly opposing [Fortas] and helping to defeat him." Smelling blood, some conservatives targeted Justice William Brennan, another well-established liberal force on the court, for a real estate investment he had made with Fortas and some lower court judges. Brennan responded by giving up all activities outside his duties on the Supreme Court, including not only the real estate investment but also his future speaking plans and a part-time teaching post at New York University.[9]

With the third notable event to take place during May 1969, Thurmond reaped the benefits of his hard work in preventing Abe Fortas from becoming chief justice. Southern members of the Senate Judiciary Committee praised Nixon's appointment of Judge Warren Burger as the new chief justice of the United States, with John McClellan of Arkansas claiming that Burger's record on the US Court of Appeals for the District of Columbia Circuit "commends itself to the endorsement of the American people and American jurisprudence," and Sam Ervin of North Carolina arguing that the appointment "affords us the guarantee that we will have to return to constitutional government in the United States as far as the Supreme Court is concerned." Adding his voice to the chorus of praise, which culminated in the committee's unanimous vote of approval, a delighted Thurmond told a constituent that "the President has made an excellent choice in Judge Burger as Chief Justice. Hopefully, with him in this vital position, we will see a marked improvement in the direction of the Court."[10]

The Burger nomination marked the first occasion on which Thurmond seemed genuinely satisfied with a presidential nomination of a Supreme Court justice since his arrival in the Senate in 1955. His role in the nomination process, as he had come to see it, was no longer a simple matter of opposing nominees with dangerous liberal ideologies: by 1968, his influence had advanced markedly through his invaluable contribution to Richard Nixon's "southern strategy" and his prominent role in galvanizing conservative forces during a period of civil unrest. With Earl Warren gone and Warren Burger in place, the impact of Strom Thurmond and South Carolina's Republican movement in influencing the Supreme Court's lineup was undeniable.

The fourth and final reason for the significance of May 1969 was the manner in which Fritz Hollings, rather than Thurmond, influenced Nixon's selection of a South Carolina judge. As Fortas's resignation required Nixon to fill another vacancy, Hollings saw an opportunity to mention the name of Clement Furman Haynsworth, of the US Court of Appeals for the Fourth Circuit, during a meeting with the president at the White House on May 28. Given the junior senator's low-key involvement in the nomination process prior to May 1969, it might have seemed more logical that Thurmond, with his rapidly inflating confidence, would have influenced Nixon's selection of a South Carolinian, particularly as he had led the campaign against Fortas and attempted to trigger Douglas's impeachment, while also pushing for the appointment of a "strict constructionist" in the form of Burger. Yet the Nixon administration welcomed Hollings's recommendation of Judge Haynsworth: by linking the South Carolina nominee to the charismatic Hollings rather than the abrasive Thurmond, the administration hoped to avoid resurrecting Drew Pearson's accusations of the political "deal" that allegedly took place between Nixon and Thurmond during the previous year's Republican National Convention in Miami. Hollings believed that Thurmond's controversial reputation had become problematic for the Republican Party, claiming in his memoirs that "we had some fine judges in South Carolina, but Thurmond at this point was no help in influencing the decision process. His zealousness over the years had alienated even some fellow Republicans. They worried that he was hurting the image of the GOP."[11]

Nonetheless, Thurmond was not shy in offering Nixon his own preference for a South Carolina nominee, namely, former governor and senator Donald

S. Russell, who had famously appointed himself to the late Olin D. Johnston's senate seat before Fritz Hollings defeated him in the 1966 Democratic primary. By Thurmond's logic, Nixon's appointment of a conservative Democrat such as Russell would actually prove more useful to Republican Party growth in South Carolina than the appointment of the Republican Clement Haynsworth. As John Spratt, then president of the South Carolina State Bar, recalls:

> [Thurmond] knew that the Republican Party, if it was going to succeed in South Carolina, didn't need more country club Republicans and aristocratic types, they needed down-to-earth people, like he was. So he didn't come out for [Haynsworth]. Instead, he came out for Donald Russell. And Donald Russell was a wonderful guy, smart as he could be . . . . He was smart, he was very conservative, and everybody in the Senate had the highest regard for him, Democrat and Republican.[12]

Thurmond's disagreement with Hollings over the best candidate to fill the Fortas vacancy suggests that the party dimension was more relevant than ever in influencing the attitudes of South Carolina's senators in the nomination of Supreme Court justices. With each man keeping an eye on the dramatic development of a two-party system in their state, the Republican Thurmond endorsed the segregationist Democrat Russell in order to build on the Republican presence in South Carolina, while the Democrat Hollings's decision to throw his weight behind the Republican Clement Haynsworth seemed a logical tactic in preventing the defection of white conservative voters from the Democratic Party. Hollings later claimed that the Nixon administration preferred Haynsworth not only for his Republican Party affiliation, but also because the White House feared that Thurmond's involvement "would complicate its efforts to promote a judge from South Carolina to the Supreme Court." As Hollings recalls:

> It appeared that they got the message to him to be circumspect, lie low, and essentially confine himself in the Senate to written comments other than a few perfunctory remarks. I would handle the nomination . . . . I reassured my Democratic colleagues of Haynsworth's character and went out of my way to make it clear that he was not Thurmond's man.[13]

The fact that Hollings went out of his way to play down links between Thurmond and Haynsworth suggests that Thurmond's "achievements" as the antagonist of the Supreme Court nomination process had come at a price for the senior senator's popularity. By June 1969, it seemed that Thurmond's influence in the process had peaked: he was reportedly "embarrassed" that the Nixon administration opted for Fritz Hollings's preference rather than his own, and he ultimately withdrew to a backseat role in the process of promoting Haynsworth's confirmation.[14] He would prove even less successful in the impeachment of Justice Douglas. As Harry Ashmore, former editor of the *Arkansas Gazette*, pointed out, the senator's "charges" against Douglas did not seem credible given that Warren Burger had recently presided over a conference held by the Center for the Study of Democratic Institutions, the very same "overtly political" institution to which Douglas belonged. Few others took the accusations against Douglas seriously. Senator Edward M. Kennedy of Massachusetts argued in the Senate that Thurmond could not cite "one example here on the floor, where he can be challenged, during all the thirty years Justice Douglas has been on the Supreme Court, where he has had to disqualify himself from a case that came up because of prior kinds of activities." The controversy over Justice Douglas's supposed ethical impropriety prompted him to resign from the Parvin Foundation on May 21, but the attempted impeachment only encouraged the aging Roosevelt appointee to remain on the Supreme Court for another six years, by which time he was wheelchair-bound and on the verge of senility.[15]

Thurmond remained on the sidelines while Hollings led the campaign for Haynsworth's confirmation, but Nixon's hope of a southern nomination free from controversy would prove short-lived. Hollings, like his predecessors Thurmond and Johnston, would now become the face of South Carolina controversy in the nomination process for Supreme Court justices.

In the words of John P. Frank, "there can't be an older 'Old South' than Judge Haynsworth." Born in Greenville, South Carolina, in 1912, Clement Haynsworth represented the fifth generation in a direct succession of Haynsworth lawyers. After graduating from Harvard, he joined the family law firm back in Greenville, which developed into one of the major law practices in the South Carolina upcountry. Having overcome a speech impediment to become a highly successful corporate lawyer and "business-getter," Haynsworth remained with the family firm, spending three years serving in World War II before President Dwight

D. Eisenhower nominated him, shortly after the Simon Sobeloff controversy, to the US Court of Appeals for the Fourth Circuit in 1957. Prominent South Carolinians sent many endorsements of Haynsworth to Olin Johnston, the senior senator from South Carolina and Senate Judiciary Committee member. These included the president of the South Carolina Bar Association; the secretaries of the Spartanburg, Anderson, and Greenwood County Bar Associations; the managing director of the Hotel Greenville; and Charles E. Daniel, chairman of the Daniel Construction Company.[16]

With Johnston chairing the three-man subcommittee considering his nomination in March 1957, Haynsworth corresponded with the chairman for several days, assuring Johnston that "I shall be only too happy to inform you of any detail of my personal and public life which may be of interest to you." When Mississippi's James Eastland, chairman of the full Judiciary Committee, contacted Strom Thurmond, then South Carolina's junior senator, to request that he return his "blue slip"—the device by which senators indicate to the chairman their approval or disapproval of a nominee—Thurmond responded, "Mr. Haynesworth [*sic*] was not my choice for the position but I intend to vote for his confirmation." Shortly after, Bernard Segal, of the American Bar Association's Standing Committee on the Federal Judiciary, wrote to Eastland to advise him that "we consider Mr. Haynsworth qualified for this appointment, and this is the present unanimous view of the Committee." Following the Senate's approval of his appointment, Haynsworth wrote again to Johnston on April 8 to show appreciation "for your kindness in calling me on the telephone on Thursday to report the action of the Senate in confirming my appointment to the Court of Appeals." As the new judge on the Fourth Circuit, Haynsworth sat alongside Simon Sobeloff, and also John J. Parker, who had made history when the Senate defeated his nomination to the US Supreme Court in 1930, marking the only formal rejection of a Supreme Court nominee throughout a period of more than seventy years.[17]

According to Hollings, when he reminded President Nixon that he had met Clement Haynsworth at an investment meeting in Haynsworth's hometown of Greenville, the president recalled, "Oh, that little fella that stuttered." After Nixon requested that Hollings outline Haynsworth's qualifications by letter, the senator complied the very same day, enclosing a biographical sketch and informing the president that "Judge Haynsworth has inspired us all to greater service. His decisions reflect a thorough understanding of legal principles, and his outstanding analyses of complex legal questions would instill stability in the nation's highest Court."[18] Hollings succeeded in winning over Nixon with his assurances of Haynsworth's conservatism, the nature of which would later lead to an amusing exchange during his confirmation hearings. When someone used the phrase "strict constructionist" during questioning, the aforementioned Philip Hart of Michigan commented that although he was uncertain as to what a "strict constructionist" was, he assumed Haynsworth to be one. The nominee remarked, "I have been said to be one. I don't know—I don't know what it is and I certainly do not know that I am one. . . . The term has not been defined to me by anyone, sir."[19] Two days on from Hollings's letter to Nixon, Haynsworth sent the senator a note to thank him for his endorsement. While acknowledging that "Supreme Court appointments are so rare, the available choice so broad, and the uncertainties of political affairs so great that anyone would be foolish to acknowledge the slightest expectation," Haynsworth was barely able to contain his excitement, adding that "if the President is looking for experienced judges, however, I am in the rather enviable position of having as much as twelve years' experience as an appellate judge, while so far avoiding attaining a state of very advanced years."[20]

By August 21, 1969, when Richard Nixon formally nominated Haynsworth to replace Abe Fortas on the Supreme Court, the nominee benefited from what seemed to be a sympathetic lineup on the Judiciary Committee. In 1969, four senators from the Fourth Circuit—comprising the states of Maryland, Virginia, West Virginia, North Carolina, and South Carolina—sat on the committee: Millard Tydings of Maryland, Robert C. Byrd of West Virginia, Sam Ervin of North Carolina, and Strom Thurmond of South Carolina. John Frank has argued that "because of an almost family quality of the bar of the Fourth Circuit, these Senators had a special feeling of knowing their judges, and Senator Tydings, early to question Haynsworth, was very much of that family."[21] Before long, however, Hollings learned of lukewarm feelings toward the nominee elsewhere in the Senate. The remarks of Democratic Senate Majority Leader Mike Mansfield of Montana ("I don't know anything about the fellow") and also Philip Hart ("I don't know a thing about him") encouraged Hollings to argue that while Haynsworth favored a "strict constructionist" interpretation of the Constitution, he was also a "moderate" who "had followed what the Supreme Court says the law is." By linking Haynsworth to two positions that some would have believed to be mutually exclusive, Hollings's opening gambit proved ineffective, with the *New York Times* reporting liberal concerns regarding the nominee's sympathy with the segregationist cause but also conservative complaints that Haynsworth was not sufficiently conservative.[22]

Significantly, one of the first senators to oppose Haynsworth openly was Republican Jacob Javits of New York, who had shown more enthusiasm than most in resisting the actions of South Carolina's senators in the recent past. Javits had stood up to Thurmond and Johnston when the pair had tried to curb the Supreme Court's power during the 1950s, and was also one of the more outspoken figures during Johnston's determination to block John F. Kennedy's nomination of Thurgood Marshall to the Second Circuit in 1962. Javits wrote to Nixon shortly before the president announced the Haynsworth nomination, describing the nominee's position in a series of civil rights cases as "an approach to the problem of racial segregation which, if injected into the Supreme Court at this time . . . could only be viewed as a staggering blow to the cause of civil rights." Senators were particularly concerned by Haynsworth's decision to uphold Virginia's "freedom of choice" statutes relating to segregated schools, in a ruling which the Supreme Court later struck down in *Green v. County School Board of New Kent County* in 1968. One week later, Roy Wilkins, executive director of the NAACP, wrote to Hollings to offer another indication that Haynsworth's record on civil rights would prove a tough sell to northern senators. Wilkins argued that Haynsworth's sympathy with "the system of racially segregated public education that was upset by the *Brown* case ruling of May 17, 1954" was illustrated by the fact that the Supreme Court had reversed four of his decisions on civil rights cases, with the justices "repudiating" his views on one other occasion. Echoing Javits's concerns, Wilkins claimed that Haynsworth's "elevation to the Supreme Court will retard the progress toward improved racial conditions in the nation," and urged Hollings to vote against confirmation.[23]

Before long, George Meany, head of the American Federation of Labor and Congress of Industrial Organizations (AFL-CIO), announced that he would oppose Haynsworth on the basis of the nominee's supposed hostility to organized labor. While Hollings may have been correct that the AFL-CIO—then engaged in a struggle against membership losses as companies outsourced their jobs to the South—had sent investigators to South Carolina to "dig up dirt" on the nominee, he later conceded that the union's opposition to Haynsworth was a "wake-up call" that shook his initial confidence in the success of the nomination. Just in case Hollings was not sufficiently alarmed by the negative reaction to the nominee's civil rights record and the active opposition of the largest union federation in the United States, a third hammer blow landed on September 7, when Republican Senate leader Everett Dirksen of Illinois—the man who Hollings genuinely believed would guarantee Haynsworth's confirmation—died suddenly of a heart attack, delaying the hearings for a week. The South Carolinian was dismayed when Senator Hugh Scott of Pennsylvania replaced Dirksen as minority leader. As Hollings later recalled, "Hugh Scott, he just said Philadelphia and labor just don't like Thurmond. . . . He wouldn't handle it." Furthermore, the AFL-CIO position meant that Hollings could not rely on support from Bob Griffin of Michigan, the new Senate minority whip, who would be seeking reelection in 1972 in a state with a significant union influence.[24]

Despite the huge setbacks, Hollings set out to convince senators to throw their support behind the controversial South Carolina nominee. Working closely with Attorney General John Mitchell and also William Rehnquist, assistant attorney general for the Office of Legal Counsel, Hollings and Haynsworth pursued a charm offensive with wavering senators. According to John Spratt, "every day, Clement Haynsworth would show up at Fritz's office and Fritz would give him his marching orders and say, 'I've called so-and-so, I've done this, I've done that, you go see them, they expect you.'" At a press conference, Hollings began laying the groundwork for a defense of Haynsworth's civil rights record by arguing that the nominee had ruled that the North Carolina Dental Association could not exclude black dentists from its membership. Introducing the nominee to the Senate Judiciary Committee on September 16, Hollings began by acknowledging the growing opposition to Haynsworth, declaring, "I find that in presenting him, I must defend him. I do so with pride, because I first suggested him to President Nixon last May." The senator later admitted that "I felt as though I was presenting an indicted defendant rather than the Chief Judge of the US Court of Appeals for the Fourth Circuit."[25]

Following Hollings's introduction, Chairman James Eastland kicked off the questioning by addressing the issue of whether Haynsworth should have recused himself from the *Darlington Manufacturing Company v. NLRB* case, which had involved a company with business connections to a vending machine firm by the name of Carolina Vend-A-Matic, in which Haynsworth owned one-seventh of the stock. The case of *Brunswick Corp. v. Long* came under discussion following revelations that Haynsworth had purchased one thousand shares in the Brunswick firm, supposedly while he and the other judges of the Fourth

Circuit were considering the case. While no senator ever proved the charges of ethical impropriety, some did succeed in planting seeds of doubt by continuing to discuss the two cases. Prominent Haynsworth opponents from outside the Senate only added to the skepticism, among them George Meany, who claimed that the nominee lacked "the legal ethics of straightforward honesty."[26]

With "Fourth Circuit" senators Tydings and Ervin giving the nominee every opportunity to make his case, and Eastland concluding that "I will not make a final determination on the confirmation of the nominee before us based on the criticism that has been levelled at him," the first day of hearings concluded with little discussion of how Haynsworth's confirmation would affect the jurisprudence of the Supreme Court.[27] This changed on the following day, when Philip Hart questioned the nominee on his judicial philosophy. Sam Ervin, in one of the few highlights of the hearings, could not resist interjecting:

Senator Ervin: If the senator will pardon me for committing an unpardonable sin, I am glad at long last the senator from Michigan agrees with me that a senator has a right to ascertain the view of a nominee for the Supreme Court.

Senator Hart: I am ascertaining whether he agrees with Earl Warren.

Senator Ervin: And I would like to say that I am glad to have a convert to my philosophy. However, I never did get one of the previous nominees to ever reveal any of his political or constitutional philosophy. And I was told at the time that it was highly improper for me to seek to ascertain it. Excuse me. I won't interrupt you anymore.[28]

Ervin's interjection no doubt amused senators who recalled his and Hart's differing views on previous nominees, but his remarks may also have highlighted the fact that the southern members of the Judiciary Committee were apparently, for the first time, on the defensive. Shortly after a further round of questions from Senator Edward Kennedy of Massachusetts, it was the turn of Senator Birch Bayh of Indiana, who interrogated Haynsworth mercilessly, returning to the theme of judicial ethics with regard to Carolina Vend-A-Matic.[29] When attorney John P. Frank appeared before the committee to clarify the issue of whether or not Judge Haynsworth had behaved unethically, Senator Bayh pursued the Carolina Vend-A-Matic issue further:

Senator Bayh: Let me ask you why in the well-documented information you have given us, there was little or no reference to the canons of judicial ethics? Why were the canons not significant enough to be considered in your brief?

Mr. Frank: Because I did not deal with the canons. Because I think for purposes of the federal courts they are simply immaterial. They merely are reflective of, in this highly general language of, what is in the code anyway, and the rule for the federal judges is adequately, I think, covered by the statutes and the cases and I don't think the canons really add anything other than a confirming note or echo.[30]

Unconvinced by Frank's rather awkward form of diplomacy, Bayh was determined to oppose Clement Haynsworth's confirmation with the same energy and dedication displayed by Strom Thurmond in his fight against Abe Fortas. Following George Meany's statement on the AFL-CIO's opposition to Haynsworth on September 18, Bayh resumed his questioning of the nominee five days later. Sam Ervin failed to ease the tension by quoting a line from Henry Wadsworth Longfellow's "A Psalm of Life": "Time is fleeting, and our hearts, though stout and brave, still, like muffled drums, are beating funeral marches to the grave."[31]

Senator Bayh: What is that supposed to mean?

Senator Ervin: It means that apparently we are going to be in the funeral march to the grave before we get through this proceeding.

Senator Bayh: I hope not. I am concerned and I suppose I should ask the question if you had to do it over again whether you would still maintain that kind of relationship with Carolina Vend-A-Matic. You feel that there is absolutely nothing that was improprietous here?

Judge Haynsworth: I don't know what you mean by that kind of relationship. I was a stockholder, as I have said.

Senator Bayh: Stockholder, vice president, and your wife is secretary, and you were on the board of directors and you own $450,000 worth of stock. You are doing business with one of the litigants.

Judge Haynsworth: Well now, Senator—

Senator Bayh: A significant amount of business of the corporation was done with textile companies, and the case involved was a textile case. This is what concerns me. It is a matter of appearance.

Judge Haynsworth: Senator, I was a director until 1963. I was an inactive vice president. We have been into all of this.[32]

One can only imagine how South Carolina's Strom Thurmond felt as he sat in silence listening to Birch Bayh's interrogation. Nonetheless, the senior senator complied with the administration's wishes and limited himself to a tiny number of interventions during the hearings, speaking up to ask John Frank, and later Judge Harrison Winter, Haynsworth's colleague on the Fourth Circuit, if either of them believed that Haynsworth had ever behaved unethically. During testimony from Clarence Mitchell and Joseph Rauh, of the Leadership Conference on Civil Rights, Thurmond made one further intervention, declaring that "I have no questions of these witnesses, but I want to inquire at what time are we going to recess for lunch and at what time are we going to come back?"[33]

In his 1991 study of the Haynsworth nomination, John Frank claimed that the coalition of groups opposing Haynsworth effectively selected Senator Birch Bayh as their leader. Having initially approached Philip Hart to lead the campaign, they settled on Bayh after Hart declined the responsibility, on the grounds that he had backed Abe Fortas enthusiastically the previous year.[34] Bayh's rigorous questioning of Clement Haynsworth during the Judiciary Committee hearings—which concluded with seven members voting against the nominee—culminated, on October 8, in his announcement of a "bill of particulars," which outlined a total of twenty arguments for why the Senate should reject the nomination. These ranged from the allegation that Haynsworth had cast the deciding vote in the infamous *Darlington* decision, favoring Carolina Vend-A-Matic ("Charge 3"), to the fact that the judge had sat on six cases involving Vend-A-Matic customers ("Charge 7"), and the accusation that he had used his office to promote the vending business ("Charge 16"), in addition to a detailed graph showing the sudden increase in gross annual sales for Vend-A-Matic since Haynsworth became a judge on the Fourth Circuit. Bayh sent the full list of charges to Fritz Hollings's office, enclosing an explanatory letter that concluded, in a handwritten line at the bottom, "Fritz—I haven't relished this matter, but the facts should be out in the open. Birch."[35]

Horrified by the "bill of particulars," and convinced that Bayh was pursuing payback for the Republican treatment of Fortas the previous year, Hollings called a press conference, during which he conceded that "an aura has been created that a judge is on the run" but insisted that the charges were "grossly exaggerated," and that "no actual conflict of interest had been proved." On the Senate floor, Hollings, in a bid to offset charges brought by a fellow Democrat, was now calling on a group of Republican senators to help him defend the Haynsworth nomination, including Marlow Cook of Kentucky, Howard Baker of Tennessee, Roman Hruska of Nebraska, Barry Goldwater of Arizona, and even his South Carolina colleague, Strom Thurmond. Hollings challenged Bayh to a televised debate on the accusations he had leveled against Haynsworth, and produced his own document, in which he responded in detail to each of Bayh's twenty charges while also noting the "calculated" nature of the accusations.[36]

Hollings's response ensured that a comprehensive defense of the nominee would go on record as a rebuttal of Bayh's charges, but his attempt to drag Bayh in front of television cameras proved less straightforward. In a letter dated October 9, Hollings formally challenged the Indiana senator to a televised debate, pointing out that he would contact various TV networks to arrange a suitable time. True to his word, Hollings sent a telegram to the president of news at the Columbia Broadcasting System (CBS), the president of news at the American Broadcasting Corporation (ABC), and the vice president in charge of news at the National Broadcasting Corporation (NBC).[37]

In his response, sent on the same day, Bayh advised Hollings that "in light of the serious nature of our responsibility to advise and consent to the nomination of a Justice who will sit on the Supreme Court for life and dispense justice for all of our citizens in that capacity . . . we should do our best to debate this matter in a deliberate and dispassionate manner on the floor of the Senate." The following day, an agitated Hollings responded by pointing out that "it was you who took the debate from senatorial processes to the headlines and TV tube and now there is no alternative because both public opinion and Senate opinion is formulating." Hollings remained unconvinced that Bayh would even face him in the Senate, let alone in a television studio. As he recalled in his memoirs, "Bayh refused to stay on the floor. He would make a charge and then leave." Referring to an offer from *Meet the Press* to stage a televised debate, Hollings claimed in his correspondence with Bayh that he had accepted the invitation "because I believe that an answer to your charges is the only way that we can protect the reputation of the United States Senate and of the Court."[38]

The very same day, an unfazed Bayh tried a different tack:

Dear Fritz:

I have just received your telegram relative to our debating the Haynsworth matter on national television. In re-reading it a second and third time, I still feel very much as I did in response to your first inquiry.

Fritz, so many different sources have been responsible for various statements and allegations throughout this entire distasteful affair that I am returning your wire without disclosing its contents in the hopes that someone other than yourself was the author.

I have too much respect for you and for the service you have performed and will continue to perform for your state in the Senate to let others goad us into this type of personal acrimony.

Best regards,
Birch Bayh[39]

In his terse response, Hollings began by claiming ownership of the words in his telegram before complaining to Bayh that "I don't get this pedestal of personal acrimony that you have assumed. You attack Judge Haynsworth in a nine-page 'bill of particulars,' then when someone wants to defend him and go down the list of charges, you assume the 'don't let's get personal' attitude." He urged Bayh once again to "please reconsider your position." In the final communication from Bayh's office—undated, and scrawled in Bayh's own hand rather than typed—the senator from Indiana informed his South Carolina colleague that "one thing you should know is that I did not disclose your last letter. In fact, a member of the press walked into my office with a copy of it . . . before I had even received it. Where it originated, I don't know!" When Clement Haynsworth wrote to Fritz Hollings the following month to show his appreciation for the senator's energetic support for his confirmation, he commented that "you performed superbly, your only failure being your futile attempt to entice Senator Bayh into a debate in which you would have demolished him."[40]

As bullish as his attitude may have seemed, Hollings was beginning to sense defeat during the month of October, albeit in the unlikely form of newspaper cartoons. An illustration from the *Raleigh (NC) News and Observer* showing Haynsworth sitting before the Judiciary Committee while an angry-looking Birch Bayh clenched his fist and asked, "Judge Haynsworth, it is true that you owned three boxes of Oaties Cereal when you ruled in their case?" offered a clear example of press ridicule of the perceived triviality of Bayh's charges but nonetheless highlighted the manner in which the Indianan's fight against the nominee had infiltrated the public consciousness. Far more serious was an illustration by Herblock in the *Washington Post,* which showed Haynsworth as a schoolboy carrying a book bag with Carolina Vend-A-Matic stock falling out of it, with Attorney General John Mitchell standing beside him, claiming, "But your honor, my client hasn't done anything wrong—and he promises to stop doing it."

According to John Spratt, "Fritz said he knew then it was all over."[41]

11. THE ASTONISHING AND PUZZLING SENATOR HOLLINGS

Republican senators began calling on the Nixon administration to withdraw the Haynsworth nomination. The president took no action, and Attorney General Mitchell even refused a request from Haynsworth himself that he be withdrawn from consideration. As a means of counterattack, the administration urged Republican chairmen in the South to argue that Haynsworth's opponents were acting solely out of a personal prejudice against the South. Harry Dent, who had served on Strom Thurmond's staff before becoming one of Richard Nixon's crucial southern political strategists, approached eight Washington, DC, correspondents from southern newspapers to convince them to pursue a "southern angle" in their coverage. Nonetheless, in Fritz Hollings's view, the efforts of the southern writers who happily played up the supposed antisouthern bias, such as James J. Kilpatrick, failed to dilute the impact of Herblock's "Vend-A-Justice" cartoons, which Hollings condemned on the Senate floor.[1]

With the ethics question, the civil rights record, and the alleged hostility to organized labor, Haynsworth had unwittingly created a smorgasbord of controversy, guaranteed to unite a diverse coalition of senators in opposing him. Before long, Hollings and the Nixon administration realized that they had underestimated the ability of organized labor and the NAACP to influence the Senate in a campaign referred to by Joel Grossman and Stephen Wasby as a "desperate effort to save the Court's prevailing liberal policies from destruction."[2] As each day went by, senators from both parties communicated to Hollings differing views toward the nominee. Republican Wallace Bennett of Utah concluded that "the charges against the judge are political and based on revenge rather than factual, and I have decided to vote for his confirmation," while Democrat Daniel Inouye of Hawaii stated flatly, "as you know, I have publicly announced that I intend to vote against Judge Haynsworth's nomination," and Republican Ted Stevens of Alaska declared solemnly, "I think you should know that I have a persistent doubt developing concerning Judge Haynsworth." Republican Lee Jordan of Idaho expressed his concern that Haynsworth was in fact Strom Thurmond's "stalking horse for the Supreme Court." As Kentucky's Marlow Cook would later point out in his "new standards" speech, "[Haynsworth's] South Carolina residence was construed as conclusive proof that he was a close friend of the widely criticized senior senator from that state" despite the fact that Haynsworth and Thurmond barely knew each other, and despite Hollings's effort to work closely with the Nixon administration to minimize Thurmond's role in the confirmation process.[3]

President Nixon finally called a press conference on October 20, 1969, during which he asserted that Haynsworth had never gained personally from any of his rulings. The president claimed that he did not believe that a judge's philosophy constituted an appropriate basis for the Senate's rejection of a Supreme Court nominee, before concluding that "it is not proper to turn down a man because he is a Southerner, because he is a Jew, because he is a Negro, or because of his philosophy." This statement, an obvious reference to the troubled Supreme Court nominations of Louis Brandeis in 1916 and Thurgood Marshall in 1967, suggested the extent to which Nixon would push the "southern" aspect of the Haynsworth controversy, but the president's decision to address these issues ultimately failed to save the nomination. Some Republicans, already unhappy with Nixon's failure to screen Haynsworth adequately prior to announcing his nomination, resented the administration putting pressure on them to support the controversial nominee.[4]

Speculation in the press over Haynsworth's prospects was mixed: David Lawrence wrote, in an article published in the *Richmond News Leader,* that Haynsworth's opponents were constructing an organized effort to block his confirmation "because he is from the South," while other newspapers, including the *Charlotte Observer,* predicted a grim outcome, and others, such as the *Washington Post* and South Carolina's *The State,* expected the Senate to confirm Haynsworth by a narrow margin.[5] By the final day of the Senate debate, Hollings had become so despondent that his comments bordered on sarcasm. Referring to himself as "the undistinguished Senator from South Carolina," he declared that "with two people on the press gallery, with everybody waiting around for the last two hours to go home, with every Senator for the last two weeks having made up his mind, suffice it to say that we could continue to try to make it look like we are making a record."[6] Hollings later summed up the harrowing experience of the Haynsworth affair—which clearly informed his opinion on the transformation of the Supreme Court nomination process during the late 1960s—when he asked, in his memoirs, "What good person wants to put himself and his family through the horrific treatment that has become a routine part of the Senate's 'advice and consent' process?"[7] One might add that those who had supported Simon Sobeloff, Thurgood Marshall, and Abe Fortas may have asked the same question following South Carolina's treatment of those nominees during their own hearings.

Following the Senate's rejection of Clement Haynsworth's confirmation, by a vote of 45–55, southern senators capitalized on the administration's claim that the attack on the nominee constituted an attack on the South. Strom Thurmond's supporters expressed disgust at the perceived antisouthern bias, with one writer asking, "How many more times will the South get slapped in the face before the people wake up?" and another complaining that "all of South Carolina is sick and angry about the treatment given Haynsworth. It was an insult to every South Carolinian, and every Southerner. . . . This is as bad as 'Reconstruction.' We need another HAMPTON to save us—and we are looking to you, Senator Thurmond, to be that Hampton." While Thurmond no doubt appreciated one of his supporters comparing him to Wade Hampton, the Civil War hero and former South Carolina governor, he sounded inconsolable in a letter to Clement Haynsworth, in which he claimed that "the lamentable failure of the Senate to confirm your nomination was the greatest disappointment I have had since I have been in the Senate." In a newsletter, Thurmond compared Haynsworth to the last rejected Supreme Court nominee, namely, John J. Parker, Haynsworth's former colleague on the Fourth Circuit. Certainly there were remarkable similarities between the two cases, in that Parker's record on civil rights and his opposition to the "yellow dog contract" also ensured the resistance of an unlikely coalition of the NAACP and the AFL. However, it was the fact that Parker was from the South that provided the ultimate cause for a comparison, with Thurmond arguing that Haynsworth, like Parker, "was born and bred to a more exacting tradition of law and history than liberals would accept."[8] Predictably, Thurmond was not the only one to point to the obvious similarities between Haynsworth and Parker: shortly before the Senate torpedoed Haynsworth's nomination, James J. Kilpatrick had made the same comparison, speaking of a South "where defeat is an old companion."[9]

Nonetheless, others remained unconvinced by the "anti-South" arguments. Southern Republican senator Bill Brock recalls, "I was not aware of any resentment or bitterness towards the South from senators from other regions during this period. . . . There certainly was concern about [Republican] gains, but those were the concerns of those whose interests lay in maintaining a majority for Democrats in the Senate." Ironically, Brock's view that Haynsworth's opponents in the Senate were motivated by party concerns rather than regional prejudice provides a further comparison with the Parker rejection: in 1969, some senators resented Nixon's appointment of a South Carolina judge as part of a Republican "southern strategy," in the same way that, in 1930, several southern Democrats voted against the North Carolinian Parker in order to prevent Republican president Herbert Hoover from building on his success in winning the state of North Carolina in the 1928 presidential election.[10] Furthermore, given that Nixon had won only one Deep South state—South Carolina—it may have been Haynsworth's association with that particular state, rather than the South, that alienated wavering senators.

The administration's effort to minimize Thurmond's role in the Haynsworth nomination had failed to erase memories of the senator's influence over Richard Nixon's 1968 election victory, and his leadership of the successful campaign to deny Abe Fortas the chief justiceship. Senator Millard Tydings of Maryland summed up the relevance of the Fortas rejection on the fate of Clement Haynsworth when he claimed: "The Fortas affair cast over the Court a shadow of suspicion and mistrust from which the Court has not fully emerged. This aura hangs most noticeably over Mr. Fortas's vacant seat, the very one to which Judge Haynsworth has been nominated. We must recognize that the ultimate decision in the present matter cannot realistically be insulated from this specter."[11]

With his successful campaign against Fortas in 1968, the formidable Thurmond may unwittingly have sabotaged a golden opportunity to engineer the appointment of a conservative South Carolina Supreme Court justice in 1969. However, the man himself saw the situation very differently, telling a married couple from Columbia, South Carolina, "Frankly, I do not think there is any comparison between the Fortas situation and the Haynsworth case, and the record clearly substantiates this position."[12] In a further reminder of the growing public interest in the politicization of the Supreme Court nomination process, two political science students from the University of Minnesota, Sue Shepard and Jerry Jensen, wrote to senators to ask them to complete a brief questionnaire on the Haynsworth vote, for use in a term paper. Claiming that "our final grade in the class depends on this survey," the students asked senators to "please rate as '10' those factors that were of absolute value in your decision to vote for conformation [*sic*] and rate as '0' those factors that were completely neutral in helping you formulate your decision." With a fountain pen, Thurmond filled in his ratings as follows:

Voted for:

0 A. Because he was a Southerner
10 B. Because the President wanted him for the job
10 C. Because he was known for his strict constructionist approach
10 D. Because he is a man of integrity
10 E. Because the opinion of my home constituents appeared to be in favor of conformation [*sic*]
10 F. Because a more proper balance would have been restored to the court
10 G. Because he appeared to be a man of excellent judicial experience
10 H. Because the mood of the nation seemed to desire his conformation [*sic*]
0 I. Because legislation important to me would have been hampered if I had voted against
0 J. Because his opponents were trying to run a smear campaign
0 K. Because he appeared to be pro-business[13]

It is not clear if Thurmond interpreted the request to mean that "0" and "10" were the only options available to him, but his failure to record anything falling between the two most extreme ratings seems a fitting summary of his approach toward the nomination process over the preceding fifteen years. Although he would modify his references to the South in his public statements over the next three decades, his enthusiasm for advancing southerners on the federal judiciary would remain. Although he happily supported Ronald Reagan's controversial Supreme Court nomination of Robert Bork, he made no secret of his preference for South Carolina's Judge William Wilkins Jr., and pushed Wilkins's candidacy further following the Senate's rejection of Bork in October 1987.[14]

Fritz Hollings remained outspoken following the Haynsworth rejection. In a letter to W. C. Boyd, the senator played down his feud with fellow Democrat

Birch Bayh and instead complained bitterly that the Republicans were responsible for derailing the nomination:

> Daily we had their leader, Scott of Pennsylvania, and the Republican Whip, Griffin of Michigan, shouting for the President to withdraw the appointment. In the month-long debate, our leader, Mike Mansfield, by contrast, never said one word against Haynsworth and only made his decision known the afternoon before the vote. It so happens that the Attorney General of the United States commented to me only last week that the Republicans defeated Clement and all you have to do is ask Clement. I handled the appointment. I know this better than anyone.[15]

To the president of Dan River Mills in Greenville, the senator claimed that "Clement was a good product, but we just couldn't sell. You will remember my desperation in August and September. I could see the gathering storm and then Senator Dirksen died and we had to move fast. The Administration sat back as if they knew how to handle the situation and we never got back in the ball game." When Hollings went public with his criticism, J. Drake Edens, Republican national committeeman for South Carolina, offered a stinging rebuke, claiming that "Senator Hollings has been demagoguing and has been demagoguing from the beginning," adding that Hollings had succeeded in influencing only one vote for Haynsworth, "and I'm not sure he was responsible for that." Edens pointed out that while Thurmond had remained in Washington, DC, to defend the Haynsworth nomination, Hollings had spent three weeks on a "junket" to India, adding, "I don't know if Senator Hollings was in India to round up votes for Judge Haynsworth . . . but if he was, the Indian delegation didn't show up in our corner on Friday." Hollings continued to insist that the nomination would have succeeded had Everett Dirksen lived, despite Dirksen's failure to corral support among Republican senators for Lyndon Johnson's attempt to promote Abe Fortas the previous year.[16]

Although Hollings's disappointment after weeks of intensive campaigning on behalf of the Nixon administration may have put him in an indignant mood, he was not alone in his view that the administration was to blame for the Haynsworth debacle. Senator Russell Long of Louisiana claimed in a letter to Robert Stoddard, mayor of Spartanburg, South Carolina, that "the South stood solidly behind the President on the Haynsworth vote. If he had done his homework on his side of the aisle, he would have prevailed." Furthermore, history has not been kind to Richard Nixon's role in the Haynsworth affair: John Maltese has argued that the administration's lobbying effort degenerated into "strong-arm tactics that ultimately did more harm than good." Nixon's enthusiasm in backing Haynsworth before the nation's press—despite allegedly nominating him without consulting the American Bar Association (ABA) or the Republican National Committee or any senator other than Fritz Hollings—did indeed suggest that he may have been less concerned with Haynsworth's suitability as a Supreme Court justice, and more focused on rewarding the South and continuing to build a strong Republican Party in that region.[17]

With the Haynsworth nomination in ruins, Thurmond claimed in a newsletter that "knowledgeable people have confidence that the President will nominate another conservative, hopefully one from the South." This hope appeared to have some credibility: on November 21, Nixon wrote to Hollings to thank the senator for supporting the Haynsworth nomination, pointing out that "the Court needs men of Judge Haynsworth's philosophy to restore the proper balance to this great institution, and I propose that we continue our effort to provide the Court with such men."[18] Few, including an already disappointed Fritz Hollings, could have anticipated Nixon's next selection of a nominee to fill the vacancy on the Supreme Court.

The Senate's defeat of Clement Haynsworth's nomination only reinforced the belief of many conservative white southerners that no president would succeed in appointing a Supreme Court justice with any degree of sympathy for the South. To make matters worse for those southerners, the Haynsworth controversy occurred just as the Supreme Court was hammering the final nails into the coffin of southern segregation. On October 29, 1969, the justices handed down the critical decision in *Alexander v. Holmes County School Board,* which ordered the complete and immediate desegregation of Mississippi's schools. The *Brown* (1954) and "Brown II" (1955) decisions had legitimized desegregation "with all deliberate speed," allowing state officials to drag their heels, while *Green v. County School Board* (1968) had been open to interpretation with regard to the speed of transition to a unitary system. But the *Alexander* ruling, thanks largely to the aging Justice Hugo Black's insistence, ensured no ambiguity whatsoever in ordering school districts to desegregate throughout the South.[19]

In joining with Mississippi's James Eastland in condemning *Alexander,*

Thurmond claimed that "the Nixon Administration stood with the South in this case . . . but the Court has chosen to override both the state of Mississippi and the Justice Department. I hope something can be done to overcome the effects of this pernicious ruling." Despite a march of over three thousand white residents of Greenville and Darlington counties to the South Carolina State House in protest at the desegregation ruling, the state's governor, Robert McNair, showed no indication that he would reverse the careful transition to racial order that Fritz Hollings, his predecessor, had initiated. Announcing that he would oppose any attempt to close down public schools, the governor declared that "we don't want federal troops in South Carolina. We've built a reputation for obedience to the law." Sixteen years on from *Brown,* the issue of segregated southern schools continued to rage in the Senate following the *Alexander* ruling, with Hollings using a debate with South Carolina's old nemesis, Jacob Javits of New York, to reiterate his claims of an antisouthern bias following the Haynsworth rejection. As the *Charleston News and Courier* reported, "Hollings said that 200,000 Negro children are attending segregated schools in New York, but that the Federal Government's efforts have been directed only against the South. 'They've developed busing,' Hollings said, 'to mix children—where? In North Carolina and South Carolina. Not in New York. Not in Chicago.'"[20]

Richard Nixon's selection of segregationist judge G. Harrold Carswell of Florida—in his second attempt to name a southerner to replace Abe Fortas on the Supreme Court—only exacerbated southern tension over the segregation issue in the years 1969 and 1970. Unlike the Haynsworth episode, during which no senator had questioned the nominee's competence as a judge, skeptics raised serious questions regarding Carswell's legal ability, particularly given his lack of published work and the fact that other judges rarely, if ever, cited his opinions.

With a track record of defending white supremacy and a painfully lukewarm ABA rating, Carswell's nomination appeared doomed from the start, and very quickly united the very same forces that had opposed Haynsworth. In his lengthy statement of opposition, George Meany of the AFL-CIO claimed that "the Administration's sole guide in making its selection was its Southern political strategy." A now-legendary ham-fisted defense offered by Republican Roman Hruska only damaged Carswell's chances even further, with the senator from Nebraska arguing that "even if he is mediocre, there are a lot of mediocre judges and people and lawyers. They are entitled to a little representation, aren't they, and a little chance? We can't have all Brandeises, Cardozos, and Frankfurters, and stuff like that there." Peter Fish has argued that Nixon, in naming Carswell, responded to the Senate's rejection of Clement Haynsworth with a "spite" nomination, defined as "an ill-disguised strategy of vengeance against the upper chamber—a strategy intended . . . to force the Senate into a posture of ironic acceptance of a second-choice nominee possessing professional credentials widely perceived as inferior to those of the original nominee." The consequences of Nixon's antagonistic strategy would be catastrophic.[21]

Thurmond, having taken a back seat during the Haynsworth confirmation hearings, was happy to air his opinions on the new nominee, telling one constituent that "Judge Carswell is a comparatively young man and should be on the Court a long time. I am pleased that President Nixon turned South again to fill this vacancy." The senator was quick to address the growing criticism, making the predictable argument that, "although they will not admit it, the people who have raised arguments against Judge Carswell's confirmation are opposed to him primarily on the basis of his being from the South."[22] By complete contrast, Hollings had very little to say. The state's press took a great interest in his sudden silence, particularly as he had been so openly critical of the Nixon administration following the Senate's rejection of Haynsworth. Speculative articles started to appear in the *News and Courier*, beginning with an observation that "Senator Hollings' hesitation on whether he'll vote for or against confirmation of Judge G. Harrold Carswell as a Supreme Court nominee is, to put it mildly, both astonishing and puzzling."[23]

Shortly after, Hollings gave an interview in which he made the extraordinary suggestion that if the Senate rejected Carswell, he would recommend to President Nixon that he renominate Clement Haynsworth. If Fish is correct that Nixon hoped the Senate would confirm Carswell because senators did not believe they would get away with a second rejection, it seems ironic that Hollings thought it possible that the senators who had rejected Haynsworth would react so negatively to the Carswell nomination that Haynsworth might end up winning them over if Nixon nominated him a second time. Nonetheless, South Carolina's political journalists expressed little enthusiasm for Hollings's position: the *News and Courier* urged him to back Carswell unequivocally, while *The State* noted that "the Senator's indecision on Carswell might produce damage that could take years to repair." The sense of frustration was also evident in letters from Hollings's South Carolina constituents, some of whom joined with the state's press in urging him to make his position known.[24]

Privately, Hollings was holding out little hope of a second Haynsworth nomination. In a letter to Fulton B. Creech, he claimed, "I have withheld taking a public position on Carswell until after the debates because this was exactly the trouble I found myself in, handling the Haynsworth nomination. Everybody had committed before they listened to the facts. I did not want to be guilty of the same thing." Describing Carswell as "nothing to get enthused about," the senator declared, "I am proud of the South and, when we put our foot forward, it should be our very best foot. Carswell can't even carry Haynsworth's law books." Regarding the upcoming vote in the Senate, Hollings confessed, "in confidence, I will probably vote for him but I am not proud of the vote. I don't believe he is a racist or any of these charges generally about him. I just believe that he is a mediocre lawyer and judge and that if I had a case, I would not associate him in it. Therefore, I see no reason why I should promote him to the highest court." Hollings discussed the possibility of resubmitting Haynsworth in a letter to the senior vice president of the Fidelity Federal Savings and Loan Association, pointing out that "re-submitting the name of a Supreme Court nominee is not without precedent," citing President Andrew Jackson's successful renomination of Roger Taney in 1835, but added that he did not believe "that this is a realistic consideration about Clement Haynsworth in our present political climate." To another constituent, he declared, "I have given some thought to this, but concluded that to re-nominate him would serve to resurrect the same charges by his opponents. I would doubt that the Judge should be expected to undergo this again."[25]

Hollings eventually endorsed Carswell in a brief, lukewarm statement in the Senate—in which he claimed that his initial silence had "opened a Pandora's box of editorial nonsense in many of the South Carolina newspapers"—before declaring his intention to vote for Carswell's confirmation. Following the Senate's rejection of Carswell the same week, by a vote of 45–51, President Nixon sent Hollings another letter of thanks, commending him "for standing by this fine jurist despite the heated campaign of misrepresentation and scurrility that ultimately cost him his confirmation." With his southern Supreme Court strategy shot down in flames for a second time, Nixon nominated Minnesotan judge Harry A. Blackmun to fill the Fortas vacancy. Thurmond remained supportive of the president and the new nominee, claiming in a statement to the Senate Judiciary Committee that "Judge Blackmun is a man of high ethical conduct and competence, as were Judge Haynsworth and Judge Carswell." In an interview reported in the *Sarasota Herald Tribune,* Thurmond referred to the Carswell rejection as "a black day in the history of the United States," yet, despite his view that "it will be impossible to get a judge from the South with strict constructionist views appointed to the Supreme Court," the senator concluded optimistically that he was confident in President Nixon naming a southern judge before the end of his presidency.[26]

By complete contrast, Hollings portrayed Blackmun's confirmation as further evidence of an antisouthern prejudice. Complaining of "the double standard employed by my colleagues in the Senate as a body, apparently, on whether or not a judge is from South Carolina or Minnesota," Hollings concluded that "apparently, if one is from South Carolina, the standards or qualifications . . . are higher than would be required of a Minnesota judge." Following the Senate's confirmation of his appointment, Blackmun would disappoint conservatives with his record on the court, not least with his authorship of the majority opinion in *Roe v. Wade* (1973), which established a constitutional right to an abortion and made the mild-mannered Minnesotan an unlikely hero of the women's movement.[27]

On May 15, 1970, Marlow Cook declared to the Senate that "with the confirmation of Harry A. Blackmun by the Senate this week, I believe we have come to the end of an era in Supreme Court history. . . . To the extent that the recent controversial period has eroded respect for our legal institutions, it has been a disaster." The senator from Kentucky reasserted that Clement Haynsworth had not in fact violated the judicial code, and echoed Hollings's complaints of a double standard when pointing out that Judge Blackmun had also presided over cases involving firms in which he owned stock, yet senators had raised no objections. Cook's response to the Senate's treatment of Haynsworth was to offer five criteria to be used when considering future nominees: 1. Competence; 2. Achievement; 3. Temperament; 4. Judicial integrity; and 5. Non-judicial record. Cook may not have foreseen the trouble that lay ahead for the nomination process in the 1980s and 1990s, but his "Haynsworth test" does provide another indication of Haynsworth's huge significance during a tumultuous political period, and the influence this episode would have on subsequent nominations.[28]

Cook's Senate aide, Mitch McConnell, was the primary author of the "new standards" speech, and the text later formed the basis for his article "Haynsworth and Parker: A New Senate Standard of Excellence," published in the *Kentucky Law Journal.* McConnell later served as deputy attorney general during Gerald Ford's presidency before winning election to the US Senate in 1984. As Senate minority leader from 2007, McConnell led Republican senators during the heated confirmation battles over President Barack Obama's nominations of Sonia Sotomayor and Elena Kagan to the Supreme Court, and became Senate majority leader in January 2015. Following Obama's nomination of Merrick Garland to the court in March 2016, McConnell insisted that the Republican-controlled Senate would not consent to Judiciary Committee hearings or a vote until after the presidential election in November. Seizing upon McConnell's 1970 article, in which he had argued that politics should play no part in the confirmation process, Democrats threw accusations of hypocrisy at the majority leader. Meanwhile, political commentators began comparing the McConnell-led Republican opposition to Obama in 2016 with the Thurmond-led Republican opposition to Lyndon Johnson, who, in 1968, was also in the final year of his presidency. In the event, McConnell led Senate Republicans in the "nuclear option" of removing the 60-vote majority required to confirm Supreme Court nominees. The controversial move, engineered on April 7, 2017, to confirm President Donald Trump's nomination of Judge Neil Gorsuch, cemented the Kentuckian's vitally important role in the history of the US judicial nominations process. His Republican colleague, Mississippi's Roger Wicker, commented, "When the final chapter in Mitch McConnell's book is written, this will place very prominently . . . it's a huge victory [and] consequential for decades."[29]

The Haynsworth controversy spilled over into the 1970 congressional elections. In the Tennessee senatorial election, Republican congressman Bill Brock succeeded in defeating three-term incumbent Democratic senator Albert Gore, partly through reminding Tennesseans of Gore's opposition to Haynsworth. Over in South Carolina, James B. Edwards, chairman of the Republican Party in the First Congressional District, made the same allegation, unsuccessfully, of Lieutenant Governor John C. West, the Democratic candidate in that year's gubernatorial contest. The moderate lieutenant governor would succeed Robert McNair in the governor's mansion after defeating his Republican opponent, the Thurmond-endorsed Congressman Albert Watson. West later commented that "the Southern elections of 1970 were the first elections with racial overtones where the moderates won." Three African American candidates won election to the state House in a further suggestion of a changing South Carolina.[30]

President Nixon later considered, albeit briefly, nominating Albert Watson to the US Court of Military Appeals, but backed down after Republican leaders warned him that a Watson nomination would fare no better than those of Haynsworth and Carswell. According to the *New York Times,* Strom Thurmond's announcement that Nixon had "tentatively" approved a Watson nomination immediately triggered opposition among senators.[31] Watson's failed gubernatorial bid, and senators' refusal to even consider him for a judicial position, only confirmed the toxic nature of Thurmond's influence in the Senate by 1971. Just as he would adopt more moderate positions on race relations during the 1970s, the senator's role as antagonist in the nomination process for Supreme Court justices would transform peacefully into that of a quiet elder statesman. Having functioned as an obstruction to the liberal and moderate appointments of the 1950s and 1960s, Thurmond would now perform the function of shepherding conservative judges through an increasingly partisan nominations process, acting as a crucial sounding board for Ronald Reagan throughout his presidency. Perhaps the most striking example of Thurmond's transformation appeared during hearings into Reagan's nomination of Robert Bork in 1987, by which time Thurmond had become the most senior Republican senator on the Judiciary Committee. Those who recalled him dismissing the noncommittal responses of Thurgood Marshall and Abe Fortas might have been struck by his objection, twenty years later, to a question from Alabama's Senator Howell Heflin on *Roe v. Wade,* on the grounds that it required Bork "to express an opinion on a matter that may come before the Supreme Court, and I would think that would be improper."[32]

Following his resignation from the court, Abe Fortas returned to private practice, appearing before his old colleagues on the Supreme Court on several occasions. Laura Kalman has claimed that, on the first of these occasions, Fortas made eye contact with Harry Blackmun. Standing before the man who had replaced him on the Supreme Court, Fortas appeared to acknowledge Blackmun with a nod. A curious Blackmun later asked Fortas if he recalled that moment, to which the soft-spoken Tennessean responded, "I'll never forget it."[33] It was by no means the only unforgettable moment in an extraordinary life, which came to an end on April 5, 1982, when Fortas died from a ruptured aorta, aged seventy-one. Clement Haynsworth—who would remain on the Fourth Circuit until his own death at the age of seventy-seven, on November 22, 1989—would not be the final victim claimed by the Supreme Court nomination process. The Haynsworth fiasco had showcased South Carolina's rapid and volatile political development before the rest of the nation. The attitude of the state's senators toward the nominations process was perfectly compatible with the conservative backlash embodied by Richard Nixon's election victories, yet the drive for a "strict constructionist" appointment was woefully at odds with the efforts of other senators to protect the liberal gains of the past three decades. Furthermore, the unusual prominence of South Carolina in Nixon's "southern strategy" only poisoned the Haynsworth nomination for many others.

From Olin Johnston's defense of white supremacy in the fight against *Smith v. Allwright* in the mid-1940s to John C. West's triumph at the start of the 1970s in "the first Southern elections with racial overtones where the moderates won," South Carolina's confrontational relationship with the Supreme Court had sparked a war of many battles. In explaining South Carolina's civil rights journey, scholars of "massive resistance" have typically focused on the most obvious historical signposts, among them the Rock Hill protests, the peaceful desegregation of Clemson, the Orangeburg Massacre, and the troubled gubernatorial election of 1970.[34] The fact that the state's politicians acted as persistent pugilists within the walls of the US Senate has gone largely overlooked. From 1954 until 1970, the distinguished upper chamber of Congress became a battlefield in which South Carolina's senators fought the appointment of Simon Sobeloff to the Fourth Circuit; established a record-breaking filibuster against civil rights legislation; obstructed Thurgood Marshall's rise to the Second Circuit and, later, to the Supreme Court; triggered the landmark Senate rejection of Abe Fortas as chief justice; and, finally, failed to engineer the appointment of one of their own to the nation's highest court. To borrow Marlow Cook's words once again, this proved to be a truly unforgettable era for the US Supreme Court.

Although Thurmond was unhappy that the Senate had refused to confirm a South Carolina judge for the Fortas vacancy, his contentment with the conservative nominees offered by Republican presidents would continue throughout his remaining years in the Senate, while Hollings's lingering bitterness was palpable in his attitude toward subsequent judicial nominations. As will become clear, the junior senator's approach toward nominations remained strangely unaltered despite the enormous changes taking place in South Carolina, many of which he had initiated as the state's governor prior to arriving in the Senate. Hollings would ensure, throughout the 1970s and 1980s, and into the 1990s, that the state of South Carolina would continue to play a unique role in the complicated process of judicial nominations.

12. "DYNAMIC CONSERVATISM"

In his 1959 inaugural address following his election as governor of South Carolina, Ernest "Fritz" Hollings insisted that he would ensure the continuation of racial segregation in the state's public schools. His argument that the maintenance of segregation was the only means of ensuring fair educational opportunities is remarkable if only for the fact that, four years later, Hollings would preside over Clemson University's highly symbolic desegregation. In his memoirs, he claimed that a visit to an elementary school for African American children early in his career inspired him to reform the state's education system in the sense that, "given what I had just seen, I realized that minority education was separate but certainly not equal." While Hollings had advocated resistance to the Supreme Court in January 1959, arguing that education, as a practical matter, "can only be done in the segregated pattern," the governor ended his term in 1963 with a legendary farewell address, describing acceptance of *Brown v. Board of Education* as "a hurdle that brings little progress to either side. But the failure to clear it will bring us irreparable harm."[1]

Scholars have attributed Fritz Hollings's significance as a southern political figure to three aspects of his career. Firstly, they have acknowledged his role in guiding South Carolina through a period of political transition via a coordinated acceptance of desegregation. Tony Badger has claimed that Hollings's contribution warrants a measure of "self-congratulation," while Robert Mickey has argued that Hollings's success in negotiating with federal officials and repressing the state's white supremacist forces achieved "a peaceful, if token, desegregation." Secondly, scholars have characterized Hollings's introduction of a comprehensive system of technical training as a vitally important development in South Carolina's history, with Jack Bass and W. Scott Poole praising his skill in convincing the state legislature to help him finance the creation of "a willing, inexpensive and trained workforce," a process that constituted, in the words of James C. Cobb, "one of the pioneering responses to the need for a flexible but effective industrial training program." Finally, Hollings's survival as a Democratic senator over a thirty-eight-year period in an increasingly conservative state provides one of the more significant examples of Nicol Rae's characterization of southern Democrats as an ideologically flexible faction, focused primarily on local and regional concerns. Perhaps the most notable remark from Hollings's 1959 inaugural address is his claim that "it is our mission to put forward a dynamic conservatism as an asset, not a liability."[2] A combination of conservatism and progress was present throughout Hollings's Senate career, explaining his survival as a southern Democrat despite the Republican Party's political dominance of South Carolina by the time of his retirement in 2005.

With his Brylcreemed hair, boyish good looks, and verbal eloquence, the dynamic young governor was an obvious contender for a US Senate seat, and it is perhaps curious that most of the literature recognizing Hollings's importance has overlooked much of his lengthy career as a senator. Nicol Rae has noted the significance of Hollings's aborted 1984 presidential run and his support for Robert Bork's 1987 Supreme Court nomination, yet the South Carolinian was not among Rae's sizable cohort of interviewees during the completion of his study *Southern Democrats* (1994). Similarly, John P. Frank, who has produced the most comprehensive study of the Clement Haynsworth nomination, noted the significance of Hollings in recommending and promoting Haynsworth, yet he did not interview the senator, nor did he scrutinize his personal papers. With most scholars of southern political history focusing on state-level activities, black protest movements, massive white resistance, and other political activity prior to the early 1970s, the existing Hollings–related literature has focused largely on his four years as governor without bringing the story of his fascinating involvement in racial politics up to date. A more recent study—of "Ernest F. Hollings in the Civil Rights Era"—made no mention of his vote for the Bork nomination, or his support for Jesse Jackson in the 1988 Democratic Party presidential primaries.

Hollings was one of the more distinctive characters in the US Senate, not least through the rich, stirring tones of his voice, which contrasted markedly with Olin Johnston's deep, "slow-as-molasses" baritone, and especially with Strom Thurmond's unyielding nasal bark. Hollings used his inimitable voice to devastating effect, with references to "ponying up" sums of money, terms such as "shenanigans" and "accoutrements," and also the occasional malapropism. In his questioning, as a member of the Senate Commerce Committee, of Attorney General Janet Reno during hearings into violence on television in 1993, Hollings singled out the anarchic animated show *Beavis and Butthead* for criticism, declaring, "We've got this, what is it, *Buffcoat and Beaver,* or *Beaver* and something else, that they had—I haven't seen it, I don't watch it, but whatever it is, it was at seven o'clock—*Buffcoat*—and they put it on now at ten-thirty, I think. They've pleaded guilty, and they'll do it as long as you and I have hearings." In a remarkable showcase of his heavy Charleston accent, Hollings argued that "we just can't have hearings like we've had now for forty yee-ahs and get no-wee-ah." On other occasions, his idiosyncratic comments resulted in a number of gaffes: Hollings responded to the claims of Japanese leaders that Americans are "lazy" by reminding them that the atomic bomb was "made in the United States and tested in Japan" and apologized to Senator Howard Metzenbaum of Ohio for referring to him as "the Senator from B'nai Brith."[3]

Political contradictions seemed to characterize Hollings's complex ideology. Alongside his concern for African Americans living in poverty, as indicated by his "hunger tours" of 1969–1970, was his lengthy battle for fiscal conservatism, evidenced by the Gramm-Rudman-Hollings Balanced Budget Act of 1985, a collaboration with Republican senators Phil Gramm of Texas and Warren Rudman of New Hampshire. Hollings's brand of "dynamic conservatism" often led him to vote against a majority of his fellow Democrats in the Senate: he was one of only two Democratic senators to vote in favor of Robert Bork's confirmation as a Supreme Court justice in 1987, and one of only two Democrats to vote against the Family and Medical Leave Act of 1993, which aimed to ensure the provision of unpaid leave for employees requiring time off due to medical or family-related circumstances.[4]

The view of scholars that Hollings established a track record of forward-looking racial moderation has obscured the extension of his conservative ideology throughout his lengthy career. Yet Hollings's voting record in the Senate offers a classic example of how postwar southern Democrats saw electoral incentives in working across party lines in order to separate themselves from the national Democratic Party, in contrast to southern Republicans, who, as Frances E. Lee has argued, "do not need or seek any cross-party alliances in order to improve their political credibility with constituents." While he has been candid in discussing his passion for balancing the federal budget, the senator has been far less vocal on the issue of his voting record in the nomination of Supreme Court justices. Hollings utilized his record in the federal judicial nominations process as a means of displaying his conservative credentials to his South Carolina constituents in a manner that illustrates his attention to local and regional concerns. In so doing, he proved successful in solidifying his support among white conservatives but also tested frequently the patience and loyalty of his African American supporters. Despite his willingness to distance himself from Strom Thurmond, Hollings's voting record in the nominations process highlights the often overlooked fact that the two senators were products of the same South Carolina political tradition, and shared many ideological similarities long before Hollings arrived in the Senate. Only four years prior to Hollings's claim in his inaugural address that "we in South Carolina see no conflict between such conservatism and progress; indeed, we think they go hand in hand toward bringing us a better life," Thurmond had outlined his belief in "forward-looking moderation," claiming that "some call it conservatism. Some condemn it as reactionary, but I believe it to be a sound approach to most of the problems which we have faced in the past and which we must face in the future."[5]

As explained in previous chapters, Hollings's responses to President Lyndon Johnson's Supreme Court nominations proved to be ambiguous. His skill in choosing his political targets carefully and refusing to associate himself too closely with any particular group or institution reflects not only South Carolina's tendency toward independence, but also a mastery of diplomacy, which ensured his survival during an unpredictable era of racial unrest and political transition.

Hollings developed an ability to navigate his way across a complex political landscape during his turbulent four years as governor of South Carolina. On the one hand, he expressed a commitment to racial segregation and frequently condemned the NAACP, expressing the view that "if the Supreme Court can declare certain organizations as subversive, I believe South Carolina can declare the NAACP both subversive and illegal."[6] On the other hand, Hollings ensured the safety of black protestors and prepared the state for Clemson University's desegregation while at the same time maintaining cordial relationships with white conservatives engaged in "massive resistance." The governor's communications with the white Citizens' Councils—set up in response to the Supreme

Court's order to desegregate public schools—offer a useful example of the Hollings brand of diplomacy. In public, Hollings made clear his support, stating that "the Citizens' Councils, by mobilizing the best leadership at the community level, can help to restore decency in government and maintain peace and security for all people, both white and Negro." On December 2, 1960, Ralph B. Kolb, chairman of the South Carolina Citizens' Council, asked Hollings to back the governors of Mississippi, Alabama, and Georgia in "strengthening the position" of Louisiana's Governor Jimmie Davis during the crisis over the desegregation of William Frantz Elementary School in New Orleans. In his brief response, Hollings offered Governor Davis "sympathy and support," to which an unsatisfied Kolb replied, "we do not believe a routine expression of sympathy and support generally, under conditions now existing in Louisiana, is sufficient."[7]

Following archsegregationist Ross Barnett's victory in Mississippi's gubernatorial election of 1959, Hollings proved particularly diplomatic. The following month, Mrs. Bessie Britton, a Kingstree, South Carolina, resident and Citizens' Council member, wrote to express concern over a "rumor" that Hollings had declined to introduce Barnett at a Council meeting in South Carolina, to be held in the New Year. Hollings claimed in a particularly frank and detailed draft that "South Carolina is fortunate to be free of undue problems in racial relationships. I can best serve all South Carolinians at this time in helping to preserve this stability and way of life by maintaining separate status as Governor without identification with any groups, regardless of how worthy may be their purposes in the field of race relations. I have high personal respect and admiration for the objectives of the Citizens Councils and am greatly appreciative of their work in maintaining good relations between the races in our state."[8] Later in the month, however, when Hollings's office dispatched the response to Mrs. Britton, it was much shorter and read very differently, with Hollings declaring, "I am sorry I will not be able to attend the Citizens' Council meeting on January 29 due to other commitments. I can't tell from your letter what the rumor is, but assure you that my inability to attend is not because of an attitude against the Citizens' Council, which I have always supported."[9]

Around the same time, Farley Smith, executive secretary of the Association of Citizens' Councils, contacted Hollings over his concern that the governor did not seem to approve of the Association's invitation to Governor-elect Barnett. The governor's staff composed a suggested response, outlining that "I have the greatest admiration for Governor-elect Barnett of Mississippi and I feel that your selection of him as a speaker is an excellent one. However, I am of the opinion that you are making a mistake in having this meeting at this time and I sincerely feel that the Citizens' Council should not get in a running fight with the NAACP." However, when Hollings's office sent the response to Smith, it had been reduced to only one line, reading, "I have never had the pleasure of meeting Governor Barnett and told you of my limited knowledge when you and Mr. Dinkins were in Columbia."[10]

Hollings's decision not to align himself with Barnett ultimately proved to be an astute move. When Barnett advocated open resistance to black student James Meredith's enrollment at the University of Mississippi in September and October 1962, and expected other southern governors to back him, Hollings reverted to his usual diplomacy. As Hollings recalled years later, Barnett telephoned him and requested that he arrange for motorcades from cities in South Carolina, Georgia, and Alabama to head to Oxford, Mississippi, to undertake a united southern resistance to federal orders to integrate the university. According to Hollings, "I told Ross at the time, I said, that would be a very dangerous thing. I can't think of anybody following me in a motorcade, for a showdown to Oxford, Mississippi, that wouldn't include every kook, red-neck, crack-pot, Ku Klux Klanner, and everything else that you could find and they'd all follow me out and expect me to do something when I got there. . . . He didn't like that at all, got rather angry about it at the time." Publicly, however, Hollings acknowledged the feelings of many white conservative constituents. The *New York Times* quoted him as stating, "it is a very sad thing . . . the people of South Carolina are 100 per cent in sympathy with the people of Mississippi."[11] As with the draft of his letter to Farley Smith, criticizing the decision to hold the Citizens' Council meeting rather than criticizing Barnett himself, Hollings was careful to claim solidarity between the people of South Carolina and the people of Mississippi, rather than solidarity between himself and Barnett.

In contrast to the erratic Barnett's mismanagement of the Oxford crisis, Hollings avoided a large-scale outbreak of violence during the sit-in protests in Rock Hill, South Carolina, by replacing the town's white officers with black officers sent in from elsewhere in the state. Despite having claimed in a telegram to President Dwight D. Eisenhower that owners of private diners were not obliged to serve anyone who walked into their premises, the governor, in his own words, did not want "the little minority kids at the stools to be crowded by the white punks with peg-legged britches and ducktail haircuts who were waiting to dive and grab a seat as soon as the little black child got up to go to the bathroom." While avoiding making public his concern for the safety of "the little minority kids," Hollings did write to Farley Smith to thank the Association of Citizens' Councils for their cooperation in promoting law and order in Rock Hill during the sit-in protest, telling Smith, "You have done a fine service for the people of Rock Hill and the people of South Carolina." Even in his legendary farewell address in January 1963, Hollings maintained a similar style of diplomacy by emphasizing the importance of law and order over personal emotion, rather than making an open, and unthinkable, call for South Carolina to accept racial integration in public places.[12]

Hollings's term as governor divided black South Carolinians. Modjeska Simkins, the legendary NAACP activist who had enjoyed cordial relations with Olin Johnston, claimed in 1976 to be a Hollings opponent when she recalled a protest at South Carolina State College in Orangeburg in 1960: "They didn't have enough space in the jail. They put them in an enclosure, a wired-in enclosure around the jail. It was a cold, freezing day—well, I won't say it was freezing, but it was very bitter cold. And some of those children were water-hosed. They rolled on the ground with the force of the hose. And Hollings was governor. He did nothing about it."[13]

Alternatively, James Clyburn, another active participant in South Carolina's civil rights movement before his appointment as Governor John C. West's "minority advisor" in 1970 and election to the US House of Representatives in 1992, offers a more balanced appraisal: "I think he's a very shrewd politician. I guess every time I went to jail, he was Governor. But he never stood in the doorway of progress. This 'massive resistance' never took place in South Carolina as it did in Mississippi, Alabama, Louisiana, Arkansas, simply because people like Fritz Hollings took a different tack."[14] In his memoirs, Hollings neglected to mention the wire enclosure, and instead recalled the Orangeburg protest with his usual folksiness, joking that "Clyburn needles me about that episode; he says I hosed him down but didn't kill him," and also tells a touching story of how Clyburn met his future wife, Emily, in the courthouse after the arrests.[15]

After winning election to the Senate in November 1966, Hollings continued refining his political instincts in the practice of providing, or withholding, senatorial consent to presidential nominations to the US Supreme Court. The Haynsworth episode demonstrates the senator's perception, and acceptance, of how South Carolina's conservative white voting majority perceived federal judges during the era of civil rights. His shift from an ambiguous position on two liberal nominees (Marshall and Fortas) to an open endorsement of a conservative nominee is consistent with the style of diplomacy he had practiced as governor. In Haynsworth's case, the senator was able to play down the nominee's little-known decisions and emphasize his supposedly sound constitutional judgment. In the case of Marshall and Fortas, Hollings knew from the outset that he would never be able to "sell" a liberal judicial philosophy to southern conservatives, nor would he be able to play down the impact of *Brown* or *Miranda* or any other landmark Supreme Court decision that either man had been involved in. His success in winning reelection in November 1968 suggested that he had played his hand skillfully and diplomatically with regard to Marshall and Fortas, but his bitter disappointment following the Senate's rejection of Haynsworth would influence his actions over the course of subsequent nominations.

Hollings may not have shared Strom Thurmond's optimistic prediction of another southern Supreme Court nominee before the end of Richard Nixon's presidency, but Nixon secured an airtight justification for naming a third southern judge when Justice Hugo Black, the court's only southerner, announced his intention to retire in September 1971. The *Los Angeles Times* reported that Nixon was considering as many as seven southerners for the vacancy, noting that the president was also seeking out "a nominee who believes in a strict interpretation of the Constitution." According to former White House counsel John W. Dean, Nixon told Attorney General John Mitchell that Black's replacement must be a southerner, and "must be against busing, and against forced housing integration. Beyond that, he can do what he pleases. He can screw around on, you know, economics and et ceteras." In selecting the inoffensive Virginian Democrat Lewis F. Powell, a former president of the ABA, Nixon finally succeeded in naming a southerner with impeccable legal credentials and little or no controversy, race-related or otherwise, to his name. Yet the president's selection of William Rehnquist, assistant attorney general for the Office of Legal Counsel, to replace Justice John Marshall Harlan II, who revealed his retirement plans only one week after Hugo Black's announcement, ultimately overshadowed the Powell nomination. The president nominated Powell and Rehnquist on the same day, October 21, 1971, and senators braced themselves to scrutinize two Nixon nominees at once.[16]

Alarmed by Rehnquist's conservatism, the American Civil Liberties Union (ACLU) broke "a time-honored tradition" of never formally opposing a nomination for public office, and called openly for the Senate to reject the nominee. During confirmation hearings, Hollings's nemesis, Senator Birch Bayh of Indiana, asked the nominee if he had ever challenged or harassed black or Hispanic voters at polling booths in his home state of Arizona, which Rehnquist denied. In addition to writing to the Judiciary Committee chairman, James Eastland, to protest his innocence, Rehnquist submitted a sworn affidavit to contradict six accusations of harassment. John W. Dean, who claims responsibility for influencing Nixon's choice of Rehnquist, has conceded that a "lack of vetting left [Rehnquist] ill-prepared to fend off attacks. Even during the hearings themselves, the White House was half-asleep."[17] Before long, Judiciary Committee member John V. Tunney of California announced his opposition to confirmation, arguing that "[Rehnquist's] justification of a vast expansion of the Subversive Activities Control Board, his defense of unrestricted governmental surveillance, his rationale for preventive detention, all of these demonstrate that he is quite the reverse of a 'strict constructionist.' He, instead, seems quite willing to read into the powers of the Executive branch unrestricted latitude which threatens the very basis of individual freedoms."[18] Noting Rehnquist's relative youth and the fact that "he could still be serving on the Court in the year 2000," Tunney claimed that the nominee was ill-suited to serve on the Supreme Court during a period of "profound social and political changes in this country" and complained that "it is singularly inappropriate for those who favor Mr. Rehnquist's nomination to attempt to hold Mr. Powell hostage in their endeavor." The controversy over the Rehnquist selection meant that, finally, the president was able to get a southerner confirmed to the court without inconvenience, as one editorial noted: "The curious thing about the entire exercise is that Powell, who has come in for virtually no criticism, almost certainly is just as conservative as Rehnquist."[19]

Seeking to defend the Rehnquist nomination by offsetting the unexpected accusations of racism, Hollings contacted fellow South Carolinian Ben Holman, former director of the Community Relations Service—a wing of the Justice Department responsible for managing race-influenced community conflict—in order to probe his views. In his response, Holman explained that Rehnquist "has been highly supportive of our cause and on several occasions sought to broaden our statutory mandate," adding that "as a black man sensitive to the various forms of racist behavior, I can assure you that Bill Rehnquist will judge minorities fairly if he is confirmed to the Court." Armed with a weapon to use against Rehnquist's critics, Hollings took the time to quote "the black man who heads the Community Relations Service" in letters to constituents, and also quoted Holman in a speech on the Senate floor, requesting that the complete letter be printed for the record.[20]

In other communications to his constituents, Hollings emphasized that he had become acquainted with Rehnquist during the Justice Department's unsuccessful drive to confirm Clement Haynsworth the previous year. The senator's comments on Rehnquist's conservatism in these letters—"some attack Mr. Rehnquist for his conservatism. Yet a strong article of conservatism has always been the strong emphasis on individual liberties"—provide another example of Hollings using a "strict constructionist" approach to judicial interpretation as a selling point when defending a nominee, without reflecting on the potential consequences of the nominee's decisions. His claim that "I believe [Rehnquist] holds the First Amendment and the rights of the individual in highest respect" does not acknowledge that a judge can hold the original meaning of the First Amendment "in highest respect" while at the same time handing down decisions that fail to protect the rights of all individuals all of the time.[21]

With Thurmond and others on the Senate Judiciary Committee supporting both nominees, and in the absence of a "Vend-A-Matic"-style controversy, Birch Bayh knew that his opposition to William Rehnquist stood no chance of developing the same momentum witnessed during his campaign against Clement Haynsworth. His most potent weapon—a one-and-a-half-page memorandum Rehnquist had authored in 1952 while working as a law clerk for Justice Robert Jackson, in which the nominee had apparently advised the late justice to uphold the "separate but equal" doctrine established by *Plessy v. Ferguson*—proved ineffective in gathering support for his opposition. Rehnquist maintained that he had merely outlined only one hypothetical position for Jackson to adopt when preparing his opinion in *Brown v. Board of Education,* but many senators remained unconvinced, not least because the memo was written in the first person, with the line "I have been excoriated by my 'liberal' colleagues but I think *Plessy* was right" seeming to provide incontrovertible evidence of Rehnquist's racial conservatism. Nonetheless, with only Bayh and Senators Philip Hart of Michigan, Edward Kennedy of Massachusetts, and John Tunney of California voting against Rehnquist in committee, the Senate confirmed Powell, with only one negative vote, on December 6, 1971, and Rehnquist, by a vote of 68–26, on December 10, defeating Bayh's effort to mount a filibuster by a vote of 70–22.

John Dean considered Nixon's appointment of William Rehnquist to have "redefined the Supreme Court, making it a politically conservative bastion within our governmental system. . . . With Rehnquist, Nixon found the conservative who would sit on the high bench for three decades."[22]

Hollings's diplomacy in the federal judicial nomination process highlights once again James Cobb's theory of white southern politicians walking a tightrope when addressing African American concerns while at the same time trying to imply that white conservative interests remained paramount.[23] Influenced by his skillful management of the Clemson episode and his personal involvement in the Haynsworth rejection, the distinctive Hollings approach to Supreme Court appointments would truly stand out in the late 1980s and early 1990s, ensuring that the state of South Carolina maintained its unique involvement in the judicial nominations process.

With his enthusiastic backing of Nixon's southern Supreme Court strategy, Strom Thurmond began mellowing into the persona of a kindly elder statesman, smiling benevolently upon each Republican nominee offered by Republican Presidents Nixon, Ford, and Reagan during the 1970s and 1980s. Fritz Hollings, despite the apparent political contrast with his South Carolina colleague, remained locked into the very same process of crafting a conservative lineup of "strict constructionist" judges who would, in theory, begin dismantling the legacy of Earl Warren, Hugo Black, William O. Douglas, and the other justices of the Warren Court era. With the Senate's confirmation of Lewis Powell, Thurmond and Hollings had finally overseen a presidential appointment of a conservative southern judge to the US Supreme Court, albeit a judge from Virginia and not South Carolina. Yet by the mid-1980s, few conservatives were satisfied that the Republican appointments of the period 1969–1975 had helped to roll back the Warren Court's legacy, particularly given Harry Blackmun's authorship of *Roe v. Wade,* and Lewis Powell's centrist position on the court, as evidenced by his role in *Regents of the University of California v. Bakke* (1978), which dented yet preserved the principle of affirmative action in education institutions.

With the Republican Party back in control of the US Senate in 1981, President Ronald Reagan would benefit from a valuable Republican ally as the new chairman of the Senate Judiciary Committee—none other than South Carolina's Strom Thurmond. The senator would continue his trend of supporting presidential appointments of conservative Supreme Court justices, and, as chairman, he would oversee the Committee's approval of Sandra Day O'Connor, the first female justice of the court; Antonin Scalia, the first Italian-American justice; and also—despite a second round of controversy over the aforementioned 1952 memorandum—President Reagan's promotion of William Rehnquist to the chief justiceship following Warren Burger's retirement. In 1981, the chairman reportedly toasted Sandra Day O'Connor's confirmation in a manner "more suited for a 1950s bride than for the newest associate member for the Supreme Court," with the truly Thurmond-like declaration, "We love you for your beauty, respect you for your intelligence, adore you for your charm, and will come to love you . . . because we can't help it."[24]

Progressive-minded commentators have taken a dim view of Thurmond's dealings with the opposite sex, but his minor role in promoting women to the federal judiciary is perhaps worthy of some credit. Shortly after the Senate's rejection of Clement Haynsworth, Thurmond forwarded to Harry S. Fleming, special assistant to the president, recommendations of Judge Susie M. Sharp of the North Carolina Supreme Court, and Judge Mildred Lillie of California's Second Appellate District Court. Nixon's serious consideration of Lillie's candidacy when seeking replacements for Justices Black and Harlan in the fall of 1971 has been well-documented, but less well known is the fact that Thurmond and others had recommended both Lillie and Sharp almost two years before. Sam Ervin and B. Everett Jordan, the two senators from North Carolina, had brought Sharp's name to Nixon's attention even earlier, and they wrote to the president following the Haynsworth rejection to ask once again that he "give her every consideration in your selection of a new justice for the Supreme Court." Significantly, the administration considered Lillie and Sharp to be the only true "conservatives" on the president's list of female candidates.[25]

Nixon ultimately chose to make the disastrous nomination of G. Harrold Carswell, but his wife's influence, and the need to offset the risk of a future rejection, would bring his attention back to Mildred Lillie. Although John Dean claims that the president saw political advantages in naming Lillie as one of the Black/Harlan replacements in 1971—at one point believing that "these bastards can't vote against her"—a negative ABA rating destroyed Lillie's candidacy. David Yalof has speculated that the administration dropped Susie Sharp from consideration due to her advanced age of sixty-four, and the fact that Nixon was also weighing the nomination of Senator Robert C. Byrd of West Virginia and wished to avoid "a ticket composed entirely of Southerners," particularly after the Haynsworth and Carswell controversies. Nonetheless, Sharp's name continued to appear on presidential shortlists until Ronald Reagan appointed Sandra Day O'Connor as the court's first female justice in 1981.[26]

Caroline Davis, director of the Women's Department of the United Automobile, Aerospace and Agricultural Implement Workers of America, wrote to Thurmond, ironically just weeks after he had passed on recommendations of Lillie and Sharp, to urge the senator to oppose the Carswell nomination on the grounds that his confirmation would prove disastrous for women. Arguing that "Judge Carswell showed no concern for women or the welfare of children of working mothers when he ruled last fall in the Ida Phillips versus Martin Marietta case," Davis's letter highlighted an intensifying chorus of female dissent in the arena of judicial nominations.[27] As both Thurmond and Hollings would experience during the 1980s and 1990s, the court's willingness to address divisive issues such as abortion, capital punishment, and affirmative action would only amplify the voices of women, and minority men and women, long after the social transformation of the 1960s.

13. "TOO MUCH BLOOD ON THE FLOOR"

Shuffling down the hall of the Russell Senate Office building with his distinctive crop of bright orange hair, the aging Strom Thurmond was, by the mid-1980s, barely recognizable as the giant of southern politics who had interrogated Thurgood Marshall and engineered the destruction of Abe Fortas's promotion to chief justice twenty years previously. As chairman of the Senate Judiciary Committee, Thurmond was able to provide conservative Supreme Court nominees with a smooth passage to confirmation during the early years of the Reagan presidency, but the Democrats' success in regaining control of the Senate in the 1986 mid-term elections—which resulted in Democratic senator Joseph Biden of Delaware replacing Thurmond as chairman—suggested that senators might now challenge, if not curtail, Ronald Reagan's success in appointing conservatives to the nation's highest court. Furthermore, Thurmond knew he could not rely on his independent-minded South Carolina colleague to support his preferences for judicial positions. Just as Thurmond had offered Donald Russell as an alternative to Fritz Hollings's recommendation of Clement Haynsworth in 1969, Hollings had offered African American Judge Matthew J. Perry as an alternative to Thurmond's choice of Emory Sneeden for a newly created seat on the Fourth Circuit Court of Appeals in 1984. Ironically, Thurmond had engineered Perry's appointment to the US Court of Military Appeals back in 1976 when making one of many efforts to improve his standing among black voters.[1]

Meanwhile, Fritz Hollings was fast becoming one of the Senate's more distinctive and colorful southern characters, as evidenced by his participation as a member of the Senate Commerce Committee. One of the more bizarre moments in Senate history occurred during Commerce Committee hearings in 1985, when Hollings discussed with Frank Zappa the merits of including lyrics sheets within album packaging as an aid to parents trying to prevent their children from exposure to inappropriate sexual or violent content. While the pair seemed to agree that lyric sheets would be preferable to a ratings system, if only to respect the fact that, in Zappa's words, "not all parents want to keep their children totally ignorant," the senator claimed, "Well, what's—yeah, you and I would differ on what's ignorance and educated, I can see that," to which an unimpressed Zappa responded, "No, I happen to think you're very educated."[2]

Hollings was not one of the critical figures in the Supreme Court nominations of Robert Bork in 1987 and Clarence Thomas in 1991, yet his role in the outcome of each selection provides a further suggestion of his unique perspective on the judicial nominations process. Nearly twenty years on from his spirited defense of Clement Haynsworth, he seemed no less enthusiastic about involving himself in controversy through backing divisive nominees for the nation's highest court. In the case of Robert Bork, President Reagan had selected a judge with impeccable conservative credentials but without considering the significance of timing. As Jan Crawford has argued, the Senate might well have confirmed Bork in June 1986 had Reagan nominated him for the vacancy left by William Rehnquist when the president appointed Rehnquist chief justice (a vacancy which he ultimately filled with Antonin Scalia). But Reagan had nominated the controversial Bork after the Democrats retook control of Congress and the scandal of the Iran-Contra Affair was beginning to weaken his approval ratings. His selection of an outspoken conservative judge to replace the moderate Lewis Powell would only invite further scrutiny and controversy.[3]

The Reagan administration, overwhelmed by Bork's intellectual superiority, remained confident that the nominee would handle the Judiciary Committee confirmation hearings skillfully, and never formulated a plan to "sell" Bork to the American people.[4] One example of Bork's unexpectedly frank responses came during his exchange with Chairman Joe Biden regarding the *Griswold v. Connecticut* decision of 1965, in which the Supreme Court had struck down a statute preventing couples' use of contraceptives. Bork claimed that Justice William O. Douglas's concern for "how awful it would be to have the police pounding into the marital bedroom" was a moot point because the Fourth Amendment prevented this scenario. In other words, "the police simply could not get into the bedroom without a warrant." Biden then pressed him on the potential implications of the Connecticut statute:

The Chairman: If they had evidence that a crime was being committed—

Judge Bork: How are they going to get evidence that a couple are using contraceptives?

The Chairman: A wiretap.

Judge Bork: Wiretapping?

The Chairman: A wiretap.

Judge Bork: You mean to say that—

The Chairman: They—they have a legal wiretap.

Judge Bork: You mean to say that a magistrate is going to organize a wiretap to find out if a couple is using contraceptives?

The Chairman: They could—

Judge Bork: No, it's—

The Chairman: —couldn't they, in law?

Judge Bork: Unbelievable. Unbelievable.

The Chairman: Let—no, I understand that, but under the law, Judge, could they not have—it was a crime, correct?

Judge Bork: It was a—it was a crime in—on the statute books, which was never prosecuted.

The Chairman: No, I—

Judge Bork: Never.

The Chairman: Well, the fact that it wasn't prosecuted—

Judge Bork: Well, let me—

The Chairman: —did not mean that it wasn't a crime, doesn't it?

Judge Bork: I have—I have more to say about that, whether it was a crime or not.

Biden continued to pursue the issue by asking what would happen if a wiretap installed on the basis of a couple's involvement in illegal activity, such as drug dealing, happened to reveal that the couple had been using contraceptives. Appearing to stifle a giggle, an incredulous Bork asserted that "nobody is going to get a warrant for that, and no prosecution is going to be upheld for that."[5] Bork later sighed with frustration during questions from Senator Dennis DeConcini of Arizona on gender discrimination, and, when Senator Edward Kennedy of Massachusetts accused him of a "bias against women and minorities in favor of big business and presidential power," an agitated Bork replied, "Senator, if those charges were not so serious, the discrepancy between the evidence and what you say would be highly amusing." Thanks to the introduction of television cameras for Sandra Day O'Connor's hearings in 1981, the confirmation process had become a remarkably public series of events by the summer of 1987, with millions of Americans watching these tense exchanges live, or as reruns on C-SPAN, or in the form of extended coverage on the evening news. In Jan Crawford's view, Bork's answers "made him seem anything but witty, warm and responsive," and implied an arrogant attitude, which enabled his opponents to portray him as unsympathetic to the problems of ordinary Americans.[6]

The Bork episode showcased an explosion in interest group activity, with over three hundred groups mobilizing in opposition to the nominee. Bork's opponents outlined grave concerns over the appointment, as outlined in a dramatic television commercial chronicling his conservative record on abortion and civil rights, which advised Americans, in the sobering tones of Hollywood actor Gregory Peck, to "please urge your Senators to vote against the Bork nomination, because if Robert Bork wins a seat on the Supreme Court, it will be for life—his life and yours."[7] In addition to the growing number of groups opposing Bork for his views on abortion and gender discrimination, southern senators with sympathy for the nominee's judicial philosophy had other reasons to hesitate before declaring their support. As Ethan Bronner has explained, African American groups opposed Bork's confirmation so virulently that most southern senators felt they had little choice but to vote against confirmation. Having adjusted to a transformed political landscape by showing greater sensitivity to black voters following the passage of the landmark Voting Rights Act, southern senators now felt compelled to vote against a highly qualified yet ultraconservative Supreme Court nominee in order to offset the risk of losing black support.

Having declared, "we're gonna go with the brothers on this one," with reference to the young black men on his staff, Louisiana's three-term Democratic senator, J. Bennett Johnston, presided over a meeting with other southern Democrats, including John Breaux, his Louisiana colleague; David Pryor of Arkansas; Wyche Fowler of Georgia; Richard Shelby of Alabama; and Bob Graham of Florida. All would vote against the nominee. Breaux later admitted that he "didn't make the decision based on [Bork's] qualifications." Southern Democrats with much longer histories in the US Congress were inclined to agree with his outlook: Robert Byrd of West Virginia and John Stennis of Mississippi, both of whom had opposed the Voting Rights Act, also joined the opposition. As one advisor to Chairman Biden observed, "To see the reaction of white Southerners afraid to go back on civil rights was overwhelming." With the gradual expansion of Republican Party control throughout the southern states, the southern Democrats, as Nicol Rae has pointed out, "had to face the new reality of Democratic Party politics in the South."[8] Without solid black support, the southern Democrats' survival had become unthinkable in most instances.

It is highly significant that Fritz Hollings was the only Deep South Democrat to maintain his independence with regard to the Bork nomination. Crucially, Hollings's defense of Robert Bork suggests very personal reasons for refusing to join his southern colleagues in voting against the nominee, and, perhaps more importantly, provides another example of South Carolina's unique role in the nomination of Supreme Court justices. Shortly before outlining his support for Bork on the Senate floor, Hollings indicated in a letter to Andrew Young, Atlanta's African American mayor, his concern over Republican encroachment in the southern states, explaining that, "The situation is much like the Haynsworth nomination, which I handled. But be that as it may, I don't think we ought to hold up the judicial appointments like Thurmond did Fortas. We are being polarized too much now and we are fast losing our Democratic Party in the

South."[9] While only too happy to emphasize the differences between himself and his South Carolina colleague, Hollings understood that the Fortas and Haynsworth nomination disasters by now characterized the judicial nominations process. His involvement in both episodes influenced his highly controversial vote to confirm Robert Bork's appointment as a Supreme Court justice.

The text of Hollings's Senate speech in defense of Bork, delivered on October 8, 1987, suggests strongly that his association with Clement Haynsworth—and his personal view that the Senate committed an unpardonable sin by rejecting the South Carolina judge in 1969—virtually compelled him to support Bork's confirmation. Opening with a lengthy and detailed account of how he had recommended Haynsworth to President Nixon and then attempted to steer the nomination through the Senate, Hollings reminded his colleagues once again of the events involved in the Haynsworth debacle, utilizing his familiar tactic of blaming the Republicans entirely, before making a claim later repeated in his 2008 memoirs, that, following Haynsworth's rejection, "at least seven Senators have individually recanted to me."[10]

Later in the speech, Hollings acknowledged the increasing black pressure to vote against the nomination. Conceding that "overwhelming black support" had proved crucial in his 1986 reelection victory, he commented that the executive director of South Carolina's NAACP had declared that "if Hollings supports Bork, he might as well forget the black vote." Yet Hollings then admitted that "were it not for my experience in the Haynsworth defeat, were it not for the distinguished character and ability of Bork the man, it would be easy politically to find something wrong or puzzling and vote 'no,'" followed by the insistence that "being reminded time and again by strong supporters that this is a vote they won't forget—and they won't—makes it difficult to vote 'aye.' But vote aye I must. For somewhere, sometime in this Senate we must stand up to the onrush of contrived threats and pressure."[11] In complete contrast to his southern colleagues, who felt that African American demands constituted an entirely logical reason to vote against the nominee, Hollings appeared to be implying that the huge black opposition to Bork made it absolutely imperative that he support the nomination and resist caving in to the NAACP's "threats and pressure."

One of the more complex aspects of the speech is the bizarre manner in which Hollings attempted to portray Robert Bork as a racial moderate while at the same time praising the nominee for refusing to hide his genuine beliefs. Hollings was, of course, correct that "Judge Bork did not hide. He was forthright," but Bork's openness in articulating his judicial philosophy had exposed a deeply conservative interpretation of the US Constitution, undermining Hollings's claim that Bork had worked to increase the "opportunities of blacks and women in this country."[12] Interestingly, in an earlier draft of the speech, from October 7, the line dealing with Bork's "forthrightness" originally read "Judge Bork did not hide from his record," but the words "from his record" were removed and replaced with "He was forthright," presumably in a bid to praise Bork's honesty without drawing attention to the actual record. While it may have been true that the nominee "was downright masterful in his more than sixty hours of testimony," it seems unlikely that the extent of Bork's constitutional expertise reassured black South Carolinians, especially when articulated in such a blunt, almost confrontational manner. It is equally unlikely that they were reassured by Hollings's claim to have "lived through those turbulent, troubled times in the South."[13]

Throughout the remainder of the speech, Hollings referred to "calls from my home state" but deflected black constituents' criticisms of Bork rather than reassured the state's black community that he was listening. When he did introduce a black voice into the speech, it was that of Jewel Lafontant, former deputy solicitor general and former secretary of the Chicago branch of the NAACP, who, according to Hollings, said of Bork, "as a woman and a black woman . . . let me tell you about the heart of the man. . . . I have no fear of entrusting my rights and my privileges to Robert Bork. . . . I sincerely believe he is devoid of racial prejudice." His use of Lafontant's sentiments to defend Bork recalled his earlier use of Ben Holman's words as a means of defending William Rehnquist following his controversial associate justice nomination in 1971.[14]

Approaching the end of the speech, Hollings was careful to avoid offending fellow Democrats by removing a line arguing that "Senators lining up against Bork are now suddenly becoming constitutional experts. The attempt is to dignify and obscure their local politics and dignify their decisions." He also removed the argument that "we become a lesser body when we trash a distinguished judge. . . . It says to the country 'give us Roman Hruska's mediocrity,'" which, had that line been left in, would have reminded his colleagues of the Senate's rejection of the undistinguished G. Harrold Carswell and also Senator Hruska's catastrophic attempt to defend that nominee. The most famous line from the speech, later repeated in Hollings's memoirs, is the judgment that "We are governing by political poll. The most deliberative body in the world is becoming a rigged jury." The line originally appeared, in the October 7 draft, in the section dealing with the NAACP's "contrived threats and pressure," but Hollings or one of his staff relocated the line to a new section dealing with the manner in which the nation's Founding Fathers "crafted a disciplined, representative democracy," suggesting strongly that Hollings believed the line to contain his most powerful political point and wanted to maximize the impact on his colleagues.[15] After including Winston Churchill's claim that "There is only one duty, one safe course, and that is to try to be right," Hollings concluded by quoting political commentator David Broder's view that "it's something else when judges are lynched to appease the public."[16] Aside from reminding those listening of a barbaric practice frequently associated with the American South, the final line of Hollings's speech would prove rather prescient, as those involved in the chaotic Clarence Thomas nomination would discover during the late summer of 1991.

In the meantime, Hollings's characterization of the Bork opposition as a "lynch mob" provoked a public row with the NAACP national board chairman, William Gibson, and confusion among Hollings's supporters, many of whom recalled that the very groups now opposing Bork had approved of many of the senator's past actions. The day after he made the speech, the *Spartanburg Herald-Journal* chronicled the debate within the southern political science community over Hollings's position. South Carolina academics appeared to agree that the junior senator's behavior did in fact seem logical, in the sense that, firstly, Hollings's vote to confirm Bork would succeed in proving his conservative credentials, and, secondly, he would have sufficient time in which to make amends prior to his 1992 reelection campaign. As Charles Dunn of Clemson University argued, "When the dust settles, both sides are going to understand and respect one another once again."[17]

Although Dunn's prediction ultimately proved correct, Hollings felt compelled to compose a second speech in defense of Bork. Clearly upset that his black constituents had "publicly vilified" him, Hollings claimed to be "hurt," and declared solemnly that "after nearly four decades in public service, it is painful to have my civil rights bona fides impeached." In one of the most significant, yet overlooked, statements of his lengthy career, Hollings argued that Robert Bork, during his tenure as solicitor general, "argued more pro–civil rights cases than any Supreme Court nominee since Thurgood Marshall."[18] On the one hand, it may seem incredible that Hollings would seek to defend Bork by comparing him to Marshall, particularly given that Bork, as solicitor general, had argued on behalf of the state of Michigan before the Supreme Court in *Milliken v. Bradley* (1974), which, as Bob Woodward and Scott Armstrong have pointed out, resulted in "the first major cutback in desegregation remedies by the Court since [Marshall] argued the *Brown* case nearly twenty years before."[19] Had this second speech been delivered, some of Hollings's colleagues may have recalled his 1967 vote to reject Marshall's confirmation for a seat on the Supreme Court and felt that this gesture had damaged his "civil rights bona fides" far more than his support for Bork.

On the other hand, with the chorus of condemnation drowning out the detail of the nominee's record, Hollings's defense did highlight some of the lesser-known cases that Bork had been involved in as solicitor general, the results of which betrayed the ruthless conservative persona portrayed on the evening news. Hollings offered, as one example, the case of *Runyon v. McCrary,* in which Bork had upheld civil rights laws preventing private schools from denying admission to black children. James Clyburn, then serving as South Carolina's human affairs commissioner, later claimed that his opposition to Bork "may have been a horrible mistake." With regard to Bork's role in *Runyon,* Clyburn expressed the view that "I find it a bit hard to believe Mr. Bork would have reversed himself on this very important issue. I admit, however, that I have no feel for what he may have done in other instances."[20]

In a third speech—intended to be delivered prior to the vote on the nomination, on October 23—Hollings outlined his view that judges have a duty to interpret the US Constitution without considering the political outcome of their decisions. This is evident in his claim that interest groups were opposing Bork through a belief that he would not "bend or ignore the Constitution in order to reach results they want but cannot achieve through the political process." In a blistering display of his conservative credentials, Hollings referred back to the "marital bedroom" issue debated by Bork and Biden, insisting that "when the ACLU and law professors like Larry Tribe say 'right to privacy,' they mean rights to obtain an abortion and engage in homosexual sodomy. You may be surprised to hear this because no one opposing Judge Bork wants to talk about it." As with the equally provocative second speech, there is no trace of the third speech in the *Congressional Record.*[21]

Regardless of his own personal feelings, the unique political realities of South Carolina ultimately motivated Hollings's willingness to stand alone while his southern Democratic colleagues pursued a very different path. As Charles Dunn argued during the Senate's deliberations over Bork's confirmation, "the damage to Hollings would have been greater had he hailed from another Southern state, where many Democratic incumbents were carried to office by an overwhelming black vote and little of the white vote."[22] In contrast to Alabama's Richard Shelby, elected as a senator in 1986 with a 50 percent share of the vote, winning 88 percent of the black vote and 38 percent of the white vote, Hollings had won election with 63 percent of the vote, taking 96 percent of the black vote and a whopping 56 percent of the white vote. Senators John Breaux of Louisiana and Wyche Fowler of Georgia won election in 1986 with numbers similar to those of Shelby, with Breaux winning with 53 percent, taking 86 percent of the black vote, and Fowler winning with 51 percent, taking 82 percent of the black vote, and each man taking only 39 percent of the white vote in their respective states.[23]

On October 23, the Senate rejected the Bork nomination by a devastating vote of 42–58, with Hollings and David Boren of Oklahoma the only two Democrats to vote in favor of confirmation. In making allowances for errors within their "probabilistic" model of congressional voting, Keith Poole and Howard Rosenthal have cited the ill-fitting votes of "maverick" senators such as Hollings, but offered some perspective on these errors by concluding that a Hollings vote to confirm the Bork nomination "was a less serious error than a vote to confirm by Ted Kennedy." Furthermore, it is significant that the aforementioned Breaux, Fowler, and Shelby were all freshman senators during the Bork episode, whereas Hollings, armed with seniority on Senate committees (including the chairmanship of the Commerce Committee) was serving his fourth term. The fact remains that although Hollings acknowledged the potential dangers of alienating black support, his seniority—combined with the makeup of the South Carolina electorate in the late 1980s—resulted in a situation where he simply had less to lose than his fellow Deep South Democrats when supporting the nomination of Robert Bork and, four years later, the nomination of the equally controversial Clarence Thomas. In explaining the key to Democratic success in South Carolina's elections, Jon Kuzenski has advised against overestimating the impact of African American voter turnout, arguing that "the substantially more important factor is what *white* voters are doing—particularly among the great blocs of the state's white evangelical and/or racial conservatives."[24]

Following Reagan's second unsuccessful attempt to replace Lewis Powell—with Judge Douglas Ginsburg, whose name he withdrew following the revelation that Ginsburg had smoked marijuana while working as an assistant professor at Harvard University in the 1960s—the president and the Senate finally settled on Judge Anthony Kennedy as the new justice of the Supreme Court. Senators declined to fight the nomination, with John McCain of Arizona declaring, "Nobody wants to go through that again. There's too much blood on the floor." According to Jan Crawford, when Kennedy arrived on the court, Justice Harry Blackmun sent him a friendly note, welcoming him to the "good old Number Three Club," in reference to the fact that both had been chosen following the failure of two previous nominations.[25]

Four years on from the Bork debacle, Fritz Hollings displayed his sense of judicial conservatism once again as he set out to defend President George H. W. Bush's nomination of Clarence Thomas to replace Thurgood Marshall on the Supreme Court. African Americans reacted negatively to the president's selection of a deeply conservative, anti–affirmative action African American as a replacement for the civil rights hero who had argued the *Brown* case—film director Spike Lee famously referred to Thomas as "a chicken and biscuit–eating Uncle Tom"—and Democrats in the Senate were divided, with many happy to see the continuation of the court's "black seat" but others underwhelmed by Thomas's judicial record and also the first notably lukewarm ABA rating since the ill-fated Carswell nomination in 1970.[26]

Prominent southern African Americans were divided in their reaction: James Clyburn overcame his "concerns" to speak favorably of Thomas's confirmation, stating, "if not Clarence Thomas, who? It is unrealistic to even think George Bush will nominate someone more sympathetic than Clarence is to the civil rights community's agenda," while Alabama's Congressman John Lewis, former head of the Student Non-Violent Coordinating Committee (SNCC), announced that he opposed Thomas, claiming "some have asked, 'If not him, who?' That, to me, is not the issue. I would oppose any nominee who espouses the views that Thomas has espoused." To complicate matters further, the confirmation hearings descended into chaos when law professor Anita Hill alleged that Thomas had behaved inappropriately and made sexually explicit comments to her on a regular basis when she worked for him at the US Department of Education, and later, when he served as chairman of the US Equal Employment Opportunity Commission. Thomas defended himself before the Judiciary Committee, describing his nomination hearings as "a national disgrace," and adding the now-famous description of his ordeal as "a high-tech lynching for uppity blacks who in any way deign to think for themselves." The Thomas nomination, in the words of David Bositis, "checkmated black activists, making it difficult for them to aggressively oppose a black nominee even though they dislike his views" and also presented southern Democrats with another complex political dilemma. Furthermore, as Michael Comiskey has shown, Thomas's supporters could easily condemn as racism the senators' attempts to hold the nominee to a high standard, with Strom Thurmond's interrogation of Thurgood Marshall perhaps offering a useful and rather ironic historical reference point.[27]

Fritz Hollings appeared to agree with Clyburn's "if not Thomas, who?" perspective. On September 25, 1991, he responded to a constituent who had criticized the forty-three-year-old Thomas's limited judicial experience and urged the senator to "tell Bush to try again." Hollings argued that "if you tell Bush to try again, you can bet your boots you're going to get a Hispanic of the same ilk. Otherwise, take your criticism and go to the Marshall nomination. While Marshall argued more cases of a specific nature, no one would have called him profound." The Senate confirmed Thomas on October 15, by a wafer-thin margin of 52–48, after which Senator John Danforth of Missouri, who had guided Thomas through the hearings, sent Hollings a note of thanks, claiming that "during a time of glaring national attention and sometimes heated battle, I appreciate your support." Nonetheless, Hollings had to compose numerous "I'm sorry you feel as you do" letters in response to far less appreciative communications from disappointed supporters, offering typically a Hollingsesque assurance that "my decision was not based on any poll. I've long since felt that polls are a curse of this profession and couldn't agree more about your analysis of the Bush Administration."[28]

Hollings's support for Bork had tested the patience of his African American supporters, but with his vote to confirm Clarence Thomas, he risked alienating a far bigger section of the electorate. Judith L. Lichtman, president of the Women's Legal Defense Fund, sent to Hollings a highly critical report of Thomas's record on "issues that have life-shaping importance to women and their families." Lichtman's assertion, in her accompanying letter, that "this is a time when women, especially women of color who face double discrimination based on gender *and* race are even more vulnerable to invidious discrimination that threatens their security and personal freedom," injected a sudden nonwhite female point of view into the Supreme Court nomination process.[29] Anita Hill's allegations added a new dimension to this development two months later. In another, equally notable, correspondence, Carolyn Hoover Sung, a native of Chester, South Carolina, complained to Hollings: "The pictures of Strom arm in arm with Thomas were so revolting when I remember asking him to vote for the Civil Rights Bill in 1964 when I was a junior at Winthrop College. I just am sorry to see you on the same side as that old lecherous coot, who has harassed six generations of women (my aunt knew him in the early 1930s and he was still 'hands on' with the scholarship recipients in the 1960s at Winthrop). Next time will you try to remember the women?"[30]

Hollings laid on thick his brand of idiosyncratic folksiness in his two-line response—"Thanks for your letter. I enjoyed it and my secretary especially loved it!"—yet his female constituents became only more vigilant in their scrutiny following the Supreme Court's announcement in 1992 of *Planned Parenthood v. Casey,* which maintained, by a five-to-four majority, a constitutional right to an abortion, but also stoked liberal fears that a growing number of justices were prepared to overturn *Roe v. Wade.* Attorney Debra A. Faulkner, of Greenville, South Carolina, wrote to the Women's Alliance for Hollings on September 9, 1992, to announce that, despite supporting Hollings consistently over the years, she would not be voting for him in future on account of his vote to confirm Clarence Thomas, citing Thomas's alignment with "the right-wing conservative Justices who consistently chip away at *Roe v. Wade.*" In sections highlighted by a member of Hollings's staff, Ms. Faulkner claimed that the senator "will never receive my vote, the vote of any of my friends and colleagues who care about women's issues, or the vote of anyone that I can contact about this," adding that "Senator Hollings ought to address this issue with his female constituency." A Ms. S. J. Conner returned to Hollings a letter he had sent her on August 17, in which he had highlighted his support for *Roe* and endorsed "efforts to improve the choices available to women and to promote their economic and social equality." At the bottom of the letter, Conner had scrawled in pen her "strong disagreement" with Hollings over the Thomas nomination, and outlined her concern that President Bush might appoint another anti-*Roe* justice if reelected in that year's presidential election. In the event, Hollings defeated a strong Republican challenge from former Republican congressman Thomas F. Hartnett, winning by 591,030 votes to 554,175, his narrowest margin of victory since defeating Marshall Parker in 1966.[31] As he had discovered when Olin Johnston defeated him in 1962, seniority and incumbency have consistently proved to be the most powerful reelection weapons in South Carolina politics. Thirty years later, the seventy-year-old Hollings—still the junior senator due to Strom Thurmond's continued service—enjoyed the benefit of these important political assets, securing his fifth term in the US Senate.

Black South Carolina voters' disappointment in Hollings's conservative record on judicial nominations continued through the 1990s. In the *Spartanburg Herald-Journal,* Fred Davis criticized Hollings's endorsement of Patrick Martin Duffy to replace the outgoing Matthew J. Perry on the US District Court for the District of South Carolina, complaining that "you don't just make a half-hearted effort to replace the state's only black federal judge, as the South Carolina junior US Senator has done, then expect the state's African American community to look the other way."[32] On the other hand, Hollings did attempt to prioritize female voters during his final election campaign in 1998. The Citizens' Committee for Ernest F. Hollings ran a television spot featuring two women from Camden, South Carolina, who had been diagnosed with breast cancer. Fran DiBiase and Susan Makla claimed that Senator Hollings intervened personally on their behalf when the US Food and Drug Administration terminated their treatment. According to Ms. DiBiase, "When Senator Hollings came to my home, I was so excited. He entered my front door and I ran to him, and I grabbed him, and I just hugged him. He reminded me so much of my father. And the care, and the love, that he felt, was easy to see." With a huge campaign war chest ensuring blanket coverage of spots such as these, Hollings won reelection to the Senate for his sixth and final term, during which he would briefly serve as the state's senior US senator following Strom Thurmond's retirement in January 2003.[33]

Hollings's supporters had good reasons for their confusion over his unusually conservative positions on judicial nominations throughout the course of his thirty-eight-year career in the US Senate. Despite his claim to support the abortion rights established in *Roe v. Wade,* Hollings voted to confirm the nomination of Clarence Thomas, who later argued in his dissent in *Stenberg v. Carhart* (2000) that the US Constitution contained no right to an abortion. Despite his repeated complaints regarding the overwhelming influence of lobbying in US politics, Hollings voted to confirm the nomination of Lewis Powell, the author of the "Powell Memorandum," a document sent by the future justice to a friend at the US Chamber of Commerce, which later became massively influential in the rise of conservative lobbying organizations. As recently as 2012, Hollings was complaining that "the lobbyists fix the vote now on the important issues and they absolutely—well, what's his name, Grover Norquist, he takes pledges and says not only that you can't vote for taxes, anything that affects taxes and an increase in taxes, you can't vote for it. . . . I mean, they run it. They run it. It's cash and carry government."[34]

On the other hand, Hollings's conservative position on Supreme Court nominations seems quite logical. Having become personally involved in Clement Haynsworth's failed nomination, and so openly bitter about the Senate's rejection of the man he had recommended personally to Richard Nixon, Hollings may well have felt bound to vote for Robert Bork, partly because he had frequently endorsed judicial restraint, and partly as a means of reminding senators of the injustice done to Haynsworth, who, like Bork, was in fact an experienced and well-respected judge. His endorsement of judicial restraint, strict constructionism, and the Founding Fathers' original intentions was part of a careful agenda to build a conservative profile to contain the Republican threat and assert a traditional South Carolina style of independence from the national Democratic Party. Hollings's actions in the Supreme Court nomination process suggest that he retained the conservative traits of his early career, although no longer in the form of a pro-segregation ideology. The frequent scholarly portrayal of Hollings as a forward-looking racial moderate—at least when compared to Strom Thurmond and Olin Johnston—has partly obscured a lengthy, distinctive conservative voting record which ensured his popularity with white conservatives and consistently disappointed his African American supporters.

In addition, the influence of the party dimension proved significant: Hollings was motivated throughout so much of his career by a need to maintain a significant Democratic Party presence in South Carolina. Knowing that he could not guarantee his survival simply by securing a huge majority of black voters in his state, Hollings regularly endorsed Republican Supreme Court nominees in order to retain Democrat-leaning white South Carolinians who felt alienated by the national party. Just as Thurmond had endorsed Donald Russell—a Democratic judge with a segregationist background—in order to further the Republican party-building effort in the state, Hollings had endorsed Republican Clement Haynsworth as a means of preventing white conservatives from deserting the Democratic Party. The impact of the confusing and ironic yet revolutionary changes in South Carolina's two-party system on the behavior of the state's senators in the nomination process for Supreme Court justices cannot be overstated.

Hollings's assertion that judges have a duty to interpret the Constitution, without regard to the outcome of their interpretations, may seem puzzling to those who praise his contribution to South Carolina's peaceful desegregation. On the other hand, this view is in itself a conservative perspective shared by the Supreme Court's strict constructionists. For Justice Antonin Scalia, the court's most outspoken conservative until his death in February 2016, judges must interpret the words of the US Constitution according to their original meaning, leaving legislators to determine the impact of a Court's decisions on US society. As Scalia claimed in 1997, "it certainly cannot be said that a constitution naturally suggests changeability; to the contrary, its whole purpose is to prevent change—to embed certain rights in such a manner that future generations cannot readily take them away." During the bicentennial celebration of the US Constitution in 1987, Justice Thurgood Marshall, only two months prior to Robert Bork's nomination to the Supreme Court, had offered a radically different perspective in a controversial speech, arguing that the nation's Founding Fathers created a system of government that "was defective from the start, requiring several amendments, a civil war and momentous social transformation to attain the system of constitutional government, and its respect for individual freedoms and human rights, we hold as fundamental today."[35] The text of Hollings's Bork defense suggests that the senator was no more willing to associate himself publicly with Thurgood Marshall's views in 1987 than he had been twenty years earlier when opposing his confirmation as a Supreme Court justice. The unique manner in which Hollings stood by his principles is in itself a useful example of South Carolina's brand of independence, which has characterized the behavior of the state's politicians for generations.

The South Carolina senators' war on the US Supreme Court is in many ways the story of the Democratic Party in the South, from the era of Jim Crow segregation to the present. The state may have accomplished its transition to a more enlightened era of race relations with comparatively few incidents of violence, and with a measure of responsible leadership that may have been sorely absent in George Wallace's Alabama, Orval Faubus's Arkansas, and Ross Barnett's Mississippi. On the other hand, Olin Johnston, Strom Thurmond, and Fritz Hollings opted to pursue an altogether more unique form of resistance within a different arena of battle, with their defiance of the court's desegregation order in *Brown v. Board of Education* offering the historian only part of the story. Although the Voting Rights Act and the court's *Stevenson v. West* decision, which ensured the reapportionment of the state's legislature, finally broke the ironclad control of South Carolina's segregationist political establishment, it is clear that the uniquely defiant South Carolina approach to judicial nominations remained intact.

CONCLUSION

A War on the Judiciary in the Southern Secessionist Tradition?

> I hope all Americans understand how important their vote is when it comes to picking a new Supreme Court Justice.
>
> —LINDSEY GRAHAM, quoted in Emma Dumain, "In Selecting Scalia Successor, S.C. Congressional Delegation Puts Obama on Notice," *Post and Courier,* February 13, 2016

> Since I have been in the Senate, I have made it a policy to have as little as possible to do with the Supreme Court.
>
> —STROM THURMOND TO SAMUEL C. CRAVEN, June 14, 1965

> Leave South Carolina's affairs to South Carolinians, or the consequences are apt to be disastrous from several viewpoints, not the least of which might be the smashing of the solid political South.
>
> —EDGAR A. BROWN, Statement Before Sub-Committee of US Senate Judiciary Committee on Proposed Civil Rights Legislation, 1959

> The President regrets that he is compelled to withdraw the invitation to you tonight at the White House.
>
> —GEORGE B. CORTELYOU TO BENJAMIN R. TILLMAN, 1902, quoted in Francis Butler Simkins, *Pitchfork Ben Tillman, South Carolinian*

When, in June 2015, South Carolina's Republican senator, Lindsey Graham, announced that he was campaigning to secure the Republican nomination for the US presidential election of 2016, he made the unintentionally amusing comment, "I won't run just to win in South Carolina."[1] To some, this may have appeared to be a grand statement of the obvious, but the notion of a South Carolina politician campaigning for the presidency solely for the benefit of his appeal to voters in South Carolina is hardly inconceivable to those with an unusual passion for the state's political history. From the drama of the state's threat to secede from the Union during the Nullification Crisis of the 1830s, to Strom Thurmond's breakaway run for president on a third-party ticket in 1948, to the aborted 2008 Democratic Party primary campaign of satirist and TV presenter Stephen Colbert—who announced that he would run only in South Carolina—the political history of the Palmetto State suggests that anything is politically possible. South Carolina's involvement at the center of important and surprising political events, particularly those relating to the state's struggle with its history of segregation, has been especially evident within a fairly recent period of eight months. In December 2014, a South Carolina judge finally vacated the 1944 conviction of George Stinney, the black teenager executed for the rape and murder of two white girls in a case widely believed to be a miscarriage of justice, while in January 2015, an official pardon nullified the convictions of the "Friendship Nine" protesters. The fatal shooting of Walter Scott on April 4, 2015, drew South Carolina into the activities of the grassroots movement Black Lives Matter. The killing of nine people only two months later at the Emanuel African Methodist Episcopal Church in Charleston rocked the state to its foundations, resulting in a remarkable political consensus that ensured the controversial removal of the Confederate battle flag from the statehouse grounds on July 11, 2015.

South Carolina's dramatic political history suggests that a war of the state's politicians on the US Supreme Court was simply inevitable. The very fact that the name "Palmetto State" recalls the spongy log walls of Fort Sumter, which absorbed the impact of British cannonballs in 1776, further suggests South Carolina pride in gestures of defiance and defense. The frequent scholarly observation of the state's comparatively smooth desegregation during the 1960s has obscured the South Carolina senators' particularly abrasive behavior within the walls of the US Congress. The horror of Preston Brooks's savage beating of Charles Sumner on the Senate floor in 1856 established a pattern of violence and confrontation that became evident in the behavior of subsequent notorious figures, albeit in diluted form, during the twentieth century. "Cotton Ed" Smith's angry jabs at the arm of his chair with a penknife to get the Speaker's attention, Coleman Blease's recitation of "N——s in the White House," and Strom Thurmond's desperate attempt to physically drag Senator Ralph Yarborough of Texas into the Senate chamber to vote against his will all suggest that the behavior of South Carolina's politicians within the dignified institution of the US Senate has been anything but peaceful, and, some might add, anything but dignified. Tony

Badger's characterization of South Carolina defiance as a "top-down" phenomenon, in which the state's leaders worked "to convince South Carolinians that the Supreme Court could be defied," ought to have shed more light on the striking manner in which these leaders pursued this agenda in Washington, DC. With senators taking the lead in resisting the order to desegregate, it seems logical that the US Senate, rather than the state itself, became the battleground for the state's gestures of defiance. The state's war on the Supreme Court illustrates best this largely overlooked phenomenon.[2]

Vice President John C. Calhoun's threat to lead his state out of the Union in 1832 proved to be the landmark political event that defined South Carolina, and the state's many flamboyant politicians, for generations. With Calhoun's belief that the Tariff of 1828 would compromise South Carolina's powerful slave economy, the Nullification Crisis began as a dramatic gesture of belief in South Carolina exceptionalism, and the manner in which it concluded, in the form of the Compromise Tariff of 1833, implied that Calhoun had achieved success by standing up to a popular president and protecting his state's autonomy. On the other hand, as Walter Edgar has shown, the Nullification Crisis made South Carolina deeply unpopular, with the state acquiring "a reputation for rashness that lingered for a generation." When contrasted with the era of *Brown v. Board of Education,* during which South Carolina maintained solidarity with other Deep South states in the fight to preserve segregation, the manner in which Calhoun's actions provoked unfavorable responses from states such as Mississippi and Georgia may seem extraordinary. With the tensions between Nullifiers and Unionists only worsening during the 1830s, Calhoun urged moderation, but, as Edgar notes, he would forever consider opponents of Nullification to be men "who had not done their duty," a perspective which supports Badger's claim of the state's politicians acting less through their convictions over the race issue, and more through a concern that they were "too quiescent and resigned." James O. Farmer has argued that Olin Johnston and state legislators need not have acted so rashly in defying the *Smith* ruling in 1944, but he concedes that a restrained response would have been out of character given their history, which taught them that "anything less than full vigilance against the black peril" would undermine reelection prospects. As in other southern states, racial moderates assumed a preference for extremism on the part of their constituents, as Keith Finley has argued, and "frequently paid lip service to the reactionaries or remained silent," thus allowing demagogic figures, Thurmond among them, to shape the region's response to court-ordered desegregation.[3]

Calhoun's expectation that southern men would "do their duty" in defending their region's independence has clearly influenced several generations of South Carolina leaders. Long after the Civil War and the southern implementation of Jim Crow segregation as a means of rolling back Reconstruction, the spirit of Calhoun lived on in the behavior of South Carolina's senators. "Cotton Ed" Smith's uncompromising stand on segregation proved to be his trump card in defeating Olin Johnston's challenge to his Senate seat in 1938. When Smith reminded crowds of his infamous walkout at the 1936 Democratic Convention in Philadelphia in protest at the presence of a black clergyman, he claimed that "John Calhoun leaned down from his mansion in the sky and whispered in my ear, 'You did right, Ed.'" Senator Wayne Morse of Oregon responded to Strom Thurmond's aggressive promotion of the Southern Manifesto with the observation, "You would think today Calhoun was walking and speaking on the floor of the Senate." According to Robert Mann, Senator Russell Long of Louisiana donated to Olin Johnston a desk that once belonged to Calhoun in order to secure Johnston's support for his promotion to assistant majority leader.[4] While the state's leaders may have opted to remain in the Union rather than make a dramatic secessionist gesture worthy of Calhoun, their desire to recapture South Carolina's authoritative voice in national affairs, which congressmen and senators had defended aggressively prior to the Civil War, remained a key motivator in the state's war on the Supreme Court.

More than one hundred years on from the Nullification Crisis, with the *Brown* ruling presenting an equally imposing threat to South Carolina's autonomy, it may seem surprising that South Carolina did not join the legislatures of Mississippi, Alabama, Georgia, and Florida in declaring the court's decision null and void.[5] The failure to invoke the spirit of Calhoun during this critical moment in the state's history may suggest that South Carolina's political establishment felt no pressure to remind others in the Union of the state's defiant past. Alternatively, of the five Deep South states, only South Carolina had been involved in one of the decisions that formed the *Brown* case, and to respond by unleashing an outright claim of nullification might have undermined the repeated argument of the state's leaders that the court had created a problem that affected the entire southern region. In March 1956, during the peak of southern resistance to *Brown,* Governor James Byrnes appealed for calm with the statement that "South Carolina is not thinking in terms of secession. Fort Sumter is now a national monument to the opening battle of the Civil War and South Carolina is content to let it go at that."[6] With his claim that "the interposition resolution confines itself to protest and avoids any mention of 'nullification,'" Byrnes seemed to be restraining his South Carolina colleagues while also reassuring the rest of the country that the state would not repeat the rebellious actions characterizing its past.

The determination of Johnston, Thurmond, and Hollings to win election to the US Senate suggests their recognition of the need to work within the federal system, and their use of secessionist language for rhetorical impact (and the purpose of securing reelection) magnified not only their inability to exert the kind of influence they claimed to wield, but also their tendency to take matters into their own hands without the full support of the southern delegation—a tradition that Hollings would continue by supporting Republican Supreme Court nominations in the 1980s and 1990s. The senators' struggle to influence the judicial nominations process remains an important yet overlooked chapter in the southern political effort to impose a regional agenda on a national scale. Furthermore, South Carolina's role in that story highlights the relevance of state (in addition to regional) traditions during the most tumultuous period of social and political transformation in twentieth-century US race relations.

The inevitable claims of political historians that southern segregationist politicians lacked a genuine belief that any form of "massive resistance" would succeed will no doubt complicate any attempt to determine whether South Carolina's senators were successful in their war on the Supreme Court. This problem is particularly relevant when analyzing the politics of the nomination process: as explained previously, senators can engineer the rejection of a nominee only through an extraordinary collective effort, and, while presidents enjoy a wide range of administrative tools and a large team of staff to promote a nominee, an individual senator will carry the burden of proof when setting out to convince colleagues that a rejection is necessary.[7] Given that these conditions offer only a bleak chance of defeating a nomination, particularly when the objection rests on regional or state concerns, it seems logical that southern senators held out little hope of achieving victory in their obstruction to nominees.

On the other hand, despite the scholarly assumptions made regarding a lack of belief in any satisfying outcome for "massive resistance," there remains a degree of exceptionalism in the case of Strom Thurmond. Anecdotal evidence suggests that Thurmond's Senate colleagues viewed him as a law unto himself, at least in terms of the extent of his belief in the sanctity of racial segregation. In addition to Olin Johnston's alleged remark that Thurmond "*believes* that shit," Robert Mann claims that Hubert Humphrey once remarked that he did not think Russell Long believed "a single word he said" during a stirring attack on the 1957 Civil Rights bill, adding, "But that S.O.B., Strom Thurmond, does."[8]

Others remain more skeptical. Robert Mickey has argued that Thurmond pursued his "Dixiecrat" run for president in 1948 as a means of laying the groundwork for his challenge to Johnston in the 1950 Senate primary. With Johnston having established an unbreakable base of support in the upcountry, Thurmond's only real chance of toppling his opponent lay in his ability to win over the conservative white voters of the state's "black belt" region through a grand gesture of commitment to segregation. John Spratt recalls that Thurmond "was out there early on, with the issue of civil rights at the 1948 Convention. Clearly this helped him, he knew it was helping him; he was taking this position because it was advantageous to him politically. Strom would tell you he believed all this." Few would dispute the evidence indicating Thurmond's willingness to push the race issue when seeking power and influence. Joseph Crespino, his recent biographer, has suggested that Thurmond may have pursued his orthodox brand of segregationist posturing in part to offset criticism in the event of his mixed-race daughter becoming public knowledge.[9]

The existence of serious political constraints in the Supreme Court nomination process only highlights Thurmond's remarkable achievement in leading a successful crusade to defeat Abe Fortas's nomination as chief justice. Nonetheless, even with this groundbreaking victory, the task of portraying South Carolina's war on the Supreme Court as a success remains challenging. On the one hand, Thurmond and Johnston succeeded, throughout the events discussed in chapters two and three, in creating a comprehensive anti–Supreme Court agenda that garnered support from several senators outside the South, with their arguments over the court's threat to national, rather than simply regional, interests provoking greater scrutiny over nominees while encouraging wider support for court-curbing legislation. On the other hand, they remained ineffective in reducing the justices' power, and unsuccessful in forcing President Eisenhower to reevaluate his methods of judicial selection, at least with regard to Supreme Court nominations. Neither Eisenhower nor Kennedy agreed to nominate Supreme Court justices who would jeopardize *Brown*'s safety, although their willingness to appoint southern senators' preferred judges to the lower courts did assist in constructing a segregationist firewall, which would in theory protect the South from a federal erosion of states' rights. Yet the passage of the Voting Rights Act effectively destroyed the firewall, forcing even Thurmond to accept the reality of the desegregated South Carolina that Fritz Hollings had chosen to acknowledge years earlier.

In addition to alienating northern senators, and aside from the practical difficulties involved in overcoming challenges in the judicial selection process, there remains a more compelling case for South Carolina's failure in waging war on the Supreme Court. In the early 1960s, a new generation of voters began communicating with Olin Johnston, one telling him, "I am 22—young America is watching more than you know," and another informing him that "the reactionary forces of bigotry and prejudice are on the wane." As noted in chapter six, a *New York Times* article from October 1963 even speculated that an increasing African American voting bloc would in fact relieve South Carolina politicians of "the necessity of having to run on a racist platform."[10] The confrontational and obstructive approach was consistent with the defiant tradition of the state's politicians, yet the story told in these pages suggests that South Carolina's senators conducted their war on the US Supreme Court in a manner that often infuriated and embarrassed a great many South Carolinians over several decades.

The choices made by historians over which method to use in analyzing the politics of judicial nominations will ultimately determine the debate over South Carolina's success or failure in waging a war on the court. If they are to continue the existing trend of emphasizing the outcome of confirmation votes in the Senate, they are bound to characterize South Carolina's attempt to influence the nominations process as an abject failure, given that senators rejected only one unfavorable liberal nomination, that of Abe Fortas, but also rejected South Carolina's Clement Haynsworth, supposedly an ideal candidate in the eyes of the state's conservative senators. Furthermore, if Thurmond hoped to encourage a greater degree of scrutiny in the nominations process by presenting a smorgasbord of criticisms aimed at Abe Fortas—none of which related to the nominee's qualifications—it is difficult to argue against the theory that this venture backfired in the short term, with senators retaliating by applying to Haynsworth a similarly rigorous form of scrutiny. As noted above, a senator carries a heavy burden of proof when opposing a presidential nomination, and requires superior powers of persuasion and overwhelming evidence of the nominee's lack of suitability when making a genuine effort to engineer a Senate rejection.[11] To complicate matters, the Parker, Fortas, Haynsworth, and Bork examples suggest that a rejection occurs only when a variety of powerful interest groups object to the nominee's position on more than one political issue, or where ethical considerations exist on more than one level. Thurmond's campaign against Fortas was successful in that it incorporated a wide range of criticisms, including the nominee's unusually close relationship with President Johnson; claims of the nominee's role in facilitating the spread of "obscene" materials; objections over the questionable payments made for his lecturing services; and, of course, his views on interpreting the Constitution, which supposedly leaned toward the Warren court's much-derided "judicial activism."

Scholars have made clear distinctions between the lives and political careers of Olin Johnston, Strom Thurmond, and Fritz Hollings, but the final votes on each Supreme Court nomination during this period imply that no ideological difference existed between them whatsoever. The standard method of analyzing the nomination process by emphasizing the outcome of each confirmation vote has proved particularly unhelpful in gaining a true understanding of the politics of the Supreme Court nomination process. In looking at the record of Senate rejections, the historian learns surprisingly little about the substance of the process and how it has evolved over time. This is unfortunate because, throughout the period under study in this work, the nomination process developed into an arena of political debate that would transcend all notions of the Senate's function as a "rubber stamp" for presidential nominations. Even in the absence of a controversial or divisive nominee, the Supreme Court nomination process continues to function as one of the most powerful—and, since the introduction of television cameras in 1981, also one of the most public—outlets for senators, interest groups, and other public figures to debate the court's influence on the political issues of the day. When considered from this perspective, the actions of Johnston, Thurmond, and Hollings did succeed in putting South Carolina at the forefront of a much wider campaign to check the power of the Supreme Court. With the increasing willingness of the nine justices to exercise political influence in a multitude of policy areas, the southern senators' emphasis on nominees' judicial experience gained legitimacy, and their frequent criticism of the justices for not applying the "strict constructionist" approach of following the words of the Constitution as intended by the Founding Fathers only gained momentum in the coming decades. Despite failing to hold back the dramatic expansion of the court's power during this era, South Carolina's war did contribute to the development of a new level of senatorial scrutiny while at the same time raising awareness of the court's growing influence in all areas of the American polity.

Given that their actions seem to be entirely consistent with South Carolina's reputation for rebellion and nonconformity, it seems ironic that the state's senators appeared to enjoy some success, perhaps unwittingly, in building a degree of consensus with regard to a much wider debate regarding the Supreme Court. Through the repeated reminder of the justices' role in threatening national security by allowing the spread of Communist subversion, South Carolina's war on the court attracted the interest of conservative Republicans during the era of the McCarthy crusade. Later, during the 1960s, conservative Americans engaged in a drive for "decency" were drawn into the war by the argument that radical interpretations of the First Amendment were allowing the proliferation of pornographic material on newsstands and in movie theaters. Similarly, the accusation that the court was undermining Christian values through the infamous school prayer decision struck a chord with an equally sizable religious element in US society. Liberal northern senators proved to be just as opposed to recess appointments as conservative southerners, and the outbreaks of racial violence occurring in the 1960s convinced many others of the credibility of southern claims that the justices were prioritizing the constitutional rights of criminals over the safety of law-abiding citizens. Under the circumstances, it is perhaps unsurprising that the comprehensive anti–Supreme Court agenda crafted by Johnston and Thurmond became a crucial component of the highly politicized nomination process that was firmly in place by the late 1960s. The impact of South Carolina's crusade is also evident in the near-success of the HR3 bill in the summer of 1958, and in the senatorial pressure exerted on Justices Brennan and Douglas to scale down their extracurricular activities in 1969.

The controversial nature of the state's influence on the federal nominations process was perhaps more evident than at any time since the Fortas episode when, in February 2016, Senate Republicans braced themselves for President Barack Obama to announce whom he would nominate to replace the late Justice Antonin Scalia on the Supreme Court. An intellectual powerhouse of unrelenting originalist dissent, Scalia dominated the court's conservative faction for thirty years, and his unexpected death allowed Obama, in the final months of his presidency, an opportunity to tip the balance of the court with the appointment of a liberal justice. With Senate Republicans insisting that the vacancy should be filled not by Obama but by the victor of the 2016 presidential election, Majority Leader Mitch McConnell and Judiciary Committee Chairman Chuck Grassley insisted that no hearings would be held to scrutinize the nominee.

South Carolina's Lindsey Graham, one of the more outspoken Senate Republicans on the issue of judicial nominations, was not shy in expressing his refusal to accommodate Obama's selection of a new justice. Although far different in temperament from Thurmond, whom he succeeded in the Senate in 2003, the soft-spoken upcountryman adopted a confrontational tone by claiming that his refusal to cooperate could be considered "payback" for Majority Leader Harry Reid changing the threshold to approve judicial nominees (but not Supreme Court candidates) from 60 votes to 50 when Democrats held the majority in the Senate: "I told the President and the Democratic leadership that if you abuse power and change the rules for appellate judges and executive appointments, going to a majority, you'll pay a price with me." Following Obama's announcement on March 16, 2016, that he had selected Judge Merrick Garland to fill the Scalia vacancy, Graham grudgingly consented to a "courtesy" meeting with the nominee but held firm on refusing to advise and consent, despite his earlier support for Obama's first two Supreme Court nominees, Sonia Sotomayor and Elena Kagan. Graham's South Carolina colleague, Senator Tim Scott, maintained, in terms worthy of Thurmond, that "the next President should fill the open seat on the Supreme Court, not a lame duck." As in the Fortas episode, Republican senators ultimately triumphed. Shortly after his inauguration as president, on February 1, 2017, Donald Trump announced his selection of conservative judge Neil Gorsuch to replace Scalia.[12]

The troubling scene of Obama in a standoff with senators determined to deprive him of the right to appoint a Supreme Court justice in his final few months in office provided sufficient comparisons with the 1968 Abe Fortas affair for journalists and political commentators to begin discussing the concept of a "Thurmond rule," which, according to Dean Rutkus and Kevin Scott of the Congressional Research Service, holds that "at some point in a Presidential Election year, the Judiciary Committee and the Senate no longer act on judicial nominations."[13] Despite the uncompromising Republican arguments for obstructing Merrick Garland's confirmation, most senators are keen to remove any notions of legitimacy from a "Thurmond rule." In the election year of 2004, Republican senator Orrin Hatch of Utah (who served with Thurmond on the

Judiciary Committee), claimed that "Strom Thurmond acted unilaterally . . . when he was Chairman, he could say whatever he wanted to, but that didn't bind the whole Committee, and it doesn't bind me." In 2008 (another election year), Alabama's Jeff Sessions stated, "Let me say this about the Thurmond rule. It is a myth. It does not exist."[14]

The ongoing debate over whether or not the principle even constitutes a "rule" has showcased a great deal of skepticism: newspaper reports continue to maintain that the rule is "not official or binding," while Rutkus and Scott have failed to identify any "consistently observed" cutoff point for the Senate to cease deliberations on a nomination during an election year. Others have highlighted a lack of historical precedent other than the chaotic summer of 1968, with Stuart Eizenstat noting in the *Washington Post* that the Judiciary Committee—including Thurmond, who was next in line for the chairmanship—did not block President Jimmy Carter's nomination of Stephen Breyer to the US Court of Appeals for the First Circuit, only weeks after Carter's loss to Ronald Reagan in the 1980 presidential election.[15]

However, while the nominations process has not ground to a halt during presidential election years, confirmation rates have certainly slowed generally in recent years. The American Constitution Society, despite referring to the "Thurmond Myth," has noted that Republican threats of invoking the "Thurmond rule" form part of the party's much broader arsenal of obstructionist tactics. As ranking Republican and later, as chairman, of the Judiciary Committee, Senator Grassley has been particularly active in reducing the number of hearings and delaying votes on nominations, aided in some cases by senators returning their "blue slips" at a snail's pace. During Barack Obama's first term as president, nearly eighty judicial vacancies—approximately 10 per cent of the federal judiciary—remained unfilled for a period of more than three years.[16]

Although the almost universal characterization of the "Thurmond rule" as nonexistent or inapplicable suggests that the extent of Thurmond's legacy in the nominations process is indeed somewhat mythical, it does seem significant that, throughout the Obama presidency—and the Garland controversy in particular—politicians, commentators, reporters, bloggers, the legal establishment, and other interested parties would debate, in such depth and with such interest, something that apparently "doesn't exist." In June 2012, Bill Robinson, president of the ABA, wrote to the majority and minority leaders in the Senate to point out that, despite considering the Thurmond rule "neither a rule nor a clearly defined event," the ABA was concerned that "recent news stories have cast it as a precedent under which the Senate, under a specified date in a presidential election year, ceases to vote on nominees to the federal circuit courts of appeal." Clearly, the frequent dismissals of the "Thurmond rule" have done little to remove the specter of Strom Thurmond from the judicial nominations process. The "rule" may not exist in any substantive form, but Thurmond's overwhelming influence in the history of senatorial obstruction to judicial nominees is clearly very real in the American public consciousness, and also in the everyday practices of senators in that most complex, controversial process. As Sarah A. Binder of the Brookings Institute has explained, "the persistence of the idea of a Thurmond rule or doctrine that compels and justifies opposition party tactics is a telling element of the modern Senate."[17]

South Carolina's war on the Supreme Court was, of course, a rhetorical war first and foremost, allowing senators to "do their duty" by defending their state and the "southern way of life." The court provided the most obvious, and most convenient, target for condemnation, enabling the three senators to portray the justices as a threat to national interests in a manner that made clear their commitment to segregation but without descending into the unfiltered racist demagoguery of a Benjamin Tillman or a Coleman Blease. The "court-baiting" tactic seemed particularly logical to the three senators when evaluating their prospects for reelection: Johnston escalated his lengthy obstruction to Thurgood Marshall's Second Circuit appointment while engaged in a lively primary contest, followed by an unusually strong Republican challenge in November 1962, while Hollings opted to vote against Marshall's 1967 appointment to the Supreme Court while looking ahead to his reelection battle in 1968.

However, the war on the court also proved highly significant in two very different party-building strategies. Following his party defection, Thurmond worked hard to maintain his base of segregationist support while building a solid Republican Party in South Carolina, while Johnston and Hollings spent much of their careers discouraging white conservative voters from deserting the Democratic Party, with each succeeding in antagonizing the state's African American population without compromising their share of the black vote. Thurmond, in guiding a string of Republican nominees safely through a Supreme Court confirmation process in which he had once behaved as a titan of obstructionism, was able to promote the idea of the Republican Party as the natural home for southern conservatives. During the same era, Hollings used his support for the very same Republican nominees to assure the state's Democratic loyalists that "South Carolina Democrats" would continue to stand apart from the national Democratic Party.

Through their unique participation in the judicial nominations process, the South Carolina senators found a powerful means of rallying the folks back home against a common enemy in a manner that would invoke the spirit of Calhoun, ensure reelection, and solidify seniority on Senate committees. Richard Nixon's preference for "strict constructionist" judges may have ushered in the final phase of South Carolina's war on the court, but the need to push back against Earl Warren's legacy ensured that the rhetoric used by South Carolina's senators in the nomination of new justices remained largely unchanged thereafter.

This work may have showcased an overlooked chapter in the history of southern resistance to *Brown v. Board of Education,* but the story told in the preceding chapters also suggests that South Carolina's war on the Supreme Court transcended the issues of race and states' rights that informed "massive resistance" and instead emphasized a radical and groundbreaking response to the court's consistent role as the final arbiter of policy in US society.

NOTES

INTRODUCTION: *The Story of South Carolina and the Supreme Court*

1. See Laurence Tribe, *God Save This Honorable Court* (London: Random House, 1985), 100–3, for a brief discussion of the relevance of these terms in the nomination process for Supreme Court justices. See also Bob Woodward and Scott Armstrong, *The Brethren* (New York: Simon and Schuster, 1979); Ronald Kahn and Kenneth I. Kersch, eds., *The Supreme Court and American Political Development* (Lawrence: University Press of Kansas, 2006); Michael J. Klarman, *From Jim Crow to Civil Rights: The Supreme Court and the Struggle for Racial Equality* (Oxford: Oxford University Press, 2004); Alpheus T. Mason, *The Supreme Court from Taft to Warren* (New York: W. W. Norton, 1958); John R. Schmidhauser, *The Supreme Court: Its Politics, Personalities and Procedures* (New York: Holt, Rinehart and Winston, 1960); and John R. Schmidhauser and L. L. Berg, *The Supreme Court and Congress* (New York: Free Press, 1972).

2. See, generally, L. A. Scot Powe, "The Senate and the Court: Questioning a Nominee," *Texas Law Review* 54 (1975–1976): 891–902.

3. *Buffalo Progressive Herald*, Saturday, April 19, 1930, Manuscript Division, Library of Congress, Hoover NAACP Records, Parker Hearings, Box 1: C398.

4. "Carolinian Seen in Line for Court," *New York Times*, August 13, 1969; "Nixon Gave Thurmond Supreme Court Veto," *Lewiston Daily Sun* (ME), April 20, 1968.

5. James F. Byrnes, "The Supreme Court Must Be Curbed!," originally published by *US News and World Report*, May 18, 1956, Herman E. Talmadge Collection, Subgroup C, Series 3: Civil Rights, Box 17, Folder 6.

6. Transcript of James Eastland's Senate speech regarding introduction of Resolution 104, Richard B. Russell Collection Subgroup E, Series 4: Vertical Files, Box 4, Folder 64; Olin D. Johnston to James Eastland, March 15, 1956; Olin D. Johnston to James Eastland, March 15, 1956; from Olin D. Johnston to Speaker Solomon Blatt, telegram, February 9, 1955, Olin D. Johnston Collection, Senate Papers, Legislative Files, Box 46, Civil Rights, School Segregation; "Impeach Justices, Thurmond Urges," *New York Times*, July 8, 1957, 15; Strom Thurmond to Reverend Henry J. Gambrell, June 6, 1969, Strom Thurmond Collection, Subject Correspondence Series, Mss.0100.18, Year 1969, Nominations, 3 (United States District, Circuit and Supreme Court), Box 28, Folder 1; correspondence between Olin D. Johnston and George Bell Timmerman, February 2–11, 1955; draft of statement in Senate regarding Supreme Court Justice Qualification Bill, January 29, 1959, Strom Thurmond Collection, Mss.0100.11, Speeches Series 1935–1998, Subseries A, General File (1935–1983), Statements on the Senate Floor, Box 8, Folder 690; "Thurmond Warns of a Third Party," *New York Times*, August 21, 1955, 53; Keith M. Finley, *Delaying the Dream: Southern Senators and the Fight against Civil Rights, 1938–1965* (Baton Rouge: Louisiana State University Press, 2008), 4.

7. See, generally, Henry J. Abraham, *Justices, Presidents, and Senators: A History of the U.S. Supreme Court Appointments from Washington to Clinton* (Lanham, MD: Rowman and Littlefield, 1999). David A. Yalof, *Pursuit of Justices: Presidential Politics and the Selection of Supreme Court*

Nominees (Chicago: University of Chicago Press, 1999), offers comparisons of the varying style of judicial selection employed by Presidents Truman through to Clinton. Also, contrast the portrayal of President Herbert Hoover as antagonistic in Peter G. Fish, "Spite Nominations to the United States Supreme Court: Herbert C. Hoover, Owen J. Roberts and the Politics of Presidential Vengeance in Retrospect," *Kentucky Law Journal* 77 (1988): 545–76, with the portrayal of him as deferential to the Senate two years later, in Ira H. Carmen, "The President, Politics and the Power of Appointment: Hoover's Nomination of Mr. Justice Cardozo," *Virginia Law Review* 55 (1969): 616–59.

8. The full text of the paragraph in question is as follows: "He shall have power, by and with the advice and consent of the Senate, to make treaties, provided two-thirds of the senators present concur; and he shall nominate, and by and with the advice and consent of the Senate, shall appoint ambassadors, other public ministers and consuls, judges of the supreme court, and all other officers of the United States, whose appointments are not herein otherwise provided for, and which shall be established by law. But the Congress may by law vest the appointments of such inferior officers, as they think proper, in the president alone, in the courts of law, or in the heads of departments." Cited in F. G. Cullop, *The Constitution of the United States: An Introduction* (New York: Penguin, 1969), 99.

9. Some presidents have made nominations with little or no chance of Senate confirmation, and others have made "spite" nominations under the (usually mistaken) belief that senators would not dare to reject two or more nominees consecutively. However, it does not appear that anyone has identified a case in which a president has intentionally made a nomination in the knowledge that the Senate will reject the nominee.

10. See Abraham, *Justices, Presidents;* Jan Crawford Greenburg, *Supreme Conflict: The Inside Story of the Struggle for Control of the United States Supreme Court* (New York: Penguin Press, 2007); Yalof, *Pursuit;* H. P. Monaghan, "The Confirmation Process: Law or Politics?," *Harvard Law Review* 101, no. 6 (April 1988): 1202–12; Joel B. Grossman and Stephen L. Wasby, "The Senate and Supreme Court Nominations: Some Reflections," *Duke Law Journal* 560, no. 3 (August 1972): 557–91.

11. Telephone conversation between Lyndon B. Johnson and Olin D. Johnston, April 14, 1964, Lyndon B. Johnston Presidential Recordings, Miller Center, University of Virginia, WH6404.09, http://millercenter.org/scripps/archive/presidentialrecordings/Johnson.

12. *US News and World Report,* March 21, 1960, Edgar A. Brown Papers, Mss.0091, Johnston, Olin D., Box 30, Folder 390; Russell Merritt, "The Senatorial Election of 1962 and the Rise of Two-Party Politics in South Carolina," *South Carolina Historical Magazine* 98, no. 3 (1997): 254–55.

13. Harry N. Johnson to Olin D. Johnston, June 18, 1962; press release from the office of Senator Kenneth B. Keating, April 30, 1962, Olin D. Johnston Collection, Senate Papers, Legislative Files, Box 101, Judiciary Committee, Appointments, Marshall, Thurgood, Folder 4; David A. Nichols, *A Matter of Justice: Eisenhower and the Civil Rights Revolution* (New York: Simon and Schuster, 2007), 86; "Nominee Marshall," *New York Times,* August 26, 1962, 152.

14. Bruce Allen Murphy, *Fortas* (New York: William Morrow, 1988), 426; "Carolina Negroes Cool to Hollings," *New York Times,* November 4, 1968, 38; Ernest F. Hollings and Kirk Victor, *Making Government Work* (Columbia: University of South Carolina Press, 2008), 128; Nicol C. Rae, *Southern Democrats* (Oxford: Oxford University Press, 1994), 105.

15. Jack Bass and Marilyn W. Thompson, *Strom: The Complicated Personal and Political Life of Strom Thurmond* (New York: Public Affairs, 2005), 165; Anthony J. Badger, "From Defiance to

Moderation: South Carolina Governors and Racial Change," in *New Deal/New South: An Anthony J. Badger Reader* (Fayetteville: University of Arkansas Press, 2007), 128; interview with Liz Patterson, September 29, 2014; Strom Thurmond to Walter Brown, April 14, 1962, Strom Thurmond Collection, Subject Correspondence Series, Mss.0100.18, 3 (United States Court and Supreme Court Judges), Year 1962, Box 19, Folder 1; Hollings and Victor, *Making Government Work,* 210–11.

16. Joseph Crespino, *Strom Thurmond's America* (New York: Hill and Wang, 2012), 118–19; Strom Thurmond to J. R. McVicker, July 8, 1957, Strom Thurmond Collection, Subject Correspondence Series, Mss.0100.18, Legislature, Year 1957, Box 27, Supreme Court January 3–July 2, 1957; Strom Thurmond to Henry T. Chance, July 10, 1957, Strom Thurmond Collection, Subject Correspondence Series, Mss.0100.18, Legislature, Year 1957, Box 27, Supreme Court July 3–13, 1957; "Russell Leads Attack on Thurmond," *Augusta Chronicle,* August 31, 1957, Strom Thurmond Collection, Legislative Assistant Series, Mss.0100.15, Box 140, Richard Russell, August 1957–May 1964; Hollings and Victor, *Making Government Work,* 142.

17. Interview with John Spratt, September 28, 2014; Juan Williams, *Thurgood Marshall: American Revolutionary* (New York: Random House, 198), 337–38.

18. Crespino, *Strom Thurmond's America.*

19. Ibid., 109–10.

1. "TOTAL AND UNREMITTING WAR"

1. Charles W. Joyner, "Shared Traditions: South Carolina as a Folk Culture," in *Proceedings of the South Carolina Historical Association,* ed. Roger Figueira and Stephen Lowe (Columbia: South Carolina Historical Association), 9; Jack Bass and Marilyn W. Thompson, *Strom: The Complicated Personal and Political Life of Strom Thurmond* (New York: Public Affairs, 2005), 42; V. O. Key, *Southern Politics in State and Nation* (New York: Vintage, 1949), 150; Jamie W. Moore, "The Lowcountry in Economic Transition: Charleston since 1865," *South Carolina Historical Magazine* 80, no. 2 (April 1979): 157; Robert Mickey, *Paths out of Dixie: The Democratization of Authoritarian Enclaves in America's Deep South, 1944–1972* (Princeton, NJ: Princeton University Press, 2015), 65; Peter Coclanis, *In the Shadow of a Dream: Economic Life and Death in the South Carolina Low Country, 1670–1920* (Oxford: Oxford University Press, 1989), 90–91.

2. Walter Edgar, *South Carolina: A History* (Columbia: University of South Carolina Press, 1998), 337–38; Jack Bass and W. Scott Poole, *The Palmetto State: The Making of Modern South Carolina* (Columbia: University of South Carolina Press, 2009), 42.

3. Key, *Southern Politics,* 143; John W. White, "The White Citizens' Councils of Orangeburg County, South Carolina," in Winfred B. Moore Jr. and Orville Vernon Burton, eds., *Toward the Meeting of the Waters: Currents in the Civil Rights Movement of South Carolina during the Twentieth Century* (Columbia: University of South Carolina Press, 2008), 261; Bass and Poole, *Palmetto State,* 93; Mickey, *Paths,* 223; C. Vann Woodward, *The Strange Career of Jim Crow* (Oxford: Oxford University Press, 1974), 32.

4. Kari Frederickson, "'The Slowest State' and 'Most Backward Community': Racial Violence in South Carolina and Federal Civil Rights Legislation, 1946–48," *South Carolina Historical Magazine* 98, no. 2 (1997): 198; Bruce Baker, *This Mob Will Surely Take My Life: Lynchings in the Carolinas,*

1871–1947 (London: Continuum, 2008), 4; Stan Opotowsky, "Dixie Dynamite: The Inside Story of the White Citizens' Councils," reprinted from *New York Post,* January 6–20, 1957, 12.

5. Key, *Southern Politics,* 150–55; Bryant Simon, "The Devaluation of the Vote: Legislative Apportionment and Inequality in South Carolina, 1890–1962," *South Carolina Historical Magazine* 101, no. 3 (July 2000): 247–48.

6. Key, *Southern Politics,* 139, 151; Frank E. Jordan, *The Primary State: A History of the Democratic Party in South Carolina, 1896–1962* (self-published, n.d.), 162–63; Simon, "The Devaluation," 248; John E. Huss, *Senator for the South: A Biography of Olin D. Johnston* (New York: Doubleday, 1961), 64–72; Bass and Thompson, *Strom,* 78–79; Bass and Poole, *Palmetto State,* 112.

7. Key, *Southern Politics,* 131; Anthony J. Badger, "From Defiance to Moderation: South Carolina Governors and Racial Change," in *New Deal/New South: An Anthony J. Badger Reader* (Fayetteville: University of Arkansas Press, 2007), 133; Mickey, *Paths,* 224; Numan V. Bartley, *The Rise of Massive Resistance: Race and Politics in the South during the 1950's* (Baton Rouge: Louisiana State University Press, 1999), 46.

8. Key, *Southern Politics,* 130.

9. See David Herbert Donald, *Charles Sumner and the Coming Civil War* (New York: Alfred A. Knopf, 1960) for a thorough account of the Brooks-Sumner Incident.

10. Orville Vernon Burton et al., "Seeds in Unlikely Soil: The *Briggs v. Elliott* School Desegregation Case," in *Toward the Meeting of the Waters,* ed. Moore and Burton, 190.

11. *The Atlanta Constitution,* May 18, 1954, 1, Richard B. Russell Collection, Subgroup C, Series 3: Speech/Media, Box 27, Folder 9.

12. Jim Newton, *Justice for All: Earl Warren and the Nation He Made* (New York: Riverhead, 2007), 460–61.

13. James O. Farmer, "Memories and Forebodings: The Fight to Preserve the White Democratic Primary in South Carolina," in *Toward the Meeting of the Waters,* ed. Moore and Burton, 244.

14. Simon, "The Devaluation," 251; Edgar, *South Carolina,* 551.

15. Ernest F. Hollings and Kirk Victor, *Making Government Work* (Columbia: University of South Carolina Press, 2008), 167.

16. Charles L. Zelden, *The Battle for the Black Ballot: Smith v. Allwright and the Defeat of the Texas All-White Primary* (Lawrence: University Press of Kansas, 2004), 112; Key, *Southern Politics,* 627.

17. "Judge Vacates Conviction in 1944 Execution," *New York Times,* December 18, 2014, A28.

18. Huss, *Senator,* 158–59.

19. Telephone conversation between Lyndon B. Johnson and Olin D. Johnston, December 26, 1963, Lyndon B. Johnston Presidential Recordings, Miller Center, University of Virginia, K6312.18.

20. Wim Roefs, "The Impact of 1940s Civil Rights Activism on the State's 1960s Scene: A Hypothesis and Historiographical Discussion," in *Toward the Meeting of the Waters,* ed. Moore and Burton, 161; Joseph Crespino, *Strom Thurmond's America* (New York: Hill and Wang, 2012), 92.

21. Bass and Poole, *Palmetto State,* 70–74; Bass and Thompson, *Strom,* 25.

22. Crespino, *Strom Thurmond's America,* 118.

23. See, generally, Bass and Thompson, *Strom.*

24. Hollings and Victor, *Making Government Work,* 82.

25. Dewey W. Grantham, *The Life and Death of the Solid South: A Political History* (Lexington:

University Press of Kentucky, 1988), 118, 131; Bass and Thompson, *Strom*, 3–18, 156; Badger, "From Defiance," 128; Crespino, *Strom Thurmond's America*, 102–4; Hollings and Victor, *Making Government Work*, 84–110.

26. Interview with Elizabeth J. Patterson, September 29, 2014; interview with John Spratt, September 28, 2014.

27. "Herman Talmadge, Georgia Senator and Governor, Dies at 88," *New York Times*, March 22, 2002.

28. Dale Duckworth to Strom Thurmond, October 7, 1958, Strom Thurmond Collection, Subject Correspondence Series, Mss.0100.18, Year 1958, Box 7, Folder 4–1 (Supreme Court), July 3–December 31, 1958; J. H. Bickley to Olin D. Johnston, July 6, 1957; Olin D. Johnston to J. H. Bickley, July 9, 1957, Olin D. Johnston Collection, Senate Papers, Legislative Files, Box 61, Judiciary Committee, Supreme Court; R. Victor Brannon to Strom Thurmond, undated; Strom Thurmond to Mr. and Mrs. R. Victor Brannon, December 1, 1958, Strom Thurmond Collection, Subject Correspondence Series, Mss.0100.18, Year 1962, Box 7, Folder 4–1 (Supreme Court), July 3–December 31, 1958.

29. Strom Thurmond to A. L. McKenzie, January 1, 1958, Strom Thurmond Collection, Subject Correspondence Series, Mss.0100.18, Year 1958, Box 7, Folder 4–1 (Supreme Court), January 1–June 23, 1958.

2. THE MAN FROM MARYLAND

1. Nadine Cohodas, *Strom Thurmond and the Politics of Southern Change* (Macon, GA: Mercer University Press, 1995), 254; W. D. Smyth, "Segregation in Charleston in the 1950s: A Decade of Transition," *South Carolina Historical Magazine* 92, no. 2 (1991): 108; "School Case Decision Occupies Candidates," *News and Courier*, May 19, 1954, 1; "Governor Byrnes 'Shocked' By High Court Ruling," *News and Courier*, May 18, 1954, 1; "Decision is Denounced by S.C. Congressmen," *News and Courier*, May 18, 1954, 1.

2. Michael J. Klarman, *From Jim Crow to Civil Rights: The Supreme Court and the Struggle for Racial Equality* (Oxford: Oxford University Press, 2004), 247; Grace Elizabeth Hale, "Of the Meaning of Progress: A Century of Southern Race Relations," in *The American South in the Twentieth Century*, ed. Craig S. Pascoe et al. (Athens: University of Georgia Press, 2005), 58; J. Harvie Wilkinson III, *From Brown to Bakke: The Supreme Court and School Integration, 1954–1978* (Oxford: Oxford University Press, 1979), 26; Anthony J. Badger, "From Defiance to Moderation: South Carolina Governors and Racial Change," in *New Deal/New South: An Anthony J. Badger Reader* (Fayetteville: University of Arkansas Press, 2007), 132.

3. Jack Bass and Walter DeVries, *The Transformation of Southern Politics* (Athens: University of Georgia Press, 1995), 254; Robert Mickey, *Paths out of Dixie: The Democratization of Authoritarian Enclaves in America's Deep South, 1944–1972* (Princeton, NJ: Princeton University Press, 2015), 217; Jason Morgan Ward, *Defending White Democracy* (Chapel Hill: University of North Carolina Press, 2011), 121; Badger, "From Defiance," 131.

4. Juan Williams, *Thurgood Marshall: American Revolutionary* (New York: Random House, 1988), 149–51, 175–76; James T. Patterson, *Brown v. Board of Education: A Civil Rights Milestone and Its Troubled Legacy* (Oxford: Oxford University Press, 2002), 17–18; Adam Fairclough, *Better Day Coming: Blacks and Equality, 1890–2000* (London: Penguin, 2001), 218; Barbara A. Perry, *A*

"Representative" Supreme Court? The Impact of Race, Religion and Gender on Appointments (London: Greenwood Press, 1991), 97.

5. Marcia Synnott interview with Ernest F. Hollings, July 8, 1980, South Carolina Political Collections, Oral History Project, University of South Carolina, http://library.sc.edu/file/1786.

6. James F. Byrnes, "The Supreme Court Must Be Curbed!," *US News and World Report,* May 18, 1956, 52.

7. Ward, *Defending,* 122–23, 142; Badger, "From Defiance," 132; Keith M. Finley, *Delaying the Dream: Southern Senators and the Fight against Civil Rights, 1938–1965* (Baton Rouge: Louisiana State University Press, 2008), 7; Jane Dailey, Glenda Elizabeth Gilmore, and Bryant Simon, eds., *Jumpin' Jim Crow: Southern Politics from Civil War to Civil Rights* (Princeton, NJ: Princeton University Press, 2000), 4–5.

8. Finley, *Delaying the Dream,* 69; Charles S. Bullock and Janna Deitz, "Transforming the South: The Role of the Federal Government," in *The American South in the Twentieth Century,* ed. Craig S. Pascoe et al. (Athens: University of Georgia Press, 2005), 247.

9. Joseph Crespino, *Strom Thurmond's America* (New York: Hill and Wang, 2012), 71.

10. Fairclough, *Better Day Coming,* 210.

11. Jack Bass and Marilyn W. Thompson, *Strom: The Complicated Personal and Political Life of Strom Thurmond* (New York: Public Affairs, 2005), 146; Frank E. Jordan, *The Primary State: A History of the Democratic Party in South Carolina, 1896–1962* (self-published, n.d.), 81; Dewey W. Grantham, *The Life and Death of the Solid South: A Political History* (Lexington: University Press of Kentucky, 1988), 136; Crespino, *Strom Thurmond's America,* 98–99.

12. Finley, *Delaying the Dream,* 5, 23, 53; Richard B. Russell to Olin D. Johnston, June 7, 1949; Olin D. Johnston to Richard B. Russell, June 9, 1949, Olin D. Johnston Collection, Senate Papers, Legislative Files, Box 17.

13. Ward, *Defending,* 82, 119, 153.

14. Michael L. Gillette interview with Strom Thurmond, May 7, 1979, Lyndon B. Johnson Oral Histories, Miller Center, University of Virginia, http://web2.millercenter.org/lbj/oralhistory/thurmond_strom_1979_0507.pdf; Virginia Van der Veer Hamilton, *Lister Hill: Statesman from the South* (Chapel Hill: University of North Carolina Press, 1987), 195.

15. Olin D. Johnston to Speaker Solomon Blatt, January 20, 1956, Olin D. Johnston Collection, Senate Papers, Legislative Files, Box 56; Bryant Simon, *A Fabric of Defeat* (Chapel Hill: University of North Carolina Press, 1998), 233.

16. Keith M. Finley, "Balancing Liberal and Conservative Policy Preferences: Russell B. Long's Early United States Senate Career, 1948–1957," *Louisiana History* 45, no. 1 (Winter 2004): 17, 30; Ward, *Defending,* 113–14. See also Finley, *Delaying the Dream,* 139.

17. Henry J. Abraham, *Justices, Presidents, and Senators: A History of the U.S. Supreme Court Appointments from Washington to Clinton* (Lanham, MD: Rowman and Littlefield, 1999), 194; "Senate Confirms Warren by Voice," *New York Times,* March 2, 1954; "Opposition to Warren Inspired by Fred Howser," *San Francisco Chronicle,* February 14, 1954; "Langer v. Warren," *New York Times,* February 18, 1954; "Judiciary Committee Approves Warren Nomination, 12 to 3," *Baltimore Sun,* February 25, 1954; "Low in the Smear Line," *St. Louis Post-Dispatch,* February 21, 1954; Laurence H. Tribe, *God Save This Honorable Court* (London: Random House, 1985), 91.

18. Patterson, *Brown v. Board,* 55–57; Klarman, *From Jim Crow,* 301; Tribe, *God Save,* 37–38; Patterson, *Brown v. Board,* 60–65; Briggs v. Elliott Descendants Reunion Banquet Keynote Address by Senator Ernest F. Hollings, May 11, 2002, Summerton, South Carolina, South Carolina Political Collections, Oral History Project, University of South Carolina, http://digital.tcl.sc.edu/cdm/compoundobject/collection/how/id/552/show/547/rec/1.

19. Gunnar Myrdal, *An American Dilemma: The Negro Problem and American Democracy* (New York: Harper and Brothers, 1944); Jim Newton, *Justice for All: Earl Warren and the Nation He Made* (New York: Riverhead, 2007), 298, 327; Patterson, *Brown v. Board,* 67–69.

20. Transcript of James Eastland's Senate speech regarding introduction of Resolution 104, Richard B. Russell Collection, Subgroup E, Series 4: Vertical Files, Box 4, Folder 64; Olin D. Johnston to James Eastland, March 15, 1956, Olin D. Johnston Collection, Senate Papers, Legislative Files, Box 46, Civil Rights, School Segregation.

21. "Thurmond Warns of a Third Party," *New York Times,* August 21, 1955, 53.

22. Jim Newton, *Eisenhower: The White House Years* (New York: Anchor, 2011), 116, 252; Dwight D. Eisenhower, *Mandate for Change: The White House Years, 1953–1956* (New York: Signet, 1962), 284; Newton, *Justice for All,* 113–14; David A. Yalof, *Pursuit of Justices: Presidential Politics and the Selection of Supreme Court Nominees* (Chicago: University of Chicago Press, 1999), 47–49.

23. David A. Nichols, *A Matter of Justice: Eisenhower and the Civil Rights Revolution* (New York: Simon and Schuster, 2007), 79.

24. Abraham, *Justices, Presidents,* 197.

25. Hearings before the Committee of the Judiciary, United States Senate, Eighty-Fourth Congress, First Session on Nomination of John Marshall Harlan, of New York, to be Associate Justice of the Supreme Court, printed for the use of the Committee on the Judiciary, US Government Printing Office (1967), February 24, 1955, 140.

26. "Senate Confirms Harlan to Bench," *New York Times,* March 17, 1955, 1.

27. Ibid., 1; Michael A. Kahn, "Shattering the Myth about President Eisenhower's Supreme Court Appointments," *Presidential Studies Quarterly* 22, no. 1 (Winter 1992): 51; "Harlan Hearing Held by Senators," *New York Times,* February 25, 1955, 8; Remarks of Senator Richard B. Russell before the United States Senate on March 16, 1955 on Nomination of John Marshall Harlan to be Associate Justice of the Supreme Court, Richard B. Russell Collection Subgroup C, Series 10: Civil Rights, Box 27, Folder 11.

28. Weekly radio report by Senator Strom Thurmond, July 15, 1955, 4, Strom Thurmond Collection, Mss.0100.11, Speeches Series 1935–1998, Subseries B, Originals (1947–1970), Statements, Box 4, Folder 48; Address by Senator Strom Thurmond before the Southern Society at the Plaza Hotel, New York, January 14, 1955, 22–24, Strom Thurmond Collection, Mss.0100.11, Speeches Series 1935–1998, Subseries A, General File (1935–1983), Addresses 1955, Box 7, Folder 604.

29. "Senate Confirms Harlan to Bench," *New York Times,* March 17, 1955, 1; Olin D. Johnston to Reverend John H. Wrenn, February 8, 1955, Olin D. Johnston Collection, Senate Papers, Legislative Files, Box 46, Civil Rights, General; Newton, *Justice for All,* 341.

30. Wilkinson, *From Brown to Bakke,* 81; Fairclough, *Better Day Coming,* 220; Bullock and Deitz, "Transforming the South," 251; Bob Woodward and Scott Armstrong, *The Brethren* (New York: Simon and Schuster, 1979), 40.

31. J. W. Peltason, *58 Lonely Men: Southern Federal Judges and School Desegregation* (Chicago: University of Illinois Press, 1971), 22–23; Weekly radio report by Senator Strom Thurmond, July 15, 1955, 1, Strom Thurmond Collection, Mss.0100.11, Speeches Series 1935–1998, Subseries B, originals (1947–1970), Statements 1955, Box 4, Folder 48; Nichols, *A Matter of Justice,* 70; "Decision Pleases Many in Congress," *News and Courier,* June 1, 1955, 26.

32. Olin D. Johnston to William Langer, June 25, 1956, Olin D. Johnston Collection, Senate Papers, Legislative Files, Box 54, Judiciary Committee, General, Folder 4; Nichols, *A Matter of Justice,* 86.

33. Nichols, *A Matter of Justice,* 86.

34. "Obstructionism," *Washington Post–Times Herald,* July 28, 1955, 14; Olin D. Johnston to Harley M. Kilgore, January 13, 1956, Olin D. Johnston Collection, Senate Papers, Legislative Files, Box 54, Judiciary Committee, General, Folder 3.

35. Nichols, *A Matter of Justice,* 86.

36. Ibid., 87; Olin D. Johnston to Harley M. Kilgore, January 11, 1956, Olin D. Johnston Collection, Senate Papers, Legislative Files, Box 54, Judiciary Committee, General, Folder 3.

37. Olin D. Johnston to Harley M. Kilgore, January 13, 1956, Olin D. Johnston Collection, Senate Papers, Legislative Files, Box 54, Judiciary Committee, General, Folder 3; "Inquiry by Senate on Sobeloff Urged," *New York Times,* January 15, 1956, 31.

38. Finley, *Delaying the Dream,* 21.

39. Newsletter from the office of Olin D. Johnston, April 12, 1956; speech delivered by Senator Olin D. Johnston on the floor of the Senate, May 17, 1956; Simon E. Sobeloff to Joseph C. O'Mahoney, May 20, 1956, Olin D. Johnston Collection, Senate Papers, Legislative Files, Box 54, Judiciary Committee, General, Folder 4; "Sobeloff Supported at Hearing," *Washington Post–Times Herald,* May 6, 1956, B5

40. Newsletter from the office of Olin D. Johnston, June 8, 1956; "Johnston Raps Sobeloff Appointment," *Washington Post–Times Herald,* June 5, 1956, 17; notes of Olin D. Johnston on letter from John Gregg McMaster to Olin D. Johnston, May 1, 1956, Olin D. Johnston Collection, Senate Papers, Legislative Files, Box 54, Judiciary Committee, General, Folder 4; Nichols, *A Matter of Justice,* 87; "Sobeloff Reports Go to Senate; Way Clear for Judgeship Action," *New York Times,* July 7, 1956, 34.

41. "Johnston Raps Sobeloff Appointment," *Washington Post–Times Herald,* June 5, 1956, 17, Olin D. Johnston Collection, Senate Papers, Legislative Files, Box 54, Judiciary Committee, General, Folder 4; Excerpt from Minutes of Full Committee Meeting Held on Monday, June 25, 1956, Olin D. Johnston Collection, Senate Papers, Legislative Files, Box 54, Judiciary Committee, General, Folder 4; Nichols, *A Matter of Justice,* 88.

42. Herbert Brownell to James O. Eastland, June 8, 1956, in excerpt from Minutes of Full Committee Meeting Held on Monday, June 25, 1956, 2; excerpt from Minutes of Full Committee Meeting Held on Monday, June 25, 1956, 3, Olin D. Johnston Collection, Senate Papers, Legislative Files, Box 54, Judiciary Committee, General, Folder 4.

43. Olin D. Johnston to William Langer, June 25, 1956, Olin D. Johnston Collection, Senate Papers, Legislative Files, Box 54, Judiciary Committee, General, Folder 4.

44. Card from anonymous writer to Olin D. Johnston, n.d.; Samuel B. George to Olin D. Johnston, June 10, 1956; Olin D. Johnston to Samuel B. George, June 14, 1956; George W. Thomas to Olin D. Johnston, July 19, 1956, Olin D. Johnston Collection, Senate Papers, Legislative Files,

Box 54, Judiciary Committee, General, Folder 4; "Senate Action on Sobeloff Blocked," *Spartanburg Herald-Journal,* June 29, 1956, 1.

45. "Senate Unit Delays Voting on Sobeloff," *New York Times,* June 28, 1956, 11; Nichols, *A Matter of Justice,* 87; Olin D. Johnston to Mr. and Mrs. O.K. McDaniel (telegram), June 29, 1956; Olin D. Johnston to C. Allen Ashley Jr., June 29, 1956.

46. Speech of Hon. Olin D. Johnston of South Carolina in the Senate of the United States, In Opposition to Confirmation of Mr. Simon E. Sobeloff for Judge of United States Fourth Circuit Court of Appeals, Congressional Record, Proceedings and Debates of the 84th Congress, Second Session, 8–10; letters from Olin D. Johnston to various, July 16, 1956, Olin D. Johnston Collection, Senate Papers, Legislative Files, Box 54, Judiciary Committee, General, Folder 4; "Sobeloff Is Opposed," *New York Times,* July 15, 1956, 42; "Two Senators Delay Sobeloff Confirmation," *Washington Post–Times Herald,* July 28, 1956, 23.

47. "Senate Confirms Sobeloff, 64 to 19," *New York Times,* July 17, 1956, 1; Nichols, *A Matter of Justice,* 87; L. Marion Gressette to Olin D. Johnston, July 20, 1956; Huger Sinkler to Olin D. Johnston, July 18, 1956, Olin D. Johnston Collection, Senate Papers, Legislative Files, Box 54, Judiciary Committee, General, Folder 1.

48. Olin D. Johnston to James H. Hammond, July, 20 1956; Olin D. Johnston to Huger Sinkler, July 20, 1956, Olin D. Johnston Collection, Senate Papers, Legislative Files, Box 54, Judiciary Committee, General, Folder 3; George Bell Timmerman to Olin D. Johnston, July 18, 1956, Olin D. Johnston Collection, Senate Papers, Legislative Files, Box 54, Judiciary Committee, General, Folder 1; Nichols, *A Matter of Justice,* 88; Walter Brown to Strom Thurmond, July 13, 1962, Strom Thurmond Collection, Subject Correspondence Series, Mss.0100.18, Year 1962, Box 19, 3 (United States Court and Supreme Court Judges), Folder 1; Peltason, *58 Lonely Men,* 24.

49. "Case Asks No Delay in Brennan Okay," *Daytona Beach Morning Journal,* November 20, 1956, 4; "Brennan Check Urged," *New York Times,* November 20, 1956, 57; "Sen. Johnston to Examine Justice Brennan's Record," *St. Petersburg Times,* November 19, 1956, 2.

50. Yalof, *Pursuit,* 55–58; Perry, *A "Representative" Supreme Court?,* 40; Stephen J. Wermiel, "The Nomination of Justice Brennan: Eisenhower's Mistake?," *Constitutional Commentary* 11 (1994–1995), 533; Clarence F. Anderson to Olin D. Johnston, November 21, 1956; anonymous to Olin D. Johnston, November 19, 1956, Olin D. Johnston Collection, Senate Papers, Legislative Files, Box 60, Judiciary Committee, Appointments, Brennan, William J., Folder 101.

51. Excerpt from Congressional Record, March 19, 1957, Herman E. Talmadge Collection Subgroup C, Series 8: Legislation, Box 426, Folder 7.

52. See Wermiel, "The Nomination of Justice Brennan," for a thorough study of Brennan's record prior to his nomination; Yalof, *Pursuit,* 42–43; Mark Silverstein, *Judicious Choices: The Politics of Supreme Court Appointments* (London: Norton, 2004), 31.

3. "A RENDEZVOUS WITH REALITY"

1. "Will Johnston or Thurmond Lead?," *News and Courier,* April 9, 1956, 8A; Frank E. Jordan, *The Primary State: A History of the Democratic Party in South Carolina, 1896–1962,* 82; interview with Elizabeth J. Patterson, September 29, 2014.

2. Joseph Crespino, *Strom Thurmond's America* (New York: Hill and Wang, 2012), 105; Jim Newton, *Justice for All: Earl Warren and the Nation He Made* (New York: Riverside, 2007), 339–40; "South Must Take Offensive in Race Fight, Eastland Says," *News and Courier,* January 27, 1956, 1; Anthony J. Badger, "From Defiance to Moderation: South Carolina Governors and Racial Change," in *New Deal/New South: An Anthony J. Badger Reader* (Fayetteville: University of Arkansas Press, 2007), 127–43, 134–35.

3. Speech by Senator John Sparkman, Alabama Statewide Radio Hook-Up originating from Mobile, Alabama, April 17, 1950, Olin D. Johnston Collection, Senate Papers, Reference Files, Box 116, Civil Rights, 1950–56; Anthony J. Badger, "Southerners Who Refused to Sign the Southern Manifesto," in *New Deal/New South: An Anthony J. Badger Reader* (Fayetteville: University of Arkansas Press, 2007), 72–80; Robert Mann, *When Freedom Would Triumph: The Civil Rights Struggle in Congress, 1954–1968* (Baton Rouge: Louisiana State University Press, 2007), 19; Richard B. Russell to Hayes Mizell, April 30, 1962, Richard B. Russell Collection Subgroup C, Series 10: Civil Rights, Box 195, Folder 10; "Senators Chart High Court Fight," *New York Times,* February 10, 1956, 10; Crespino, *Strom Thurmond's America,* 108; Badger, "From Defiance," 135. The extent of Thurmond's role in the creation of the Southern Manifesto has been debated exhaustively in previous studies. See, for example, Crespino, *Strom Thurmond's America,* 105–7; Keith M. Finley, *Delaying the Dream: Southern Senators and the Fight against Civil Rights, 1938–1965* (Baton Rouge: Louisiana State University Press, 2008), 142–45; and Robert Mann, *The Walls of Jericho: Lyndon Johnson, Hubert Humphrey, Richard Russell, and the Struggle for Civil Rights* (New York: Harcourt Brace, 1996), 161–63.

4. Jason Morgan Ward, *Defending White Democracy* (Chapel Hill: University of North Carolina Press, 2011), 152–53. For examples of support from outside the South, see Ewing E. Clemons to Olin D. Johnston, October 23, 1957, Olin D. Johnston Collection, Senate Papers, Legislative Files, Box 60, Judiciary Committee, Appointments, Haynsworth, Clement F., Folder 103; Stanley Walling to Olin D. Johnston, September 4, 1959, Olin D. Johnston Collection, Senate Papers, Legislative Files, Box 70, Civil Rights, Reaction to ODJ Speech, Folder 2; John R. Schmidhauser, *The Supreme Court: Its Politics, Personalities and Procedures* (Austin, TX: Holt, Rinehart and Winston, 1960), 149; Report of the Committee on Federal-State Relationships as Affected by Judicial Decisions, August 1958, Conference of Chief Justices, 1313 East Sixtieth Street, Chicago 37, Illinois, Herman E. Talmadge Collection Subgroup C, Series 3: Civil Rights, Box 17, Folder 4; "Hearing on Two Judicial Appointees Tones Down 'Oath' to a Question," *Washington Post–Times Herald,* April 22, 1958, A8.

5. Address by Senator Strom Thurmond on a Declaration of Principles, in the United States Senate, March 12, 1956, 6, Strom Thurmond Collection, Mss.0100.11, Speeches Series 1935–1998, Subseries B, originals (1947–1970), Addresses 1956, Box 4, Folder 53; Crespino, *Strom Thurmond's America,* 107–8; Olin D. Johnston to Jay E. Darlington, October 20, 1958, Olin D. Johnston Collection, Senate Papers, Legislative Files, Box 65, Judiciary Committee, General, Appointments; Strom Thurmond to Mr. and Mrs. R. Victor Brannon, December 1, 1958; Strom Thurmond to O. L. Andrews, October 27, 1958, Strom Thurmond Collection, Subject Correspondence Series, Mss.0100.18, Year 1958, Box 7, Folder 4–1 (Supreme Court), July 3–December 31, 1958.

6. Strom Thurmond to J. R. McVicker, July 8, 1957, Strom Thurmond Collection, Subject Correspondence Series, Mss.0100.18, Year 1957, Box 27, Supreme Court July 3–13, 1957. For examples of southerners maintaining solidarity in the Senate, see Richard B. Russell to Olin D. Johnston, June

7, 1949; Olin D. Johnston to Richard B. Russell, June 9, 1949, Olin D. Johnston Collection, Senate Papers, Legislative Files, Box 17, Civil Rights; Finley, *Delaying the Dream,* 177; Crespino, *Strom Thurmond's America,* 114–15; "Won't Use Act to Punish Dixie, Ike Tells Russell," *Washington Post–Times Herald,* July 11, 1957, A1; "Russell Leads Attack on Thurmond," *Augusta Chronicle,* August 31, 1957, 1, Strom Thurmond Collection, Legislative Assistant Series, Mss.0100.15, Box 140, Richard Russell, August 1957–May 1964.

7. Crespino, *Strom Thurmond's America,* 108; statement by Senator Strom Thurmond in the Senate with reference to the Supreme Court decision in the *Mallory* case, June 27, 1957, 3, Strom Thurmond Collection, Mss.0100.11, Speeches Series 1935–1998, Subseries B, originals (1947–1970), Statements on Senate Floor 1957, Box 5, Folder 73; statement by Senator Strom Thurmond on *Mallory* decision and *Star* Editorial, January 9, 1958, Strom Thurmond Collection, Mss.0100.11, Speeches Series 1935–1998, Subseries B, originals (1947–1970), Statements on Senate Floor 1958, Box 8, Folder 84; Irving Dilliard, "Thomas C. Hennings Jr. and the Supreme Court," *Missouri Law Review* 26, no. 4 (1961): 432; Stephen M. Engel, *American Politicians Confront the Court: Opposition Politics and Changing Responses to Judicial Power* (Cambridge: Cambridge University Press, 2011), 296; "4 Democrats Offer Bill on Confessions," *New York Times,* April 26, 1960, 13.

8. Ward, *Defending,* 162; Robert Mickey, *Paths out of Dixie: The Democratization of Authoritarian Enclaves in America's Deep South, 1944–1972* (Princeton, NJ: Princeton University Press, 2015), 186; Olin D. Johnston to Leroy Collins, September 27, 1957, Olin D. Johnston Collection, Senate Papers, Legislative Files, Box 60, Judiciary Committee, NAACP, Folder 107A; John E. Huss, *Senator for the South: A Biography of Olin D. Johnston* (New York: Doubleday, 1961), 207.

9. Statement by Senator Strom Thurmond in opposition to the confirmation of W. Wilson White as Assistant Attorney General for Civil Rights Division, on Senate floor, August 13, 1958, 3–4, Strom Thurmond Collection, Mss.0100.11, Speeches Series 1935–1998, Subseries B, originals (1947–1970), Statements on Senate Floor 1958, Box 8, Folder 85; "Southerners Hold Up Vote On White's Rights Job," *Washington Post–Times Herald,* August 7, 1958, A16.

10. "Senators Assail and Praise Court," *New York Times,* September 30, 1958, 22.

11. "Wanted! Earl Warren for Impeachment for giving aid and comfort to the Communist Conspiracy, the mortal Enemy of the United States and the American People!," leaflet, September 1957, Strom Thurmond Collection, Subject Correspondence Series, Mss.0100.18, Year 1957, Box 27, Supreme Court July 15–December 19, 1957; Louis L. Loeb to Richard B. Russell, October 15, 1957, Richard B. Russell Collection Subgroup C, Series 3: Speech/Media, Box 27, Folder 9; Roland A. Ouellette to Herman Talmadge, May 8, 1958 and handwritten notes; Ernest S. Griffith to Herman Talmadge, June 10, 1958, Herman E. Talmadge Collection Subgroup C, Series 3: Civil Rights, Box 8, Folder 18; Herman E. Talmadge and Mark Royden Winchell, *Talmadge: A Political Legacy, A Politician's Life—A Memoir* (Atlanta: Peachtree Publishers, 1987), 157.

12. "Impeach Justices, Thurmond Urges," *New York Times,* July 8, 1957, 15; Crespino, *Strom Thurmond's America,* 109–10; "Heat Raised in Senate Debate on Court," *Washington Post–Times Herald,* June 27, 1957, A2; Huss, *Senator,* 207–8.

13. "S.C. Senators Seek Court Power Limits," *News and Courier,* February 10, 1955, 1; "State Segregation Bills Attacked by Senator," *Sarasota Herald-Tribune,* February 11, 1955, 3; Engel, *American Politicians,* 297–98; Mann, *Walls of Jericho,* 231–32.

14. "Senate Group Votes Curbs on High Court," *Washington Post–Times Herald,* May 1, 1958, A1; Engel, *American Politicians,* 298; Mann, *Walls of Jericho,* 233–34.

15. "A Group with Real Power," *US News and World Report,* March 21, 1961, Edgar A. Brown Papers, Mss.0091, Johnston, Olin D., Box 30, Folder 390; "Wear Down South, LBJ Says of Rights," *Atlanta Journal,* June 18, 1963; Strom Thurmond Collection, Legislative Assistant Series, Mss.0100.15, Box 140, Lyndon Johnson, July 1957–October 1966.

16. Newton, *Justice for All,* 356–57; David A. Nichols, *A Matter of Justice: Eisenhower and the Civil Rights Revolution* (New York: Simon and Schuster, 2007), 240.

17. Olin D. Johnston to Thomas C. Hennings, March 17, 1959; Thomas C. Hennings to Olin D. Johnston, March 18, 1959, Olin D. Johnston Collection, Senate Papers, Reference Files, Civil Rights, 1959: April: General, Box 116.

18. Olin D. Johnston to Burnet R. Maybank, Thomas R. Waring, Thomas H. Pope, Robert E. McNair, L. Marion Gressette, Edgar A. Brown, Solomon Blatt, James F. Byrnes, Daniel R. McLeod, George Bell Timmerman Jr., and Ernest F. Hollings, March 25, 1959; Olin D. Johnston to Strom Thurmond and L. Mendel Rivers, April 20, 1959; Olin D. Johnston to Arthur J. Limehouse, April 20, 1959, Olin D. Johnston Collection, Senate Papers, Reference Files, Civil Rights, 1959: April: General, Box 116.

19. James F. Byrnes to Olin D. Johnston, April 9, 1959; George Bell Timmerman Jr. to Olin D. Johnston, April 13, 1959, Olin D. Johnston Collection, Senate Papers, Reference Files, Civil Rights, 1959: April: General, Box 116.

20. Olin D. Johnston to Thomas R. Waring, Robert E. McNair, and Solomon Blatt, April 6, 1959, Olin D. Johnston Collection, Senate Papers, Reference Files, Civil Rights, 1959: April: General, Box 116.

21. Statement of The Honorable Ernest F. Hollings, Governor of South Carolina, before the Subcommittee on Constitutional Rights Legislation of the Judiciary Committee of the United States House of Representatives, Washington, DC, April 14, 1959, 1–6, Olin D. Johnston Collection, Senate Papers, Reference Files, Civil Rights, 1959: April: General, Box 116; Address by Governor Ernest F. Hollings to the General Assembly of South Carolina, January 9, 1963, South Carolina Political Collections, Oral History Project, University of South Carolina, http://digital.tcl.sc.edu/cdm/compoundobject/collection/how/id/291/rec/14; "Hollings Says Farewell, Sees Desegregation," *Times-News,* (Hendersonville, NC), January 10, 1963, 3.

22. Statement of The Honorable Ernest F. Hollings, 3.

23. Statement of Reverend I. DeQuincy Newman of Spartanburg, South Carolina, before the Senate Subcommittee on Constitutional Rights, April 16, 1959, 1–5; Olin D. Johnston to Ernest F. Hollings, April 20, 1959, Olin D. Johnston Collection, Senate Papers, Reference Files, Civil Rights, 1959: April: General, Box 116; Wim Roefs, "The Impact of 1940s Civil Rights Activism on the State's 1960s Scene: A Hypothesis and Historiographical Discussion," in *Toward the Meeting of the Waters: Currents in the Civil Rights Movement of South Carolina during the Twentieth Century,* ed. Winifred B. Moore and Orville Vernon Burton (Columbia: University of South Carolina Press, 2008), 160–61.

24. Dwight D. Eisenhower to William P. Rogers, September 17, 1958, William P. Rogers Papers, Series I: General Correspondence, 1952–61, Box 4; Nichols, *A Matter of Justice,* 86.

25. "Stewart OK'd for High Court by Senate, 70–17," *Philadelphia Inquirer,* May 6, 1959; "Senate Confirms Justice Stewart," *New York Times,* May 6, 1959, William P. Rogers Papers, Series VII: Scrapbook, 1938–61, Box 66, Folder 3.

26. Nichols, *A Matter of Justice,* 82–83; "Stewart Is Confirmed—On Job since October," *Washington Evening Star,* May 6, 1959; "Senate Confirms Justice Stewart," *New York Times,* May 6, 1959, William P. Rogers Papers, Series VII: Scrapbook, 1938–61, Box 66, Folder 3; Kahn, "Shattering the Myth," 48, 51; Nichols, *A Matter of Justice,* 82.

27. The United States Senate, Report of Proceedings, Hearings Held before Committee on the Judiciary, Nomination of Potter Stewart to be Associate Justice of the Supreme Court of the United States, April 9, 1959, 28.

28. Ibid., 41.

29. Ibid., 46.

30. Unknown headline, *Washington Post–Times Herald,* April 10, 1959, William P. Rogers Papers, Series VII: Scrapbook, 1938–61, Box 66, Folder 3; L. A. Scot Powe, "The Senate and the Court: Questioning a Nominee," *Texas Law Review* 54 (1975–1976): 898.

31. Unknown headline, *Washington Post–Times Herald,* April 30, 1959, William P. Rogers Papers, Series VII: Scrapbook, 1938–61, Box 66, Folder 3.

32. Statement of Senator Strom Thurmond on Senate Floor Opposing Confirmation of Potter Stewart to be an Associate Justice of the United States Supreme Court, May 5, 1959; Strom Thurmond Collection, Mss.0100.11, Speeches Series 1935–1998, Subseries B, originals (1947–1970), Statements on Senate Floor, Box 8, Folder 93.

33. "Roll Call Vote in Senate on Stewart Nomination," *New York Times,* May 6, 1959, William P. Rogers Papers, Series VII: Scrapbook, 1938–61, Box 66, Folder 3; "Stewart Is Confirmed—On Job since October," *Washington Evening Star,* May 6, 1959, William P. Rogers Papers, Series VII: Scrapbook, 1938–61, Box 66, Folder 3.

34. Unknown headline, *Washington Post–Times Herald,* April 10, 1959, William P. Rogers Papers, Series VII: Scrapbook, 1938–61, Box 66, Folder 3.

4. HOME OF THE WHITE MAN'S SOUL

1. "Was Misquoted Says Thurgood Marshall," *Richmond Times-Dispatch,* August 21, 1962, Olin D. Johnston Collection, Senate Papers, News Clippings, Box 136, Marshall, Thurgood.

2. Nadine Cohodas, *Strom Thurmond and the Politics of Southern Change* (Macon, GA: Mercer University Press, 1995), 365.

3. Bob Woodward and Scott Armstrong, *The Brethren* (New York: Simon and Schuster, 1979), 52; Juan Williams, *Thurgood Marshall: American Revolutionary* (New York: Random House, 1988), 175–76; James T. Patterson, *Brown v. Board of Education: A Civil Rights Milestone and Its Troubled Legacy* (Oxford: Oxford University Press, 2002), 17–18; Adam Fairclough, *Better Day Coming: Blacks and Equality, 1890–2000* (London: Penguin, 2001), 218; Barbara A. Perry, *A "Representative" Supreme Court? The Impact of Race, Religion and Gender on Appointments* (London: Greenwood Press, 1991), 97.

4. Williams, *Thurgood Marshall,* 199.

5. John Monk, Preface to *Toward the Meeting of the Waters: Currents in the Civil Rights Movement of South Carolina during the Twentieth Century,* ed. Winfred B. Moore Jr. and Orville Vernon Burton (Columbia: University of South Carolina Press, 2008), xxii; David Robertson, *Sly and Able: A Political Biography of James F. Byrnes* (New York: W. W. Norton, 1994), 506; Patterson, *Brown v.*

Board, 26; V. O. Key, *Southern Politics in State and Nation* (New York: Vintage, 1949), 628; Peter F. Lau, *Democracy Rising: South Carolina and the Fight for Black Equality since 1865* (Louisville: University Press of Kentucky, 2006), 95; Williams, *Thurgood Marshall,* 199–203.

6. Earl Black and Merle Black, *Politics and Society in the South* (Cambridge, MA: Harvard University Press, 1987), 93; James L. Felder, *Civil Rights in South Carolina* (Charleston, SC: History Press, 2012), 48.

7. Robertson, *Sly and Able,* 509–10; Williams, *Thurgood Marshall,* 202.

8. J. W. Peltason, *58 Lonely Men: Southern Federal Judges and School Desegregation* (Chicago: University of Illinois Press, 1971), 10, 73; Felder, *Civil Rights,* 49; Williams, *Thurgood Marshall,* 201; Thurgood Marshall and Robert Carter, "Real Heroes in S.C.," *Baltimore Afro-American,* June 16, 1951, 4, cited in Williams, *Thurgood Marshall,* 201; Orville Vernon Burton et al., "Seeds in Unlikely Soil: The *Briggs v. Elliott* School Desegregation Case," in *Toward the Meeting of the Waters,* ed. Moore and Burton, 188; William Henry Harbaugh, *Lawyer's Lawyer: The Life of John W. Davis* (New York: Oxford University Press, 1973), cited in Williams, *Thurgood Marshall,* 203.

9. Williams, *Thurgood Marshall,* 229.

10. Bryant Simon, *A Fabric of Defeat* (Chapel Hill: University of North Carolina Press, 1998), 200, 205–10; Key, *Southern Politics,* 130–31, 143; Dewey G. Grantham, *The Life and Death of the Solid South: A Political History* (Lexington: University Press of Kentucky, 1988), 98–99; G. C. Waldrep III, *Southern Workers and the Search for Community* (Chicago: University of Chicago Press, 2000), 49–50; Timothy Minchin, *Hiring The Black Worker: The Racial Integration of the Southern Textile Industry, 1960–1980* (Chapel Hill: University of North Carolina Press, 1999), 217; Bruce J. Schulman, *From Cotton Belt to Sunbelt* (Durham, NC: Duke University Press, 1994), 52–53; K. Michael Prince, *Rally Round the Flag, Boys!* (Columbia: University of South Carolina Press, 2004), 28; Wim Roefs, "The Impact of 1940s Civil Rights Activism on the State's 1960s Scene: A Hypothesis and Historiographical Discussion," in *Toward the Meeting of the Waters,* ed. Moore and Burton, 160; J. P. Shannon, "Presidential Politics in the South—1938, II," *Journal of Politics* 1, no. 3 (August 1939): 288.

11. Simon, *Fabric of Defeat,* 221; Charles L. Zelden, *The Battle for the Black Ballot: Smith v. Allwright and the Defeat of the Texas All-White Primary* (Lawrence: University Press of Kansas, 2004), 112; Key, *Southern Politics,* 627–30; draft of speech by Governor Olin D. Johnston, June 14, 1944; draft of speech by Governor Olin D. Johnston, July 24, 1944, Olin D. Johnston Collection, Senate Papers, Legislative Files, Box 120, 1944, June–July.

12. James O. Farmer, "Memories and Forebodings: The Fight to Preserve the White Democratic Primary in South Carolina," in *Toward the Meeting of the Waters,* ed. Moore and Burton, 249; Robert Mickey, *Paths out of Dixie: The Democratization of Authoritarian Enclaves in America's Deep South, 1944–1972* (Princeton, NJ: Princeton University Press, 2015), 103–8; Key, *Southern Politics,* 628; Felder, *Civil Rights,* 42; press release from the office of Senator Olin D. Johnston, October 23, 1956; Olin D. Johnston Collection, Senate Papers, Legislative Files, Box 54, Folder 4.

13. Virginia Van der Veer Hamilton, *Lister Hill: Statesman from the South* (Chapel Hill: University of North Carolina Press, 1987), 213; Anthony J. Badger, "Southerners Who Refused to Sign the Southern Manifesto," in *New Deal/New South: An Anthony J. Badger Reader* (Fayetteville: University of Arkansas Press, 2007), 72–73; Grantham, *The Life and Death,* 135.

14. Perry, *A "Representative" Supreme Court?,* 96–97; Mark V. Tushnet, *Making Constitutional*

Law: Thurgood Marshall and the Supreme Court, 1961–1991 (Oxford: Oxford University Press, 1997), 9; Perry, *A "Representative" Supreme Court?*, 97; Williams, *Thurgood Marshall*, 292, 296, 298; Henry J. Abraham, *Justices, Presidents, and Senators: A History of the U.S. Supreme Court Appointments from Washington to Clinton* (Lanham, MD: Rowman and Littlefield, 1999).

15. Williams, *Thurgood Marshall*, 111, 298; Perry, *A "Representative" Supreme Court?*, 95; Abraham, *Justices, Presidents*, 209; David A. Yalof, *Pursuit of Justices: Presidential Politics and the Selection of Supreme Court Nominees* (Chicago: University of Chicago Press, 1999), 75–79; Perry, *A "Representative Supreme Court?*," 98–99; Christine L. Nemacheck, *Strategic Selection* (Charlottesville: University of Virginia Press, 2008), 51; Abraham, *Justices, Presidents*, 209; Orville Vernon Burton et al., "South Carolina," in *Quiet Revolution in the South: The Impact of the Voting Rights Act, 1965–1990*, ed. Chandler Davidson and Bernard N. Grofman (Princeton, NJ: Princeton University Press, 1994), 195; Darlene Clark Hine, *Black Victory: The Rise and Fall of the White Primary in Texas* (Columbia: University of Missouri Press, 2003), 244; Key, *Southern Politics*, 146; Nancy J. Weiss, *Farewell to the Party of Lincoln: Black Politics in the Age of FDR* (Princeton, NJ: Princeton University Press, 1983), 137–38; Mickey, *Paths*, 99.

16. Olin D. Johnston to Dora K. Fogartie, June 23, 1961, Olin D. Johnston Collection, Senate Papers, Legislative Files, Box 83, Folder 101B; Olin D. Johnston to E. G. Schuler, January 13, 1961, Olin D. Johnston Collection, Senate Papers, Legislative Files, Box 83, Folder 101B.

17. Newsletter from the office of Olin D. Johnston, March 30, 1962, Edgar A. Brown Collection, MSS 381–393, Johnston, Olin D., Box 30, Folder 390.

18. Gordon Silverstein, *Law's Allure: How Law Shapes, Constrains, Saves and Kills Politics* (Cambridge: Cambridge University Press, 2009), 33–34, 51–53.

19. Mark Silverstein, *Judicious Choices: The Politics of Supreme Court Appointments* (London: Norton, 1994), 54; G. Silverstein, *Law's Allure*, 51.

20. Bryant Simon, "The Devaluation of the Vote: Legislative Apportionment and Inequality in South Carolina, 1890–1962," *South Carolina Historical Magazine* 101, no. 3 (July 2000): 247–48.

21. William H. Frist and J. Lee Annis Jr., *Tennessee Senators, 1911–2001: Portraits of Leadership in a Century of Change* (New York: Derrydale Press, 1999), 66; Charles S. Bullock and Ronald Keith Gaddie, *Georgia Politics in a State of Change* (Boston: Longman, 2010), 26, 34; Douglas Smith, "Into the Political Thicket: Reapportionment and the Rise of Suburban Power," in *The Myth of Southern Exceptionalism*, ed. Matthew Lassiter and Joseph Crespino (Oxford: Oxford University Press, 2009), 278; Simon, "The Devaluation," 251.

22. M. Silverstein, *Judicious Choices*, 55; G. Silverstein, *Law's Allure*, 53; and generally, Felder, *Civil Rights.*

23. Newsletter from the office of Olin D. Johnston, June 9, 1961, Edgar A. Brown Collection, Mss.0091, Johnston, Olin D., Box 30, Folder 390; Olin D. Johnston, "The Good Side of the South," *New York Times*, September 3, 1961, SM17; Herbert Hartsook interview with Thomas W. Chadwick, June 26, 1995, University of South Carolina, South Carolina Political Collections, Oral History Project, http://library.sc.edu/file/1751).

24. "Senate in Clash over Court Curb," *New York Times*, May 2, 1958, 16; "Should Supreme Court Appointees Have Five Years' Experience on the Bench?," *American Legion Magazine*, December 1961, Strom Thurmond Collection, MSS100 Speeches, General File, sub-series A, Articles 1961, Box

10, Folder 794; television address by Senator Kenneth Keating ("Senate Report," April 29, 1962, WNEW-TV, New York City), April 20, 1962, Olin D. Johnston Collection, Senate Papers, Legislative Files, Box 101, Judiciary Committee, Appointments, Marshall, Thurgood, Folder 4; "Sen. Keating to Denounce Sen. Johnston," *News and Courier,* April 28, 1962, 6A.

25. Williams, *Thurgood Marshall,* 300; "Marshall Gets Senate Hearing but Absentees Delay Decision," *New York Times,* May 2, 1962, 16.

26. Arthur Schlesinger, *Robert Kennedy and His Times* (New York: Ballantine Books, 1978), 330–31; Robert Dallek, *Flawed Giant: Lyndon Johnson and His Times, 1961–1973* (Oxford: Oxford University Press, 1998), 439; Perry, *A "Representative" Supreme Court?,* 97; Williams, *Thurgood Marshall,* 299; Tushnet, *Making Constitutional Law,* 12, 13n; Schlesinger, *Robert Kennedy,* 330–31; Victor S. Navasky, *Kennedy Justice* (New York: Atheneum, 1971), 256.

27. Earl Black, *Southern Governors and Civil Rights* (Cambridge, MA: Harvard University Press, 1976), 80–82; Anthony J. Badger, "From Defiance to Moderation: South Carolina Governors and Racial Change," in *New Deal/New South: An Anthony J. Badger Reader* (Fayetteville: University of Arkansas Press, 2007), 135–36; James C. Cobb, *The Selling of the South* (Chicago: University of Illinois Press, 1993), 141; "Sen. Olin Johnston in Landslide S.C. Victory," *Ocala Star-Banner,* June 13, 1962, 27; "Voters Show Belief in Sen. Olin Johnston," *Spartanburg Herald,* June 14, 1962, 4; Frank E. Jordan, *The Primary State: A History of the Democratic Party in South Carolina, 1896–1962* (self-published, n.d.), 83; Ernest F. Hollings and Kirk Victor, *Making Government Work* (Columbia: University of South Carolina Press, 2008), 103.

28. "Eastland Offers Amendment," *New York Times,* June 30, 1962, 20; Newsletter from the office of Senator Olin D. Johnston, July 27, 1962, Edgar A. Brown Papers, Mss.0091, Johnston, Olin D., Box 30, Folder 390; "Senators Ask Action on Prayer Decision," *Washington Post,* July 27, 1962, A2; newsletter from the office of Senator Strom Thurmond, June 30, 1962, Strom Thurmond Collection, Mss.0100.11, Speeches Series 1935–1998, Subseries A, General File (1935–1983), Press Releases 1962, Box 13, Folder 1109.

29. Hearings before a Subcommittee of the Judiciary, United States Senate, Eighty-Seventh Congress, Second Session of Nomination of Thurgood Marshall, of New York, to be United States Circuit Judge for the Second Circuit, printed for the use of the Committee on the Judiciary, July 12, 1962, 46–47.

30. Ibid., 49.

31. Olin D. Johnston to Mrs. E. Sinclair Eaton, August 21, 1962; Olin D. Johnston to L. P. B. Lipscomb, August 21, 1962, Olin D. Johnston Collection, Senate Papers, Legislative Files, Box 101, Judiciary Committee, Appointments, Marshall, Thurgood, Folder 3.

32. "Sen. Johnston Blocks GOP Move to Conduct Marshall Hearings," *News and Courier,* August 7, 1962, Edgar A. Brown Papers, Mss.0091, Johnston, Olin D., Box 30, Folder 390; "Johnston and Marshall," *News and Courier,* July 17, 1962, 8A, Olin D. Johnston Collection, Senate Papers, News Clippings, Box 136, Marshall, Thurgood.

33. Walter Brown to Strom Thurmond, July 13, 1962, Strom Thurmond Collection, Subject Correspondence Series, Mss.0100.18, 3 (United States Court and Supreme Court Judges), Year 1962, Box 19, Folder 1; "Voters Show Belief in Sen. Olin Johnston," *Spartanburg Herald,* June 14, 1962, 4; "Johnston and Marshall," *News and Courier,* July 17, 1962, 8A, Olin D. Johnston Collection, Senate Papers, News Clippings, Box 136, Marshall, Thurgood.

5. "THE BOYS DOWN THERE"

1. Harry N. Johnson to Olin D. Johnston, June 18, 1962; Mabel B. Sheldon to Olin D. Johnston, July 9, 1962, Olin D. Johnston Collection, Senate Papers, Legislative Files, Box 101, Judiciary Committee, Appointments, Marshall, Thurgood, Folder 4.

2. Boston Brice to Olin D. Johnston, July 20, 1962; Olin D. Johnston to Calhoun Thomas, August 16, 1962, Olin D. Johnston Collection, Senate Papers, Legislative Files, Box 101, Judiciary Committee, Appointments, Marshall, Thurgood, Folder 4; Calhoun Thomas to Olin D. Johnston, August 9, 1962, Olin D. Johnston Collection, Senate Papers, Legislative Files, Box 101, Judiciary Committee, Appointments, Marshall, Thurgood, Folder 4.

3. Olin D. Johnston to Calhoun Thomas, August 16, 1962; J. M. Hinton to Olin D. Johnston, July 20, 1962; Olin D. Johnston to Calhoun Thomas, August 16, 1962, Olin D. Johnston Collection, Senate Papers, Legislative Files, Box 101, Judiciary Committee, Appointments, Marshall, Thurgood, Folder 4.

4. "Johnston and Marshall," *News and Courier,* July 17, 1962, 8A, Olin D. Johnston Collection, Senate Papers, News Clippings, Box 136, Marshall, Thurgood; Rock Hill Chapter N.A.A.C.P. to Olin D. Johnston, June 28, 1962; John H. McCray to Olin D. Johnston, July 20, 1962; C. B. Bailey to Olin D. Johnston, July 27, 1962; Emory O. Jackson to Olin D. Johnston, June 26, 1962; Eustace Gay to Olin D. Johnston, July 2, 1962; E. Lewis Ferrell to Olin D. Johnston, July 4, 1962, Olin D. Johnston Collection, Senate Papers, Legislative Files, Box 101, Judiciary Committee, Appointments, Marshall, Thurgood, Folder 4.

5. Jason Morgan Ward, *Defending White Democracy* (Chapel Hill: University of North Carolina Press, 2011), 166, 170–71.

6. See Russell Merritt, "The Senatorial Election of 1962 and the Rise of Two-Party Politics in South Carolina," *South Carolina Historical Magazine* 98, no. 3 (1997): 281–301.

7. Edgar A. Brown to Olin D. Johnston, October 15, 1962; Charles A. Lafitte to Olin D. Johnston, October 4, 1962; Charles E. Simons to Solomon Blatt, October 13, 1962; Edgar A. Brown to Charles A. Lafitte, October 6, 1962, Edgar A. Brown Papers, Mss.0091, Johnston, Olin D., Box 30, Folder 390.

8. Walter Brown to Strom Thurmond, April 11, 1962, Strom Thurmond Collection, Subject Correspondence Series, Mss.0100.18, 3 (United States Court and Supreme Court Judges), Year 1962, Box 19, Folder 1.

9. Walter Brown to Strom Thurmond, April 11, 1962, Strom Thurmond Collection, Subject Correspondence Series, Mss.0100.18, 3 (United States Court and Supreme Court Judges), Year 1962, Box 19, Folder 1; Edgar A. Brown to Olin D. Johnston, July 18, 1962, Edgar A. Brown Papers, Mss.0091, Johnston, Olin D., Box 30, Folder 390; Roger K. Newman, *Hugo Black: A Biography* (New York: Pantheon, 1994), 538.

10. Edgar A. Brown to Olin D. Johnston, June 14, 1962, Edgar A. Brown Papers, Mss.0091, Johnston, Olin D., Box 30, Folder 390.

11. Hearings before a Subcommittee of the Judiciary, United States Senate, Eighty-Seventh Congress, Second Session of Nomination of Thurgood Marshall, of New York, to be United States Circuit Judge for the Second Circuit, printed for the use of the Committee on the Judiciary, August 8, 1962, 55; "Dixie Senators Stall Appointment of Negro," *Nashua Telegraph,* August 27, 1962, 14; Juan Williams, *Thurgood Marshall: American Revolutionary* (New York: Random House, 1988), 301.

12. Hearings, August 8, 1962, 56, 117; "Marshall Hearing May End Next Week," *News and Cou-*

rier, August 9, 1962, Olin D. Johnston Collection, Senate Papers, News Clippings, Box 136, Marshall, Thurgood.

13. Williams, *Thurgood Marshall,* 301–2; Mabel B. Sheldon to Olin D. Johnston, July 9, 1962; Ralph B. Kolb to Olin D. Johnston, August 7, 1962, Strom Thurmond Collection, Subject Correspondence Series, Mss.0100.18, 3 (United States Court and Supreme Court Judges), Year 1962, Box 19, Folder 1.

14. Hearings, July 19, 1967, 182.

15. Ralph B. Kolb to Olin D. Johnston, August 7, 1962, Strom Thurmond Collection, Subject Correspondence Series, Mss.0100.18, 3 (United States Court and Supreme Court Judges), Year 1962, Box 19, Folder 1.

16. Hearings, August 20, 1962, 178.

17. "Senators Still in Row over Negro Federal Judge," August 21, 1962, *Tampa Tribune,* Olin D. Johnston Collection, Senate Papers, News Clippings, Box 136, Marshall, Thurgood; Williams, *Thurgood Marshall,* 302.

18. Ibid., 301; "Nominee Marshall," *New York Times,* August 26, 1962, 52; Hearings, August 24, 1962, 183; Bob Woodward and Scott Armstrong, *The Brethren* (New York: Simon and Schuster, 1979), 67; "Marshall's Humor Backfires on Him," *Atlanta Constitution,* August 28, 1962; "Inexcusable Stalling," *Washington Post,* August 22, 1962, Olin D. Johnston Collection, Senate Papers, News Clippings, Box 136, Marshall, Thurgood.

19. Hearings, August 24, 1962, 207.

20. Ibid., 208–9; "Nominee Marshall," *New York Times,* August 26, 1962, 152.

21. "Senate Fight on Marshall Forecast," *Washington Post,* August 26, 1962, A6; Williams, *Thurgood Marshall,* 303.

22. David A. Yalof, *Pursuit of Justices: Presidential Politics and the Selection of Supreme Court Nominees* (Chicago: University of Chicago Press, 1999), 80–81; Mark Silverstein, *Judicious Choices* (London: Norton, 2004), 55; Jim Newton, *Justice for All: Earl Warren and the Nation He Made* (New York: Riverhead, 2007), 393.

23. "Areas of Inquiry by the Senate Judiciary Committee," 1–14, Manuscript Division, Library of Congress, Arthur Goldberg Papers, Box 2, Folder 45.

24. James A. Thorpe, "The Appearance of Supreme Court Nominees before the Senate Judiciary Committee," *Journal of Public Law* 18 (1969), 387; Newton, *Justice for All,* 393.

25. Mrs. A. A. Feder to Olin D. Johnston, August 22, 1962; Robert G. Ervin to Olin D. Johnston, August 22, 1962; Charles J. Turck to Olin D. Johnston, August 27, 1962, Olin D. Johnston Collection, Senate Papers, Legislative Files, Box 101, Judiciary Committee, Appointments, Marshall, Thurgood, Folder 4.

26. "South Can't Afford 2-Party Luxury, Sen. Johnston Says," *News and Courier,* May 11, 1962, Edgar A. Brown Papers, Mss.0091, Johnston, Olin D., Box 30, Folder 390.

27. See Merritt, "The Senatorial Election of 1962," 281–301; "Johnston Labels GOP Votes Protests against President," *News and Courier,* November 8, 1962; Numan V. Bartley and Hugh D. Graham, *Southern Politics and the Second Reconstruction* (Baltimore: Johns Hopkins University Press, 1975), 97–98; "Johnston Wins County Vote," *Newberry Observer,* November 6, 1962, 1; "Johnston Labels GOP Votes Protests against President," *News and Courier,* November 8, 1962; "Influence of Negro

Vote Grows," *News and Courier,* January 17, 1963, 1, Edgar A. Brown Papers, Mss.0091, Johnston, Olin D., Box 30, Folder 390; Hollings and Victor, *Making Government Work,* 102–3.

28. "Johnston's Victory Attributed to Negroes, *News and Courier,* December 3, 1962, Edgar A. Brown Papers, Mss.0091, Johnston, Olin D., Box 30, Folder 390.

29. Thom Hiers to Olin D. Johnston, September 4, 1962, Olin D. Johnston Collection, Senate Papers, Legislative Files, Box 101, Judiciary Committee, Appointments, Marshall, Thurgood, Folder 1.

30. Frank E. Jordan, *The Primary State: A History of the Democratic Party in South Carolina* (self-published, n.d.), 83.

31. Dewey W. Grantham, *The Life and Death of the Solid South: A Political History* (Lexington: University Press of Kentucky, 1988), 169; Bartley and Graham, *Southern Politics,* 123.

32. Telephone conversation between Lyndon B. Johnson and James Eastland, November 29, 1963, Lyndon Johnson Presidential Recordings, Miller Center, University of Virginia, K6311.06; telephone conversation between Lyndon Johnson and Richard Russell, November 29, 1963, Lyndon B. Johnson Presidential Recordings, Miller Center, University of Virginia, K6311.06. An official reason for Eastland and Russell both offering Justice Harlan as an alternative to Chief Justice Warren has never materialized, but it is likely that both senators appreciated Harlan's moderate voice on the court, and his dissent in the notorious *Baker v. Carr* would also have been noted. See Gordon Silverstein, *Law's Allure: How Law Shapes, Constrains, Saves and Kills Politics* (Cambridge: Cambridge University Press, 2009), 53.

33. George Bell Timmerman to Olin D. Johnston and Strom Thurmond, September 18, 1962, Strom Thurmond Collection, Subject Correspondence Series, Mss.0100.18, 3 (United States Court and Supreme Court Judges), Year 1962, Box 19, Folder 2; Edgar A. Brown to Olin D. Johnston (note), December 4, 1963, Edgar A. Brown Collection, MSS 381–393, Johnston, Olin D., Box 30, Folder 390.

6. "A COLORED MAN WITH THE NAME OF MARSHALL"

1. Address by Governor Ernest F. Hollings to the General Assembly of South Carolina, January 9, 1963, South Carolina Political Collections, Oral History Project, University of South Carolina, http://digital.tcl.sc.edu/cdm/compoundobject/collection/how/id/291/rec/14; "Hollings Says Farewell, Sees Desegregation," *Times-News* (Hendersonville, NC), January 10, 1963, 3; Francis M. Wilhoit, *The Politics of Massive Resistance* (New York: George Braziller, 1973), 198; George McMillan, "Integration with Dignity," in *Perspectives in South Carolina History: The First 300 Years,* ed. Ernest M. Lander Jr. and Robert K. Ackerman (Columbia: University of South Carolina Press, 1973), 389; Walter Edgar, *South Carolina: A History* (Columbia: University of South Carolina Press, 1998), 538; Ernest F. Hollings and Kirk Victor, *Making Government Work* (Columbia: University of South Carolina Press, 2008), 76; statement of The Honorable Ernest F. Hollings, Governor of South Carolina, before the Subcommittee on Constitutional Rights Legislation of the Judiciary Committee of the United States House of Representatives, Washington, DC, April 14, 1959, 2, Olin D. Johnston Collection, Senate Papers, Reference Files, Civil Rights, 1959: April: General, Box 116.

2. "Sen. Olin Johnston in Landslide S.C. Victory," *Ocala Star-Banner,* June 13, 1962, 27; "Voters Show Belief in Sen. Olin Johnston," *Spartanburg Herald,* June 14, 1962, 4; Hollings and Victor, *Making Government Work,* 72.

3. Marcia Synnott interview with Ernest F. Hollings, July 8, 1980, South Carolina Political Collections, Oral History Project, University of South Carolina, http://library.sc.edu/scpc/Hollings-Synnott1980.pdf.

4. Anthony J. Badger, "From Defiance to Moderation: South Carolina Governors and Racial Change," in *New Deal/New South: An Anthony J. Badger Reader* (Fayetteville: University of Arkansas Press, 2007), 138; "Influence of Negro Vote Grows," *News and Courier,* January 17, 1963, Edgar A. Brown Papers, Mss.0091, Johnston, Olin D., Box 30, Folder 390; "South Carolina Shuns Militancy," *New York Times,* October 26, 1963, 13; Numan V. Bartley and Hugh D. Graham, *Southern Politics and the Second Reconstruction* (Baltimore: Johns Hopkins University Press, 1975), 97–102.

5. Joseph Crespino, *Strom Thurmond's America* (New York: Hill and Wang, 2012), 133–34; Keith M. Finley, *Delaying the Dream: Southern Senators and the Fight against Civil Rights, 1938–1965* (Baton Rouge: Louisiana State University Press, 2008), 237; Jack Bass and Walter DeVries, *The Transformation of Southern Politics* (Athens: University of Georgia Press, 1995), 25, 256; Dewey W. Grantham, *The Life and Death of the Solid South: A Political History* (Lexington: University Press of Kentucky, 1988), 169, 188–89; Numan V. Bartley and Hugh D. Graham, *Southern Politics and the Second Reconstruction* (Baltimore: Johns Hopkins University Press, 1975), 123; Edgar, *South Carolina,* 546.

6. Jack Bass and Marilyn W. Thompson, *Strom: The Complicated Personal and Political Life of Strom Thurmond* (New York: Public Affairs, 2005), 156; Crespino, *Strom Thurmond's America,* 104.

7. Telephone conversation between Lyndon B. Johnson and Olin D. Johnston, December 26 1963, Lyndon Johnson Presidential Recordings, Miller Center, University of Virginia, (K6312.18) 25, http://millercenter.org/scripps/archive/presidentialrecordings/Johnson.

8. "S. Carolina Democrats Seek to Blunt Civil Rights Issue," *Washington Post–Times Herald,* October 7, 1964, A7; interview with Elizabeth J. Patterson, September 29, 2014; telephone conversation between Lyndon B. Johnson and Olin D. Johnston, January 5, 1965, Lyndon Johnson Presidential Recordings, Miller Center, University of Virginia, (WH6501.01) 6707; Edgar A. Brown to Olin D. Johnston, April 10, 1965, Edgar A. Brown Papers, Mss.0091, Johnston, Olin D., Box 30, Folder 390; "Sen. Johnston Remains Gravely Ill," *Sumter Daily-Item,* April 16, 1965, 1; "Sen. Olin Johnston Dies of Pneumonia," *Sarasota Herald Tribune,* April 19, 1965, 4.

9. "Opinions Mixed about Donald in His Bailiwick"; "Mrs. Johnston Not Consulted," *Spartanburg Herald-Journal,* April 23, 1965, 1; "House, Senate Approve"; "Russell Becomes a Senator Today," *Spartanburg Herald-Journal,* April 22, 1965, 1; Bass and DeVries, *Transformation,* 261; Frank E. Jordan, *The Primary State: A History of the Democratic Party in South Carolina, 1896–1962* (self-published, n.d.), 49; Hollings and Victor, *Making Government Work,* 116; "S. Carolina to Vote after Dull Campaign," *Washington Post–Times Herald,* June 13, 1966, A8.

10. James C. Cobb, "From the First New South to the Second: The Southern Odyssey through the Twentieth Century," in *The American South in the Twentieth Century,* ed. Craig S. Pascoe et al. (Athens: University of Georgia Press, 2005), 6–7; "2 Parties Court Carolina Negro," *New York Times,* May 1, 1966, 61.

11. Badger, "From Defiance," 136; "Senator Russell Loses in S.C.," *Eugene Register-Guard,* June 15, 1966, 4A; Hollings and Victor, *Making Government Work,* 131.

12. Bartley and Graham, *Southern Politics,* 125; Bass and DeVries, *Transformation,* 255; James C. Cobb, *The South and America since World War II* (Oxford: Oxford University Press, 2012), 115.

13. Orville Vernon Burton et al., "South Carolina," in *Quiet Revolution in the South: The Impact of the Voting Rights Act, 1965–1990*, ed. Chandler Davidson and Bernard N. Grofman (Princeton, NJ: Princeton University Press, 1994), 191–92, 215; James O. Farmer, "Memories and Forebodings: The Fight to Preserve the White Democratic Primary in South Carolina," in *Toward the Meeting of the Waters: Currents in the Civil Rights Movement of South Carolina during the Twentieth Century*, ed. Winfred B. Moore Jr. and Orville Vernon Burton (Columbia: University of South Carolina Press, 2008), 244; McKenzie Webster, "The Warren Court's Struggle with the Sit-In Cases and the Constitutionality of Segregation in Places of Public Accommodations," *Journal of Law and Politics* 17 (2001): 394; Jim Newton, *Justice for All: Earl Warren and the Nation He Made* (New York: Riverhead, 2007), 460-461.

14. Ernest F. Hollings to Tunis Harber, February 10, 1967, Ernest F. Hollings Collection, Senate Papers, Legislative Files and Constituent Correspondence, Box 105, Judiciary, Supreme Court; Strom Thurmond to T. K. Mowbray, January 22, 1965, Strom Thurmond Collection, Subject Correspondence Series, Mss.0100.18, 4–1 Supreme Court Year 1965, Box 5, Folder 1.

15. David A. Yalof, *Pursuit of Justices: Presidential Politics and the Selection of Supreme Court Nominees* (Chicago: University of Chicago Press, 1999), 82; telephone conversation between Lyndon B. Johnson and Nicholas Katzenbach, August 6, 1965, Lyndon Johnson Presidential Recordings, Miller Center, University of Virginia, (WH6508.02); telephone conversation between Lyndon B. Johnson and Abe Fortas, August 10, 1965, Lyndon Johnson Presidential Recordings, Miller Center, University of Virginia, (WH6508.03).

16. Bass and Thompson, *Strom*, 199.

17. Yalof, *Pursuit*, 87–89; Robert Dallek, *Flawed Giant: Lyndon Johnson and His Times, 1961–1973* (Oxford: Oxford University Press, 1998), 232; Bob Woodward and Scott Armstrong, *The Brethren* (New York: Simon and Schuster, 1979), 52.

18. Strom Thurmond to President Lyndon Johnson, March 2, 1967, Strom Thurmond Collection, Subject Correspondence Series, Mss.0100.18, Nominations, Year 1967, Box 26, Folder 1; Barbara A. Perry, *A "Representative" Supreme Court? The Impact of Race, Religion and Gender on Appointments* (London: Greenwood Press, 1991), 100; Nadine Cohodas, *Strom Thurmond and the Politics of Southern Change* (Macon, GA: Mercer University Press, 1995), 388; Yalof, *Pursuit*, 90.

19. News release from the office of Senator Strom Thurmond, June 13, 1967, Ernest F. Hollings Collection, Senate Papers, Legislative Files and Constituent Correspondence, Box 105, Judiciary, Judges, Selection and Appointment, Marshall, Thurgood; Strom Thurmond to Mr. and Mrs. Ed Hall, June 15, 1967, Strom Thurmond Collection, Subject Correspondence Series, Mss.0100.18, Nominations, Year 1967, Box 26, Folder 1.

20. News release from the office of Senator Strom Thurmond, June 13, 1967, Ernest F. Hollings Collection, Senate Papers, Legislative Files and Constituent Correspondence, Box 105, Judiciary, Judges, Selection and Appointment, Supreme Court, Marshall, Thurgood; Strom Thurmond to Mr. and Mrs. Guy H. Rouse, June 20, 1967; Strom Thurmond to Mr. J. N. Frank, June 20, 1967; Strom Thurmond to Edward R. Cusick, June 23, 1967; Strom Thurmond to D. E. Burns, June 27, 1967, Strom Thurmond Collection, Subject Correspondence Series, Mss.0100.18, 3 (United States Court and Supreme Court Judges), Year 1967, Box 26, Folder 1.

21. John R. Buch to Strom Thurmond, June 20, 1967; Frank P. Stelling to Strom Thurmond,

June 20, 1967; R. C. Moore to Strom Thurmond, July 15, 1967; Carrie Pauley Stevenson to Strom Thurmond, July 15, 1967; Strom Thurmond Collection, Subject Correspondence Series, Mss.0100.18, 3 (United States Court and Supreme Court Judges), Year 1967, Box 26, Folders 1–2.

22. Edward R. Cusick to Strom Thurmond, July 13 and 26, 1967; Strom Thurmond Collection, Subject Correspondence Series, Mss.0100.18, 3 (United States Court and Supreme Court), Year 1967, Box 26, Folder 2; "Important for Regular Masons!" bulletin, undated [letter from Edward R. Cusick, dated June 26, 1967], Strom Thurmond Collection, Subject Correspondence Series, Mss.0100.18, 3 (United States Court and Supreme Court Judges), Year 1967, Box 26, Folder 1.

23. Fritz Hollings to Thurgood Marshall, June 19, 1967, Ernest F. Hollings Collection, Senate Papers, Legislative Files and Constituent Correspondence, Box 105, Judiciary, Judges, Selection and Appointment, Supreme Court, Marshall, Thurgood.

24. Thurgood Marshall to Ernest "Fritz" Hollings, June 20, 1967, Ernest F. Hollings Collection, Senate Papers, Legislative Files and Constituent Correspondence, Box 105, Judiciary, Judges, Selection and Appointment, Supreme Court, Marshall, Thurgood.

25. Ernest "Fritz" Hollings to Thurgood Marshall, June 21, 1967, Ernest F. Hollings Collection, Senate Papers, Legislative Files and Constituent Correspondence, Box 105, Judiciary, Judges, Selection and Appointment, Supreme Court, Marshall, Thurgood.

26. James J. Kilpatrick, "Race Immaterial On Marshall Bid," *Sarasota Journal,* June 12, 1967, 6.

27. Thurgood Marshall to Ernest "Fritz" Hollings, June 27, 1967, Ernest F. Hollings Collection, Senate Papers, Legislative Files and Constituent Correspondence, Box 105, Judiciary, Judges, Selection and Appointment, Supreme Court, Marshall, Thurgood.

28. Draft of speech dated June 20, 1967, Ernest F. Hollings Collection, Senate Papers, Legislative Files and Constituent Correspondence, Box 105, Judiciary, Judges, Selection and Appointment, Supreme Court, Marshall, Thurgood.

29. Ernest "Fritz" Hollings to E. B. Woodward, June 29, 1967; Ernest "Fritz" Hollings to E. B. Woodward (draft of letter), June 23, 1967, Ernest F. Hollings Collection, Senate Papers, Legislative Files and Constituent Correspondence, Box 105, Judiciary, Judges, Selection and Appointment, Supreme Court, Marshall, Thurgood.

30. Huger Sinkler to Ernest "Fritz" Hollings, June 20, 1967, Ernest F. Hollings Collection, Senate Papers, Legislative Files and Constituent Correspondence, Box 105, Judiciary, Judges, Selection and Appointment, Supreme Court, Marshall, Thurgood.

31. Earl Black and Merle Black, *Politics and Society in the South* (Cambridge, MA: Harvard University Press, 1987), 139–40.

7. BETWEEN THURMOND AND THURGOOD

1. Juan Williams, *Thurgood Marshall: American Revolutionary* (New York: Random House, 1988), 336; Joseph Crespino, *Strom Thurmond's America* (New York: Hill and Wang, 2012), 215.

2. Hearings before the Committee of the Judiciary, United States Senate, Ninetieth Congress, First Session on Nomination of Thurgood Marshall, of New York, to be an Associate Justice of the Supreme Court, printed for the use of the Committee on the Judiciary, US Government Printing Office (1967), July 13, 1967, 3; Williams, *Thurgood Marshall,* 334.

3. Hearings, July 13, 1962, 13.

4. Ibid., 13.

5. Hearings, July 14, 1967, 53–54.

6. F. G. Cullop, *The Constitution of the United States: An Introduction* (New York: Penguin, 1969), 104.

7. Hearings, July 14, 1967, 54.

8. Ibid., 56, 66; Williams, *Thurgood Marshall,* 335.

9. Hearings, July 19, 1967, 160–61.

10. Ibid., 161.

11. Ibid., 162.

12. Roy Lucas to Strom Thurmond, September 30, 1967; Strom Thurmond to Roy Lucas, October 5, 1967, Strom Thurmond Collection, Subject Correspondence Series, Mss.0100.18, 3 (United States Court and Supreme Court Judges), Year 1967, Box 26, Folder 3.

13. Hearings, July 19, 1967, 163.

14. Ibid., 163.

15. Ibid., 163.

16. Ibid., 163–64.

17. Ibid., 163–64.

18. Keith M. Finley, *Delaying the Dream: Southern Senators and the Fight against Civil Rights, 1938–1965* (Baton Rouge: Louisiana State University Press, 2008), 8–9; Jason Morgan Ward, *Defending White Democracy* (Chapel Hill: University of North Carolina Press, 2011), 113–14; Crespino, *Strom Thurmond's America,* 139.

19. Hearings, July 19, 1967, 165.

20. Ibid., 172.

21. Ibid., 172–73.

22. Ibid., July 19, 1967, 179.

23. Ibid., July 19, 1967, 179–83.

24. Ernest F. Hollings to Walter T. Cardwell, July 21, 1967, Ernest F. Hollings Collection, Senate Papers, Legislative Files and Constituent Correspondence, Box 105, Judiciary, Judges, Selection and Appointment, Supreme Court, Marshall, Thurgood.

25. One particular example is Wally McNamee's photograph of Marshall from the *Washington Post,* reproduced in Williams, *Thurgood Marshall,* and dated July 21, 1967.

26. Hearings, July 24, 1967, 187.

27. Ibid., 197.

28. "King, Carmichael Pleas Annoy Marshall," *Star-Ledger* (Newark, NJ), April 16, 1967; "Marshall Raps 'Black Anarchy,'" *Chattanooga Times,* April 16, 1967; "Negro Leader Unhappy with King, SNCC," *Vindicator* (Youngstown, OH), April 16, 1967; Ernest F. Hollings Collection, Senate Papers, Legislative Files and Constituent Correspondence, Box 105.

29. Ernest "Fritz" Hollings to Thurgood Marshall, July 26, 1967; Ernest "Fritz" Hollings to I. P. Stanback, August 16, 1967; Ernest "Fritz" Hollings to Virginia Payne, August 23, 1967, Ernest F. Hollings Collection, Senate Papers, Legislative Files and Constituent Correspondence, Box 105, Judiciary, Judges, Selection and Appointment, Supreme Court, Marshall, Thurgood.

30. I. P. Stanback to Ernest "Fritz" Hollings, August 14, 1967; Samuel B. Hudson to Ernest "Fritz" Hollings, August 6, 1967, Ernest F. Hollings Collection, Senate Papers, Legislative Files and Constituent Correspondence, Box 105, Judiciary, Judges, Selection and Appointment, Supreme Court, Marshall, Thurgood.

31. Office memo from "Betty" to Ernest "Fritz" Hollings, August 10, 1967; Ernest "Fritz" Hollings to Samuel B. Hudson, August 11, 1967; Ernest "Fritz" Hollings to Virginia Payne, August 23, 1967; office memo, undated, August 1967; Ernest "Fritz" Hollings to James W. McPherson, August 14, 1967, Ernest F. Hollings Collection, Senate Papers, Legislative Files and Constituent Correspondence, Box 105, Judiciary, Judges, Selection and Appointment, Supreme Court, Marshall, Thurgood; Ernest F. Hollings and Kirk Victor, *Making Government Work* (Columbia: University of South Carolina Press, 2008), 132.

32. Ernest "Fritz" Hollings to Samuel B. Hudson, August 11, 1967; Ernest "Fritz" Hollings to Virginia Payne, August 23, 1967; I. P. Stanback to Ernest "Fritz" Hollings, August 14, 1967; draft of speech dated June 20, 1967; Ernest "Fritz" Hollings to Virginia Payne, August 23, 1967, Ernest F. Hollings Collection, Senate Papers, Legislative Files and Constituent Correspondence, Box 105, Judiciary, Judges, Selection and Appointment, Supreme Court, Marshall, Thurgood; "Hollings to Vote against Marshall," *Washington Post–Times Herald,* August 5, 1967, A6.

33. Mrs. Arthur B. Ward to Strom Thurmond, July 22, 1967; Strom Thurmond to Mrs. Arthur B. Ward, July 27, 1967, Strom Thurmond Collection, Subject Correspondence Series, Mss.0100.18, 3 (United States Court and Supreme Court Judges), Year 1967, Box 26, Folder 3.

34. "Marshall on the Stand," *New York Times,* July 30, 1967, 142; Alan R. Willis to Strom Thurmond, July 21, 1967; Strom Thurmond Collection, Subject Correspondence Series, Mss.0100.18, 3 (United States Court and Supreme Court Judges), Year 1967, Box 26, Folder 2; Strom Thurmond to Mrs. R. Kenneth Fairman, August 14, 1967, Strom Thurmond Collection, Subject Correspondence Series, Mss.0100.18, 3 (Unites States Court and Supreme Court Judges), Year 1967, Box 26, Folder 3.

35. "Marshall Rises to Top Tribunal," editorial, *Deseret News,* July 1, 1967, 14B; James J. Kilpatrick, "Race Immaterial on Marshall Bid," *Sarasota Journal,* June 12, 1967, 6; "The Thurgood Marshall Appointment," editorial, *Times Daily,* June 15, 1967, 4.

36. "Marshall Backed by Senate Panel," *New York Times,* August 4, 1967, 60.

37. Address by Senator Strom Thurmond on Senate Floor in opposition to Confirmation of Thurgood Marshall to be an Associate Justice of the Supreme Court of the United States," August 30, 1967, 5, 17, Strom Thurmond Collection, Mss.0100.11, Speeches Series 1935–1998, Subseries B, originals (1947–1970), Statements on Senate Floor, Box 13, Folder 158.

38. Ibid., 8.

39. Ibid., 14–15.

40. Ibid., 28.

41. Barbara A. Perry, *A "Representative" Supreme Court? The Impact of Race, Religion and Gender on Appointments* (London: Greenwood Press, 1991), 102; "Roll-Call Vote in Senate on Marshall Nomination," *New York Times,* August 31, 1967, 19; Williams, *Thurgood Marshall,* 337–38; Henry J. Abraham, *Justices, Presidents, and Senators: A History of the U.S. Supreme Court Appointments from Washington to Clinton* (Lanham, MD: Rowman and Littlefield, 1999), 221.

42. Keith T. Poole and Howard Rosenthal, eds., *Ideology and Congress: A Political Economic History of Roll Call Voting* (New Brunswick, NJ: Transaction Publishers, 2009), 145; Robert Mann,

The Walls of Jericho: Lyndon Johnson, Hubert Humphrey, Richard Russell, and the Struggle for Civil Rights (New York: Harcourt Brace, 1996), 401.

43. Hollings and Victor, *Making Government Work*, 128.

44. "South Carolina Negroes Meet to Push for Voter Registration," *New York Times*, September 25, 1967, 30.

45. Abraham, *Justices, Presidents*, 194; W. J. Cash, *The Mind of the South* (New York: Alfred A. Knopf, 1949), 86.

46. Williams, *Thurgood Marshall*, 338.

47. Richard Parker to Strom Thurmond, September 5, 1967; Strom Thurmond to Richard Parker, September 13, 1967, Strom Thurmond Collection, Subject Correspondence Series, Mss.0100.18, 3 (United States Court and Supreme Court Judges), Year 1967, Box 26, Folder 3.

8. "AND YOU REFUSE TO ANSWER THAT QUESTION?"

1. Hearings before the Committee on the Judiciary, United States Senate, Ninetieth Congress, Second Session on Nomination of Abe Fortas, of Tennessee, to be Chief Justice of the United States and Nomination of Homer Thornberry, of Texas, to be Associate Justice of the Supreme Court of the United States, printed for the use of the Committee on the Judiciary, US Government Printing Office, Washington: 1968, July 19, 1968, 219–20.

2. Ibid., 219–20.

3. Mark Silverstein, *Judicious Choices: The Politics of Supreme Court Appointments* (London: Norton, 1994), 31–32.

4. Joseph Crespino, *Strom Thurmond's America* (New York: Hill and Wang, 2012), 214; Strom Thurmond to President Lyndon Johnson, March 2, 1967, Strom Thurmond Collection, Subject Correspondence Series, Mss.0100.18, 3 (United States Court and Supreme Court Judges), Year 1967, Box 26, Folder 2; "Thurmond Urges Johnson Not to Fill Court Vacancy," *News and Courier*, June 22, 1968, 6A.

5. Timothy R. Johnson and Jason M. Roberts, "Presidential Capital and the Supreme Court Nomination Process," *Journal of Politics* 66, no. 3 (2004): 663–83.

6. David Stebenne, *Arthur J. Goldberg: New Deal Liberal* (Oxford: Oxford University Press, 1996), 371; Hearings before the Committee on the Judiciary, United States Senate, Ninetieth Congress, Second Session on Nomination of Abe Fortas, of Tennessee, to be Chief Justice of the United States and Nomination of Homer Thornberry, of Texas, to be Associate Justice of the Supreme Court of the United States, printed for the use of the Committee on the Judiciary, US Government Printing Office, Washington: 1968, 12–13, 22–23.

7. Crespino, *Strom Thurmond's America*, 213; Strom Thurmond to Mayor Allan L. Luke, Jr., May 2, 1968, Strom Thurmond Collection, Subject Correspondence Series, Mss.0100.18, 3 (United States District, Circuit, and Supreme Court Judges), Year 1968, Box 20, Folder 1.

8. Ernest "Fritz" Hollings to William W. Kelly, July 12, 1968; Ernest "Fritz" Hollings to Walter Brown, July 9, 1968, Ernest F. Hollings Collection, Senate Papers, Legislative Files and Constituent Correspondence, Box 104, Judiciary, Judges, Selection and Appointment, Supreme Court, Fortas, Abe, Statements, Hollings.

9. Calhoun Thomas to Ernest "Fritz" Hollings, July 10, 1968; Ernest "Fritz" Hollings to Calhoun Thomas, July 15, 1968, Ernest F. Hollings Collection, Senate Papers, Legislative Files and Constituent Correspondence, Box 104, Judiciary, Judges, Selection and Appointment, Supreme Court, Fortas, Abe, Statements, Hollings.

10. Strom Thurmond to C. A. Vines, July 19, 1968; Jack C. Hawe to Strom Thurmond, July 24, 1968; Strom Thurmond to Jack C. Hawe, August 2, 1968, Strom Thurmond Collection, Subject Correspondence Series, Mss.0100.18, 3 (United States District, Circuit, and Supreme Court Judges), Year 1968, Box 21, Folder 4.

11. Newsletter from the office of Senator Ernest "Fritz" Hollings, June 20, 1968, Ernest F. Hollings Collection, Senate Papers, Legislative Files and Constituent Correspondence, Box 104, Judiciary, Judges, Selection and Appointment, Supreme Court, Fortas, Abe, Statements, Hollings.

12. Walter Edgar, *South Carolina: A History* (Columbia: University of South Carolina Press, 1998), 542; Jack Bass and W. Scott Poole, *The Palmetto State: The Making of Modern South Carolina* (Columbia: University of South Carolina Press, 2009), 118–19.

13. Laurence H. Tribe, *God Save This Honorable Court* (London: Random House, 1985), 71; Crespino, *Strom Thurmond's America,* 220–21.

14. Robert E. McNair to Lyndon Johnson, January 30, 1964, Robert E. McNair Collection, Lieutenant Governor Files, Box 2, Judicial Endorsements for Charles Simons and Robert Hemphill as US District Judges, 1962–1964.

15. Strom Thurmond to Walter Brown, April 14, 1962, Strom Thurmond Collection, Subject Correspondence Series, Mss.0100.18, (United States Court and Supreme Court Judges), Year 1962, Box 19, Folder 1.

16. Walter Brown to Strom Thurmond, July 13, 1962, Strom Thurmond Collection, Subject Correspondence Series, Mss.0100.18, (United States Court and Supreme Court Judges), Year 1962, Box 19, Folder 1.

17. Strom Thurmond to John C. West, October 3, 1963, Strom Thurmond Collection, Subject Correspondence Series, Mss.0100.18, 3 (United States District, Circuit, and Supreme Court Judges), Year 1963, Box 25, Folder 3.

18. Telephone conversation between Lyndon B. Johnson and Olin D. Johnston, April 14, 1964, Lyndon Johnson Presidential Recordings, Miller Center, University of Virginia, (WH6404.09) 3029, http://millercenter.org/scripps/archive/presidentialrecordings/Johnson.

19. Telephone conversation between Lyndon B. Johnson and Olin D. Johnston, April 14, 1964, Lyndon Johnson Presidential Recordings, Miller Center, University of Virginia, (WH6404.09) 3031.

20. Telephone conversation between Lyndon B. Johnson and Strom Thurmond, April 14, 1964, Lyndon Johnson Presidential Recordings, Miller Center, University of Virginia, (WH6404.09) 3032.

21. Strom Thurmond to Robert McNair (telegram), April 14, 1964, Robert McNair Collection, Lieutenant Governor Papers, Box 2, Judicial Endorsements for Charles Simons and Robert Hemphill as US District Judges, 1962–1964.

22. Letter from Bill Brock to the author, April 22, 2014.

23. Robert Mickey, *Paths out of Dixie: The Democratization of Authoritarian Enclaves in America's Deep South, 1944–1972* (Princeton, NJ: Princeton University Press, 2015), 232–33; David Robertson, *Sly and Able: A Political Biography of James F. Byrnes* (New York: W. W. Norton, 1994), 536–37; Billy B. Hathorn, "The Changing Politics of Race: Congressman Albert William Watson and the S.C.

Republican Party, 1965–1970," *South Carolina Historical Magazine* 89, no. 4 (October 1988): 230.

24. Crespino, *Strom Thurmond's America,* 225.

25. Robert Dallek, *Lyndon B. Johnson: Portrait of a President* (London: Penguin, 2004), 68–69; Barbara A. Perry, *A "Representative" Supreme Court? The Impact of Race, Religion and Gender on Appointments* (London: Greenwood Press, 1991), 77; Bruce Allen Murphy, *Fortas* (New York: William Morrow, 1988), 50–51.

26. Hearings before the Committee on the Judiciary, United States Senate, Ninetieth Congress, Second Session on Nomination of Abe Fortas, of Tennessee, to be Chief Justice of the United States and Nomination of Homer Thornberry, of Texas, to be Associate Justice of the Supreme Court of the United States, printed for the use of the Committee on the Judiciary, US Government Printing Office, Washington: 1968, July 11, 1968, 8, 12, 22–23.

27. Ibid., 38.

28. Murphy, *Fortas,* 365.

29. William G. Ross, "The Functions, Roles and Duties of the Senate in the Supreme Court Appointment Process," *William and Mary Law Review* 28 (1986–1987): 655; Michael Comiskey, *Seeking Justices: The Judging of Supreme Court Nominees* (Lawrence: University Press of Kansas, 2004), 67.

30. Hearings, July 12, 1968, 47.

31. Ibid., 52.

32. Ibid., 56.

33. Ibid., 61.

34. Telephone conversation between Lyndon B. Johnson and Everett Dirksen, July 15, 1968, Lyndon Johnson Presidential Recordings, Miller Center, University of Virginia, (WH6807.01).

35. Hearings, July 16, 1968, 100.

36. Ibid., 104–5.

37. Hearings, July 17, 1968, 173.

38. Hearings, July 18, 1968, 180.

39. Ibid., 181.

40. Murphy, *Fortas,* 370.

41. Hearings, July 18, 1968, 182–83.

42. Ibid., 183–84.

43. Ibid., 189.

44. Crespino, *Strom Thurmond's America,* 108.

45. Jim Newton, *Justice for All: Earl Warren and the Nation He Made* (New York: Riverhead, 2007), 495.

46. Hearings, July 18, 1968, 191.

47. W. J. Cash, *The Mind of the South* (New York: Alfred A. Knopf, 1941), 260.

48. Jack Bass and Marilyn W. Thompson, *Strom: The Complicated Personal and Political Life of Strom Thurmond* (New York: Public Affairs, 2005), 204; Laura Kalman, *Abe Fortas: A Biography* (New Haven, CT: Yale University Press, 1992), 340; Crespino, *Strom Thurmond's America,* 217.

49. Hearings, July 18, 1968, 191–92.

50. Ernest F. Hollings and Kirk Victor, *Making Government Work* (Columbia: University of South Carolina Press, 2008), 142.

51. Speech of Hon. Ernest F. Hollings of South Carolina in the Senate of the United States, July

18, 1968, Congressional Record, Proceedings and Debates of the 90th Congress, Second Session, Ernest F. Hollings Collection, Senate Papers, Legislative Files and Constituent Correspondence, Box 104, Judiciary, Judges, Selection and Appointment, Supreme Court, Fortas, Abe, Statements, Hollings.

52. John R. Allen to Ernest "Fritz" Hollings, July 2, 1968, Ernest F. Hollings Collection, Senate Papers, Legislative Files and Constituent Correspondence, Box 104, Judiciary, Judges, Selection and Appointment, Supreme Court, Fortas, Abe, Statements, Hollings.

53. Briefing of news release from Greenville paper, July 11, 1968, Ernest F. Hollings Collection, Senate Papers, Legislative Files and Constituent Correspondence, Box 104, Judiciary, Judges, Selection and Appointment, Supreme Court, Fortas, Abe, Statements, Hollings.

54. Hearings, July 19, 1968, 219; Kalman, *Fortas,* 341.

55. Hearings, July 19, 1969, 219–20.

56. James A. Thorpe, "The Appearance of Supreme Court Nominees before the Senate Judiciary Committee," *Journal of Public Law* 18 (1969): 394.

57. Ibid., 247.

9. NO ORDINARY TIME

1. Richard R. Zukowski to Strom Thurmond, July 24, 1968; Mrs. Clarence A. Watkins to Strom Thurmond, October 3, 1968; Strom Thurmond Collection, Subject Correspondence Series, Mss.0100.18, 3 (United States District, Circuit, and Supreme Court Judges), Year 1968, Box 23, Folders 3[-1] and 3[-2]; note from Arthur Ravenel Jr. to Strom Thurmond, July 19, 1968, Strom Thurmond Collection, Subject Correspondence Series, Mss.0100.18, 3 (United States District, Circuit, and Supreme Court Judges), Year 1968, Box 21, Folder 4; Kenneth W. Akers to Strom Thurmond, July 26, 1968; Strom Thurmond to Kenneth W. Akers, July 30, 1968, Strom Thurmond Collection, Subject Correspondence Series, Mss.0100.18, 3 (United States District, Circuit, and Supreme Court Judges), Year 1968, Box 21, Folder 5.

2. Hearings before the Committee on the Judiciary, United States Senate, Ninetieth Congress, Second Session on Nomination of Abe Fortas, of Tennessee, to be Chief Justice of the United States and Nomination of Homer Thornberry, of Texas, to be Associate Justice of the Supreme Court of the United States, printed for the use of the Committee on the Judiciary, US Government Printing Office, Washington: 1968, July 11, 1968, 282.

3. Ibid., 291, 294–97.

4. Ibid., 306.

5. Ibid., 300, 304.

6. Hearings, July 23, 1968, 359.

7. Ibid., 360.

8. Bob Woodward and Scott Armstrong, *The Brethren* (New York: Simon and Schuster, 1979), 11, 242; Hugo Black interview with Eric Sevareid and Martin Agronsky, CBS News, The Phoenix Learning Group, Inc., https://www.youtube.com/watch?v=HAgQdeup2vo. The very public use of the line "I know it when I see it" was by no means exclusive to Potter Stewart in the year 1964. James Bond (played by Sean Connery) uses the very same expression when his boss, M (Bernard Lee), asks him what he knows about gold in *Goldfinger* (1964).

9. Joseph Crespino, *Strom Thurmond's America* (New York: Hill and Wang, 2012), 218; newsletter from the office of Senator Strom Thurmond, August 5, 1968, Strom Thurmond Collection, Subject Correspondence Series, Mss.0100.18, 3 (United States District, Circuit, and Supreme Court Judges), Year 1968, Box 21, Folder 6.

10. "Harry Dent, The President's Political Co-Ordinator, Says: 'I Gave Thurmond 100% Loyalty and Now I Give Mr. Nixon 100%,'" *New York Times*, February 1, 1970, SM7; "Nixon Gave Thurmond Supreme Court Veto," *Lewiston Daily Sun*, August 20, 1968, 4.

11. Strom Thurmond to Reverend W. Y. Cooley, September 9, 1968, Strom Thurmond Collection, Subject Correspondence Series, Mss.0100.18, 3 (United States District, Circuit, and Supreme Court Judges), Year 1968, Box 22, Folder 11.

12. Bruce Allen Murphy, *Fortas* (New York: William Morrow, 1988), 466.

13. Strom Thurmond to John Mitchell, September 18, 1968, Strom Thurmond Collection, Subject Correspondence Series, Mss.0100.18, 3 (United States District, Circuit, and Supreme Court Judges), Year 1968, Box 22, Folder 13; Strom Thurmond to George M. Forte, September 23, 1968, Strom Thurmond Collection, Subject Correspondence Series, Mss.0100.18, 3 (United States District, Circuit, and Supreme Court Judges), Year 1968, Box 22, Folder 14.

14. Crespino, *Strom Thurmond's America*, 225.

15. Murphy, *Fortas*, 481; Laurence H. Tribe, *God Save This Honorable Court* (London: Random House, 1985), 91; Mrs. Clarence A. Watkins to Strom Thurmond, October 3, 1968, Strom Thurmond Collection, Subject Correspondence Series, Mss.0100.18, 3 (United States District, Circuit, and Supreme Court Judges), Year 1968, Box 23, Folder 17.

16. Alan Banov to William Hoffman, August 6, 1968, Ernest F. Hollings Collection, Senate Papers, Legislative Files and Constituent Correspondence, Box 104, Judiciary, Judges, Selection and Appointment, Supreme Court, Fortas, Abe, Statements, Hollings.

17. "Senate Action on Sobeloff Blocked," *Spartanburg Herald*, June 29, 1956, 1.

18. Murphy, *Fortas*, 366.

19. Ibid., 481; Crespino, *Strom Thurmond's America*, 222; Murphy, *Fortas*, 480.

20. "Threat to Fortas Nomination," *The Times*, July 26, 1968, Ernest F. Hollings Collection, Senate Papers, Legislative Files and Constituent Correspondence, Box 104, Judiciary, Judges, Selection and Appointment, Supreme Court, Fortas, Abe, Statements, Hollings; Murphy, *Fortas*, 484–85.

21. Ibid., 478; Paul A. Freund, "Appointment of Justices: Some Historical Perspectives," *Harvard Law Review* 101 (1988): 1155; Strom Thurmond to David G. Jennings, September 23, 1968, Strom Thurmond Collection, Subject Correspondence Series, Mss.0100.18, 3 (United States District, Circuit, and Supreme Court Judges), Year 1968, Box 22, Folder 14.

22. Crespino, *Strom Thurmond's America*, 218–19; Murphy, *Fortas*, 490–91.

23. Laura Kalman, *Abe Fortas: A Political Biography* (New Haven, CT: Yale University Press, 1992), 351; Crespino, *Strom Thurmond's America*, 224; Murphy, *Fortas*, 497–98, 521; cartoon from *The State*, September 13, 1968, Strom Thurmond Collection, Subject Correspondence Series, Mss.0100.18, 3 (United States District, Circuit, and Supreme Court Judges), Year 1968, Box 22, Folder 12; Jim Newton, *Justice for All: Earl Warren and the Nation He Made* (New York: Riverside, 2007), 496.

24. Murphy, *Fortas*, 365; Roger K. Newman, *Hugo Black: A Biography* (New York: Pantheon, 1994), 589–90; Murphy, *Fortas*, 364–65, 535–41; Newton, *Justice for All*, 474–76.

25. Robert Mann, *The Walls of Jericho: Lyndon Johnson, Hubert Humphrey, Richard Russell, and the Struggle for Civil Rights* (New York: Harcourt Brace, 1996), 494–99; Neil D. McFeeley, *Appointment of Judges: The Johnson Presidency* (Austin: University of Texas Press, 1987), 219; news release from the office of Senator Richard B. Russell, September 26, 1968, Richard B. Russell Collection Subgroup C, Series 1: Dictation, Box 9, Folder 1.

26. R. Sam Garrett and Denis Steven Rutkus, *Speed of Presidential and Senate Actions on Supreme Court Nominations, 1900–2009* (Washington, DC: Congressional Research Service, May 8, 2009), 36–37; Tribe, *God Save*, 90–91; Freund, "Appointment of Justices," 1155; Mark Silverstein, "The People, the Senate, and the Court: The Democratization of the Judicial Confirmation System," *Constitutional Commentary* 9 (1992): 42.

27. Mark Silverstein, *Judicious Choices: The Politics of Supreme Court Appointments* (London: Norton, 1994), 27–28.

28. Ibid., 31–32.

29. Crespino, *Strom Thurmond's America*, 102–4; telephone conversation between Lyndon B. Johnson and Everett Dirksen, July 15, 1968, Lyndon Johnson Presidential Recordings, Miller Center, University of Virginia, (WH6807.01).

30. Strom Thurmond to Commander Howard K. Williamson, October 3, 1968, Strom Thurmond Collection, Subject Correspondence Series, Mss.0100.18, 3 (United States District, Circuit, and Supreme Court Judges), Year 1968, Box 23, Folder 16; Murphy, *Fortas*, 525; Jack Bass and Marilyn W. Thompson, *Strom: The Complicated Personal and Political Life of Strom Thurmond* (New York: Public Affairs, 2005), 207.

31. "Politics: Nixon, after Tour in South, Goes to Hartford Rally and Assails Inflation," *New York Times*, October 5, 1968, 20.

32. Conrad Black, *Richard M. Nixon: A Life in Full* (New York: Public Affairs, 2007), 558.

33. "Carolina Negroes Cool to Hollings," *New York Times*, November 4, 1968, 38.

34. Draft of statement by Ernest "Fritz" Hollings, July 18, 1968, 3, Ernest F. Hollings Collection, Senate Papers, Legislative Files and Constituent Correspondence, Box 104, Judiciary, Judges, Selection and Appointment, Supreme Court, Fortas, Abe, Statements, Hollings; Strom Thurmond to John J. Tarpey, September 18, 1968, Strom Thurmond Collection, Subject Correspondence Series, Mss.0100.18, 3 (United States District, Circuit, and Supreme Court Judges), 3 (United States District, Circuit, and Supreme Court Judges), Year 1968, Box 22, Folder 13.

35. Newsletter from the office of Senator Ernest "Fritz" Hollings, September 18, 1968, Ernest F. Hollings Collection, Senate Papers, Legislative Files and Constituent Correspondence, Box 104, Judiciary, Judges, Selection and Appointment, Supreme Court, Fortas, Abe, Statements, Hollings.

36. Walter Edgar, *South Carolina: A History* (Columbia: University of South Carolina Press, 1998), 546.

37. David Stebenne, *Arthur J. Goldberg: New Deal Liberal* (Oxford: Oxford University Press, 1996), 373.

38. McFeeley, *Appointment of Judges*, 207; telephone conversation between Lyndon B. Johnson and Everett Dirksen, undated, October 1968, Lyndon Johnson Presidential Recordings, Miller Center, University of Virginia, (WH6810.01).

39. McFeeley, *Appointment of Judges*, 225; "Thurmond Reports a Johnson Retreat," *New York Times*, December 10, 1968, 40.

40. Stebenne, *Arthur J. Goldberg,* 371; telephone conversation between Lyndon B. Johnson and Earl Warren, December 10, 1968, Lyndon Johnson Presidential Recordings, Miller Center, University of Virginia, (WH6812.01).

41. Ibid. (WH6812.01).

42. David A. Yalof, *Pursuit of Justices: Presidential Politics and the Selection of Supreme Court Nominees* (Chicago: University of Chicago Press, 1999), 99–100; McFeeley, *Appointment of Judges,* 229.

43. Newton, *Justice for All,* 496.

10. "THE LITTLE FELLA THAT STUTTERED"

1. Statement by Senator Marlow W. Cook on the floor of the Senate, May 15, 1970, 7, 15, Ernest F. Hollings Collection, Senate Papers, Legislative Files and Constituent Correspondence, Box 126, Judiciary, Judges, Selection and Appointment, Supreme Court, General.

2. See, for example, A. Mitchell McConnell, "Haynsworth and Carswell: A New Senate Standard of Excellence," *Kentucky Law Journal* 59 (1970–1971): 7–34; Edward N. Beiser, "The Haynsworth Affair Reconsidered: The Significance of Conflicting Perceptions of the Judicial Role," *Vanderbilt Law Review* 23 (1969–1970): 263–90; and Joel B. Grossman and Stephen L. Wasby, "Haynsworth and Parker: History Does Live Again," *South Carolina Law Review* 23 (1971): 345–59.

3. David Robertson, *Sly and Able: A Political Biography of James F. Byrnes* (New York: W. W. Norton, 1994), 318–19.

4. See Richard L. Watson, "The Defeat of Judge Parker: A Study in Pressure Groups and Politics," *Mississippi Valley Historical Review* 50, no. 2 (1963): 213–34; Mark Silverstein, *Judicious Choices: The Politics of Supreme Court Appointments* (London: Norton, 2004); John Anthony Maltese, *The Selling of Supreme Court Nominees* (Baltimore: Johns Hopkins University Press, 1995).

5. Ernest F. Hollings and Kirk Victor, *Making Government Work* (Columbia: University of South Carolina Press, 2008), 149.

6. In addition to the Griffin and Hart articles discussed in this section of the chapter, examples include Luis Kutner, "Advice and Dissent: Due Process of the Senate," *DePaul Law Review* 23 (1973–1974): 658–90; John D. Felice and Herbert F. Weisberg, "The Changing Importance of Ideology, Party, and Region in Confirmation of Supreme Court Nominees, 1953–1988," *Kentucky Law Journal* 77 (1988–1989): 509–30; James E. Gauch, "The Intended Role of the Senate in Supreme Court Appointments," *University of Chicago Law Review* 65, no. 1 (1989): 337–65; Albert P. Melone, "The Senate's Confirmation Role in Supreme Court Nominations and the Politics of Ideology Versus Impartiality," *Judicature* 75, no. 2 (1991–1992): 68–79; William Bradford Reynolds, "The Confirmation Process: Too Much Advice and Too Little Consent," *Judicature* 75, no. 2 (1991–1992): 80–82; Mark Silverstein, "The People, The Senate and the Court: The Democratization of the Judicial Confirmation System," *Constitutional Commentary* 9 (1992): 41–58; P. S. Ruckman Jr., "The Supreme Court, Critical Nominations, and the Senate Confirmation Process," *Journal of Politics* 55, no. 3 (1993): 793–805; and, crucially, the aforementioned McConnell, "Haynsworth and Carswell," which is discussed later in the chapter.

7. Robert P. Griffin, "The Broad Role," *Prospectus* 2 (1968–1969): 285–87, 291; Philip A. Hart, "The Discriminating Role," *Prospectus* 2 (1968–1969): 307–8.

8. Nadine Cohodas, *Strom Thurmond and the Politics of Southern Change* (Macon, GA: Mercer University Press, 1995), 403. See also Bruce Allen Murphy, *Fortas* (New York: William Morrow, 1988), 195–200; Bob Woodward and Scott Armstrong, *The Brethren* (New York: Simon and Schuster, 1979), 14–17.

9. Laura Kalman, *Abe Fortas: A Political Biography* (New Haven, CT: Yale University Press, 1992), 374; "Thurmond Urges Douglas to Quit," *New York Times*, May 30, 1969, 11; Strom Thurmond to Claude Ragsdale Jr., May 28, 1969; Strom Thurmond to Thomas J. Robertson, May 9, 1969, Strom Thurmond Collection, Subject Correspondence Series, Mss.0100.18, 3 (United States District, Circuit, and Supreme Court Judges), Year 1969, Box 28, Folder 1; Woodward and Armstrong, *The Brethren*, 17–18.

10. "Burger Nomination is Lauded by Conservative Members of Senate Judiciary Panel," *New York Times*, May 22, 1969, 37; Strom Thurmond to Rex L. Blanton, May 26, 1969, Strom Thurmond Collection, Subject Correspondence Series, Mss.0100.18, 3 (United States District, Circuit, and Supreme Court Judges), Year 1969, Box 28, Folder 1.

11. John P. Frank, *Clement Haynsworth, the Senate, and the Supreme Court* (Charlottesville: University Press of Virginia, 1991), 23; Hollings and Victor, *Making Government Work*, 143–44; "Nixon Gave Thurmond Supreme Court Veto," *Lewiston Daily Sun*, August 20, 1968, 4.

12. Interview with John Spratt, September 28, 2014.

13. Hollings and Victor, *Making Government Work*, 143–44.

14. "Dirksen Says Haynsworth Will Get Court Post," *New York Times*, August 14, 1969, 17.

15. "Thurmond Urges Douglas to Quit," *New York Times*, May 30, 1969, 11; "Kennedy, Thurmond Squabble on Justice Douglas, Education," *Milwaukee Journal*, June 10, 1969, 4; Woodward and Armstrong, *The Brethren*, 476–80.

16. Frank, *Clement Haynsworth*, 17–18; nomination of Clement F. Haynsworth, Jr. [list of submissions of endorsements], February 20, 1957, Olin D. Johnston Collection, Senate Papers, Legislative Files, Box 60, Folder 101; Charles E. Daniel to Olin D. Johnston, March 8, 1957; Wake H. Myers to Olin D. Johnston, February 25, 1957; Arthur Magill to Olin D. Johnston, February 25, 1957, Olin D. Johnston Collection, Senate Papers, Legislative Files, Box 60, Folder 103.

17. Clement Haynsworth to Olin D. Johnston, March 11, 1957; Clement Haynsworth to Olin D. Johnston, April 8, 1957, Olin D. Johnston Collection, Senate Papers, Legislative Files, Box 60, Judiciary Committee, Appointments, Haynsworth, Clement F., Folder 101; "Blue slip" communication between James O. Eastland and Strom Thurmond, February 21, 1957; Bernard G. Segal to James O. Eastland, March 1, 1957; Ernest F. Hollings Collection, Senate Papers, Legislative Files and Constituent Correspondence, Box 127, Judiciary, Judges, Selection and Appointment, Supreme Court, Haynsworth, Clement F. Jr., Hearings and Committee Report: Hearings, 1957; Laurence H. Tribe, *God Save This Honorable Court* (London: Random House, 1985), 90–91; Silverstein, "The People, The Senate," 42.

18. Interview with Ernest "Fritz" Hollings by Andrea L'Hommedieu, June 20, 2012, George J. Mitchell Oral History Project, Bowdoin Digital Commons, http://digitalcommons.bowdoin.edu/mitchelloralhistory/200/; Ernest "Fritz" Hollings to President Richard Nixon, May 28, 1969, Ernest F. Hollings Collection, Senate Papers, Legislative Files and Constituent Correspondence, Box 127, Judiciary, Judges, Selection and Appointment, Supreme Court, Haynsworth, Clement F. Jr., General, Pro, Folder 4.

19. L. A. Scot Powe, "The Senate and the Court: Questioning a Nominee," *Texas Law Review* 54 (1975–1976): 894.

20. Clement Haynsworth to Ernest "Fritz" Hollings, May 30, 1969, Ernest F. Hollings Collection, Senate Papers, Legislative Files and Constituent Correspondence, Box 127, Judiciary, Judges, Selection and Appointment, Supreme Court, Haynsworth, Clement F. Jr., General, Pro, Folder 2.

21. Timothy R. Johnson and Jason M. Roberts, "Presidential Capital and the Supreme Court Nomination Process," *Journal of Politics* 66, no. 3 (2004): 664n; Frank, *Clement Haynsworth,* 37.

22. "Dirksen Says Haynsworth Will Get Court Post," *New York Times,* August 14, 1969, 17.

23. Ibid.; John Massaro, *Supremely Political: The Role of Ideology and Presidential Management in Unsuccessful Supreme Court Nominations* (Albany: State University of New York Press, 1990), 3; Charles S. Bullock and Janna Deitz, "Transforming the South: The Role of the Federal Government," in *The American South in the Twentieth Century,* ed. Craig S. Pascoe et al. (Athens: University of Georgia Press, 2005), 251; J. Harvie Wilkinson III, *From Brown to Bakke: The Supreme Court and School Integration, 1954–1978* (Oxford: Oxford University Press, 1979), 117; Roy Wilkins to Ernest "Fritz" Hollings, August 22, 1969, Ernest F. Hollings Collection, Senate Papers, Legislative Files and Constituent Correspondence, Box 127, Judiciary, Judges, Selection and Appointment, Supreme Court, Haynsworth, Clement F. Jr., General, Con, Folder 2.

24. Hollings and Victor, *Making Government Work,* 145–46; Frank, *Clement Haynsworth,* 26, 31; Andrea L'Hommedieu Interview with Ernest "Fritz" Hollings, June 20, 2012, George J. Mitchell Oral History Project, Bowdoin Digital Commons; "Griffin's Stand against Haynsworth Sideswipes Kelley's Senate Dream," *Detroit Free Press,* October 11, 1969, Strom Thurmond Collection, Subject Correspondence Series, Mss.0100.18, 3 (United States District, Circuit, and Supreme Court Judges), Year 1969, Box 28, Folder 4.

25. Hollings and Victor, *Making Government Work,* 144–45; interview with John Spratt, September 28, 2014; "Liberal Democrats Reserve Comments on Nomination," *Sarasota Herald Tribune,* August 14, 1969, 7; statement by Senator Ernest F. Hollings in introduction of Judge Clement Haynsworth before Judiciary Committee, September 16, 1969, Ernest F. Hollings Collection, Senate Papers, Legislative Files and Constituent Correspondence, Box 128.

26. Hearings before Committee on the Judiciary, United States Senate, Ninety-First Congress, First Session on Nomination of Clement F. Haynsworth Jr., of South Carolina, to be Associate Justice of the Supreme Court of the United States, September 16, 1969, 39; Statement by Senator Marlow W. Cook on the floor of the Senate, May 15, 1970, 15, Ernest F. Hollings Collection, Senate Papers, Legislative Files and Constituent Correspondence, Box 126, Judiciary, Judges, Selection and Appointment, Supreme Court, General; Frank, *Clement Haynsworth,* 32.

27. Hearings, September 16, 1969, 58.

28. Hearings, September 17, 1969, 75.

29. Ibid., 80–100.

30. Ibid., 129.

31. Hearings, September 23, 1969, 291.

32. Ibid., 292.

33. Hearings, September 17, 1969, 135–36; Hearings, September 23, 1969, 256; Hearings, September 25, 1969, 458.

34. Frank, *Clement Haynsworth,* 30.

35. Senator Birch Bayh's Bill of Particulars and Senator Ernest F. Hollings's Detailed Answer, November 18, 1969; Birch Bayh to Ernest "Fritz" Hollings, October 8, 1969, Ernest F. Hollings Collection, Senate Papers, Legislative Files and Constituent Correspondence, Box 128, Judiciary, Judges, Selection and Appointment, Supreme Court, Haynsworth, Clement F. Jr., Statements, Hollings.

36. "Senator Defends Haynsworth Acts," *New York Times*, October 8, 1969, 32; "Haynsworth Backers in Senate Hold Preview of Floor Debate," *New York Times*, October 14, 1969, 40; Bill of Particulars and Detailed Answer, November 18, 1969, Ernest F. Hollings Collection, Senate Papers, Legislative Files and Constituent Correspondence, Box 128, Judiciary, Judicial Conflict of Interest.

37. Ernest "Fritz" Hollings to Birch Bayh, October 9, 1969; telegram from Ernest "Fritz" Hollings to Mr. Richard J. Salant, Mr. Elmer W. Lower and Mr. Reuven Frank, October 9, 1969, Ernest F. Hollings Collection, Senate Papers, Legislative Files and Constituent Correspondence, Box 127, Judiciary, Judges, Selection and Appointment, Supreme Court, Haynsworth, Clement F. Jr., General, Con, Folder 3.

38. Birch Bayh to Ernest "Fritz" Hollings, October 9, 1969; Ernest "Fritz" Hollings to Birch Bayh (telegram), October 10, 1969, Ernest F. Hollings Collection, Senate Papers, Legislative Files and Constituent Correspondence, Box 127, Judiciary, Judges, Selection and Appointment, Supreme Court, Haynsworth, Clement F. Jr., General, Con, Folder 3; Hollings and Victor, *Making Government Work*, 147–48.

39. Birch Bayh to Ernest "Fritz" Hollings, October 10, 1969, Ernest F. Hollings Collection, Senate Papers, Legislative Files and Constituent Correspondence, Box 127, Judiciary, Judges, Selection and Appointment, Supreme Court, Haynsworth, Clement F. Jr., General, Con, Folder 3.

40. Ernest "Fritz" Hollings to Birch Bayh, October 13, 1969; Birch Bayh to Ernest "Fritz" Hollings, undated, Ernest F. Hollings Collection, Senate Papers, Legislative Files and Constituent Correspondence, Box 127, Judiciary, Judges, Selection and Appointment, Supreme Court, Haynsworth, Clement F. Jr., General, Con, Folder 3; Clement Haynsworth to Ernest "Fritz" Hollings, November 25, 1969, Ernest F. Hollings Collection, Senate Papers, Legislative Files and Constituent Correspondence, Box 127, Judiciary, Judges, Selection and Appointment, Supreme Court, Haynsworth, Clement F. Jr., General, Con, Folder 1.

41. Cartoon from *News and Observer* (Raleigh, NC), October 9, 1969, Ernest F. Hollings Collection, Senate Papers, Legislative Files and Constituent Correspondence, Box 127, Judiciary, Judges, Selection and Appointment, Supreme Court, Haynsworth, Clement F. Jr., General, Con, Folder 2; Hollings and Victor, *Making Government Work*, 148–49; interview with John Spratt, September 28, 2014.

11. THE ASTONISHING AND PUZZLING SENATOR HOLLINGS

1. Joel B. Grossman and Stephen L. Wasby, "Haynsworth and Parker: History Does Live Again," *South Carolina Law Review* 23 (1971): 348; John Anthony Maltese, *The Selling of Supreme Court Nominees* (Baltimore: Johns Hopkins University Press, 1995), 78; John Massaro, *Supremely Political: The Role of Ideology and Presidential Management in Unsuccessful Supreme Court Nominations* (New York: State University of New York Press, 1990), 99; John P. Frank, *Clement Haynsworth, the Senate, and the Supreme Court* (Charlottesville: University Press of Virginia, 1991), 85.

2. Grossman and Wasby, "Haynsworth and Parker," 352.

3. Wallace F. Bennett to Ernest "Fritz" Hollings, October 10, 1969; Daniel K. Inouye to Ernest "Fritz" Hollings, October 9, 1969; Ted Stevens to Ernest "Fritz" Hollings, October 25, 1969, Ernest F. Hollings Collection, Senate Papers, Legislative Files and Constituent Correspondence, Box 127, Judiciary, Judges, Selection and Appointment, Supreme Court, Haynsworth, Clement F. Jr., General, Pro, Folder 2; Massaro, *Supremely Political,* 21; Statement by Senator Marlow W. Cook on the floor of the Senate, May 15, 1970, 15, Ernest F. Hollings Collection, Senate Papers, Legislative Files and Constituent Correspondence, Box 126, Judiciary, Judges, Selection and Appointment, Supreme Court, General.

4. Edward M. Beiser, "The Haynsworth Affair Reconsidered: The Significance of Conflicting Perceptions of the Judicial Role," *Vanderbilt Law Review* 23 (1969–1970): 270–71; Massaro, *Supremely Political,* 98–99.

5. "Haynsworth Defeat Could Prompt Resentment Vote in Next Election," *Richmond News Leader,* November 12, 1969; "Ethics Paradox in Haynsworth Case," *Evening Star* (Washington, DC), November 10, 1969; "Thin Haynsworth Victory Predicted," *The State,* Ernest F. Hollings Collection, Senate Papers, Legislative Files and Constituent Correspondence, Box 127, Judiciary, Judges, Selection and Appointment, Supreme Court, Haynsworth, Clement F. Jr., General, Pro, Folder 3; Frank, *Clement Haynsworth,* 83–84.

6. Frank, *Clement Haynsworth,* 87.

7. Ernest F. Hollings and Kirk Victor, *Making Government Work* (Columbia: University of South Carolina Press, 2008), 150.

8. Newsletter from the office of Senator Strom Thurmond, December 1, 1969, Strom Thurmond Collection, Subject Correspondence Series, Mss.0100.18, 3 (United States District, Circuit, and Supreme Court Judges), Year 1970, Box 21, Folder 7.

9. Carl W. Porter to Strom Thurmond, November 21, 1969; Sara Sullivan Ervin to Strom Thurmond, November 24, 1969; Strom Thurmond to Clement Haynsworth, December 2, 1969, Strom Thurmond Collection, Subject Correspondence Series, Mss.0100.18, 3 (United States District, Circuit, and Supreme Court Judges), Year 1969, Box 29, Folder 7; Kenneth W. Goings, *The NAACP Comes of Age: The Defeat of Judge John J. Parker* (Bloomington: Indiana University Press, 1990), 25; Richard Kluger, "The Story of John Johnston Parker: The First Demonstration of Negro Political Power since Reconstruction," *Journal of Blacks in Higher Education* 46 (Winter 2004–2005): 125; Richard L. Watson, "The Defeat of Judge Parker: A Study in Pressure Groups and Politics," *Mississippi Valley Historical Review* 50, no. 2 (1963): 220; "Thin Haynsworth Victory Predicted," *The State,* n.d., Ernest F. Hollings Collection, Senate Papers, Legislative Files and Constituent Correspondence, Box 127, Ernest F. Hollings Collection, Senate Papers, Legislative Files and Constituent Correspondence, Box 127, Judiciary, Judges, Selection and Appointment, Supreme Court, Haynsworth, Clement F. Jr., General, Pro, Folder 3.

10. Bill Brock to the author, April 22, 2014. The Parker controversy is covered extensively in Donald J. Lisio, *Hoover, Blacks, and Lily-Whites: A Study of Southern Strategies* (Chapel Hill: University of North Carolina Press, 1985).

11. Massaro, *Supremely Political,* 81.

12. Strom Thurmond to Mr. and Mrs. P. M. Smurthwaite, January 8, 1970, Strom Thurmond

Collection, Subject Correspondence Series, Mss.0100.18, 3 (United States District, Circuit, and Supreme Court Judges), Year 1970, Box 21, Folder 1.

13. Survey request from Sue Shepard and Jerry Jensen to Strom Thurmond, January 30, 1970, Strom Thurmond Collection, Subject Correspondence Series, Mss.0100.18, 3 (United States District, Circuit, and Supreme Court Judges), Year 1970, Box 21, Folder 1.

14. Ethan Bronner, *Battle for Justice; How the Bork Nomination Shook America* (New York: Sterling, 1989), 197–98; Jan Crawford Greenburg, *Supreme Conflict: The Inside Story of the Struggle for Control of the United States Supreme Court* (New York: Penguin Press, 2007), 58.

15. Ernest "Fritz" Hollings to W. C. Boyd, March 24 1970, Ernest F. Hollings Collection, Senate Papers, Legislative Files and Constituent Correspondence, Box 127, Judiciary, Judges, Selection and Appointment, Supreme Court, Carswell, George Harrold, 1970, Folder 2.

16. Ernest "Fritz" Hollings to Robert S. Small, November 28 1969, Ernest F. Hollings Collection, Senate Papers, Legislative Files and Constituent Correspondence, Box 127, Judiciary, Judges, Selection and Appointment, Supreme Court, Haynsworth, Clement F. Jr., General, Pro, Folder 3; Massaro, *Supremely Political,* 99; "Edens Charges Hollings with Playing 'Both Sides,'" undated, Ernest F. Hollings Collection, Senate Papers, Legislative Files and Constituent Correspondence, Box 127, Judiciary, Judges, Selection and Appointment, Supreme Court, Haynsworth, Clement F. Jr., General, Con, Folder 5; Andrea L'Hommedieu Interview with Ernest "Fritz" Hollings, June 20, 2012, George J. Mitchell Oral History Project, Bowdoin Digital Commons; Hollings and Victor, *Making Government Work,* 145.

17. Russell Long to Robert L. Stoddard, December 10, 1969, Strom Thurmond Collection, Subject Correspondence Series, Mss.0100.18, 3 (United States District, Circuit, and Supreme Court Judges), Year 1969, Box 29, Folder 7; Maltese, *The Selling,* 77; Frank, *Clement Haynsworth,* 27.

18. Newsletter from the office of Senator Strom Thurmond, December 1, 1969, Strom Thurmond Collection, Subject Correspondence Series, Mss.0100.18, 3 (United States District, Circuit, and Supreme Court Judges), Year 1970, Box 21, Folder 7; Richard Nixon to Ernest "Fritz" Hollings, November 21, 1969, Ernest F. Hollings Collection, Senate Papers, Legislative Files and Constituent Correspondence, Box 127; Judiciary, Judges, Selection and Appointment, Supreme Court, Haynsworth, Clement F. Jr., General, Pro, Folder 4.

19. J. Harvie Wilkinson III, *From Brown to Bakke: The Supreme Court and School Integration, 1954–1978* (Oxford: Oxford University Press, 1979), 119–20; Bob Woodward and Scott Armstrong, *The Brethren* (New York: Simon and Schuster, 1979), 38–63; "Officials Say Court Order Could Affect Most of South," *New York Times,* October 30, 1969, 34.

20. "Officials Say Court Order Could Affect Most of South," *New York Times,* October 30, 1969, 34; Joseph Crespino, *Strom Thurmond's America* (New York: Hill and Wang, 2012), 238; "South Carolina Governor to Obey Court on Schools," *New York Times,* January 28, 1970, 1; "Hollings, Javits Clash on Schools," *News and Courier,* February 7, 1970, 3A.

21. A. Mitchell McConnell, "Haynsworth and Carswell: A New Senate Standard of Excellence," was published in *Kentucky Law Journal* 59 (1970–1971): 23; Peter G. Fish, "Spite Nominations to the United States Supreme Court: Herbert C. Hoover, Owen J. Roberts and the Politics of Presidential Vengeance in Retrospect," *Kentucky Law Journal* 77 (1988): 552–53; Laurence H. Tribe, *God Save This Honorable Court* (London: Random House, 1985), 89; Statement of George Meany, President,

American Federation of Labor and Congress of Industrial Organizations, submitted to the Senate Judiciary Committee on the Nomination of G. Harrold Carswell to be an Associate Justice of the United States Supreme Court, February 2, 1970, Strom Thurmond Collection, Subject Correspondence Series, Mss.0100.18, 3 (United States District, Circuit and Supreme Court Judges), Year 1970, Box 21, Folder 1; Henry J. Abraham, *Justices, Presidents, and Senators: A History of the U.S. Supreme Court Appointments from Washington to Clinton* (Lanham, MD: Rowman and Littlefield, 1999), 11; Michael Comiskey, *Seeking Justices: The Judging of Supreme Court Nominees* (Lawrence: University Press of Kansas, 2004), 67–68.

22. Strom Thurmond to Mrs. Donald W. McCarter, February 6, 1970, Strom Thurmond Collection, Subject Correspondence Series, Mss.0100.18, 3 (United States District, Circuit, and Supreme Court Judges), Year 1970, Box 21, Folder 1; news release from the office of Strom Thurmond, March 26, 1970, Strom Thurmond Collection, Mss.0100.11, Speeches Series 1935–1998, Subseries B, originals (1947–1970), Press Releases 1970 (January 6, 1970–May 6, 1970), Box 16, Folder 197.

23. "Hollings Hesitates," *News and Courier*, March 22, 1970, 14A, Ernest F. Hollings Collection, Senate Papers, Legislative Files and Constituent Correspondence, Box 127, Judiciary, Judges, Selection and Appointment, Supreme Court, Carswell, George Harrold, 1970, Folder 1.

24. "Sen. Hollings Temporises While Carswell Dangles," *The State*, April 1, 1970, 14A; W. M. Hodge and Robert E. Graham to Ernest "Fritz" Hollings, April 3, 1970; Mrs. Robert Hume Lucas to Ernest "Fritz" Hollings, April 2, 1970, Ernest F. Hollings Collection, Senate Papers, Legislative Files and Constituent Correspondence, Box 127, Judiciary, Judges, Selection and Appointment, Supreme Court, Carswell, George Harrold, 1970, Folder 3.

25. Ernest "Fritz" Hollings to Fulton B. Creech, March 24, 1970, Ernest F. Hollings Collection, Senate Papers, Legislative Files and Constituent Correspondence, Box 127, Judiciary, Judges, Selection and Appointment, Supreme Court, Carswell, George Harrold, 1970, Folder 2; Ernest "Fritz" Hollings to William R. Merritt, December 5, 1969, Ernest F. Hollings Collection, Senate Papers, Legislative Files and Constituent Correspondence, Box 127, Judiciary, Judges, Selection and Appointment, Supreme Court, Haynsworth, Clement F. Jr., General, Pro, Folder 4; Ernest "Fritz" Hollings to David Karesh, October 19, 1971, Ernest F. Hollings Collection, Senate Papers, Legislative Files and Constituent Correspondence, Box 154, Judiciary, Judges, Selection and Appointment, General.

26. Statement by Senator Ernest F. Hollings on Judge G. Harrold Carswell, April 6, 1970, Ernest F. Hollings Collection, Senate Papers, Legislative Files and Constituent Correspondence, Box 127, Judiciary, Judges, Selection and Appointment, Supreme Court, Carswell, George Harrold, 1970, Folder 3; Richard Nixon to Ernest "Fritz" Hollings, April 11, 1970, Ernest F. Hollings Collection, Senate Papers, Legislative Files and Constituent Correspondence, Box 127, Judiciary, Judges, Selection and Appointment, Supreme Court, Carswell, George Harrold, 1970, Folder 2; newsletter from the office of Strom Thurmond, April 29, 1970, Strom Thurmond Collection, Mss.0100.11, Speeches Series 1935–1998, Subseries B, originals (1947–1970), Press Releases 1970 (January 6, 1970–May 6, 1970), Box 16, Folder 197; "Nixon Will Get Southerner on Court, Predicts Thurmond in Sarasota Talk," *Sarasota Herald Tribune*, April 11, 1970, 2B.

27. Frank, *Clement Haynsworth*, 124; Linda Greenhouse, *Becoming Justice Blackmun: Harry Blackmun's Supreme Court Journey* (New York: Henry Holt, 2005), 222–24.

28. Statement by Senator Marlow W. Cook on the floor of the Senate, May 15, 1970, 15, Ernest

F. Hollings Collection, Senate Papers, Legislative Files and Constituent Correspondence, Box 126, Judiciary, Judges, Selection and Appointment, Supreme Court, General.

29. "McConnell's Shining Moment," *The Hill,* April 7, 2017. See also Paul Kane, "Why Sen. Mitch McConnell Won't Budge on the Supreme Court Nomination," *Washington Post,* March 16, 2016. For a fuller discussion of the "Thurmond rule," see the concluding chapter.

30. Letter from Bill Brock, April 22, 2014; Billy B. Hathorn, "The Changing Politics of Race: Congressman Albert William Watson and the S.C. Republican Party, 1965–1970," *South Carolina Historical Magazine* 89, no. 4 (October 1988): 232, 237; "New Mood in South," *New York Times,* April 25, 1971, E15; Philip G. Grose, *Looking for Utopia: The Life and Times of John C. West* (Columbia: University of South Carolina Press, 2011), 148–59; Dewey W. Grantham, *The Life and Death of the Solid South: A Political History* (Lexington, KY: University Press of Kentucky, 1988), 183; Nadine Cohodas, *Strom Thurmond and the Politics of Southern Change* (Macon, GA: Mercer University Press, 1995), 412.

31. "Nixon Reportedly Drops Plans to Nominate Watson as Judge," *New York Times,* May 28, 1971, 8.

32. Christine L. Nemacheck, *Strategic Selection* (Charlottesville: University of Virginia Press, 2008), 69; Footage of Bork Supreme Court confirmation hearings, 1987, https://www.youtube.com/watch?v=5ffTtOMIJAk.

33. Laura Kalman, *Abe Fortas: A Biography* (New Haven, CT: Yale University Press, 1992), 392.

34. For more on scholarly interpretations of South Carolina's civil rights era, see John Monk, Preface to *Toward the Meeting of the Waters: Currents in the Civil Rights Movement of South Carolina during the Twentieth Century,* ed. Winfred B. Moore Jr. and Orville Vernon Burton (Columbia: University of South Carolina Press, 2008), xxi–xxiv.

12. "DYNAMIC CONSERVATISM"

1. Ernest F. Hollings and Kirk Victor, *Making Government Work* (Columbia: University of South Carolina Press, 2008), 16; Earl Black, *Southern Governors and Civil Rights* (Cambridge, MA: Harvard University Press, 1976), 80–82; Anthony J. Badger, "From Defiance to Moderation: South Carolina Governors and Racial Change," in *New Deal/New South: An Anthony J. Badger Reader* (Fayetteville: University of Arkansas Press, 2007), 135–36; James C. Cobb, *The Selling of the South* (Chicago: University of Illinois Press, 1993), 141; inaugural address of The Honorable Ernest F. Hollings as Governor of South Carolina, Columbia, January 20, 1959, 4–5, South Carolina Political Collections, Oral History Project, University of South Carolina, http://digital.tcl.sc.edu/cdm/compoundobject/collection/how/id/349/show/340/rec/2; address by Governor Ernest F. Hollings to the General Assembly of South Carolina, January 9, 1963, South Carolina Political Collections, Oral History Project, University of South Carolina; "Hollings Says Farewell, Sees Desegregation," *Times-News,* (Hendersonville, NC), January 10, 1963, 3.

2. Badger, "From Defiance," 143; Robert Mickey, *Paths out of Dixie: The Democratization of Authoritarian Enclaves in America's Deep South, 1944–1972* (Princeton, NJ: Princeton University Press, 2015), 239; Jack Bass and W. Scott Poole, *The Palmetto State: The Making of Modern South Carolina* (Columbia: University of South Carolina Press, 2009), 112; Jack Bass and Walter DeVries,

The Transformation of Southern Politics (Athens: University of Georgia Press, 1995), 250; Cobb, *The Selling,* 166; Nicol C. Rae, *Southern Democrats* (Oxford: Oxford University Press, 1994), 4; inaugural address, 5.

3. Hollings and Victor, *Making Government Work,* 103; footage of Commerce Committee hearings into violence on television, 1993, https://www.youtube.com/watch?v=310bkzXRt-0; "A Bitter Rivalry in South Carolina," *New York Times,* October 30, 1992.

4. Walter Edgar, *South Carolina: A History* (Columbia: University of South Carolina Press, 1998) 542; Rae, *Southern Democrats,* 105; US Senate Roll Call Votes, 103rd Congress—1st Session, HR1—Family and Medical Leave Act, February 4, 1993.

5. Frances E. Lee, "The Challenge of Bipartisanship: A Historical Perspective," in *Working Congress: A Guide for Senators, Representatives, and Citizens,* ed. Robert Mann (Baton Rouge: Louisiana State University Press, 2014), 46–58; address by Senator Strom Thurmond before the Southern Society at the Plaza Hotel, New York, January 14, 1955, 22, Strom Thurmond Collection, Mss.0100.11, Speeches Series 1935–1998, Subseries A, General File (1935–1983), Addresses 1955, Box 7, Folder 604.

6. Badger, "From Defiance," 135.

7. Mickey, *Paths out of Dixie,* 223–24; Ralph B. Kolb to Ernest "Fritz" Hollings, December 2, 1960; Ernest "Fritz" Hollings to Ralph B. Kolb, December 3, 1960; Ralph B. Kolb to Ernest "Fritz" Hollings, December 5, 1960, Ernest F. Hollings Collection, Gubernatorial Papers, Box 14, Citizens' Council, c.1959–1963.

8. Bessie S. Britton to Ernest "Fritz" Hollings, December 19, 1959; draft of response to Bessie S. Britton, undated, Ernest F. Hollings Collection, Gubernatorial Papers, Box 14, Barnett Conference, 1961.

9. Ernest "Fritz" Hollings to Bessie S. Britton, December 28, 1959, Ernest F. Hollings Collection, Gubernatorial Papers, Box 14, Barnett Conference, 1961.

10. Draft of response to Farley Smith, undated; Farley Smith to Ernest "Fritz" Hollings, December 1, 1959; Ernest "Fritz" Hollings to Farley Smith, December 7, 1959, Ernest F. Hollings Collection, Gubernatorial Papers, Box 14, Barnett Conference, 1961.

11. Marcia Synnott interview with Ernest F. Hollings, July 8, 1980, South Carolina Political Collections, Oral History Project, University of South Carolina, http://library.sc.edu/file/1786; "Vandiver Assails Barnett Stand and Calls for Obedience to Law," *New York Times,* October 1, 1962, 24.

12. Hollings and Victor, *Making Government Work,* 76–77; David A. Nichols, *A Matter of Justice: Eisenhower and the Civil Rights Revolution* (New York: Simon and Schuster, 2007), 251; Ernest "Fritz" Hollings to Farley Smith, February 24, 1960, Ernest F. Hollings Collection, Gubernatorial Papers, Box 14, Citizens' Council, c.1959–1963; "Hollings Says Farewell, Sees Desegregation," *Times-News* (Hendersonville, NC), January 10, 1963, 3.

13. Oral history interview with Modjeska Simkins, July 28, 1976, Interview G-0056-2, Documenting the American South, University Library, University of North Carolina at Chapel Hill, http://docsouth.unc.edu/sohp/playback.html?base_file=G-0056-2&duration=05:45:13.

14. Interview with James Clyburn, October 3, 2014.

15. Hollings and Victor, *Making Government Work,* 78.

16. "7 Southerners on List for Black's Court Seat," *Los Angeles Times,* September 21, 1971, Strom Thurmond Collection, Subject Correspondence Series, Mss.0100.18, 2–3 Supreme Court, Year 1971, Box 5, Folder 1; John W. Dean, *The Rehnquist Choice* (New York: Touchstone, 2001), 47; R. Sam

Garrett and Denis Steven Rutkus, "Speed of Presidential and Senate Actions on Supreme Court Nominations, 1900–2009," published by Congressional Research Service (May 8, 2009), 25.

17. Henry J. Abraham, *Justices, Presidents, and Senators: A History of the U.S. Supreme Court Appointments from Washington to Clinton* (Lanham, MD: Rowman and Littlefield, 1999), 269; Dean, *The Rehnquist Choice,* 270–71.

18. Statement of Senator John V. Tunney in Opposition to the Supreme Court Nomination of Assistant Attorney General William Rehnquist, November 18, 1971, 1; Ernest F. Hollings Collection, Senate Papers, Legislative Files and Constituent Correspondence, Box 154, Judiciary, Supreme Court, Rehnquist, William, General, Folder 1.

19. "The Advocate," *Evening Star,* November 11, 1971, Ernest F. Hollings Collection, Senate Papers, Legislative Files and Constituent Correspondence, Box 154, Judiciary, Supreme Court, General; Dean, *The Rehnquist Choice,* 1. Rehnquist became chief justice of the United States in 1986 and served until his death in 2005.

20. Ben Holman to Ernest "Fritz" Hollings, November 4, 1971; Ernest "Fritz" Hollings to Sister Bernetta Quinn, November 22, 1971; Text of Remarks by Senator Hollings on the Floor of the Senate, December 6, 1971, Ernest F. Hollings Collection, Senate Papers, Legislative Files and Constituent Correspondence, Box 154, Judiciary, Supreme Court, General.

21. Ernest "Fritz" Hollings to Peter Murray, December 10, 1971; Ernest "Fritz" Hollings to Louise G. Gasque, November 29, 1971, Ernest F. Hollings Collection, Senate Papers, Legislative Files and Constituent Correspondence, Box 154, Judiciary, Supreme Court, General.

22. Dean, The *Rehnquist Choice,* 265, 274–75; Abraham, *Justices, Presidents,* 269–70.

23. James C. Cobb, *The South and America since World War II* (Oxford: Oxford University Press, 2012), 115; Numan V. Bartley and Hugh D. Graham, *Southern Politics and the Second Reconstruction* (Baltimore: Johns Hopkins University Press, 1975), 125.

24. Joseph Crespino, *Strom Thurmond's America* (New York: Hill and Wang, 2012), 278–79, 299.

25. Letters from Harry S. Fleming to Strom Thurmond, January 10, 1970; Sam J. Ervin and B. Everett Jordan to President Richard Nixon, November 26, 1969, Strom Thurmond Collection, Subject Correspondence Series, Mss.0100.18, 3 (United States District, Circuit, and Supreme Court Judges), Year 1970, Box 21, Folder 1; David A. Yalof, *Pursuit of Justices: Presidential Politics and the Selection of Supreme Court Nominees* (Chicago: University of Chicago Press, 1999), 119.

26. Dean, *The Rehnquist Choice,* 114; Yalof, *Pursuit,* 119, 137, 251–52n.

27. Caroline Davis to Strom Thurmond, January 29, 1970, Strom Thurmond Collection, Subject Correspondence Series, Mss.0100.18, 3 (United States District, Circuit, and Supreme Court Judges), Year 1970, Box 21, Folder 1.

13. "TOO MUCH BLOOD ON THE FLOOR"

1. "Hollings Defends His Opposition to Sneeden," *Sumter Daily Item,* July 27, 1984, 4B; Jack Bass and Walter DeVries, *The Transformation of Southern Politics* (Athens: University of Georgia Press, 1995), 259.

2. Footage of Frank Zappa's testimony during Senate hearings into "obscene" lyrics in rock music, and questions, https://www.youtube.com/watch?v=MMrL1SDkJRg.

3. Jan Crawford Greenburg, *Supreme Conflict: The Inside Story of the Struggle for Control of the United States Supreme Court* (New York: Penguin Press, 2007), 46–47.

4. Ibid., 50–51.

5. Footage of Bork Supreme Court confirmation hearings, 1987, https://www.youtube.com/watch?v=5ffTtOMIJAk.

6. Ethan Bronner, *Battle for Justice: How the Bork Nomination Shook America* (New York: Sterling, 1989), 196; Greenburg, *Supreme Conflict,* 51.

7. Christine L. Nemacheck, *Strategic Selection* (Charlottesville: University of Virginia Press, 2008), 15; People for the American Way television film opposing the Supreme Court nomination of Robert Bork, 1987, https://www.youtube.com/watch?v=NpFe101kF3Y.

8. Bronner, *Battle,* 255–59; Nicol C. Rae, *Southern Democrats* (Oxford: Oxford University Press, 1994), 105–6.

9. Ernest "Fritz" Hollings to Andrew Young, October 2, 1987, Ernest F. Hollings Collection, Senate Papers, Legislative Files and Constituent Correspondence, Box 379, Judiciary, Judges, Selection and Appointment, Supreme Court, Bork, Hearings, September 15–30, 1987, Statements, Hollings.

10. Ernest "Fritz" Hollings speech on The Nomination of Judge Robert Bork [first speech], October 8, 1987, 1–4; Ernest F. Hollings Collection, Senate Papers, Legislative Files and Constituent Correspondence, Box 379, Judiciary, Judges, Selection and Appointment, Supreme Court, Bork, Hearings, September 15–30, 1987, Statements, Hollings.

11. Ibid., 3–4.

12. Ibid., 4–5.

13. Draft of Ernest "Fritz Hollings speech on The Nomination of Judge Robert Bork [first speech]," October 7, 1987, 3–4, 6; Ernest F. Hollings Collection, Senate Papers, Legislative Files and Constituent Correspondence, Box 379, Judiciary, Judges, Selection and Appointment, Supreme Court, Bork, Hearings, September 15–30, 1987, Statements, Hollings.

14. Ibid., 6, 9; Ben Holman to Ernest "Fritz" Hollings, November 4, 1971, Ernest F. Hollings Collection, Senate Papers, Legislative Files and Constituent Correspondence, Box 154, Judiciary, Supreme Court, General.

15. Draft of first speech, October 7, 1987, 4–5, 9.

16. First speech, October 8, 10.

17. "Hollings Expected to Weather Storm over Bork," *Spartanburg Herald-Journal,* October 9, 1987, B5.

18. The Nomination of Judge Robert Bork [second speech], October 22, 1987, 2–3; Ernest F. Hollings Collection, Senate Papers, Legislative Files and Constituent Correspondence, Box 379, Judiciary, Judges, Selection and Appointment, Supreme Court, Bork, Hearings, September 15–30, 1987, Statements, Hollings.

19. Bob Woodward and Scott Armstrong, *The Brethren* (New York: Simon and Schuster, 1979), 342; see also chapter nine. J. Harvie Wilkinson III, *From Brown to Bakke: The Supreme Court and School Integration, 1954–1978* (Oxford: Oxford University Press, 1979).

20. First speech, October 8, 1987, 6; "Clarence Thomas Should Be Intensely Scrutinized but His Nomination Should Not Be Derailed" [statement by Congressman James Clyburn], undated, Ernest F. Hollings Collection, Senate Papers, Legislative Files and Constituent Correspondence and

Hollings Files, Box 421, Judiciary, Judges, Selection and Appointment, Supreme Court, Clarence Thomas, Folder 2.

21. The Nomination of Judge Robert Bork [third speech], October 23, 1987, p.3; Ernest F. Hollings Collection, Senate Papers, Legislative Files and Constituent Correspondence, Box 379, Judiciary, Judges, Selection and Appointment, Supreme Court, Bork, Hearings, September 15–30, 1987, Statements, Hollings. See Congressional Record, Proceedings and Debates of the 100th Congress First Session, Volume 133, Part 21, October 22, 1987–October 29, 1987, United States Government and Printing Office, Washington, 1987.

22. "Hollings Expected to Weather Storm over Bork," *Spartanburg Herald-Journal,* October 9, 1987, B5.

23. Source: Joint Center for Political Studies, *The News,* September 10, 1991, 7A.

24. Nadine Cohodas, *Strom Thurmond and the Politics of Southern Change* (Macon, GA: Mercer University Press, 1995), 492; Rae, *Southern Democrats,* 105; Keith T. Poole and Howard Rosenthal, eds., *Ideology and Congress: A Political Economic History of Roll Call Voting* (New Brunswick, NJ: Transaction Publishers, 2009), 10; John C. Kuzenski, "South Carolina: The Heart of GOP Alignment in the South," in *The New Politics of the Old South: An Introduction to Southern Politics,* ed. Charles S. Bullock III and Mark J. Rozell (Lanham, MD: Rowman and Littlefield, 2003), 37.

25. Henry P. Monaghan, "The Confirmation Process: Law or Politics?," *Harvard Law Review* 101 (1988): 1209; Greenburg, *Supreme Conflict,* 70.

26. Dennis S. Nordin, *From Edward Brooke to Barack Obama: African American Political Success, 1966–2008* (Columbia: University of Missouri Press, 2012), 25; David A. Yalof, *Pursuit of Justices: Presidential Politics and the Selection of Supreme Court Nominees* (Chicago: University of Chicago Press, 1999), 111; Henry J. Abraham, *Justices, Presidents, and Senators: A History of the U.S. Supreme Court Appointments from Washington to Clinton* (Lanham, MD: Rowman and Littlefield, 1999), 28.

27. "Clarence Thomas Should Be Intensely Scrutinized but His Nomination Should Not Be Derailed" [statement by Congressman James Clyburn], undated; "He's Forgotten Where He's From," *Los Angeles Times,* August 12, 1991, Ernest F. Hollings Collection, Senate Papers, Legislative Files and Constituent Correspondence and Hollings Files, Box 421, Judiciary, Judges, Selection and Appointment, Supreme Court, Clarence Thomas, Folder 2; Footage of Clarence Thomas at Supreme Court confirmation hearings, 1991, https://www.youtube.com/watch?v=11EEDD2vxaE; "Southern Senators Tread Lightly on Nomination," *Orlando Sentinel,* taken from *The News,* September 10, 1991, 7A; Michael Comiskey, *Seeking Justices: The Judging of Supreme Court Nominees* (Lawrence: University Press of Kansas, 2004), 45–46.

28. Ernest "Fritz" Hollings to Bud Ferillo, September 25, 1991; John Danforth to Ernest "Fritz" Hollings, October 28, 1991; Ernest "Fritz" Hollings to John L. Williams, October 21, 1991; Ernest "Fritz" Hollings to Otis L. Guy, October 21, 1991, Ernest F. Hollings Collection, Senate Papers, Legislative Files and Constituent Correspondence and Hollings Files, Box 421, Judiciary, Judges, Selection and Appointment, Supreme Court, Clarence Thomas, Folder 1.

29. Judith L. Lichtman to Ernest "Fritz" Hollings, August 1, 1991, Ernest F. Hollings Collection, Senate Papers, Legislative Files and Constituent Correspondence and Hollings Files, Box 421, Judiciary, Judges, Selection and Appointment, Supreme Court, Clarence Thomas, Folder 3.

30. Carolyn Hoover Sung to Ernest "Fritz" Hollings, October 18, 1991, Ernest F. Hollings Collection, Senate Papers, Legislative Files and Constituent Correspondence and Hollings Files, Box 421, Judiciary, Judges, Selection and Appointment, Supreme Court, Clarence Thomas, Folder 3.

31. Ernest "Fritz" Hollings to Carolyn Hoover Sung, October 24, 1991; Ernest "Fritz" Hollings to S. J. Conner, August 27, 1992; Ernest "Fritz" Hollings to S. J. Conner, August 27, 1992, Ernest F. Hollings Collection, Senate Papers, Legislative Files and Constituent Correspondence and Hollings Files, Box 421, Judiciary, Judges, Selection and Appointment, Supreme Court, Clarence Thomas, Folder 3; Deborah A. Faulkner to Ernest "Fritz" Hollings, September 9, 1992, Ernest F. Hollings Collection, Senate Papers, Legislative Files and Constituent Correspondence and Hollings Files, Box 421, Judiciary, Judges, Selection and Appointment, Supreme Court, Clarence Thomas, Folder 2; "A Bitter Rivalry in South Carolina," *New York Times,* October 30, 1992.

32. "Hollings Should Have Expanded His Search," *Spartanburg Herald-Journal,* June 26, 1995, A8.

33. Citizens' Committee for Ernest F. Hollings television spot for reelection of Senator Ernest F. Hollings, 1998, https://www.youtube.com/watch?v=yZv_dDdaiqc; Kuzenski, "South Carolina," 37.

34. Greenburg, *Supreme Conflict,* 178–79; Andrew L'Hommedieu Interview with Ernest "Fritz" Hollings, June 20, 2012, George J. Mitchell Oral History Project, Bowdoin Digital Commons, http://digitalcommons.bowdoin.edu/mitchelloralhistory/200/.

35. Antonin Scalia, *A Matter of Interpretation: Federal Courts and the Law* (Princeton, NJ: Princeton University Press, 1997), 40; Tinsley A. Yarborough, *The Rehnquist Court and the Constitution* (Oxford: Oxford University Press, 2001), 64–65.

CONCLUSION: *A War on the Judiciary in the Southern Secessionist Tradition?*

1. "2016 Candidate Lindsey Graham Has Problems at Home in South Carolina," *Boston Globe,* June 3, 2015.

2. Joseph Crespino, *Strom Thurmond's America* (New York: Hill and Wang 2012), 173–74; "Curtains for Cotton Ed," *Time,* August 7, 1944; "Blease Poetry Is Expunged from Record," *Afro American,* June 22, 1929, 1; Anthony J. Badger, "Southerners Who Refused to Sign the Southern Manifesto," in *New Deal/New South: An Anthony J. Badger Reader* (Fayetteville: University of Arkansas Press, 2007), 79–80, and "From Defiance to Moderation: South Carolina Governors and Racial Change," in *New Deal/New South,* 134–35.

3. Walter Edgar, *South Carolina: A History* (Columbia: University of South Carolina Press, 1998), 330–31, 337–38; Badger, "From Defiance," 134; James O. Farmer, "Memories and Forebodings: The Fight to Preserve the White Democratic Primary in South Carolina," in *Toward the Meeting of the Waters: Currents in the Civil Rights Movement of South Carolina during the Twentieth Century,* ed. Winfred B. Moore Jr. and Orville Vernon Burton (Columbia: University of South Carolina Press, 2008), 249; Keith M. Finley, *Delaying the Dream: Southern Senators and the Fight against Civil Rights, 1938–1965* (Baton Rouge: Louisiana State University Press, 2008), 195.

4. Edgar, *South Carolina,* 507; Bryant Simon, *A Fabric of Defeat: The Politics of South Carolina Millhands, 1910–1948* (Chapel Hill: University of North Carolina Press, 1998), 205; Finley, *Delaying the Dream,* 148; Robert Mann, *The Walls of Jericho: Lyndon Johnson, Hubert Humphrey, Richard*

Russell, and the Struggle for Civil Rights (New York: Harcourt Brace, 1996), 163; letter from Robert Mann to the author, November 19, 2014.

5. Edgar, *South Carolina,* 528.

6. "South Carolina: New Schools Cited by Byrnes," *New York Times,* March 12, 1956, 22.

7. See, for example, Badger's comments on South Carolina's politicians in "From Defiance," 128, and also Mann's comments on Richard Russell's disillusionment in *Walls of Jericho,* 366; Henry P. Monaghan, "The Confirmation Process: Law or Politics?," *Harvard Law Review* 101, no. 6 (April 1988): 1202–12.

8. Mann, *Walls of Jericho,* 197n.

9. Robert Mickey, *Paths out of Dixie: The Democratization of Authoritarian Enclaves in America's Deep South, 1944–1972* (Princeton, NJ: Princeton University Press, 2015), 145–47; interview with John Spratt, September 28, 2014; Crespino, *Strom Thurmond's America,* 120.

10. Price Riley to Olin D. Johnston (telegram), September 5, 1962; Bruce Tremain to Olin D. Johnston, September 6, 1962, Olin D. Johnston Collection, Senate Papers, Legislative Files, Box 101, Judiciary Committee, Appointments, Marshall, Thurgood, Folder 2; "South Carolina Shuns Militancy," *New York Times,* October 26, 1963, 13.

11. Joel B. Grossman and Stephen L. Wasby, "The Senate and Supreme Court Nominations: Some Reflections," *Duke Law Journal* 560, no. 3 (August 1972): 557–91.

12. Dumain, "In Selecting Scalia Successor," and Marisa Endicott, "Graham Meets Obama's Supreme Court Nominee," *The State,* April 20, 2016; Dumain, "In Selecting Scalia Successor."

13. Russell Wheeler, "Judicial Confirmations: What Thurmond Rule?," *Issues in Governance Studies* 5 (March 2012): 1, http://www.brookings.edu/~/media/research/files/papers/2012/3/judicial-wheeler/03_judicial_wheeler.pdf.

14. Lee Davidson, "Griffith to Miss Demos' Deadline," *Deseret News,* July 21, 2004; Glenn Kessler, "A Bushel of Flip-Flops on Approving Judicial Nominees," *Washington Post,* February 23, 2016.

15. Dumain, "In Selecting Scalia Successor"; Wheeler, "Judicial Confirmations," 1, http://www.brookings.edu/~/media/research/files/papers/2012/3/judicial-wheeler/03_judicial_wheeler.pdf; Stuart E. Eizenstat, "In 1980, the GOP approved a lame-duck Democrat's nominee. He's now on the Supreme Court," *Washington Post,* March 16, 2016.

16. Eizenstat, "In 1980, the GOP Approved a Lame-Duck Democrat's Nominee," *Washington Post,* March 16, 2016; "What *Is* the Thurmond Rule?," American Constitution Society, 2012, 2, http://www.acslaw.org/sites/default/files/pdf/ACS%20Talking%20Points%20-%20The%20Thurmond%20Rule.pdf; Al Kamen, "Judicial Nominees: Beware the Thurmond Rule," *Washington Post,* February 3, 2012.

17. Sarah A. Binder, "'Tis the Season for the Thurmond Rule," Brookings Institute, June 14, 2012, http://www.brookings.edu/research/opinions/2012/06/14-judicial-thurmond-binder; Wm. T. (Bill) Robinson to The Honorable Harry Reid and The Honorable Mitch McConnell, June 20, 2012, 2; Judging the Environment (online), http://www.judgingtheenvironment.org/library/letters/ABA-Robinson-letter-to-Sen-leaders-VACs-6-2012.pdf.

BIBLIOGRAPHY

PRIMARY SOURCES

Manuscripts and Archives

Dwight D. Eisenhower Presidential Library, Abilene, KS
William P. Rogers Papers, 1938–1962
Library of Congress, Washington DC
Arthur J. Goldberg Papers, 1793–1995
National Association for the Advancement of Colored People records, 1842–1999
Richard B. Russell Library for Political Research and Studies, Russell Special Collections Building, University of Georgia, Athens, GA
Richard B. Russell Jr. Collection
Herman E. Talmadge Collection
South Carolina Political Collections, Ernest F. Hollings Special Collections Library, University of South Carolina Libraries, Columbia, SC
Ernest F. "Fritz" Hollings Papers, 1943–2009
Olin DeWitt Talmadge Johnston Papers, 1914–1965
Robert E. McNair Papers, 1953–2008
Special Collections Library, Strom Thurmond Institute Building, Clemson University, Clemson, SC
Edgar Allen Brown Papers, 1911–1975
Strom Thurmond Collection

Interviews

Clyburn, James. Columbia, S.C., October 3, 2014
Patterson, Elizabeth J. Spartanburg, S.C., September 29, 2014
Spratt, John. York, S.C., September 28, 2014

Online Sources

Documenting the American South, University Library, University of North Carolina at Chapel Hill.

Oral history interview with Modjeska Simkins, July 28, 1976, Interview G-0056-2, http://docsouth.unc.edu/sohp/playback.html?base_file=G-0056-2&duration=05:45:13.

Lyndon B. Johnson Oral Histories, Miller Center, University of Virginia.

Michael L. Gillette interview with Strom Thurmond, May 7, 1979, http://web2.millercenter.org/lbj/oralhistory/thurmond_strom_1979_0507.pdf.

Lyndon B. Johnson Presidential Recordings, Miller Center, University of Virginia.

Telephone conversations between Lyndon B. Johnson and Everett Dirksen, July 15, 1968 (WH6807.01); undated, October 1968 (WH6810.01).

Telephone conversation between Lyndon B. Johnson and Abe Fortas, August 10, 1965 (WH6508.03).

Telephone conversations between Lyndon B. Johnson and Olin D. Johnston, December 26, 1963 (K6312.18) 25; April 14, 1964 (WH6404.09) 3029, 3031.

Telephone conversation between Lyndon B. Johnson and Nicholas Katzenbach, August 6, 1965 (WH6508.02).

Telephone conversation between Lyndon B. Johnson and Strom Thurmond, April 14, 1964 (WH6404.09) 3032.

Telephone conversation between Lyndon B. Johnson and Earl Warren, December 10, 1968 (WH6812.01), http://millercenter.org/scripps/archive/presidentialrecordings/Johnson.

George J. Mitchell Oral History Project, Bowdoin Digital Commons.

Interview with Ernest "Fritz" Hollings by Andrea L'Hommedieu, June 20, 2012, http://digitalcommons.bowdoin.edu/mitchelloralhistory/200/.

University of South Carolina, South Carolina Political Collections, Digital Collections

Address by Governor Ernest F. Hollings to the General Assembly of South Carolina, January 9, 1963, http://digital.tcl.sc.edu/cdm/compoundobject/collection/how/id/291/rec/14.

Briggs v. Elliott Descendants Reunion Banquet Keynote Address by Senator Ernest F. Hollings, May 11, 2002, Summerton, South Carolina, http://digital.tcl.sc.edu/cdm/compoundobject/collection/how/id/552/show/547/rec/1.

Fritz Hollings: In His Own Words. Inaugural address of The Honorable Ernest F. Hollings as Governor of South Carolina, Columbia, January 20, 1959, http://digital.tcl.sc.edu/cdm/compoundobject/collection/how/id/349/show/340/rec/2.

University of South Carolina, South Carolina Political Collections, Oral History Project.

Herbert Hartsook interview with Thomas W. Chadwick, June 26, 1995, http://library.sc.edu/file/1751.

Marcia Synnott interview with Ernest F. Hollings, July 8, 1980, http://library.sc.edu/file/1786.

YouTube

Hugo Black interview with Eric Sevareid and Martin Agronsky, c. 1968, CBS News, The Phoenix Learning Group, Inc., https://www.youtube.com/watch?v=HAgQdeup2vo.

Citizens' Committee for Ernest F. Hollings television spot for reelection of Senator Ernest F. Hollings, 1998, https://www.youtube.com/watch?v=yZv_dDdaiqc.

Footage of Bork Supreme Court confirmation hearings, 1987, https://www.youtube.com/watch?v=5ffTtOMIJAk.

Footage of Clarence Thomas at Supreme Court confirmation hearings, 1991, https://www.youtube.com/watch?v=11EEDD2vxaE.

Footage of Commerce Committee hearings into violence on television, 1993, https://www.youtube.com/watch?v=310bkzXRt-0.

Footage of Frank Zappa's testimony during Senate hearings into "obscene" lyrics in rock music, and questions, 1985, https://www.youtube.com/watch?v=MMrL1SDk-JRg.

People for the American Way television film opposing the Supreme Court nomination of Robert Bork, 1987, https://www.youtube.com/watch?v=NpFe101kF3Y.

SECONDARY SOURCES

Books and Articles

Abraham, Henry J. *Justices, Presidents, and Senators: A History of the U.S. Supreme Court Appointments from Washington to Clinton.* Lanham, MD: Rowman and Littlefield, 1999.

Ackerman, Bruce A. "Transformative Appointments." *Harvard Law Review* 101, no. 6 (1988): 1164–84.

Ayers, Edward L. *The Promise of the New South: Life after Reconstruction.* Oxford: Oxford University Press, 1992.

Badger, Anthony J. "From Defiance to Moderation: South Carolina Governors and Racial Change." In *New Deal/New South: An Anthony J. Badger Reader,* 127–43. Fayetteville: University of Arkansas Press, 2007.

———. "Southerners Who Refused to Sign the Southern Manifesto." In *New Deal/New South: An Anthony J. Badger Reader,* 72–87. Fayetteville: University of Arkansas Press, 2007.

———. "Whatever Happened to Roosevelt's New Generation of Southerners?" In *New Deal/New South: An Anthony J. Badger Reader,* 58–71. Fayetteville: University of Arkansas Press, 2007.

Baker, Bruce. *This Mob Will Surely Take My Life: Lynchings in the Carolinas, 1871–1947.* London: Continuum, 2008.

Baker, Nancy V. *Conflicting Loyalties: Law and Politics in the Attorney General's Office, 1789–1990.* Lawrence: University Press of Kansas, 1992.

Bartley, Numan V. *The New South, 1945–1980.* Baton Rouge: Louisiana State University Press, 1996.

———. *The Rise of Massive Resistance: Race and Politics in the South during the 1950's.* Baton Rouge: Louisiana State University Press, 1999.

Bartley, Numan V., and Hugh D. Graham. *Southern Politics and the Second Reconstruction.* Baltimore: Johns Hopkins University Press, 1975.

Bass, Jack, and Marilyn W. Thompson. *Strom: The Complicated Personal and Political Life of Strom Thurmond.* New York: Public Affairs, 2005.

Bass, Jack, and W. Scott Poole. *The Palmetto State: The Making of Modern South Carolina.* Columbia: University of South Carolina Press, 2009.

Bass, Jack, and Walter DeVries. *The Transformation of Southern Politics.* Athens: University of Georgia Press, 1995.

Beiser, Edward N. "The Haynsworth Affair Reconsidered: The Significance of Conflicting Perceptions of the Judicial Role." *Vanderbilt Law Review* 23 (1969–1970): 263–90.

Black, Conrad. *Richard M. Nixon: A Life in Full.* New York: Public Affairs, 2007.

Black, Earl. *Southern Governors and Civil Rights.* Cambridge, MA: Harvard University Press, 1976.

Black, Earl, and Merle Black. *Politics and Society in the South.* Cambridge, MA: Harvard University Press, 1987.

Boller, Paul F. *Presidential Campaigns.* Oxford: Oxford University Press, 2004.

Bronner, Ethan. *Battle for Justice: How the Bork Nomination Shook America.* New York: Sterling, 1989.

Bullock, Charles S. "The South in Congress: Power and Policy." In *Contemporary Southern Politics,* edited by James F. Lea, 177–93. Baton Rouge: Louisiana State University Press, 1988.

Bullock, Charles S., and Janna Deitz. "Transforming the South: The Role of the Federal Government." In *The American South in the Twentieth Century,* edited by Craig S. Pascoe et al., 247–62. Athens: University of Georgia Press, 2005.

Bullock, Charles S., and Ronald Keith Gaddie. *Georgia Politics in a State of Change.* Boston: Longman, 2010.

Bullock, Charles S., III, and Mark J. Rozell, eds. *The New Politics of the Old South: An Introduction to Southern Politics.* Lanham, MD: Rowman and Littlefield, 2003.

Burton, Orville Vernon, et al. "South Carolina." In *Quiet Revolution in the South: The Impact of the Voting Rights Act, 1965–1990,* edited by Chandler Davidson and Bernard N. Grofman, 191–232. Princeton, NJ: Princeton University Press, 1994.

Byrnes, James F. "The Supreme Court Must Be Curbed!" *US News and World Report*, May 18, 1956, pp. 50–58.

Califano, Joseph A. *The Triumph and Tragedy of Lyndon Johnson*. New York: Simon and Schuster, 1991.

Carmen, Ira H. "The President, Politics and the Power of Appointment: Hoover's Nomination of Mr. Justice Cardozo." *Virginia Law Review* 55 (1969): 616–59.

Caro, Robert J. *The Years of Lyndon Johnson: Master of the Senate*. London: Jonathan Cape, 2002.

Carter, Stephen. "The Confirmation Mess." *Harvard Law Review* 101, no. 6 (1988): 1185–1201.

Cash, W. J. *The Mind of the South*. New York: Alfred A. Knopf, 1941.

Cobb, James C. "From the First New South to the Second: The Southern Odyssey through the Twentieth Century." In *The American South in the Twentieth Century*, edited by Craig S. Pascoe et al., 1–18. Athens: University of Georgia Press, 2005.

———. *The Selling of the South*. Chicago: University of Illinois Press, 1993.

———. *The South and America since World War II*. Oxford: Oxford University Press, 2012.

Coclanis, Peter. *In the Shadow of a Dream: Economic Life and Death in the South Carolina Low Country, 1670–1920*. Oxford: Oxford University Press, 1989.

Cohodas, Nadine. *Strom Thurmond and the Politics of Southern Change*. Macon, GA: Mercer University Press, 1995.

Comiskey, Michael. "Can a President Draft—or Pack—the Supreme Court? FDR and the Court in the Great Depression and World War II." *Albany Law Review* 57 (1993): 1043–60.

———. *Seeking Justices: The Judging of Supreme Court Nominees*. Lawrence: University Press of Kansas, 2004.

Cooper, William J., Jr. "Economics or Race: An Analysis of the Gubernatorial Election of 1890 in South Carolina." *South Carolina Historical Magazine* 73, no. 4 (1972): 209–19.

Crespino, Joseph. *Strom Thurmond's America*. New York: Hill and Wang, 2012.

Cullop, F. G. *The Constitution of the United States: An Introduction*. New York: Penguin, 1969.

Dailey, Jane, Glenda Elizabeth Gilmore, and Bryant Simon, eds. *Jumpin' Jim Crow: Southern Politics from Civil War to Civil Rights*. Princeton, NJ: Princeton University Press, 2000.

Dallek, Robert. *Flawed Giant: Lyndon Johnson and His Times, 1961–1973*. Oxford: Oxford University Press, 1998.

———. *John F. Kennedy: An Unfinished Life*. London: Penguin, 2003.

———. *Lyndon B. Johnson: Portrait of a President*. London: Penguin, 2004.

Danelski, David. *A Supreme Court Justice Is Appointed*. New York: Random House, 1964.

Davidson, Chandler, and Bernard N. Grofman, eds. *Quiet Revolution in the South: The Impact of the Voting Rights Act, 1965–1990.* Princeton, NJ: Princeton University Press, 1994.

Dean, John W. *The Rehnquist Choice.* New York: Touchstone, 2001.

Dilliard, Irving. "Thomas C. Hennings Jr. and the Supreme Court." *Missouri Law Review* 26, no. 4 (1961): 429–40.

Donald, David Herbert. *Charles Sumner and the Coming Civil War.* New York: Alfred A. Knopf, 1960.

Edgar, Walter. *South Carolina: A History.* Columbia: University of South Carolina Press, 1998.

Eisenhower, Dwight D. *Mandate for Change: The White House Years, 1953–1956.* New York: Signet, 1962.

Engel, Stephen M. *American Politicians Confront the Court: Opposition Politics and Changing Responses to Judicial Power.* Cambridge: Cambridge University Press, 2011.

Fairclough, Adam. *Better Day Coming: Blacks and Equality, 1890–2000.* London: Penguin, 2001.

Farhang, Sean, and Ira Katznelson. "The Southern Imposition: Congress and Labor in the New Deal and Fair Deal." *Studies in American Political Development* 19 (2005): 1–30.

Felder, James L. *Civil Rights in South Carolina: From Peaceful Protests to Groundbreaking Rulings.* Charleston, SC: History Press, 2012.

Felice, John D., and Herbert F. Weisberg. "The Changing Importance of Ideology, Party, and Region in the Confirmation of Supreme Court Nominees, 1953–1988." *Kentucky Law Journal* 77 (1988–1989): 509–30.

Finley, Keith M. "Balancing Liberal and Conservative Policy Preferences: Russell B. Long's Early United States Senate Career, 1948–1957." *Louisiana History* 45, no. 1 (Winter 2004): 5–35.

———. *Delaying the Dream: Southern Senators and the Fight against Civil Rights, 1938–1965.* Baton Rouge: Louisiana State University Press, 2008.

Fish, Peter G. "Spite Nominations to the United States Supreme Court: Herbert C. Hoover, Owen J. Roberts and the Politics of Presidential Vengeance in Retrospect." *Kentucky Law Journal* 77 (1988): 545–76.

Fox, Edward J., Jr. "The Selection of Federal Judges: The Work of the Federal Judiciary Committee." *American Bar Association Journal* 43 (1957): 685–88.

Frank, John P. "The Appointment of Supreme Court Justices: Prestige, Principles and Politics 1." *Wisconsin Law Review* (1941a): 172–210.

———. "The Appointment of Supreme Court Justices: Prestige, Principles and Politics 2." *Wisconsin Law Review* (1941b): 343–79.

———. "The Appointment of Supreme Court Justices: Prestige, Principles and Politics 3." *Wisconsin Law Review* (1941c): 461–512.

———. *Clement Haynsworth, the Senate, and the Supreme Court*. Charlottesville: University Press of Virginia, 1991.

Frederickson, Karl. "'The Slowest State' and 'Most Backward Community': Racial Violence in South Carolina and Federal Civil Rights Legislation, 1946–48." *South Carolina Historical Magazine* 98, no. 2 (1997): 177–202.

Freund, Paul A. "Appointment of Justices: Some Historical Perspectives." *Harvard Law Review* 101 (1988): 1146–63.

Friedman, Richard D. "The Transformation in Senate Response to Supreme Court Nominees: From Reconstruction to the Taft Administration and Beyond." *Cardozo Law Review* 5, no. 1 (1983): 1–95.

Frist, William H., with J. Lee Annis Jr. *Tennessee Senators, 1911–2001: Portraits of Leadership in a Century of Change*. New York: Derrydale Press, 1999.

Garrett, R. Sam, and Denis Steven Rutkus. "Speed of Presidential and Senate Actions on Supreme Court Nominations, 1900–2009." Washington, DC: Congressional Research Service, May 8, 2009.

Gauch, James E. "The Intended Role of the Senate in Supreme Court Appointments." *University of Chicago Law Review* 65, no. 1 (1989): 337–65.

Gerhart, Eugene C. *America's Advocate: Robert H. Jackson*. Indianapolis: Bobbs-Merrill, 1958.

Gerhart, Michael J. *The Federal Appointments Process: A Constitutional and Historical Analysis*. Durham, NC: Duke University Press, 2000.

Goings, Kenneth W. *The NAACP Comes of Age: The Defeat of Judge John J. Parker*. Bloomington: University of Indiana Press, 1990.

Goldwater, Barry. "Political Philosophy and Supreme Court Justices." *American Bar Association Journal* 58 (February 1972): 135–40.

Grantham, Dewey W. *The Life and Death of the Solid South: A Political History*. Lexington: University Press of Kentucky, 1988.

Greenburg, Jan Crawford. *Supreme Conflict: The Inside Story of the Struggle for Control of the United States Supreme Court*. New York: Penguin Press, 2007.

Greenhouse, Linda. *Becoming Justice Blackmun: Harry Blackmun's Supreme Court Journey*. New York: Henry Holt, 2005.

Griffin, Robert P. "The Broad Role." *Prospectus* 2 (1968–1969): 285–303.

Grose, Philip G. *Looking for Utopia: The Life and Times of John C. West*. Columbia: University of South Carolina Press, 2011.

———. *South Carolina at the Brink: Robert McNair and the Politics of Civil Rights*. Columbia: University of South Carolina Press, 2006.

Grossman, Joel B. *Lawyers and Judges: The ABA and the Politics of Judicial Selection*.

New York: John Wiley and Sons, 1965.

———. "The Role of the American Bar Association in the Selection of Federal Judges: Episodic Involvement to Institutionalized Power." *Vanderbilt Law Review* 17 (1963): 785–814.

Grossman, Joel B., and Stephen L. Wasby. "Haynsworth and Parker: History Does Live Again." *South Carolina Law Review* 23 (1971): 345–59.

———. "The Senate and Supreme Court Nominations: Some Reflections." *Duke Law Journal* 560, no. 3 (1972): 557–91.

Hale, Grace Elizabeth. "Of the Meaning of Progress: A Century of Southern Race Relations." In *The American South in the Twentieth Century,* edited by Craig S. Pascoe et al., 56–73. Athens: University of Georgia Press, 2005.

Harbaugh, William Henry. *Lawyer's Lawyer: The Life of John W. Davis.* New York: Oxford University Press, 1973.

Harris, Joseph P. *The Advice and Consent of the Senate: A Study of the Confirmation of Appointments by the United States Senate.* Berkeley: University of California Press, 1953.

Hart, Philip A. "The Discriminating Role." *Prospectus* 2 (1968–1969): 305–10.

Hathorn, Billy B. "The Changing Politics of Race: Congressman Albert William Watson and the S.C. Republican Party, 1965–1970." *South Carolina Historical Magazine* 89, no. 4 (October 1988): 227–41.

Haw, James. "'The Problem of South Carolina' Re-Examined." *South Carolina Historical Magazine* 107, no. 1 (2000): 9–25.

Hine, Darlene Clark. *Black Victory: The Rise and Fall of the White Primary in Texas.* Columbia: University of Missouri Press, 2003.

———. "The NAACP and the Supreme Court: Walter F. White and the Defeat of Judge John J. Parker, 1930." *Negro History Bulletin* 40, no. 5 (1977): 753–57.

Hine, W. C. "Civil Rights and Campus Wrongs: South Carolina State College Students Protest, 1955–1968." *South Carolina Historical Magazine* 97, no. 4 (1996): 310–31.

Hollings, Ernest F., and Kirk Victor. *Making Government Work.* Columbia: University of South Carolina Press, 2008.

Hollis, D. W. "'Cotton Ed' Smith: Showman or Statesman?," *South Carolina Historical Magazine* 71, no. 4 (1970): 235–56.

Huss, John E. *Senator for the South: A Biography of Olin D. Johnston.* New York: Doubleday, 1961.

Johnson, Timothy R., and Jason M. Roberts. "Presidential Capital and the Supreme Court Nomination Process." *Journal of Politics* 66, no. 3 (2004): 663–83.

Jordan, Frank E. *The Primary State: A History of the Democratic Party in South Carolina, 1896–1962.* Self-published, n.d.

Kahn, Michael A. "The Politics of the Appointment Process: An Analysis of Why

Learned Hand Was Never Appointed to the Supreme Court." *Stanford Law Review* 25 (1973): 251–85.

———. "Shattering the Myth about President Eisenhower's Supreme Court Appointments." *Presidential Studies Quarterly* 22, no. 1 (1992): 47–56.

Kahn, Ronald, and Kenneth I. Kersch, eds. *The Supreme Court and American Political Development.* Lawrence: University Press of Kansas, 2006.

Kalman, Laura. *Abe Fortas: A Biography.* New Haven, CT: Yale University Press, 1992.

———. "Law, Politics and the New Deal." *Yale Law Journal* 108, no. 8 (1999): 2165–2213.

Katznelson, Ira, et al. "Limiting Liberalism: The Southern Veto in Congress, 1933–1950." *Political Science Quarterly* 108, no. 2 (1993): 283–306.

Key, V. O. *Southern Politics in State and Nation.* New York: Vintage, 1949.

Klarman, Michael J. *From Jim Crow to Civil Rights: The Supreme Court and the Struggle for Racial Equality.* Oxford: Oxford University Press, 2004.

Kluger, Richard. "The Story of John Johnston Parker: The First Demonstration of Negro Political Power since Reconstruction." *Journal of Blacks in Higher Education* 46 (2004–2005): 124–25.

Krutz, Glen S. "From Abe Fortas to Zoe Baird: Why Some Presidential Nominations Fail in the Senate." *American Political Science Review* 92, no. 4 (1998): 871–81.

Kutner, Luis. "Advice and Consent: Due Process of the Senate." *DePaul Law Review* 23 (1974): 658–91.

Kuzenski, John C. "South Carolina: The Heart of GOP Alignment in the South." In *The New Politics of the Old South: An Introduction to Southern Politics,* edited by Charles S. Bullock III and Mark J. Rozell, 23–51. Lanham, MD: Rowman and Littlefield, 2003.

Lander, Ernest M., Jr., and Robert K. Ackerman, eds. *Perspectives in South Carolina History: The First 300 Years.* Columbia: University of South Carolina Press, 1972.

Lau, Peter F. *Democracy Rising: South Carolina and the Fight for Black Equality since 1865.* Louisville: University Press of Kentucky, 2006.

Lea, James F., ed. *Contemporary Southern Politics.* Baton Rouge: Louisiana State University Press, 1988.

Lee, Frances E. "The Challenge of Bipartisanship: A Historical Perspective." In *Working Congress: A Guide for Senators, Representatives, and Citizens,* edited by Robert Mann, 46–58. Baton Rouge: Louisiana State University Press, 2014.

Lisio, Donald J. *Hoover, Blacks, and Lily-Whites: A Study of Southern Strategies.* Chapel Hill: University of North Carolina Press, 1985.

Maltese, John Anthony. *The Selling of Supreme Court Nominees.* Baltimore: Johns Hopkins University Press, 1995.

Mann, Robert. *The Walls of Jericho: Lyndon Johnson, Hubert Humphrey, Richard Russell, and the Struggle for Civil Rights.* New York: Harcourt Brace, 1996.

———. *When Freedom Would Triumph: The Civil Rights Struggle in Congress, 1954–1968.* Baton Rouge: Louisiana State University Press, 2007.

Marquardt, Ronald G. "Judicial Politics in the South: Robed Elites and Recruitment." In *Contemporary Southern Politics,* edited by James F. Lea, 242–62. Baton Rouge: Louisiana State University Press, 1988.

Mason, Alpheus T. *The Supreme Court from Taft to Warren.* New York: W. W. Norton, 1958.

Massaro, John. *Supremely Political: The Role of Ideology and Presidential Management in Unsuccessful Supreme Court Nominations.* Albany, NY: State University of New York Press, 1990.

McCarty, Nolan, and Rose Razaghian. "Advice and Consent: Senate Responses to Executive Branch Nominations, 1884–1996." *American Journal of Political Science* 43, no. 4 (1999): 1122–43.

McConnell, A. Mitchell. "Haynsworth and Carswell: A New Senate Standard of Excellence." *Kentucky Law Journal* 59 (1970–1971): 7–34.

McFeeley, Neil D. *Appointment of Judges: The Johnson Presidency.* Austin: University of Texas Press, 1987.

McKenna, Marian C. *Franklin Roosevelt and the Great Constitutional War: The Court-Packing Crisis of 1937.* New York: Fordham University Press, 2002.

McMillan, George. "Integration with Dignity." In *Perspectives in South Carolina History: The First 300 Years,* edited by Ernest M. Lander Jr. and Robert K. Ackerman, 381–91. Columbia: University of South Carolina Press, 1973.

Melone, Albert P. "The Senate's Confirmation Role in Supreme Court Nominations and the Politics of Ideology Versus Impartiality." *Judicature* 75, no. 2: 68–79.

Mendelsohn, Rona H. "Senate Confirmation of Supreme Court Appointments: The Nomination and Rejection of John J. Parker." *Howard Law Journal* 14 (1968): 105–49.

Merritt, Russell. "The Senatorial Election of 1962 and the Rise of Two-Party Politics in South Carolina." *South Carolina Historical Magazine* 98, no. 3 (1997): 281–301.

Mickey, Robert. *Paths out of Dixie: The Democratization of Authoritarian Enclaves in America's Deep South, 1944–1972.* Princeton, NJ: Princeton University Press, 2015.

Minchin, Timothy. *Hiring the Black Worker: The Racial Integration of the Southern Textile Industry, 1960–1980.* Chapel Hill: University of North Carolina Press, 1999.

———. "An Uphill Fight: Ernest F. Hollings and the Struggle to Protect the South Carolina Textile Industry, 1959–2005." *South Carolina Historical Magazine* 109, no. 3 (2008): 187–211.

Mitzner, Adam. "The Evolving Role of the Senate in Judicial Nominations." *Journal of Law and Politics* 5 (1988): 387–428.

Monaghan, Henry P. "The Confirmation Process: Law or Politics?" *Harvard Law*

Review 101 (1988): 1202–12.

Moore, Jamie W. "The Lowcountry in Economic Transition: Charleston since 1865." *South Carolina Historical Magazine* 80, no. 2 (1979): 156–71.

Moore, John R. "The Conservative Coalition in the United States Senate, 1942–1945." *Journal of Southern History* 33, no. 3 (1967): 368–76.

Moore, Winfred B. "James F. Byrnes: The Road to Politics, 1882–1910." *South Carolina Historical Magazine* 84, no. 2 (1983): 72–88.

Moore, Winfred B., Jr., and Orville Vernon Burton, eds. *Toward the Meeting of the Waters: Currents in the Civil Rights Movement of South Carolina during the Twentieth Century.* Columbia: University of South Carolina Press, 2008.

Murphy, Bruce Allen. *Fortas.* New York: William Morrow, 1988.

———. *Wild Bill: The Legend and Life of William O. Douglas.* New York: Random House, 2003.

Murphy, Walter F. "In His Own Image: Mr. Chief Justice Taft and Supreme Court Appointments." *Supreme Court Review* (1961a): 159–93.

———. "Marshalling the Court: Leadership, Bargaining and the Judicial Process." *University of Chicago Law Review* 29 (1961b): 640–72.

Myrdal, Gunnar. *An American Dilemma: The Negro Problem and American Democracy.* New York: Harper and Brothers, 1944.

Navasky, Victor S. *Kennedy Justice.* New York: Atheneum, 1971.

Nemacheck, Christine L. *Strategic Selection.* Charlottesville: University of Virginia Press, 2008.

Nesbit, Dorothy Davidson. "Changing Partisanship Among Southern Party Activists." *Journal of Politics* 50, no. 2 (1988): 322–34.

Newby, I. A. *Black Carolinians.* Columbia: University of South Carolina Press, 1973.

Newman, Dorothy K., et al. *Protest, Politics and Prosperity: Black Americans and White Institutions, 1940–75.* New York: Pantheon Books, 1978.

Newman, Roger K. *Hugo Black: A Biography.* New York: Pantheon, 1994.

Newton, Jim. *Eisenhower: The White House Years.* New York: Anchor, 2001.

———. *Justice for All: Earl Warren and the Nation He Made.* New York: Riverhead, 2006.

Nichols, David A. *A Matter of Justice: Eisenhower and the Civil Rights Revolution.* New York: Simon and Schuster, 2007.

Nordin, Dennis S. *From Edward Brooke to Barack Obama: African American Political Success, 1966–2008.* Columbia: University of Missouri Press, 2012.

Opotowsky, Stan. "Dixie Dynamite: The Inside Story of the White Citizens' Councils." Reprinted from *New York Post,* January 6–20, 1957.

Patterson, James T. *Brown v. Board of Education: A Civil Rights Milestone and Its Troubled Legacy.* Oxford: Oxford University Press, 2002.

Peltason, J. W. *58 Lonely Men: Southern Federal Judges and School Desegregation.* Chicago: University of Illinois Press, 1971.

Perry, Barbara A. *A "Representative" Supreme Court? The Impact of Race, Religion and Gender on Appointments.* London: Greenwood Press, 1991.

Pickering, Charles Willis. *Supreme Chaos: The Politics of Judicial Confirmation and the Culture War.* Macon, GA: Stroud and Hall, 2005.

Pierce, Carl A. "A Vacancy on the Supreme Court: The Politics of Judicial Appointment, 1893–94." *Tennessee Law Review* 39 (1972): 555–612.

Poole, Keith T., and Howard Rosenthal, eds. *Ideology and Congress: A Political Economic History of Roll Call Voting.* New Brunswick, NJ: Transaction Publishers, 2009.

Powe, L. A. Scot. "The Senate and the Court: Questioning a Nominee." *Texas Law Review* 54 (1975–1976): 891–902.

Prince, K. Michael. *Rally Round the Flag, Boys!* Columbia: University of South Carolina Press, 2004.

Rae, Nicol C. *Southern Democrats.* Oxford: Oxford University Press, 1994.

Ratcliffe, D. "The Nullification Crisis, Southern Discontents, and the American Political Process." *American Nineteenth Century History* 47 (1981): 335–62.

Reynolds, William Bradford. "The Confirmation Process: Too Much Advice and Too Little Consent." *Judicature* 75, no. 2 (1991–1992): 80–82.

Robertson, David. *Sly and Able: A Political Biography of James F. Byrnes.* New York: W. W. Norton, 1994.

Rogers, George C. Jr. "Who is a South Carolinian?" *South Carolina Historical Magazine* 101, no. 4 (2000): 319–29.

Ross, William G. "The Functions, Roles and Duties of the Senate in the Supreme Court Appointment Process." *William and Mary Law Review* 28 (1986–1987): 633–82.

———. "The Role of Judicial Issues in Presidential Campaigns." *Santa Clara Law Review* 42 (2001–2002): 391–482.

Ruckman, Paul S. "The Supreme Court, Critical Nominations, and the Senate Confirmation Process." *Journal of Politics* 55, no. 3 (1993): 793–805.

Ruger, T. W. "The Judicial Appointment Power of the Chief Justice." *University of Pennsylvania Journal of Constitutional Law* 7 (2004–2005): 341–402.

Scalia, Antonin. *A Matter of Interpretation: Federal Courts and the Law.* Princeton, NJ: Princeton University Press, 1997.

Schlesinger, Arthur. *Robert Kennedy and His Times.* New York: Ballantine Books, 1978.

Schmidhauser, John R. *The Supreme Court: Its Politics, Personalities and Procedures.* New York: Holt, Rinehart and Winston, 1960.

Schmidhauser, John R., and L. L. Berg. *The Supreme Court and Congress.* New York: Free Press, 1972.

Schott, R. L., and D. S. Hamilton. *People, Positions and Power: The Political Appointments of Lyndon Johnson.* Chicago: University of Chicago Press, 1983.

Schulman, Bruce J. *From Cotton Belt to Sunbelt.* Durham, NC: Duke University Press, 1994.

Segal, Jeffrey, and A. D. Cover. "Ideological Values and the Votes of Supreme Court Justices." *American Political Science Review* 83 (1989): 557–65.

Shannon, J. P. "Presidential Politics in the South—1938, II." *Journal of Politics* 1, no. 3 (August 1939): 278–300.

Shipan, Charles R., and Megan L. Shannon. "Delaying Justice(s): A Duration Analysis of Supreme Court Confirmations." *American Journal of Political Science* 47, no. 4 (2003): 654–68.

Silverstein, Gordon. *Law's Allure: How Law Shapes, Constrains, Saves and Kills Politics.* Cambridge: Cambridge University Press, 2009.

Silverstein, Mark. *Judicious Choices: The Politics of Supreme Court Appointments.* London: Norton, 1994.

———. "The People, the Senate, and the Court: The Democratization of the Judicial Confirmation System." *Constitutional Commentary* 9 (1992): 41–58.

Simkins, Francis Butler. *The Tillman Movement in South Carolina.* Gloucester, MA: Peter Smith, 1964.

Simon, Bryant. "The Appeal of Cole Blease of South Carolina: Race, Class and Sex in the New South." *Journal of Southern History* 62, no. 1 (February 1996): 57–86.

———. "The Devaluation of the Vote: Legislative Apportionment and Inequality in South Carolina, 1890–1962." *South Carolina Historical Magazine* 101, no. 3 (July 2000): 234–52.

———. *A Fabric of Defeat.* Chapel Hill: University of North Carolina Press, 1998.

Simpson, T. McN., III. "Jimmy Carter and the Transformation of Southern Politics, 1953–1987." In *Contemporary Southern Politics,* edited by James F. Lea, 61–82. Baton Rouge: Louisiana State University Press, 1988.

Skowronek, Stephen. *Presidential Leadership in Political Time: Reprise and Re-appraisal.* Lawrence: University Press of Kansas, 2008.

Smith, Douglas. "Into the Political Thicket: Reapportionment and the Rise of Suburban Power." In *The Myth of Southern Exceptionalism,* edited by Matthew Lassiter and Joseph Crespino, 263–85. Oxford: Oxford University Press, 2009.

Smyth, William D. "Segregation in Charleston in the 1950s: A Decade of Transition." *South Carolina Historical Magazine* 92, no. 2 (1991): 99–123.

Songer, Donald. "The Relevance of Policy Values for the Confirmation of Supreme Court Nominees." *Law and Society Review* 13 (1979): 927–48.

St. James, W. D. *The National Association for the Advancement of Colored People: A Case Study in Pressure Groups.* New York: Exposition Press, 1958.

Stebenne, David. *Arthur J. Goldberg: New Deal Liberal.* Oxford: Oxford University Press, 1996.

Sulfridge, Wayne. "Ideology as a Factor in Senate Consideration of Supreme Court Nominations." *Journal of Politics* 42 (1980): 560–67.

Sundquist, James L. *Politics and Policy: The Eisenhower, Kennedy and Johnson Years.* Washington, DC: Brookings Institution, 1968.

Swindler, William F. "The Politics of Advice and Consent." *American Bar Association Journal* 56 (1970): 533–42.

Talmadge, Herman E., and Mark Royden Winchell. *Talmadge: A Political Legacy, A Politician's Life—A Memoir.* Atlanta: Peachtree Publishers, 1987.

Thorpe, James A. "The Appearance of Supreme Court Nominees before the Senate Judiciary Committee." *Journal of Public Law* 18 (1969): 371–402.

Tindall, George Brown. *The Persistent Tradition in New South Politics.* Baton Rouge: Louisiana State University Press, 1975.

Tribe, Laurence H. *God Save This Honorable Court.* London: Random House, 1985.

Tushnet, Mark V. *Making Constitutional Law: Thurgood Marshall and the Supreme Court, 1961–1991.* Oxford: Oxford University Press, 1997.

Van der Veer Hamilton, Virginia. *Lister Hill: Statesman from the South.* Chapel Hill: University of North Carolina Press, 1987.

Van Wingen, John, and David Valentine. "Partisan Politics: A One-and-a-Half, No-Party System." In *Contemporary Southern Politics*, edited by James F. Lea, 124–47. Baton Rouge: Louisiana State University Press, 1988.

Waldrep, G. C. III. *Southern Workers and the Search for Community.* Chicago: University of Chicago Press, 2000.

Ward, Jason Morgan. *Defending White Democracy.* Chapel Hill: University of North Carolina Press, 2011.

Watson, Richard L. "The Defeat of Judge Parker: A Study in Pressure Groups and Politics." *Mississippi Valley Historical Review* 50, no. 2 (1963): 213–34.

Webster, McKenzie. "The Warren Court's Struggle with the Sit-In Cases and the Constitutionality of Segregation in Places of Public Accommodations." *Journal of Law and Politics* 17 (2001): 373–407.

Weiss, Nancy J. *Farewell to the Party of Lincoln: Black Politics in the Age of FDR.* Princeton, NJ: Princeton University Press, 1983.

Wermiel, Stephen J. "The Nomination of Justice Brennan: Eisenhower's Mistake? A Look at the Historical Record." *Constitutional Commentary* 11 (1994–1995): 515–38.

Wheat, Edward M. "The Bureaucratization of the South: From Traditional Fragmentation to Administrative Incoherence." In *Contemporary Southern Politics,* edited by James F. Lea, 263–82. Baton Rouge: Louisiana State University Press, 1988.

Wheeler, Russell. "Judicial Confirmations: What Thurmond Rule?" *Issues in Gover nance Studies* 5 (March 2012): 1–7.

Wilhoit, Francis M. *The Politics of Massive Resistance.* New York: George Braziller, 1973.

Wilkinson, J. Harvie. *From Brown to Bakke: The Supreme Court and School Integration, 1954–1978.* Oxford: Oxford University Press, 1979.

Williams, Juan. *Thurgood Marshall: American Revolutionary.* New York: Random House, 1988.

Woodward, C. Vann. *Reunion and Reaction: The Compromise of 1877 and the End of Reconstruction.* Boston: Little, Brown, 1951.

———. *The Strange Career of Jim Crow.* Oxford: Oxford University Press, 1974.

Woodward, Robert, and Scott Armstrong. *The Brethren.* New York: Simon and Schuster, 1979.

Yalof, David A. *Pursuit of Justices: Presidential Politics and the Selection of Supreme Court Nominees.* Chicago: University of Chicago Press, 1999.

Yarborough, Tinsley A. *The Rehnquist Court and the Constitution.* Oxford: Oxford University Press, 2001.

Zelden, Charles L. *The Battle for the Black Ballot: Smith v. Allwright and the Defeat of the Texas All-White Primary.* Lawrence: University Press of Kansas, 2004.

INDEX